G000242934

CAMBRIDGE

IGCSE®

BIOLOGY

Sue Kearsey, Mike Smith, Jackie Clegg and Gareth Price

William Collins' dream of knowledge for all began with the publication of his first book in 1819. A self-educated mill worker, he not only enriched millions of lives, but also founded a flourishing publishing house. Today, staying true to this spirit, Collins books are packed with inspiration, innovation and practical expertise. They place you at the centre of a world of possibility and give you exactly what you need to explore it.

Collins. Freedom to teach

Published by Collins
An imprint of HarperCollins*Publishers*
The News Building
1 London Bridge Street
London
SE1 9GF

**Browse the complete Collins catalogue at
www.collins.co.uk**

© HarperCollins*Publishers* Limited 2014

10 9 8 7 6 5 4 3

ISBN 13 978-0-00-759252-4

Sue Kearsey, Mike Smith, Jackie Clegg and Gareth Price assert their moral rights to be identified as the authors of this work.

British Library Cataloguing in Publication Data
A Catalogue record for this publication is available from the British Library

Commissioned by **Letitia Luff**
Managed by **Caroline Green**
Project managed by **Alicia Higgins**
Copy-edited by **Amanda Harman**
Proofread by **Sophia Ktori**
Illlustrations by **Jouve India Private Limited and Ann Paganuzzi**
Typeset by **Jouve India Private Limited**
Indexed by **Jane Henley**
Cover design by **Angela English**
Cover image by **Danielo/Shutterstock**
Production by **Rachel Weaver**
Printed and bound by **Grafica Veneta S.p.A, Italy**

Fully safety checked but not trialled by CLEAPSS.

Many thanks to Andrew Young, Head Science Technician of Stewards Academy, for his safety testing and reviewing of all practical activities.

The syllabus content is reproduced by permission of Cambridge International Examinations.

Exam-style questions and sample answers have been written by the author.

® IGCSE is the registered trademark of Cambridge International Examinations.

Acknowledgements

The publishers wish to thank the following for permission to reproduce photographs. Every effort has been made to trace copyright holders and to obtain their permission for the use of copyright materials. The publishers will gladly receive any information enabling them to rectify any error or omission at the first opportunity:

(t = top, c = centre, b = bottom, r = right, l = left)

Cover and p 1 danielo/Shutterstock, p 10-11 Stephen Coburn/Shutterstock, p 12 Science Photo Library/Alamy, p 13 Aleksey Stemmer/Shutterstock, p 14 Image Point Fr/Shutterstock, p 15t Eric Isselee/Shutterstock, p 15b Ann and Steve Toon/Alamy, p 18 WorldsWildlifeWonders/Shutterstock, p 20 Hraska/Shutterstock, p 21 Ram T M/Shutterstock, p 22 Martin Fowler/Shutterstock, p 25 Aleksei Verhovski/Shutterstock, p 26 Aleksandar Todorovic/Shutterstock, p 27t Doug Ellis/Shutterstock, p 27b Brian Lasenby/Shutterstock, p 28t Sergey Popov V/Shutterstock, p 28b Matthew Cole/Shutterstock, p 29t Lehrer/Shutterstock, p 29b DMVPhotos/Shutterstock, p 30 MindStorm/Shutterstock, p 31 Sally Scott/Shutterstock, p 34l Pyty/Shutterstock, p 34lc Tabby Mittins/Shutterstock, p 34rc Dr Ajay Kumar Singh/Shutterstock, p 34r Volodymyr Burdiak/Shutterstock, p 39l Quang Ho/Shutterstock, p 39lc AmnachPhoto/Shutterstock, p 39rc Rodionov Oleg/Shutterstock, p 39r Valery121283/Shutterstock, p 40-41 Jubal Harshaw/Shutterstock, p 42 TinyDevil/Shutterstock, p 43 Ed Reschke/Getty Images, p 44 Dimarion/Shutterstock, p 45 Melba Photo Agency/Alamy, p 47tl Phototake Inc./Alamy, p 47tr Designua/Shutterstock, p 47bl Phototake Inc./Alamy, p 47br July Store/Shutterstock, p 51 Dr. Richard Kessel & Dr. Gene Shih/Getty Images, p 57 Carol and Mike Werner/Alamy, p 58-9 Shutterstock/ ZanozaRu, p 60 Dr. Stanley Flegler, Visuals Unlimited/Science Photo Library, p 61 Andrew Lambert Photography/Science Photo Library, p 63 Picsfive/Shutterstock, p 64 GIPhotoStock/Science Photo Library, p 66 David Cook/BlueShiftStudios/Alamy, p 68 Phototake Inc./Alamy, p 69l J.C. Revy, ISM/Science Photo Library, p 69r J.C. Revy, ISM/Science Photo Library, p 76-7 Olena Timashova/iStockphoto, p 80 Somersault1824/Shutterstock, p 82 Martin Shields/Alamy, p 83t Andrew Lambert Photography/Science Photo Library, p 83b David Vincent, p 84 Andrew Lambert Photography/Science Photo Library, p 87 Kenneth Eward/Biografx/Science Photo Library, p 88-9 dinsor/Shutterstock, p 90 StefanOlunardi/Shutterstock, p 96 Martyn F. Chillmaid/Science Photo Library, p 100-1 Anest/Shutterstock, p 102 MarcelClemens/Shutterstock, p 105 SciencePhotos/Alamy, p 107 A.Krotov/Shutterstock, p 112 Triff/Shutterstock, p 113 Dr Keith Wheeler/Science Photo Library, p 115l Nigel Cattlin/Science Photo Library, p 115r Nigel Cattlin/Alamy, p 120-21 Angel Andrews/Shutterstock, p 122 Adam James/Alamy, p 124t HLPhoto/Shutterstock, p 124b Images of Africa Photobank/Alamy, p 126 Cate Turton/Department for International Development, p 131 Sean Sprague/Alamy, p 144-5 Cristapper/Shutterstock, p 146 Stocktrek Images, Inc./Alamy, p 148tl Biophoto Associates/Science Photo Library, p 148tc D. Kucharski K. Kucharska/Shutterstock, p 148tr Dr Keith Wheeler/Science Photo Library, p 148b Zastolskiy Victor/Shutterstock, p 149 Nigel Cattlin/Alamy, p 150l Nigel Cattlin, Visuals Unlimited/Science Photo Library, p 150r Adam Hart-Davis/Science Photo Library, p 157 You Touch Pix of EuToch/Shutterstock, p 158-9 Vladimir Melnik/Shutterstock, p 160 Alain Pol, ISM/Science Photo Library, p 163 Yiargo/Shutterstock, p 164 LeventeGyori/Shutterstock, p 165 Beerkoff/Shutterstock, p 174 National Cancer Institute/Science Photo Library, p 175 Biophoto Associates/Science Photo Library, p 176 Science Photo Library/Getty Images, p 180 Miissa/Shutterstock, p 181-2 Nikolay Litov/Shutterstock, p 184 Danny Alvarez/Shutterstock, p 187t Henrik Larsson/Shutterstock, p 187b RioPatuca/Shutterstock, p 191 Asianet-Pakistan/Shutterstock, p 192t Dmitry Naumov/Shutterstock, p 192b Medical-on-Line/Alamy, p 196 Fredrik Renande/Alamy, p 198-9 Dream Designs/Shutterstock, p 200 Sebastian Kaulitzki/Shutterstock, p 202 Science Photo Library/Alamy, p 206 Andrew Gentry/Shutterstock, p 212-13 Catwalker/Shutterstock, p 214 Shane Gross/Shutterstock, p 216 Nickolay Vinokurov/Shutterstock, p 220 MaxiSport/Shutterstock, p 221 Adam Hart-Davis/Science Photo Library, p 223 Fdimeo/Shutterstock, p 224-5 Keith A Frith/Shutterstock, p 226 Bork/Shutterstock, p 230 Poco a poco/WikiMedia Commons, p 235 Joerg Beuge/Shutterstock, p 236-7 Pan Xunbin/Shutterstock, p 238 Tudor Stanica/Shutterstock, p 254 Anest/Shutterstock, p 264-5 Dtkutoo/Shutterstock, p 266 Mary Evans Picture Library/Alamy, p 267 UIG/Getty Images, p 270t NKBImages/Getty Images, p 270b Mubus7/Shutterstock, p 272 Blend Images/ERproductions Ltd/Getty Images, p 274 Dan Pan/Alamy, p 278-9 Volodymyr Martyniuk/Shutterstock, p 280 Phototake Inc./Alamy, p 281 Nemeziya/Shutterstock, p 282 Oksix/Shutterstock, p 283 Warmer/Shutterstock, p 285 Tran Van Thai/Shutterstock, p 287t Dr Jeremy Burgess/Science Photo Library, p 287b Glyn/Shutterstock, p 288 Piyato/Shutterstock, p 289t Wildlife GMBH/Alamy, p 289bl Phototake Inc./Alamy, p 289br Medical-on-Line/Alamy, p 290 Tim Gainey/Alamy, p 291 D. Virtser/Shutterstock, p 294t Pi-Lens/Shutterstock, p 294b Perry Mastrovito/Getty Images, p 298 Fracis Leroy, Biocosmos/Science Photo Library, p 299 Nic Cleave Photography/Alamy, p 301 Dmitry Melnikov/Shutterstock, p 302 ZouZou/Shutterstock, p 307 Charles Thatcher/Getty Images, p 310 Mknobil/WikiMedia Commons, p 313 Galyna Andrushko/Shutterstock, p 316-7 Sebastian Kaulitzki/Shutterstock, p 318 Andy Lim/Shutterstock, p 321 CNRI/Science Photo Library, p 323 Eric Isselée/Shutterstock, p 329 Mary Evans Picture Library/Alamy, p 332 Science Photo Library, p 333 Huaji/Shutterstock, p 340-1 Sebastian Kaulitzki/Shutterstock, p 342 DPA Picture Alliance Archive/Alamy, p 343 Ozgur Coskun/Shutterstock, p 345 Sebastian Kaulitzki/Shutterstock, p 346 ISM/Science Photo Library, p 347 Peter Wey/Shutterstock, p 348t David Steele/Shutterstock, p 348b Antoni Halim/Shutterstock, p 349 Nelson Sirlin/Shutterstock, p 351 M. J. Mayo/Alamy, p 354 Photocrea/Shutterstock, p 359 OutdoorsMan/Shutterstock, p 360-1 Tagstock1/Shutterstock, p 362 Colin Pickett/Alamy, p 364 Anan Kaewkhammul/Shutterstock, p 369 Frans Lanting Studio/Alamy, p 370 David Hancock/Shutterstock, p 376 Jane McIlroy/Shutterstock, p 377 Tropical Rain Forest Information Center/NASA Goddard Space Flight Center PD, p 380 Frank Vincentz/WikiMedia Commons, p 381 Fotokostic/Shutterstock, p 391 Celso Diniz/Shutterstock, p 394t Rick Wylie/Shutterstock, p 394b Péter Gudella/Shutterstock, p 396 Nadirco/Shutterstock, p 398-9 Chris Knapton/Alamy, p 400 Eye of Science/Science Photo Library, p 401 Spaxiax/Shutterstock, p 403t David Nunuk/Science Photo Library, p 403b Martyn F. Chillmaid/Science Photo Library, p 406l Vichy Deal/Shutterstock, p 406r Africa Studio/Shutterstock, p 406 Food and Drink Photos/Alamy, p 409 Chris Knapton/Alamy, p 412 Itar-Tass Photo Agency/Alamy, p 416 Carolina K. Smith MD/Shutterstock, p 417 Nick Gregory/Alamy, p 418-9 Ivan_Sabo/Shutterstock, p 420 Darrin Henry/Shutterstock, p 422 Caro/Alamy, p 423 Fotokostic/Shutterstock, p 424 Frontpage/Shutterstock, p 425t Lee Prince/Shutterstock, p 425b Blickwinkel/Alamy, p 426 Earth Observations Laboratory, Johnson Space Center, p 428 Photoshot Holdings Ltd/Alamy, p 432 Cozyta/Shutterstock, p 433 Julio Etchart/Alamy, p 434 Jeremy Sutton-Hibbert/Alamy, p 436 NASA, p 437 Martyn F. Chillmaid/Science Photo Library, p 438 Sue Kearsey, p 444 M R/Shutterstock, p 446t Timothy Epp /Shutterstock, p 446b Vanessa Miles/Alamy, p 447 Stephen Bures/Shutterstock, p 448 Topora/Shutterstock, p 449 Oxfam East Africa, p 450 Andrey Kekyalyaynen/Shutterstock, p 451 Photoshot Holdings Ltd/Alamy, p 452 Dewald Kirsten/Shutterstock, p 453 Caroline Vancoillie/Shutterstock.

Contents

Getting the best from the book

Welcome to Collins *Cambridge IGCSE Biology*.

This textbook has been designed to help you understand all of the requirements needed to succeed in the Cambridge IGCSE Biology course. Just as there are twenty one sections in the Cambridge syllabus, there are twenty one sections in the textbook.

Each section is split into topics. Each topic in the textbook covers the essential knowledge and skills you need. The textbook also has some very useful features which have been designed to really help you understand all the aspects of Biology which you will need to know for this syllabus.

SAFETY IN THE SCIENCE LESSON

This book is a textbook, not a laboratory or practical manual. As such, you should not interpret any information in this book that related to practical work as including comprehensive safety instructions. Your teachers will provide full guidance for practical work and cover rules that are specific to your school.

A brief introduction to the section to give context to the science covered in the section.

The section contents shows the separate topics to be studied matching the syllabus order.

The world's tallest known living tree, which has been named Hyperion, is a coast redwood tree growing in Northern California in the US. When it was measured in 2006 it was found to be 115.61 m tall (379.3 ft). Like all plants, from the smallest seedling to the tallest redwood giant, Hyperion makes its own food from three simple ingredients, sunlight, water and carbon dioxide. This process is known as photosynthesis, and is one of the features of plants that distinguish them from animals.

CONTENTS
a) Photosynthesis
b) Leaf structure
c) Mineral requirements of plants

6
Plant nutrition

△ Saplings growing towards a controlled light source.

Knowledge check shows the ideas you should have already encountered in previous work before starting the topic.

Learning objectives cover what you need to learn in this topic.

Organisation and maintenance of the organism

INTRODUCTION

Bringing together similar activities that have the same purpose can make things much more efficient. For example, bringing teachers and students together in a school helps more students to learn more quickly than if each teacher travelled to each student's home for lessons. The same is true in the body. Having groups of similar cells in the same place as a tissue, and grouping tissues into organs, helps the body carry out all the life processes much more efficiently and so stay alive.

△ Fig 2.1 The human body is made up of several systems of grouped organs, including the digestive system, the nervous system, the muscle/skeletal system and the respiratory system.

KNOWLEDGE CHECK

✓ State that organisms are formed from many cells.
✓ Describe how cells may be specialised in different ways to carry out different functions.
✓ Define the terms *tissue*, *organ* and *organ system*.
✓ Describe how the organisation of the body systems contributes to the seven life processes.
✓ State that a microscope can be used to magnify specimens so we can see more detail.

LEARNING OBJECTIVES

✓ Describe and compare the structures in plant and animal cells.
✓ Describe the function of each type of cell structure seen under the light microscope.
✓ Describe the function of mitochondria and ribosomes.
✓ EXTENDED Identify mitochondria and rough endoplasmic reticulum in cells, and describe the function of mitochondria and ribosomes.
✓ EXTENDED Know that the cytoplasm of all cells contain ribosomes on rough endoplasmic reticulum and vesicles.
✓ EXTENDED Know that almost all cells have mitochondria on rough endoplasmic reticulum.
✓ State that aerobic respiration occurs in mitochondria and that cells with high rates of respiration have many mitochondria to provide sufficient energy.
✓ Relate structure to function in a range of specialised cells.
✓ Define tissues as groups of similar cells with a similar function.
✓ Define organs as groups of tissues that work together for a particular function.
✓ Define organ systems as groups of organs that work together for a particular function.
✓ Give examples of tissues, organs and organ systems.
✓ Describe how to calculate the magnification of biological specimens seen under a microscope.
✓ Calculate the size of biological specimens using millimetres as units.
✓ Identify the different levels of organisation in images of familiar material.
✓ EXTENDED Identify the different levels of organisation in images of unfamiliar material.
✓ Calculate the size of biological specimens using millimetres as units.
✓ EXTENDED Calculate the size of biological specimens using micrometres as units.

CELL STRUCTURE AND ORGANISATION

The diagrams below show a typical animal cell and typical plant cells. These cells all have a nucleus and cytoplasm.

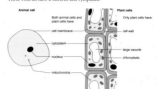

△ Fig 2.2 The basic structures of an animal cell (e.g. liver cell) and plant cells (e.g. palisade mesophyll cells).

All living organisms are made of cells. Some, such as bacteria, protoctists and some fungi, are formed from a single cell; others, such as the majority of plants and animals, are **multicellular**, with a body made of many cells. All animal and plant cells have certain features in common:

- a **cell membrane** surrounds the cell
- **cytoplasm** inside the cell, in which all the other structures are found
- a large **nucleus**.

A typical animal cell is a human liver cell.

△ Fig 2.3 Structures in animal cells seen using a light microscope. Note these cells have been stained to make some structures easier to see.

---

particularly carbohydrates but also fats and proteins, can contribute to the energy our bodies need. If we eat food that supplies more energy than we use, the extra will be deposited as energy stores of fat. This can lead to **obesity**, which is related to many health problems, such as heart disease and diabetes. Controlling the portion size at each meal, keeping between-meal snacks to a minimum, and increasing levels of exercise can help to reduce the risk of becoming overweight.

Energy requirements depend on body size, stage of development and level of exercise, as shown in Table 7.2.

	Energy used in a day (kJ)	
	Male	Female
6-year-old child	7 500	7 500
12–15-year-old teenager	12 500	9 700
adult manual worker	15 000	12 500
adult office worker	11 000	9 800
pregnant woman		10 000
breastfeeding		11 000

△ Table 7.2 Daily energy requirements for different people.

Malnutrition

The term **malnutrition** literally means 'bad nutrition' and applies to any diet that will lead to health problems. A diet that is too high in energy content, and leads to obesity, is one form of malnutrition, because obesity increases the risk of several diseases.

Malnutrition can occur if one or more nutrients is in too high a proportion in the diet. For example, a high proportion of saturated fats in the diet can lead to deposits of cholesterol forming on the inside of arteries, increasing blood pressure and also increasing the risk of coronary heart disease (see Topic 9).

Malnutrition also occurs if any of the substances needed for a healthy body are in too low a proportion in the diet. For example, a lack of a vitamin or a mineral can cause deficiency diseases, as shown in Table 7.1. Too little fibre in the diet can lead to **constipation**, in which food moves too slowly through the **alimentary canal**, increasing the risk of diseases such as diverticulitis and bowel cancer.

△ Fig 7.6 Starvation is most commonly seen in places where crops have failed due to drought (**famine**) or people are displaced as a result of war. However, it can also happen in people who choose to starve themselves, in crash diets or as a result of conditions such as anorexia.

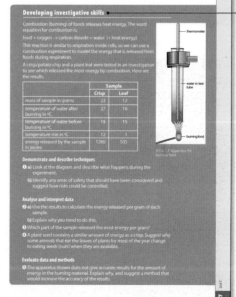

Developing investigative skills

Combustion (burning) of foods releases heat energy. The word equation for combustion is:

food + oxygen → carbon dioxide + water (+ heat energy)

This reaction is similar to respiration inside cells, so we can use a combustion experiment to model the energy that is released from foods during respiration.

A crisp/potato chip and a plant leaf were tested in an investigation to see which released the most energy by combustion. Here are the results.

	Sample	
	Crisp	Leaf
mass of sample in grams	22	12
temperature of water after burning in °C	27	16
temperature of water before burning in °C	15	15
temperature rise in °C	12	1
energy released by the sample in joules	1260	105

△ Fig 7.7 Apparatus for burning food.

Demonstrate and describe techniques

❶ a) Look at the diagram and describe what happens during the experiment.

b) Identify any areas of safety that should have been considered and suggest how risks could be controlled.

Analyse and interpret data

❷ a) Use the results to calculate the energy released per gram of each sample.

b) Explain why you need to do this.

❸ Which part of the sample released the most energy per gram?

❹ A plant seed contains a similar amount of energy as a crisp. Suggest why some animals that eat the leaves of plants for most of the year change to eating seeds (nuts) when they are available.

Evaluate data and methods

❺ The apparatus shown does not give accurate results for the amount of energy in the burning material. Explain why, and suggest a method that would increase the accuracy of the results.

Examples of investigations are included with questions matched to the investigative skills you will need to learn.

Getting the best from the book *continued*

Science in context boxes put the ideas you are learning into real-life context. It is not necessary for you to learn the content of these boxes as they do not form part of the syllabus. However, they do provide interesting examples of scientific application that are designed to enhance your understanding.

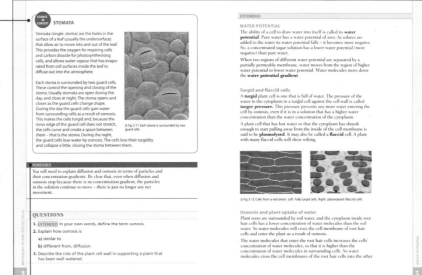

Remember boxes provide tips and guidance to help you during your course and to prepare for examination.

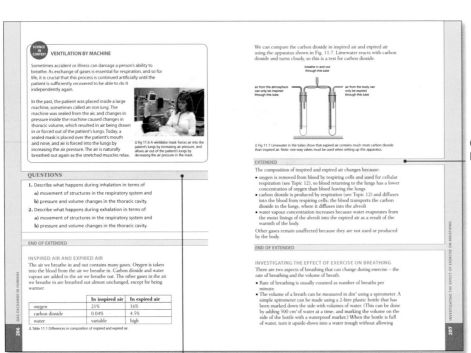

Clearly differentiated Extended material.

Questions to check your understanding.

End of topic questions allow you to apply the knowledge and understanding you have learned in the topic to answer the questions.

A full checklist of all the information you need to cover the complete syllabus requirements for each topic.

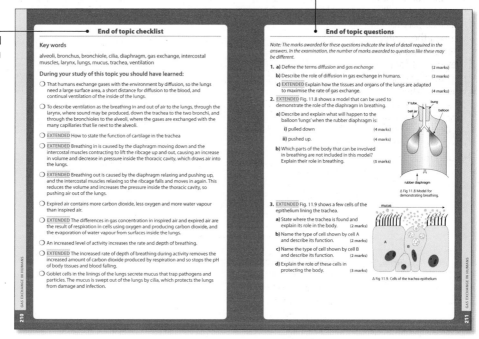

End of topic checklist

Key words

alveoli, bronchus, bronchiole, cilia, diaphragm, gas exchange, intercostal muscles, larynx, lungs, mucus, trachea, ventilation

During your study of this topic you should have learned:

○ That humans exchange gases with the environment by diffusion, so the lungs need a large surface area, a short distance for diffusion to the blood, and continual ventilation of the inside of the lungs.

○ To describe ventilation as the breathing in and out of air to the lungs, through the larynx, where sound may be produced, down the trachea to the two bronchi, and through the bronchioles to the alveoli, where the gases are exchanged with the many capillaries that lie next to the alveoli.

○ EXTENDED How to state the function of cartilage in the trachea

○ EXTENDED Breathing in is caused by the diaphragm moving down and the intercostal muscles contracting to lift the ribcage up and out, causing an increase in volume and decrease in pressure inside the thoracic cavity, which draws air into the lungs.

○ EXTENDED Breathing out is caused by the diaphragm relaxing and pushing up, and the intercostal muscles relaxing so the ribcage falls and moves in again. This reduces the volume and increases the pressure inside the thoracic cavity, so pushing air out of the lungs.

○ Expired air contains more carbon dioxide, less oxygen and more water vapour than inspired air.

○ EXTENDED The differences in gas concentration in inspired air and expired air are the result of respiration in cells using oxygen and producing carbon dioxide, and the evaporation of water vapour from surfaces inside the lungs.

○ An increased level of activity increases the rate and depth of breathing.

○ EXTENDED The increased rate of depth of breathing during activity removes the increased amount of carbon dioxide produced by respiration and so stops the pH of body tissues and blood falling.

○ Goblet cells in the linings of the lungs secrete mucus that trap pathogens and particles. The mucus is swept out of the lungs by cilia, which protects the lungs from damage and infection.

GAS EXCHANGE IN HUMANS   210

End of topic questions

Note: The marks awarded for these questions indicate the level of detail required in the answers. In the examination, the number of marks awarded to questions like these may be different.

1. **a)** Define the terms *diffusion* and *gas exchange* (2 marks)
   b) Describe the role of diffusion in gas exchange in humans. (2 marks)
   c) EXTENDED Explain how the tissues and organs of the lungs are adapted to maximise the rate of gas exchange. (4 marks)

2. EXTENDED Fig. 11.8 shows a model that can be used to demonstrate the role of the diaphragm in breathing.
   a) Describe and explain what will happen to the balloon 'lungs' when the rubber diaphragm is:
     i) pulled down (4 marks)
     ii) pushed up. (4 marks)
   b) Which parts of the body that can be involved in breathing are not included in this model? Explain their role in breathing. (5 marks)

   △ Fig 11.8 Model for demonstrating breathing.

3. EXTENDED Fig. 11.9 shows a few cells of the epithelium lining the trachea.
   a) State where the trachea is found and explain its role in the body. (2 marks)
   b) Name the type of cell shown by cell A and describe its function. (2 marks)
   c) Name the type of cell shown by cell B and describe its function. (2 marks)
   d) Explain the role of these cells in protecting the body. (3 marks)

   △ Fig 11.9. Cells of the trachea epithelium

GAS EXCHANGE IN HUMANS   211

Exam-style questions help you prepare for your exam in a focussed way and get the best results.

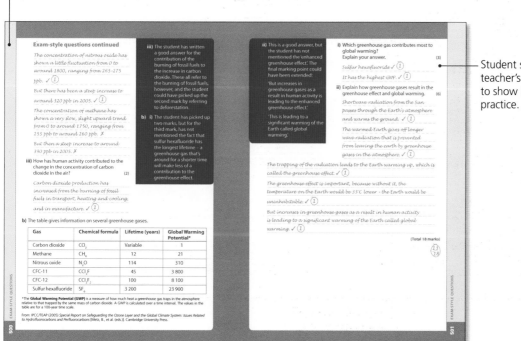

Exam-style questions continued

The concentration of nitrous oxide has shown little fluctuation from 0 to around 1800, ranging from 265-275 ppb. ✓ ①

But there has been a steep increase to around 320 ppb in 2005. ✓ ①

The concentration of methane has shown a very slow, slight upward trend from 0 to around 1750, ranging from 255 ppb to around 260 ppb. ✗

But then a steep increase to around 390 ppb in 2005. ✗

iii) How has human activity contributed to the change in the concentration of carbon dioxide in the air? (2)

Carbon dioxide production has increased from the burning of fossil fuels in transport, heating and cooling, and in manufacture. ✓ ①

b) The table gives information on several greenhouse gases.

Gas	Chemical formula	Lifetime (years)	Global Warming Potential*
Carbon dioxide	CO_2	Variable	1
Methane	CH_4	12	21
Nitrous oxide	N_2O	114	310
CFC-11	CCl_3F	45	3 800
CFC-12	CCl_2F_2	100	8 100
Sulfur hexafluoride	SF_6	3 200	23 900

*The **Global Warming Potential (GWP)** is a measure of how much heat a greenhouse gas traps in the atmosphere relative to that trapped by the same mass of carbon dioxide. A GWP is calculated over a time interval. The values in the table are over a 100-year time scale.

From: IPCC/TEAP (2005) *Special Report on Safeguarding the Ozone Layer and the Global Climate System: Issues Related to Hydrofluorocarbons and Perfluorocarbons* [Metz, B., et al. (eds.)]. Cambridge University Press.

EXAM-STYLE QUESTIONS   500

iii) The student has written a good answer for the contribution of the burning of fossil fuels to the increase in carbon dioxide. These all refer to the burning of fossil fuels, however, and the student could have picked up the second mark by referring to deforestation.

b) i) The student has picked up two marks, but for the third mark, has not mentioned the fact that sulfur hexafluoride has the longest lifetime - a greenhouse gas that's around for a shorter time will make less of a contribution to the greenhouse effect.

ii) This is a good answer, but the student has not mentioned the 'enhanced greenhouse effect'. The final marking point could have been extended:

'But increases in greenhouse gases as a result in human activity is leading to the enhanced greenhouse effect.'

'This is leading to a significant warming of the Earth called global warming.'

i) Which greenhouse gas contributes most to global warming? Explain your answer. (3)

Sulfur hexafluoride ✓ ①

It has the highest GWP. ✓ ①

ii) Explain how greenhouse gases result in the greenhouse effect and global warming. (6)

Shortwave radiation from the Sun passes through the Earth's atmosphere and warms the ground. ✓ ①

The warmed Earth gives off longer wave radiation that is prevented from leaving the earth by greenhouse gases in the atmosphere. ✓ ①

The trapping of the radiation leads to the Earth warming up, which is called the greenhouse effect. ✓ ①

The greenhouse effect is important, because without it, the temperature on the Earth would be 33°C lower - the Earth would be uninhabitible. ✓ ①

But increases in greenhouse gases as a result in human activity is leading to a significant warming of the Earth called global warming. ✓ ①

(Total 18 marks)

(13/18)

Student sample with teacher's comments to show best practice.

EXAM-STYLE QUESTIONS   501

GETTING THE BEST FROM THE BOOK

9

Around 1.74 million living species have been identified on Earth, not including bacteria. Over 320 000 of these species are classified as plants and around 1.36 million species are classified as animals. Over 62 000 of the animal species are vertebrates (animals with bony skeletons) and the rest are invertebrates (animals without backbones), of which the majority (around 1 million species) are insects.

It is difficult to know how many species are still to be discovered, although it is thought that about 15 000 new species are discovered around the world every year. The smaller the organism, the greater the chance that there are species we don't yet know about. So, although around 4000 species of bacteria have been identified, there could be many more species of bacteria than of all the other kinds of organisms put together.

CONTENTS

a) Characteristics of living organisms

b) Concept and use of a classification system

c) Methods of classification

d) Features of organisms

e) Dichotomous keys

1

Characteristics and classification of living organisms

△ Many species of different kinds of organisms live on a coral reef.

△ Fig 1.1 Tiny tardigrades (about 1 mm long) are the toughest organisms known. They can survive temperatures below −200 °C, 10 days in the vacuum of space and over 10 years without water!

Characteristics and classification of living organisms

INTRODUCTION

Sometimes it is easy to tell when something dies – an animal will stop moving around, a plant may wilt and all the green parts collapse. But does a tree die in winter, when its leaves have dropped off? Are animals 'dead' when they hibernate underground for months? As technology gets increasingly sophisticated, and we can create machines with 'brains' and new organisms from basic molecules, distinguishing between living and dead could get even more difficult. We need a set of 'rules' that work for most organisms, most of the time.

KNOWLEDGE CHECK

✓ Living organisms show a range of characteristics that distinguish them from dead or non-living material.
✓ The life processes are supported by the cells, tissues, organs and systems of the body.
✓ Living organisms show great variety.
✓ Organisms can be classified according to their characteristics.
✓ Living organisms can be grouped into species using their physical features.

LEARNING OBJECTIVES

✓ **EXTENDED** Define the seven characteristics of living organisms.
✓ Describe each of the characteristics of living organisms.
✓ Explain that not all living organisms show every characteristic all of the time.
✓ Define the term *species*.
✓ Describe how the binomial system is used to name and classify organisms.
✓ **EXTENDED** Explain why it is important to classify organisms.

✓ **EXTENDED** Explain that classification is usually based on similarities of morphology and anatomy.
✓ **EXTENDED** Describe the use of DNA in classification.

✓ **EXTENDED** State that organisms which are closely related have DNA that is more similar than organisms which are more distantly related.
✓ List the features shared by all living organisms.
✓ Identify the main features of plants and animals.
✓ Describe the main features of groups within the animal kingdom.
✓ **EXTENDED** Describe the main features of the five kingdoms of organisms.

✓ EXTENDED Describe the main features of groups within the plant kingdom.

✓ EXTENDED Describe the features of viruses.

✓ Use and construct simple dichotomous keys to identify organisms.

CHARACTERISTICS OF LIVING ORGANISMS

There are seven life processes that most living organisms will show at some time during their life.

- **Movement**: Animals may move their entire body so that it changes position or place.

EXTENDED

Organisms may also move parts of their body. For example, plants may move body parts in response to external stimuli such as light, while structures in the cytoplasm of all living cells move.

END OF EXTENDED

- **Respiration**: This is a series of chemical reactions inside living cells that break down nutrient molecules and release energy.

EXTENDED

The energy released from respiration is used for all the chemical reactions that help to keep the body alive. Together, these reactions are known as **metabolism**.

END OF EXTENDED

- **Sensitivity**: Living organisms are able to detect (or sense) and respond to changes in the environment around them. For example, we see, hear and respond to touch.

EXTENDED

Living organisms can also detect and respond appropriately to changes inside their bodies (the internal environment).

END OF EXTENDED

- **Growth**: This is the permanent increase in size of an organism.

EXTENDED

Gowth is often defined as an increase in dry mass (mass without water content) of cells or the whole body of an organism. This is because total mass can vary, depending on how much the organism eats and drinks. Dry mass only measures the amount by which the body

△ Fig 1.2 Sunflowers respond to light by tracking the Sun across the sky during the day.

increases in size when nutrients are taken into the cells and used to increase their number and size.

END OF EXTENDED

- **Reproduction**: This includes the processes that result in making more individuals of that kind of organism, such as making gametes and the fertilisation of those gametes.
- **Excretion**: This is the removal from the body of substances that are toxic (poisonous) and may damage cells if they stay in the body. Organisms also excrete substances that are in **excess**, where there is more in the body than is needed.

EXTENDED

Living cells produce many products from the metabolic reactions that take place inside them. Some of these are waste products – materials that the body does not use; for example, animals cannot use the carbon dioxide produced during respiration. These waste products may be toxic, so they must also be removed from the body by excretion.

END OF EXTENDED

- **Nutrition**: This is the absorption of nutrients into the body. The nutrients are the raw materials needed by the cells to release energy and to make more cells for growth, development and repair.

EXTENDED

Plant nutrition requires light, carbon dioxide, water and mineral ions, such as iron and magnesium. Animal nutrition requires organic compounds such as carbohydrates and proteins, mineral ions such as iron and sodium, and usually water.

END OF EXTENDED

All these characteristics will be described in greater detail in later Topics in this book.

△ Fig 1.3 Growth of a child can be measured by recording their change in height over time.

QUESTIONS

1. For each of the seven characteristics, give one example for:

   a) a human

   b) an animal of your choice

   c) a plant.

2. For each of the seven characteristics, explain why they are essential to a living organism.

An easy way to remember all seven processes is to take the first letter from each process. This spells Mrs Gren. Alternatively you may wish to make up a sentence in which each word begins with same letter as one of the processes, for example: My Revision System Gets Really Entertaining Now.

CONCEPT AND USE OF A CLASSIFICATORY SYSTEM

Classification means 'grouping things'. When we classify organisms we group them according to how similar their features are. For example, zebras are horse-like mammals that are striped.

The main classification group is the **species**. We define a species as organisms that share many features. They can also interbreed to produce **fertile** offspring. This means that the offspring are able to reproduce when they are adult. Some species, like the horse and donkey, can be bred together but they produce offspring called mules that are not fertile.

EXTENDED

The definition of species in terms of breeding to produce fertile offspring is not always true. Plains zebras and mountain zebras don't live in the same habitat, so they don't normally try to interbreed. However, in captivity they have been bred together, although the chance of a pregnancy failing is high.

END OF EXTENDED

Plains zebras and mountain zebras are so alike that we group these species together in the same **genus** (plural: genera). There are other species in this genus that also share many characteristics, including the domesticated horse and donkey.

- Genera that share many features are grouped into a **family**, so horses, donkeys and zebras are grouped in the horse family.
- Families that share key features are grouped together in an **order**. So the horse family is grouped in the perissodactyl order together with other mammals that have an odd number of toes, such as the rhinoceros family.
- Orders that share key features are grouped together in a **class**. So the odd-toed perissodactyls, even-toed ungulates and apes (including humans) are grouped in the mammal class because they all produce milk for their young.
- Classes that share key features are grouped together in a **phylum** (plural: phyla). So the mammals, birds and other organisms with a bony backbone are grouped as chordates.

△ Fig 1.4 These zebra look very similar, and can all interbreed, so they are classified in the same species – the plains zebra.

△ Fig 1.5 This is a different species of zebra, called a mountain zebra. It differs from plains zebras in a few characteristics, such as having a white belly and narrow white sripes. Plains zebras and mountain zebras do not normally interbreed.

- Phyla that share key features are grouped into a **kingdom**. So the chordates are grouped with all the other animals in the animal kingdom. There are five kingdoms, as you will see later in this topic.

The full classification for the plains zebra is shown below. Note that the names for the groups are not English words. This is because this classificatory system was started when Latin was the language used to describe science.

Kingdom	Animalia
Phylum	Chordata
Class	Mammalia
Order	Perissodactyla
Family	Equidae
Genus	*Equus*
Species	*quagga*

REMEMBER

You do not need to remember examples of each classificatory group, but you should remember the structure of the classificatory system.

Note that the genus and species names are written in italics. When we refer to a species using its Latin name we use both of these. So the plains zebra is called *Equus quagga*, whereas the mountain zebra is called *Equus zebra*.

This use of two names to identify a species is called the **binomial system**. (*Bi-* means 'two', and *nomial* relates to 'names', so *binomial* literally means 'two names'.) The binomial system is an internationally agreed system that gives a different binomial name to every species. Anyone who wants to be very clear about the species they are referring to uses the agreed binomial name.

EXTENDED

The value of classification

Classifying organisms in the way described above is called a hierarchical classification. This can be useful in helping us to understand the evolutionary relationships between organisms. Organisms within a classificatory group are usually more closely related than organisms in different groups. So we could guess that the plains zebra and mountain zebra became separate species relatively recently in evolution, but that zebras and rhinoceroses are more distantly related because they belong to a larger group – the same order rather than the same genus.

Using the binomial name helps to prevent confusion – so for example, if someone is describing zebras that they have seen, they can be much clearer about the species if they refer to *Equus quagga* or *Equus zebra*. This can be very important in **conservation** – the protection of species and habitats. For example, there are thousands of plains zebra in Africa, although most of them live in game reserves. However, the mountain zebra is considered vulnerable to extinction, as there are less than 3000 in the wild. This means that zoos and animal parks around the world are putting more effort into breeding *Equus zebra* than *Equus quagga*, to help protect the mountain zebra species.

END OF EXTENDED

QUESTIONS

1. Define the term *species*.

2. Describe how features are used to classify organisms.

3. Using an example, explain what is meant by the *binomial system* of naming organisms.

4. EXTENDED Give two reasons why classification of species is useful.

EXTENDED

METHODS OF CLASSIFICATION

In the past, scientists used the physical features of organisms to identify how similar they were and therefore decide how to classify them. These features included:

- **morphology** – the study of what organisms look like
- **anatomy** – the study of the body structure of organisms.

This works well when organisms share similar features because they evolved from a shared **ancestor**. It fails when organisms share features that are adaptations to a particular habitat.

zebras and horses evolved from a shared ancestor about 6 million years ago

Horses and zebras look similar because they share a recent ancestor.

Dolphins (mammals) and sharks (fish) are not closely related. They have a similar morphology because they are both active predators in the sea.

△ Fig 1.6 Similar features may be the result of inheritance or the result of adaptation to the same environment.

END OF EXTENDED

SCIENCE IN CONTEXT DUCK-BILLED PLATYPUS

Grouping organisms by features can cause problems because you have to use the right features to get a good classification. For example, a duck-billed platypus has a beak, webbed feet and lays eggs, which are all characteristics more commonly associated with birds. However, the platypus is not a bird but a mammal, because it has fur and the mother produces milk from mammary glands to feed her young. These two characteristics are unique to mammals. The beak and feet are adaptations to the environment, and the platypus lays eggs because it belongs to the oldest group of mammals.

△ Fig 1.7 The duck-billed platypus can be difficult to classify from its features.

EXTENDED

New techniques for comparing organisms include **DNA analysis** (sequencing of bases in DNA, Topic 4), and **protein analysis** (sequencing of amino acids in proteins, Topic 4). Offspring inherit copies of their parent's DNA, but a few changes may occur during the copying. This not only changes the DNA base sequence, but may also change the amino acid sequence in the proteins made from the DNA. More changes happen each time the DNA is copied. So the more different the DNA or protein in two organisms, the less related they are, and also the longer the time since they shared a common ancestor.

Sometimes the DNA and protein results are virtually identical to those produced from morphology and anatomy, but occasionally they are very different. For example, there are mole species on almost every continent, and they all look very alike. However, DNA and protein analysis shows that on each continent the moles evolved from other larger species and so are not closely related to moles on other continents. This helps to confirm that the new techniques are more accurate for classification than the older ones.

END OF EXTENDED

QUESTIONS

1. **EXTENDED** Define the terms *morphology* and *anatomy*.

2. **EXTENDED** Describe the advantages and disadvantages of using morphology and anatomy to classify organisms.

3. **EXTENDED** Explain how evidence from DNA and proteins is being used to classify organisms.

FEATURES OF ORGANISMS

All living organisms are formed from cells. Each cell is surrounded by a **cell membrane**, which controls what enters and leaves the cell. Within each cell is the jelly-like **cytoplasm**. This is where many reactions take place. Each cell also contains genetic material in the form of **DNA** (deoxyribonucleic acid). DNA makes it possible for cells to divide and reproduce. It also controls the processes that go on in the cell.

EXTENDED

All cells need to make proteins and they do this in a process called **protein synthesis**. Some kinds of proteins are used as parts of structures in the cell, such as the cell membrane. One particular group of proteins are the **enzymes**. Their role in the cell is to control reactions (see Topic 5), such as the reactions in the process of **respiration**. Protein synthesis is carried out on particular structures in the cell called **ribosomes**. Ribosomes are too small to be seen with a standard light microscope, but there may be millions of them within a cell.

Viruses

Viruses are very simple structures, consisting of an outer protein coat that protects the genetic material inside. They have no cell structures or cytoplasm, so they do not respire or sense their surroundings. They also do not take in substances to build more cells, or excrete anything. In many ways they behave like simple crystalline chemicals. However, when viruses infect a cell, such as a bacterial, plant or animal cell, they cause that cell to produce many copies of the virus. So they do reproduce. Not everyone agrees on whether viruses can be called *living* organisms.

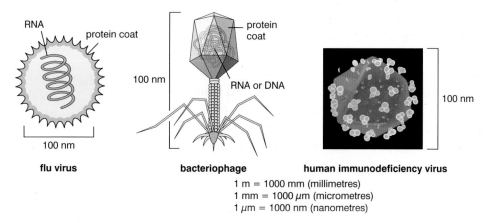

1 m = 1000 mm (millimetres)
1 mm = 1000 μm (micrometres)
1 μm = 1000 nm (nanometres)

△ Fig 1.8 Three kinds of virus. One thousand virus particles would fit across the width of one human hair.

END OF EXTENDED

SCIENCE IN CONTEXT   **HIV AND AIDS**

The HIV virus is one of a group of viruses that attack and destroy cells in the body's immune system. This leaves the body open to infection by other **pathogens** (disease-causing organisms). In the case of HIV, this results in the disease called AIDS. Many AIDS patients die not from the HIV virus, but from other diseases such as tuberculosis, which is caused by a bacterium.

The HIV virus does not survive well in the environment and is mainly transmitted from one person to another through body fluids. The most common route of transmission is sexual intercourse. However, transmission in blood is also possible, such as through blood transfusion, or the sharing of injection needles between drug users. An infected mother can pass the HIV virus to a fetus in her uterus through the placenta, or to the baby through breast milk after birth.

QUESTIONS

1. Identify three key features shared by all living organisms.

2. EXTENDED Describe the function of ribosomes in living organisms.

3. EXTENDED Name the energy-releasing process inside cells that is controlled by enzymes.

4. EXTENDED Which features of viruses are similar to cells of other kinds of organism, and which are different?

The kingdoms of life

Most of the organisms that you see around you belong to one of two kingdoms, the animals and the plants.

Plants

Plants vary greatly in size and shape, from tall rainforest trees to tiny flowers such as violets. Plants are multicellular organisms, which means they are made up of more than one cell (usually thousands or millions of cells).

Plant cells have features that are not found in animal cells. For example, plant cells may contain **chloroplasts**. These

△ Fig 1.9 The green leaves of a plant show that it is able to make its own food.

are green structures inside cells, in which the plant is able to make its own food. (You will learn more about cell structure in Topic 2.) Making their own food distinguishes plants from animals, which have to eat their food.

Plants are not usually able to move about, as animals can do. However, parts of plants may move, such as when leaves track the Sun's movements across the sky, or when seeds are spread by wind or with help from animals.

Animals

The variety of animals is huge, from enormous whales and elephants to tiny ants. Animals are also multicellular organisms. Animals differ from plants in having to find food to eat. Many animals move about to do this.

△ Fig 1.10 Animals can usually move more freely than plants.

QUESTIONS

1. Describe one difference between plant and animal cells.

2. Describe one other difference between plants and animals.

3. A new organism has been discovered. Some of its cells contain chloroplasts. Should the organism be classified as a plant or as an animal? Explain your answer.

EXTENDED

The five kingdoms of life

Living organisms can be classified into one of the five kingdoms shown in. The organisms in each kingdom have particular features that distinguish them from other kingdoms.

Prokaryote kingdom	Protoctist kingdom	Fungus kingdom	Plant kingdom	Animal kingdom
Escherichia coli *Vibrio cholerae*	*Amoeba* *Spirogyra* seaweed	yeast cells mushroom	flower shoot tree	cat ladybird newt snake snail starfish

△ Fig 1.11 The five kingdoms of living organisms.

Fungi

Some fungi (such as yeast) are single celled, but most have a structure consisting of fine threads known as **hyphae**. Several hyphae together form a **mycelium**. Many fungi can be seen without a microscope. Their cells do not contain chlorophyll, so they cannot carry out **photosynthesis**. To obtain nutrients they secrete digestive enzymes outside the cells onto living or dead animal or plant material, and absorb the digested nutrients (**saprotrophic nutrition**).

Examples of fungi include yeast, a single-celled fungus used by humans in baking and brewing, and *Mucor*, a fungus with the typical hyphal structure. *Mucor* is often seen as a mould growing on spoiled foods.

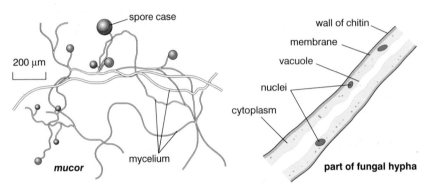

△ Fig 1.12 Left: the mycelium and spore cases of *Mucor*, a mould. Right: detail of a hypha of *Mucor*.

SCIENCE IN CONTEXT — MUSHROOMS AND TOADSTOOLS

We normally think of a mushroom or toadstool as the whole of a fungus, because this is usually all we can see. However, these are only the reproductive organs, in which spores are produced. The mycelium of the fungus is usually hidden below ground or within rotting materials, where it is moist and where the hyphae can digest the surrounding tissue and absorb the nutrients that are released. The reproductive structures have to be large enough so that the wind can carry the spores away to other places, and tough enough to survive the drying conditions of the air until the spores have been dispersed.

△ Fig 1.13 The fruiting body is often the only visible evidence of a fungus.

Prokaryotes

Prokaryotes are single-celled microscopic organisms. Their cells are much smaller than those of plants and animals.

Prokaryote cells also differ from the cells of plants and animals in that they have no **nucleus**, so their genetic material (DNA) lies free in the cytoplasm inside the cell. This feature gives the group their name: *pro* means 'before' and *karyon* is Greek for 'nucleus'. Animals, plants, fungi and protoctists are eukaryotes, from *eu* meaning 'true' and *karyon* because the DNA in their cells is within a nucleus. Many bacteria have additional circles of genetic material, called **plasmids**.

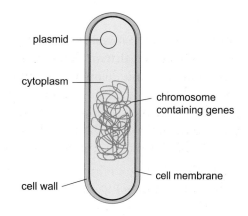

△ Fig 1.14 Generalised structure of a bacterial cell.

Prokaryotic cells are surrounded by a cell membrane. Some bacterial cells also have a **cell wall**, although in different groups of bacteria the cell wall is made of different chemicals.

The kingdom includes bacteria such as *Salmonella*, which causes food poisoning, and *Mycobacterium*, which causes a disease called tuberculosis.

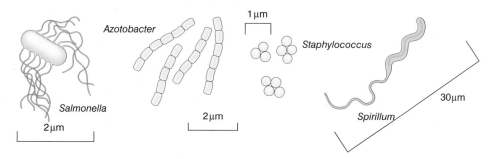

△ Fig 1.15 Different bacteria can be recognised from their shape and structure.

SCIENCE IN CONTEXT **BACTERIAL PLASMIDS**

Bacterial plasmids have become very useful to us in genetic engineering, where they are used as vectors (see Topic 20). Not all bacteria have plasmids, but those that do transfer these small circles of genetic material to other bacteria quite easily. Plasmids may even be transferred between bacteria of different species. This is not true reproduction, as the transfer is not of the main chromosome and may not lead to production of new individuals. However, this kind of transfer may be important in the spread of antibiotic resistance between bacterial species, because some of the genes for antibiotic resistance are found in the plasmids.

Protoctists

Protoctists are also single-celled microscopic organisms, but they are usually much larger than bacteria. Their cells contain a nucleus, so they are eukaryotes, and many have features of animal cells or plant cells.

One example is *Amoeba,* which looks like an animal cell, is found in ponds and feeds on other microscopic organisms. Other protoctists, such as *Chlorella*, look more like plant cells because they contain chloroplasts and so can photosynthesise. A few protoctists are pathogens, such as *Plasmodium,* the organism that causes the disease malaria in humans.

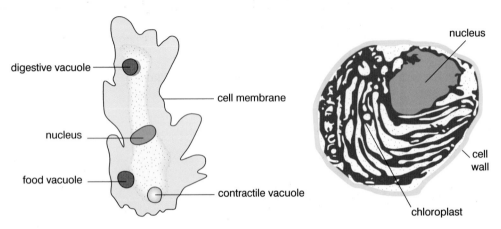

Fig 1.16 *Amoeba* (left) and *Chlorella* (right) are both protoctists because they are single celled and contain a nucleus.

SCIENCE IN CONTEXT **MALARIA**

Malaria is one of the greatest causes of death through infectious illness in the world today. Around 0.75 million people die of the disease each year, mostly young children and mostly in sub-Saharan Africa. The disease is caused by the protoctist *Plasmodium*, which has a clever way of getting from one person to the next: it hitches a lift in the alimentary canal of an *Anopheles* mosquito. The female mosquitoes suck blood from humans to get the nutrients they need to lay eggs. As a mosquito pierces into a blood vessel, it inserts a little liquid to prevent the blood from clotting. If the mosquito has fed recently on a person infected with *Plasmodium*, this liquid will contain some of the parasites and so infect the new person. This protects the protoctist from the harsh conditions of the environment.

QUESTIONS

1. Name the five kingdoms of living organisms and give an example of each kingdom.

2. Describe one key difference between a bacterial cell and an animal cell.

3. Which characteristics do fungi share with

   a) plants

   b) animals?

4. Explain why some protoctists were once classified as plants and others as animals.

END OF EXTENDED

Features of the animal kingdom

The animal kingdom can be divided into two large groups:

- **invertebrates**, which have no backbone
- **vertebrates**, which have a backbone.

The vertebrates are placed in the phylum Chordata. This phylum includes five orders:

- mammals.
- birds
- reptiles
- amphibians
- fish (including bony fish)

There are many groups of invertebrates, but some of the largest and most important groups are the insects, crustaceans, arachnids and myriapods. These groups are classified together as arthropods, which all have a tough outer shell called an **exoskeleton**.

The following sections describe the main features of these groups.

Mammals

Mammals live on land and in the water. Examples include humans, elephants, mice and whales.

- All mammals have hair or fur on their body, which can be important as insulation. Hairs can also provide sensitivity, as in whiskers.

△ Fig 1.17 Even aquatic (water-living) mammals have some hair. In the walrus, the hairs are very sensitive to touch, which helps them to find their food.

- Mammals maintain a constant internal body temperature, which is usually above that of the environment.
- Mammals have entirely internal fertilisation, with the penis of the male being inserted into the vagina of the female.
- A few mammal species lay eggs, although most give birth to live young. In the largest group of mammals the young develop inside the mother's body, supported by the placenta.
- After birth the young are fed on milk produced by mammary glands.
- In some species extensive parental behaviour also helps to protect and raise the young.

Birds

Birds exist in almost every environment and across every continent. Examples include swans, penguins and ostriches. Most birds feature:

- feathers and wings that allow them to fly and that provide good insulation against transfer of heat to the surroundings
- a well-developed circulatory system to supply oxygen to the powerful flight muscles
- a constant body temperature that is often much higher than that of the surrounding air
- bones that are modified to be strong but light
- internal fertilisation
- a reproductive process that involves producing and laying hard-shelled eggs in which the young develop outside the parent's body
- often significant parental behaviour to protect the eggs and raise the young.

△ Fig 1.18 Most birds are well adapted to flight.

Reptiles

Reptiles are found living in a wide range of environments from marine and freshwater, through to dry deserts. They include snakes, lizards, turtles and crocodiles.

- Some reptiles have legs (never more than four), whereas snakes have none.
- Reptiles have a thick scaly skin that protects them from water loss.
- Their body temperature generally varies with the temperature of the environment, although they may bask in the early morning sun to help raise body temperature quickly.
- Fertilisation is internal and occurs when the openings of the male and female reproductive tracts are brought together. This means that reptiles do not have to find water for reproduction, as amphibians do.
- Reptiles lay their eggs, which are protected by thick leathery shells, on land.

△ Fig 1.19 Snakes are legless reptiles that lay eggs on land.

Amphibians

Amphibians include frogs and toads, newts and salamanders.

- Most amphibians have two pairs of legs, although a few species have none.
- Many amphibians spend part of their life in water and part on land.
- When amphibians hatch from eggs (as tadpoles), they have gills rather like those of fish.
- As the tadpoles develop they lose their gills, the tail shortens, they develop legs and a simple lung. These changes are known as metamorphosis. Adult frogs exchange gases with the air mainly through their moist skin or lung.

△ Fig 1.20 Adult frogs usually have a short body, no tail and webbed fingers and toes to aid swimming.

- Fertilisation is external, with males shedding sperm over eggs released by the female directly into the water.

Bony fish

Bony fish are well adapted for swimming.

- Their body shape is usually streamlined, to help them swim efficiently.
- Their bony fins and tail control the direction of their movements.
- They also have a structure called a swim bladder, which allows them to control their buoyancy and remain stationary in water.
- Their skin is protected with overlapping scales.
- Many have a flap-like structure, called an operculum, which covers the gills on either side of the body. Movement of the operculum draws water across the gills even when the fish is stationary in the water.
- Fertilisation is external, with the male shedding sperm over the eggs as the female sheds the eggs directly into the water. The young usually have to fend for themselves when they hatch from the eggs.

△ Fig 1.21 Bony fish have many features for survival in water.

Myriapods

Myriapods means 'many legged ones' and this group includes centipedes and millipedes.

- Millipedes can have up to 200 pairs of legs on their body and range in size from microscopic to nearly 30 cm in length. They live in leaf litter and soil and generally eat plant debris.
- Centipedes have fewer legs and are predators.

△ Fig 1.22 Myriapods can have up to 200 pairs of legs.

Insects

Insects are the most successful group on the planet in terms of numbers. Examples include bees, beetles, flies and butterflies.

- Insect bodies have three regions: the head, thorax and abdomen.
- They have six jointed legs and many insects have pairs of wings.
- The whole of the body is covered by a tough exoskeleton made of chitin.
- The head is well supplied with sense organs, including compound eyes. The antennae can detect vibrations, and some insects have extremely sensitive chemical detectors that can sense chemicals in tiny quantities in the air.
- Some insects (e.g. ants and bees) have a complex social structure with intricate behaviour patterns. These sorts of insects often live in large communities with a single individual (the queen) who produces most of the young.

△ Fig 1.23 Bees work together to find food and care for the young in the colony.

Arachnids

The majority of arachnids are spiders, although the group also includes scorpions. Almost all arachnids live on land.

- The body plan of spiders has two main parts, with eight legs that arise from the front part. A pair of pedipalps at the front is used to manipulate food.
- Most spiders are carnivorous, catching flying insects in webs. Spider webs are made of a sticky protein that is said to be, weight for weight, stronger than steel.
- Scorpions have an elongated body. The venomous sting at the end of the tail is used for defence and to capture prey.
- Most scorpions are nocturnal and feed on a variety of smaller insects.

△ Fig 1.24 A spider's body is made up of the prosoma (the head region) and the opisthosoma (the back section).

Crustaceans

Crustaceans are a mainly marine group, including crabs, lobsters, crayfish and woodlice. Woodlice are terrestrial but need to live in cool damp places to avoid drying out.

- Crustaceans have a standard body plan with head, thorax and abdomen, although the abdomen may be made of several segments.
- The head has two pairs of antennae.
- The number of legs varies in different groups of crustaceans. Real legs are attached to the thorax but some crustaceans, such as the shrimps, have additional 'swimming legs' attached to the abdomen.
- In some species, such as crabs, a pair of front legs has been highly modified into pincers, or chelipeds.
- Marine crustaceans grow in size by moulting their hard exoskeleton, growing rapidly and then hardening the new exoskeleton. This can occur a number of times during life.

Δ Fig 1.25 The front pincers of a crab may be modified for handling food or for signalling to other crabs.

QUESTIONS

1. Use the following headings to draw up a table: Group, Key body features, Fertilisation, Production of young. Use your table to compare the following groups of vertebrates: bony fish, birds, mammals, amphibians and reptiles.

2. A new animal species has been discovered. It has a backbone, scaly legs, lungs and feathers. How should it be classified? Give a reason for your answer.

3. Myriapods, insects, arachnids and crustaceans are all classified as arthropods. Explain why.

4. Compare the body plan of myriapods, insects, arachnids and crustaceans.

Features of the plant kingdom

The plant kingdom also contains several groups. Two of these are the ferns and the flowering plants.

Ferns

Ferns usually have broad divided leaves called *fronds*. Most grow as clumps of fronds from the ground, though some produce long tough stalks that support the fronds above the ground. In some species the stalks, surrounded by the tough frond bases, form a thick trunk resulting in a tree. Roots at the base of the fern hold it firmly in the ground and absorb water and nutrients from the soil.

During the winter, the fronds die back so there is little to be seen above ground. In the spring the new fronds unfurl from the ground to the tip of the leaf.

Ferns do not have flowers or seeds. Instead they reproduce using spores that are released into the air from spore cases under the leaves.

△ Fig 1.26 Fern spore cases (brown) on the underside of a fern frond release spores into the air when the conditions are right for new ferns to grow.

Flowering plants

The flowering plants are the most obvious group of the plant kingdom. Most of the trees, woody plants, herbaceous (soft leafy) plants and grasses that you see are flowering plants.

They generally have a central stem bearing side branches with leaves that tend to be smaller than the large fronds of ferns. Roots are generally well developed for supporting the plant and absorbing water and nutrients from the soil.

Reproduction in flowering plants depends on flowers. Male gametes in pollen are usually carried from the flower in which they are produced to flowers containing the female gametes. Fertilisation results in seeds. Flowering plants may also produce fruits around the seeds. The fruit may aid the seeds in their dispersal or help to protect them.

The flowering plant group is divided in two depending on seed structure. Cotyledons are food stores that are found in the seeds of flowering plants. **Monocotyledon** flowering plants include grasses and have a single cotyledon. **Dicotyledon** flowering plants have two cotyledons, and include most of the plants with visible flowers. The two groups of plants also differ in structure, as monocotyledons often have long strap-like leaves with parallel veins, whereas dicotyledons usually have broad leaves of many shapes with branching veins.

QUESTIONS

1. Summarise the similarities and differences between ferns and flowering plants.
2. List the features that distinguish dicotyledonous plants from monocotyledonous plants.

END OF EXTENDED

DICHOTOMOUS KEYS

Identification keys consist of a series of questions that allow biologists to identify unknown organisms. The questions must have simple answers (usually yes or no) and be answerable by looking at the organism. A **dichotomous key** separates the choices into two groups each time (see Fig. 1.27). Each question results in smaller and smaller groups until the final group contains only one species. In this way an organism can be identified in the field without use of complicated equipment.

This type of key requires careful use. As well as being easily observed, the feature chosen for each question must always be present. So using flowers to identify plants can be a problem if the plant is not in flower when you find it.

Remember that living things are highly variable. Think how different one human being can be from another. It is often better to examine several examples of an organism rather than only one.

When using a key make sure you understand exactly which feature you are meant to be observing and always carefully consider both options given, especially where the answer is not a simple yes or no.

Many keys include a simple description of the organism along with its name to act as a quick check that the key has been used correctly. If, when using a key, you find that the organism you are examining does not fit this description, go back over all the questions and carefully consider your answers.

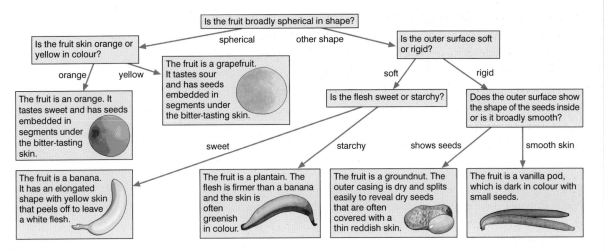

Δ Fig 1.27 A simple dichotomous key to identify some common fruits.

QUESTIONS

1. Explain what is meant by a *dichotomous key*.

2. Give two reasons why a dichotomous key may not always identify an organism.

SCIENCE IN CONTEXT

IDENTIFICATION IN THE FIELD

Scientists working in the field can now take photos of organisms that they cannot identify and email them back to museums, where they are checked against keys of organisms. If the organism is new to science, the scientist can then take further pictures, or collect an individual, to take back to the lab for further study.

Constructing A Dichotomous Key

To construct a key, you start by looking carefully at the organisms to find simple differences between them that will help to produce the groups. It is important to choose features that are fairly constant in a species, or that are so different between species that the variation within the species is not a problem for distinguishing them. Colour, shape and markings can all be useful distinguishing features, but be sure that they are not too variable between individuals.

Size of species can be used as a distinguishing feature as long as you can compare it with something standard for each species. For example, if you were making a key for identifying the different herbivores on the African grasslands, you would see that some are larger than others. Just saying one is a 'big animal' and another is a 'smaller animal' isn't helpful. So if you are about 1.5 m tall, you could use 'greater than 1.5 m tall to top of head' and 'less than 1.5 m tall to top of head', using your height to compare each species against.

Try to choose features that are present in all individuals of the species. For example, using shape of horns as a distinguishing feature for African herbivores will only work for species in which both males and females have horns of similar shape, or have no horns at all.

If you are starting with many organisms for your key, try to choose the first question or two to split the group almost equally. For example, a key for all the herbivores of the African grasslands might start: 'Does it look a bit like a horse?' This would separate out all the antelopes from animals such as the elephant, giraffe and rhinoceros.

kudu   wildebeest   zebra   Thomson's gazelle

Δ Fig 1.28 Some herbivores of the African savannah.

You can group the organisms in any way that is useful. So, for the animals shown in Fig. 1.28, we could group kudu, wildebeest and zebra with 'stripes across the back', leaving the gazelle out of the group.

This would give us this question for a key:

Does it have stripes across the back?   yes – go to next question

no – **gazelle**

We would then need a question that separates out one of kudu, wildebeest or zebra from the other two. And so on, until the key has identified each species separately.

QUESTIONS

1. Explain why it is important to use easily identifiable features when constructing a key.

2. Using the photographs above, complete the key for these four animals.

End of topic checklist

Key terms

anatomy, binomial system, cell membrane, cell wall, chloroplast, classification, conservation, cytoplasm, dichotomous key, DNA analysis, enzyme, excretion, exoskeleton, genus, growth, kingdom, morphology, movement, photosynthesis, plasmid, prokaryote, protein analysis, protein synthesis, reproduction, respiration, ribosomes, species, vertebrate

During your study of this topic you should have learned:

○ How to describe the seven characteristics of life: movement, respiration, sensitivity, growth, reproduction, excretion and nutrition.

○ EXTENDED How to define the seven characteristics of life.

○ That organisms are classified into groups by the features that they share.

○ How to define a species a group of organisms with many similar features, and know that members of a species can breed with others of the same species to produce fertile offspring.

○ How to describe the binomial system as giving organisms a genus and species name that distinguishes them from other species.

○ EXTENDED That the classification of organisms helps us to identify evolutionary relationships between them.

○ EXTENDED That the binomial system of naming organisms makes it easier for people working on the of species to be certain they are talking about the same species.

○ EXTENDED That classification used to be based just on the visible features (morphology) and body structure (anatomy) of an organism.

○ EXTENDED Scientists now also use the DNA sequence of organisms to help identify how closely related the organisms are.

○ All living organisms have cells that are surrounded by a cell membrane. Inside the cell is jelly-like cytoplasm and genetic material in the form of DNA.

○ Plants are multicellular organisms that make their own food in photosynthesis using light energy. Many of their cells contain chloroplasts, in which photosynthesis takes place. Their cells are surrounded by a cellulose cell wall.

○ Animals are multicellular organisms that get their food by eating other organisms. They coordinate their movements using nerves, and most are able to move around.

End of topic checklist continued

○ The definition of vertebrates as animals that have a backbone.

○ The definition of arthropods as invertebrates that have jointed exoskeletons in three main parts.

○ EXTENDED That all living cells contain ribosomes and to define these as the site of protein synthesis, including the formation of enzymes that control cell processes such as anaerobic respiration.

○ EXTENDED To list the main features of viruses, including know that they are infective particles made of a protein coat surrounding nucleic acid, they do not have a true cell structure, can only reproduce when inside a cell of another organism and many people think they are not true living organisms.

○ EXTENDED Living organisms can be divided into five kingdoms based on their features: animals, plants, fungi, protoctists and prokaryotes.

○ EXTENDED The plant kingdom contains the ferns, which have frond leaves and produce spores during reproduction, and flowering plants that reproduce using flowers.

○ EXTENDED Flowering plants are divided into monocotyledons, which have leaves with parallel veins and seeds containing one food store, and dicotyledons, which have leaves with branching veins and seeds containing two food stores.

○ EXTENDED Bacteria are microscopic, single-celled organisms that have no nucleus; they have a circular chromosome and some have additional genetic material in plasmids. They have cell walls and some feed off other living organisms.

○ EXTENDED Protoctists are single-celled microscopic organisms. They are eukaryotes because they have a nucleus in their cell.

○ How to use and construct a dichotomous key to identify organisms from easily identifiable features.

End of topic questions

Note: The marks awarded for these questions indicate the level of detail required in the answers. In the examination, the number of marks awarded to questions like these may be different.

1. Name and describe the seven processes of life. **(7 marks)**

2. Name two life processes necessary for an organism to release energy. **(2 marks)**

3. Explain why dry mass is used to measure growth. **(2 marks)**

4. When you place a crystal of copper(II) sulfate in a saturated solution of the same compound, the crystal will increase in size. Does this mean that the crystal is alive? Explain your answer. **(2 marks)**

5. Plants cannot move about, as animals can. Does that mean animals are more alive than plants? Explain your answer. **(2 marks)**

6. During winter, an oak tree in the UK will lose its leaves and not grow. Is the tree still living during this time? Explain your answer using all the characteristics of life. **(4 marks)**

7. The binomial name of the lion is *Panthera leo*.

   a) Which part of the name is unique to the lion? **(1 mark)**

   b) What does the other part of the name indicate? Explain your answer. **(1 mark)**

8. A zoo has a male animal and a female animal that look very alike. They put them in the same enclosure to see if they will breed.

   a) Suggest why the zoo think the animals may be of the same species. **(1 mark)**

   b) Describe what the zoo would expect to happen if the animals were of the same species. **(1 mark)**

   c) EXTENDED Describe another method that the zoo could use to check if the animals were of the same species. Explain your answer. **(2 marks)**

9. Imagine you discovered a new animal while on an expedition to a remote island in Indonesia. Explain how you would work out how to classify it. **(2 marks)**

10. EXTENDED In an exam question about classification, a student wrote:

    A bat has wings, and birds have wings, so they should be classified in the same group.

    Bats are actually classified in the class Mammalia (mammals) and birds are classified in the class Aves (birds). Mammals and birds are grouped in the phylum Chordata (organisms with a bony backbone).

End of topic questions continued

a) Identify the student's error and explain why it is a problem. **(2 marks)**

b) Explain why bats and birds are classified in different classes but in the same phylum. **(2 marks)**

11. EXTENDED DNA analysis has shown that humans share the following proportions of their genetic code with other animals: chimpanzee 96%, chicken c.60%, fly 60%, mouse c.75%.

   a) Explain what this evidence suggests about all these animals. **(1 mark)**

   b) Describe and explain the pattern of the results in relation to humans. **(2 marks)**

12. **a)** Describe three main features that are found in both plant cells and in animal cells. **(3 marks)**

   b) Describe two main features that are found in plant cells but not in animal cells. **(2 marks)**

13. Explain why a large tree and a crop such as rice or maize are both classified as plants. **(2 marks)**

14. The blue whale is the largest animal on Earth. It is classified as a mammal, although it has no fur. Suggest which other features the whale has that means it belongs to the mammal group and not another group. **(2 marks)**

15. **a)** Separate the following animals into two groups based on a main feature:
   crab   dog   shark   bee **(2 marks)**

   b) Describe the main feature you used to classify the animals. **(1 mark)**

16. EXTENDED Put the following organisms into size order, starting with the smallest:
   bacteria   protoctists   viruses **(2 marks)**

17. EXTENDED Draw up a table to compare the features of the five kingdoms. Your table should include basic cell structure, and any feature that distinguishes the group from other kingdoms. **(5 marks)**

18. EXTENDED Fungi were once classified as plants.

   a) Suggest which features were used to justify this classification. Explain your choice. **(2 marks)**

   b) Explain why fungi are no longer classified in the same kingdom as plants. **(2 marks)**

19. **EXTENDED** Some people think viruses are living organisms, other people do not.

   a) Which characteristic of living organisms do viruses have? **(1 mark)**

   b) List the other characteristics of living organisms, and for each one describe what viruses can and cannot do. **(6 marks)**

   c) Using what you know about viruses, prepare an argument for classifying them as living organisms. **(2 marks)**

   d) Using what you know about viruses, prepare an argument for *not* classifying them as living organisms. **(2 marks)**

20. Look at the key of fruits shown in Fig 1.27. List the questions and answers that would lead to an identification of a banana. **(3 marks)**

21. **a)** Give two advantages for the sort of dichotomous key shown in Fig. 1.27. **(2 marks)**

   b) Identify one problem you might have when using such a key. **(1 mark)**

22. Read the following questions carefully.

   i) Does the specimen have wings?

   ii) Does the specimen have feathers?

   iii) Does the specimen lay eggs?

   a) Which question do you think would be most useful for placing an organism in the bird group? **(1 mark)**

   b) Explain your answer. **(1 mark)**

23. Look at the pictures of flowers. Construct a simple dichotomous key to identify each flower. **(2 marks)**

| Daisy | Hibiscus | Poppy | Rose |

Multicellular organisms are made up of different cell types that each have a specific job to do. The human body is made up of about 200 different cell types, ranging from muscle and fat cells, to blood, skin and nerve cells.

All 'complex' cells (those that contain a nucleus) in all animals, plants and protoctists on Earth have the same basic structure. Scientists say that this is because we have all evolved from a single complex cell. This first complex cell evolved from a simple bacteria-like cell (without a nucleus) more than 1600 million years ago. This is the origin of all the millions of different species of plants, animals and protoctists that live on Earth today.

CONTENTS

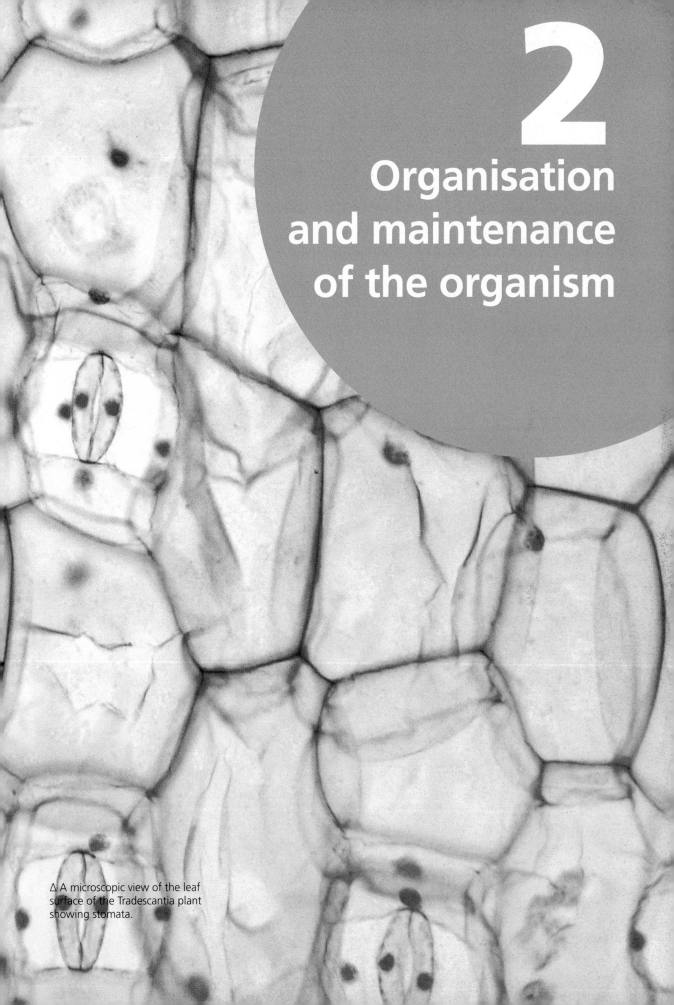

2

Organisation and maintenance of the organism

◁ A microscopic view of the leaf surface of the Tradescantia plant showing stomata.

Organisation and maintenance of the organism

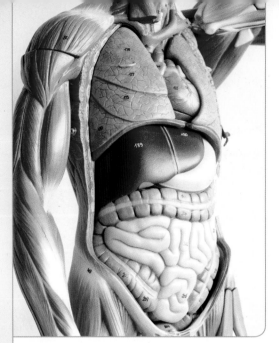

△ Fig 2.1 The human body is made up of several systems of grouped organs, including the digestive system, the nervous system, the muscle/skeletal system and the respiratory system.

INTRODUCTION

Bringing together similar activities that have the same purpose can make things much more efficient. For example, bringing teachers and students together in a school helps more students to learn more quickly than if each teacher travelled to each student's home for lessons. The same is true in the body. Having groups of similar cells in the same place as a tissue, and grouping tissues into organs, helps the body carry out all the life processes much more efficiently and so stay alive.

KNOWLEDGE CHECK

✓ State that organisms are formed from many cells.
✓ Describe how cells may be specialised in different ways to carry out different functions.
✓ Define the terms *tissue, organ* and *organ system.*
✓ Describe how the organisation of the body systems contributes to the seven life processes.
✓ State that a microscope can be used to magnify specimens so we can see more detail.

LEARNING OBJECTIVES

✓ Describe and compare the structures in plant and animal cells.
✓ Describe the function of each type of cell structure seen under the light microscope.
✓ **EXTENDED** Identify mitochondria and rough endoplasmic reticulum in cells, and describe the function of mitochondria and ribosomes.
✓ **EXTENDED** Know that the cytoplasm of all cells contain ribosomes on rough endoplasmic reticulum and vesicles.
✓ **EXTENDED** Know that almost all cells have mitochondria on rough endoplasmic reticulum.
✓ State that aerobic respiration occurs in mitochondria and that cells with high rates of respiration have many mitochondria to provide sufficient energy.
✓ Relate structure to function in a range of specialised cells.
✓ Define tissues as groups of similar cells with a similar function.
✓ Define organs as groups of tissues that work together for a particular function.
✓ Define organ systems as groups of organs that work together for a particular function.
✓ Give examples of tissues, organs and organ systems.
✓ Describe how to calculate the magnification of biological specimens seen under a microscope.
✓ Calculate the size of biological specimens using millimetres as units.
✓ Identify the different levels of organisation in images of familiar material.
✓ **EXTENDED** Identify the different levels of organisation in images of unfamiliar material.
✓ Calculate the size of biological specimens using millimetres as units.
✓ **EXTENDED** Calculate the size of biological specimens using micrometres as units.

CELL STRUCTURE AND ORGANISATION

The diagrams below show a typical animal cell and typical plant cells.
These cells all have a nucleus and cytoplasm.

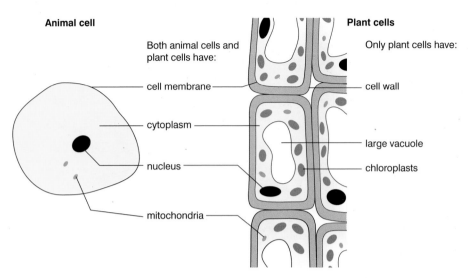

△ Fig 2.2 The basic structures of an animal cell (e.g. liver cell) and plant cells (e.g. palisade mesophyll cells).

All living organisms are made of cells. Some, such as bacteria, protoctists and some fungi, are formed from a single cell; others, such as the majority of plants and animals, are **multicellular**, with a body made of many cells. All animal and plant cells have certain features in common:

- a **cell membrane** surrounds the cell
- **cytoplasm** inside the cell, in which all the other structures are found
- a large **nucleus**.

A typical animal cell is a human liver cell.

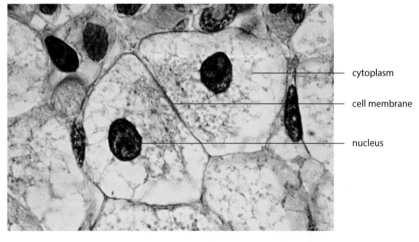

△ Fig 2.3 Structures in animal cells seen using a light microscope. Note these cells have been stained to make some structures easier to see.

Plant cells also have features that are not found in animal cells, such as:

- a **cell wall** surrounding the cell membrane
- a large central **vacuole**
- green **chloroplasts** found in some, but not all, plant cells.

A typical plant cell is a palisade cell in the upper part of a leaf.

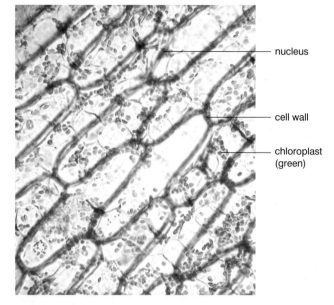

△ Fig 2.4 Structures in plant cells seen using a light microscope. Note that the cell membrane and vacuole are difficult to distinguish in this image. The chloroplasts are supported by the cytoplasm.

nucleus

cell wall

chloroplast (green)

Functions of cell structures

Each structure in a cell has a particular role.

- The cell membrane holds the cell together and controls substances entering and leaving the cell.
- The cytoplasm supports many small cell structures and is where many different chemical processes happen. It contains water, and many solutes are dissolved in it.
- The nucleus contains genetic material in the **chromosomes.** These control how a cell grows and works. The nucleus also controls cell division.
- The plant cell wall is made of cellulose, which gives the cell extra support and defines its shape.
- The plant vacuole contains cell sap. The vacuole is used for storage of some materials, and to support the shape of the cell. If there is not enough cell sap in the vacuole, the whole plant may wilt.
- Chloroplasts contain the green pigment chlorophyll, which absorbs the light energy that plants need to make food in the process known as **photosynthesis**.

SCIENCE IN CONTEXT ARTIFICIAL CELLS

Scientists have discovered so much about how the structures of cells are formed and work together that they are starting to create artificial cells. This has great potential for medicine, because these cells could be used, for example, to deliver drugs inside the body directly to the cells that need them. They could also be used in biotechnology, for example to make fuels that could replace fossil fuels.

Developing investigative skills

The photograph shows the view of some cells seen through a light microscope.

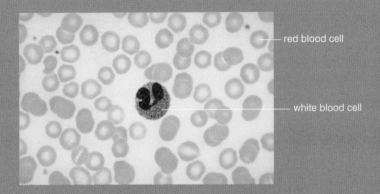

red blood cell

white blood cell

△ Fig 2.5 A photograph of blood cells taken with a light microscope.

Demonstrate and describe techniques

❶ a) Describe how to set up a slide on a microscope so that the image is clearly focused.

b) Describe and explain what precautions should be taken when viewing a slide at high magnification.

c) Describe what precaution should be taken if using natural light to illuminate the slide, and explain why this is important.

Make observations and measurements

❷ a) Draw and label a diagram of the white blood cell shown in the light micrograph above.

b) If the ×10 eyepiece was used, and the ×40 objective, calculate the magnification of the image compared with the specimen on the slide. (Use the information on page 51 to help you with this.)

Analyse and interpret data

❸ Are the cells shown plant cells or animal cells? Explain your answer.

QUESTIONS

1. a) Using the photograph in Fig. 2.3, make a careful drawing of one of the cells using a sharpened pencil to make clear lines.

  b) Label your drawing to show the three key structures of animal cells.

2. List three cell structures that are found in plant cells but not in animal cells.

3. Name the part of a plant cell that does the following:

  a) carries out photosynthesis

  b) contains cell sap

  c) stops the cell swelling if it takes in a lot of water.

Structures not visible with a light microscope

There are many structures in cells that are too small to be seen using a light microscope. However, they are visible at much higher magnifications using an electron microscope. These structures include vesicles, mitochondria, endoplasmic reticulum and ribosomes.

Vesicles

There are many small sac-like structures in the cytoplasm that are surrounded by a membrane. These structures are called **vesicles**. They can contain many different substances, such as hormones or enzymes made by the cell that are being carried to the cell membrane for release. They might also contain substances that are being stored in the cell, such as oils or fat. The surrounding membrane keeps the contents of the vesicle separate so that they do not interfere with reactions that happen in the cytoplasm.

Mitochondria

All complex cells (those found in plants, animals, protoctists and fungi) contain **mitochondria** (single: mitochondrion). These cell structures are the site of **aerobic respiration**.

Aerobic respiration releases energy for use in other cell processes (see Topic 12), such as for contraction of muscle cells, or for the production of enzymes or hormones in gland cells. Cells that are adapted for one of these purposes have much larger numbers of mitochondria than cells that carry out other roles. For example, there are many more mitochondria in a muscle cell than in a brain cell.

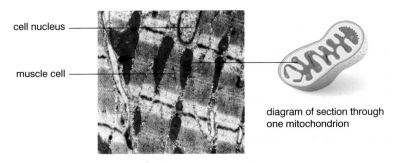

cell nucleus

muscle cell

diagram of section through
one mitochondrion

△ Fig 2.6 Electron micrograph of muscle cells, showing mitochondria (dark red) that supply energy for cell contraction.

Prokaryote cells, like those in bacteria, do not have mitochondria, but carry out respiration within the cytoplasm.

Ribosomes and rough endoplasmic reticulum

All cells contain **ribosomes**, which are tiny structures. Some ribosomes are free in the cytoplasm, but most are attached to a system of membranes inside the cell called **endoplasmic reticulum**. Proteins are produced by ribosomes during protein synthesis (Topic 17).

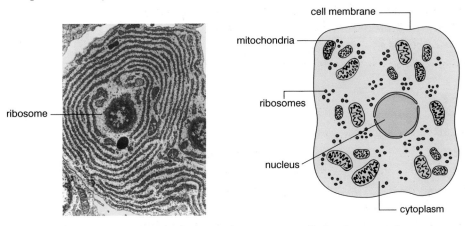

ribosome

cell membrane

mitochondria

ribosomes

nucleus

cytoplasm

△ Fig 2.7 Left: electron micrograph of a human bone marrow cell, showing many ribosomes (purple dots) lying free in the cytoplasm and attached to membranes. Right: diagram of an animal cell showing nucleus, mitochondria and ribosomes, not drawn to scale.

QUESTIONS

1. Describe the roles of vesicles, mitochondria and ribosomes in cells.

2. Explain why the structure of mitochondria and ribosomes was not well understood before the development of the electron microscope.

3. In which of these cells would you expect to find the most mitochondria: heart epithelial cell or heart muscle cell? Explain your answer.

END OF EXTENDED

LEVELS OF ORGANISATION

Cells in multicellular organisms, such as most plants and animals, rarely work independently of all other cells.

- Similar cells are grouped in **tissues**, to perform a shared function, such as muscle cells in a human, or palisade cells in a plant leaf.
- Different tissues are grouped together to form **organs**, which carry out specific functions, for example the heart in a human, or the leaf in a plant.
- Organs are arranged in **organ systems**, which carry out major body functions, such as the circulatory system, reproductive system, nervous system and respiratory system in humans.

For example, the heart is an organ in the human circulatory system that pumps blood around the body. The heart can contract to pump because it is formed from muscle tissue, which contains muscle cells that are specially adapted to contract.

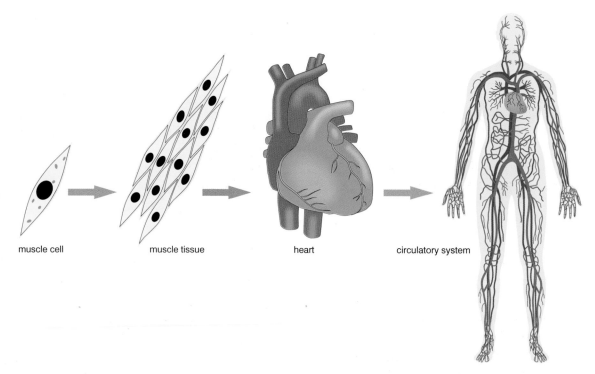

muscle cell muscle tissue heart circulatory system

△ Fig 2.8 The human body is organised at cell level. An individual muscle cell forms part of muscle tissue, which may be found in the heart, which is part of the circulatory system.

REMEMBER

As you study body systems in more detail through your course, remember to identify the organs, tissues and cell types involved in each system, so that you build a range of examples that you can use to answer questions on this topic.

QUESTIONS

1. Give two examples of each of the following in the human body:

  a) tissue   **b)** organ   **c)** system.

2. Give two examples of each of the following in a plant:

  a) tissue   **b)** organ.

Cell specialisation for function

Different types of cells carry out different jobs. Cells have special features that allow them to carry out their job. This is called **specialisation**. Good examples of specialised cells are:

- ciliated cells, nerve cells, red blood cells and sperm and egg cells in humans
- root hair cells, palisade mesophyll cells and xylem vessels in flowering plants.

SCIENCE IN CONTEXT — STEM CELLS

Every tissue in the human body contains a small number of undifferentiated cells. These are called stem cells, and their role is to divide and produce new differentiated cells within the tissue, for growth and repair. Scientists are investigating how stem cells could be given to people to mend tissue that the body cannot mend, such as the spinal cord after an accident in which it is cut. This would make it possible for a person who is paralysed following an accident to move their whole body again.

Ciliated cells

Cilia are tiny hair-like projections that cover the surfaces of certain types of cells. Cilia can move and the cell can coordinate this movement to produce waves that pass over the cell. These waves of moving cilia can move liquid in particular directions.

Ciliated epithelial cells in the lining of the respiratory tract move a liquid called mucus. Tiny particles of dust or bacteria that are trapped in the mucus are carried along in this flow and pass up the tubes. They are then emptied, along with the mucus, into the oesophagus, where they are swallowed and pass into the stomach. In this way the ciliated epithelium keeps the lungs clean. Smoking reduces the effectiveness of these cilia, which explains why smokers often have a cough – they cannot clear away the dirty mucus that collects in their lungs.

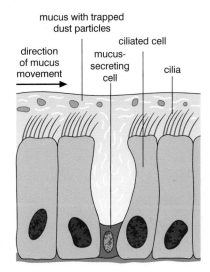

△ Fig 2.9 Secreting cells produce mucus that traps particles in the lungs. Cilia sweep the mucus out of the lungs and into the throat, where it is swallowed.

Palisade mesophyll cells

Palisade mesophyll cells are plant cells found in the upper part of a leaf. They have all the features of a plant cell (see Fig 2.4) but contain a large number of chloroplasts. This is because most photosynthesis carried out by a plant happens in these cells (see more in Topic 6).

Nerve cells

Nerve cells are specialised for conducting electrical impulses around the body. Many have a long fibre that can carry the impulses a long distance, such as from the toe to the base of the spine. The ends of the cell have many endings. Some of these connect to other nerve cells, so that the impulses can be carried to other parts of the body, such as the brain. Other endings connect to sense organs, muscles or glands, so that we can sense changes and respond to them (see more in Topic 14).

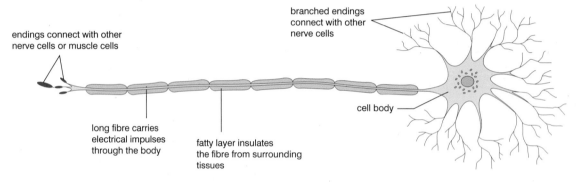

branched endings connect with other nerve cells

endings connect with other nerve cells or muscle cells

cell body

long fibre carries electrical impulses through the body

fatty layer insulates the fibre from surrounding tissues

△ Fig 2.10 This is one kind of nerve cell. All nerve cells carry electrical impulses.

Red blood cells

Red blood cells in mammals are unusual in that they do not have a nucleus and so cannot divide. The whole of the cell is filled with a chemical called haemoglobin, which can pick up oxygen in the lungs and release it near the cells that need it deep inside the body. The shape of the cell means that the innermost part of the red blood cell is never far away from the outside, so diffusion of oxygen in and out happens very rapidly. Red blood cells are made in bone marrow and last only 120 days before they are destroyed in the spleen and liver. As they have no nucleus they cannot divide.

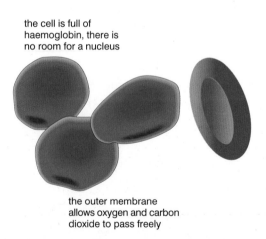

the cell is full of haemoglobin, there is no room for a nucleus

the outer membrane allows oxygen and carbon dioxide to pass freely

△ Fig 2.11 Red blood cells are specialised for carrying oxygen.

ORGANISATION AND MAINTENANCE OF THE ORGANISM

Human sex cells

The human sex cells (gametes – Topic 16) are the **sperm cell** and the **egg cell**. Sperm cells and egg cells have particular forms that are adapted to their roles in reproduction.

Sperm cells are relatively small compared with an egg cell. They have very little cytoplasm surrounding the nucleus, because they carry out few functions other than travelling to the egg cell for fertilisation. There is a small vesicle of enzymes, called the **acrosome**, at the front tip of the cell. The enzymes in the acrosome digest a hole in the egg cell membrane. This allows the nucleus of the sperm cell to enter the egg cell and fuse with its nucleus. The mid piece of the sperm cell contains many mitochondria. The mitochondria provide energy to move the tail, which moves the sperm towards the egg cell.

The human egg cell is a very large cell and almost visible without a microscope. It cannot move on its own. The large amount of cytoplasm around the nucleus provides nutrients for when the cell is fertilised and starts to divide.

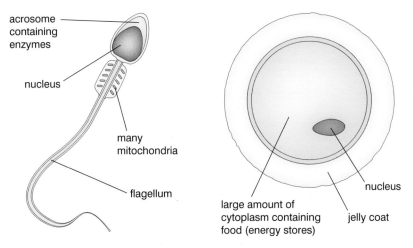

△ Fig 2.12 Diagrams of a human sperm cell (left) and human egg cell (right). Note these are not drawn to scale. An egg cell is around 20 times larger than a single sperm cell.

Root hair cells

In many plants, water and minerals are absorbed from the soil by root hairs, which penetrate the spaces between soil particles. These hairs are very fine extensions of the **root hair cells** on the root surface, just behind the growing tip of a root. The elongated shape of the cells increases the surface area available for absorption of water and dissolved mineral ions. As they age, root hairs develop a waterproof layer and become non-functional. New root hairs are constantly growing as the root pushes through the soil.

△ Fig 2.13 The root hair cells greatly increase the surface area for absorption near the tips of roots.

Xylem vessels

Xylem vessels are made when xylem cells die. Before they die, the cells produce a thick cell wall, impregnated with chemicals that make the cell wall strong and waterproof. The cells are arranged in columns in the vascular bundles (veins) in the plant root, stem and leaf. When the cells die, the cell walls form long tubes through the plant, which carry water and dissolved solutes from the roots to all the other parts of the plant. The strengthening of the vessel walls also helps to support the plant.

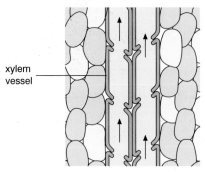

xylem
vessel

Δ Fig 2.14 Xylem vessels are long tubes of dead cells connecting the roots with all the other parts of the plant.

QUESTIONS

1. Where would you find the following cells and what do they do?

   a) ciliated cells

   b) nerve cells

   c) red blood cells

   d) root hair cells

   e) xylem vessels

2. Describe how the structure of sperm and egg cells are adapted to their functions in reproduction.

SIZE OF SPECIMENS

Magnification

Many of the structures that we study in biology are too small to be seen just using our eyes. We can use magnifying glasses and microscopes to examine details of plant and animal cells, and to take pictures and draw the diagrams you see in this book. But often we want to know the actual size of the specimen we are looking at. If we know the magnification we are using to look at a specimen then we can work out the size of a structure.

When using a microscope, the **magnification** of a specimen is calculated from the eyepiece and the objective used to view it.

- The magnification of an eyepiece for a light microscope may be ×4, ×5 or ×10.
- The magnification of an objective for a light microscope may be ×5, ×10, ×20 or ×40.

The magnification of the specimen is the magnification of the eyepiece multiplied by the magnification of the objective.

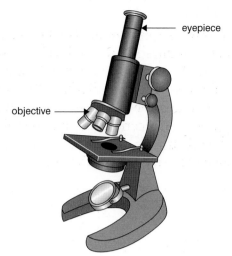

△ Fig 2.15 A light microscope.

WORKED EXAMPLES

1. If the microscope is set up with the ×5 eyepiece and ×20 objective, the magnification of a specimen viewed will be:

$$5 \times 20 = 100$$

We can work out the *size of a structure* from the image size seen under the microscope and the magnification used to view it.

actual size = observed size/magnification

The observed size is measured using a scale, such as a **graticule**, viewed through the microscope.

2. If the diameter of a cell observed under a microscope is 6 mm, and the magnification is ×400, the actual diameter of the cell is:

$$6/400 = 0.015 \text{ mm}.$$

EXTENDED

Micrometres

A micrometre is a length that is one-millionth of a metre, or 1×10^{-6} m. It is sometimes shown using the Greek lower case letter μ (prononunced *mu*). So 1×10^{-6} m may be shown as 1 μm, where the Greek lower case letter μ means 10^{-6}.

Micrometres are a useful measurement for describing objects from microscopy because they are often very small. One millimetre is 1000 micrometres. So, using the example shown above, the actual diameter of the cell in micrometres is $1000 \times 0.015 = 15$ μm.

END OF EXTENDED

QUESTIONS

1. You are looking at an object that measures 0.5 mm and the image you see is 10 mm long. Your friend is looking at an object that is 0.1 mm long using the same magnification. What size of image does your friend see?

2. Imagine you are examining a specimen of blood under a microscope to look at red blood cells. Why might it be important to know the magnification of the lens you are using?

3. The image you are looking at is 2.5 mm long and you are using a magnification of 100. Write down the calculation you would use to work out the actual size of the object.

4. EXTENDED Write down the actual size of the object in Question 3 in millimetres and in micrometres.

End of topic checklist

Key terms

aerobic respiration, cell membrane, cell wall, chloroplast, ciliated cell, cytoplasm, egg cell, endoplasmic reticulum, magnification, mitochondria, multicellular, nucleus, organ, organ system, photosynthesis, red blood cell, ribosome, root hair cell, specialisation, sperm cell, tissue, vacuole, vesicle, xylem vessel

During your study of this topic you should have learned:

○ How to describe structures inside cells including the nucleus, cytoplasm, cell membrane, cell wall, chloroplast and vacuole.

○ That the cytoplasm, cell membrane, cell wall, chloroplast and vacuole have specific roles in cells.

○ That plant and animal cells have some structures in common, but plants also have cell walls, chloroplasts and large central vacuoles that animal cells do not have.

○ EXTENDED About cell structures that are not visible with a light microscope including small storage structures called vesicles, mitochondria in which energy is released in respiration, and ribosomes, which are often on endoplasmic reticulum, and are where proteins are made.

○ EXTENDED How to state that cells with high rates of respiration have many mitochondria.

○ That within the body, cells are grouped in tissues, tissues are grouped in organs, and organs are grouped in organ systems and identify different levels of organisation on images of familiar material.

○ How to define organ systems.

○ How to define tissues, organs and systems and provide examples of each of these.

○ EXTENDED How to identify the different levels of organisation in images of unfamiliar material.

○ How these levels of organisation help the body to function more efficiently.

○ The magnification of a specimen seen under a microscope is the magnification of the eyepiece multiplied by the magnification of the objective used.

○ The size of a structure seen under a microscope is the measured size divided by the magnification.

○ How to calculate the magnification and size of biological specimens.

○ EXTENDED How to calculate the magnification and size of biological specimens using micrometres as units.

End of topic questions

Note: The marks awarded for these questions indicate the level of detail required in the answers. In the examination, the number of marks awarded to questions like these may be different.

1. Describe the role of the following cell structures:

   a) nucleus   **b)** cell membrane   **c)** cytoplasm.   **(3 marks)**

2. Draw up a table to compare the structures found in plant and animal cells.   **(12 marks)**

3. Here are some examples of statements written by students. Each statement contains an error. Identify the error and rewrite the statement so that it is correct.

   a) Animal cells are surrounded by a cell wall that controls what enters and leaves the cell.   **(1 mark)**

   b) All plant cells contain chloroplasts.   **(1 mark)**

   c) Both animal cells and plant cells contain a large central vacuole in the middle of the cell.   **(1 mark)**

4. Red blood cells are unusual because they contain no nucleus. When they are damaged, they have to be replaced with new cells from the bone marrow. Explain how this is different from other cells.   **(2 marks)**

5. Put the following in order of size, starting with the largest:

   cell   organ system   organ   tissue.   **(3 marks)**

6. Write definitions for each of these words:

   a) tissue   **b)** organ   **c)** organ system.   **(3 marks)**

7. Draw up a table with the following headings.

System	Function	Organs in this system	Tissues in these organs	Cells in these tissues

   Complete your table as fully as you can, using up to three examples of systems in the human body.   **(15 marks)**

8. The diagram shows a part of a leaf, which is a plant organ. The diagram is labelled to show some of the tissues. Describe the functions of the tissues in this organ. **(4 marks)**

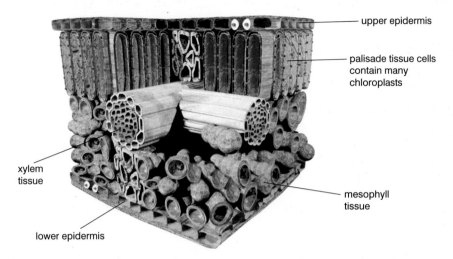

upper epidermis

palisade tissue cells contain many chloroplasts

xylem tissue

mesophyll tissue

lower epidermis

△ Fig 2.16 Section through part of a leaf.

9. Explain as fully as you can the advantage of cell differentiation and organisation for multicellular organisms. **(3 marks)**

All living organisms need to be able to transport water, oxygen, carbon dioxide and other molecules around their bodies. For simple organisms such as bacteria the distances travelled are very small, but more complex animals and plants have evolved highly specialised transport mechanisms to get vital substances from one part of the organism to another. If all the blood vessels in the human body – including arteries, veins and capillaries – were laid end to end, they would stretch for about 60 000 miles. That's nearly 100 000 km!

CONTENTS

3
Movement in and out of cells

Δ Potassium permanganate crystals dissolving in water.

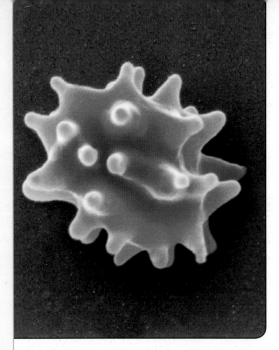

Movement in and out of cells

INTRODUCTION

If you put a red blood cell into pure water, it will eventually burst open. If you place the red blood cell into a salty solution instead, it will shrink. Surrounding every cell is the cell membrane. Imagine the cell membrane as a leaky layer that is strong enough to hold all the contents in the cell together, but that allows small particles to move through it. The cell membrane also has special 'gates' that allow certain, important particles

△ Fig 3.1 A red blood cell that has been placed in a salty solution loses water and shrinks.

through. Different cells have different kinds of 'gate' in them. So cell membranes play an essential role in controlling what goes in and out of cells, and therefore control the way that the cell functions.

KNOWLEDGE CHECK

✓ Cells need oxygen and glucose for respiration.
✓ Cells need to get rid of waste substances, such as carbon dioxide from respiration.
✓ **EXTENDED** Investigate how surface area, temperature, concentration gradient and distance affect diffusion.

LEARNING OBJECTIVES

✓ Define the term *diffusion*.
✓ Describe the importance of diffusion in gases and solutes, and in the movement of substances in and out of cells.
✓ **EXTENDED** State the energy for diffusion comes from the kinetic energy of random movement of molecules and ions.
✓ **EXTENDED** Investigate how surface area, temperature, concentration gradient and distance affect diffusion.
✓ **EXTENDED** Define the term *osmosis*.
✓ Describe the role of water in supporting plant structure.
✓ Describe the effects of osmosis on plant and animal cells and tissues.
✓ State that plants are supported by the pressure of water inside the cells pressing outwards on the cell wall.
✓ **EXTENDED** Explain the effects of osmosis on plant and animal cells and tissues.
✓ **EXTENDED** Describe and explain the importance of water potential gradient for plants and animal cells and tissues.

✓ Define *active transport* and state that it requires energy from respiration.

✓ EXTENDED Describe how active transport can occur across cell membranes.

✓ EXTENDED Discuss the importance of active transport for root hair cells and epithelial cells of villi.

DIFFUSION

Substances such as water, oxygen, carbon dioxide and food are made of particles (atoms, ions and molecules).

In liquids and gases the particles are constantly moving around. This means that they eventually spread out evenly. For example, if you dissolve sugar in a cup of water, even if you do not stir it, the sugar molecules eventually spread throughout the liquid. This is because all the molecules are moving around, colliding with and bouncing off other particles.

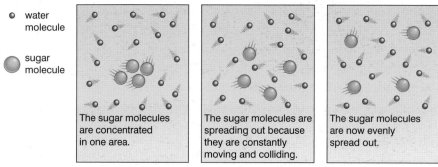

water molecule

sugar molecule

The sugar molecules are concentrated in one area.

The sugar molecules are spreading out because they are constantly moving and colliding.

The sugar molecules are now evenly spread out.

Δ Fig 3.2 Diffusion of sugar molecules in a solution.

The sugar molecules have spread out from an area of high concentration, when they were added to the water, to an area of low concentration. Eventually, although all the particles are still moving, the sugar molecules are evenly spread out and there is no longer a **concentration gradient**.

Only while there is **net movement** (where there are more particles moving in one direction than another) from an area of high concentration to an area of lower concentration is there **diffusion**.

Diffusion is the net movement of molecules from a region of their higher concentration to a region of their lower concentration.

Δ Fig 3.3 Potassium permanganate(II) diffuses through a beaker of water as the solid crystal dissolves.

Diffusion can only occur when there is a difference in concentration between two areas. Particles are said to move *down* their concentration gradient. This happens because of the random movement of particles.

Any change requires energy. The diffusion of molecules or ions through a gas or a liquid is brought about by the kinetic energy of the particles.

Diffusion is important for living organisms, as this is the process by which gases such as oxygen and carbon dioxide are exchanged between the organism and the environment. It is also the process by which solutes dissolved in water, such as mineral ions and food molecules, enter a living organism and how waste substances, such as urea, are excreted from the organism into the environment.

Diffusion in cells

Cells are surrounded by membranes. These membranes are leaky – they let tiny particles pass through them. Large particles can't get through, so cell membranes are said to be **partially permeable**.

Movement of particles across a cell membrane may happen more in one direction than the other if there is a difference in concentration on either side of the membrane (a concentration gradient). For example, in the blood vessels in the lungs there is a *low* oxygen concentration inside the red blood cells (because they have given up their oxygen to cells in other parts of the body) and a *high* oxygen concentration in the alveoli of the lungs. Therefore oxygen diffuses from the alveoli into the red blood cells.

Other examples of diffusion include:

- carbon dioxide entering leaf cells (see Topic 6)
- digested food substances from the small intestine entering the blood (see Topic 7).

Diffusion of some types of molecules and ions across the cell membrane is a **passive** process. It needs no input of energy from the cell.

Note that although diffusion requires the kinetic energy of particles in order to happen, this does not mean that diffusion is an active process in terms of cells. No energy from the cell is required for particles to diffuse into or out of a cell across the cell membrane.

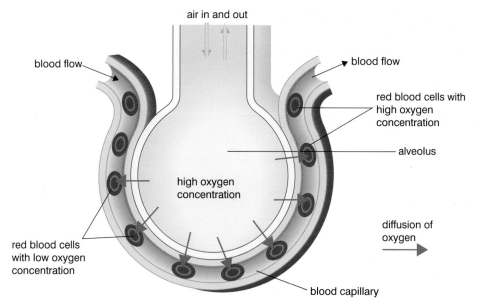

air in and out

blood flow

blood flow

red blood cells with high oxygen concentration

alveolus

high oxygen concentration

diffusion of oxygen

red blood cells with low oxygen concentration

blood capillary

Δ Fig 3.4 In blood vessels in the lungs, oxygen diffuses down its concentration gradient from the air in the lungs into red blood cells.

SCIENCE IN CONTEXT

KIDNEY FAILURE AND HAEMODIALYSIS

The kidneys are organs that depend on filtration and diffusion to produce urine and keep the concentration of many substances in the blood at a fairly constant level. People who suffer from kidney failure are unable to do this, and are very quickly at risk from the build-up of waste products, such as urea, in the body as a result of cell processes. In high concentrations these waste products can damage body cells and lead to death.

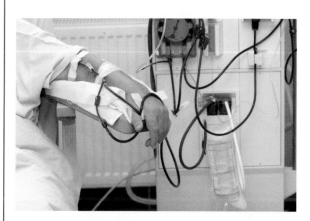

◁ Fig 3.5 A patient undergoing kidney dialysis.

Haemodialysis is an artificial way of cleaning the blood by which substances diffuse out of the blood into dialysis fluid in a machine called a dialyser. The concentration of substances in the dialysis fluid has to be correct, so that all the waste products are removed and other substances are returned to the body at the right concentration.

Investigating diffusion

Diffusion in non-living systems may be investigated in different ways.

- It can be studied simply by dropping a coloured crystal of a simple soluble substance such as potassium manganate(VII) into still water, and watching what happens. As the crystal dissolves, the particles of solute diffuse throughout the water until the concentration of solute is the same throughout the water.

Δ Fig 3.6 Left: as the crystal dissolves it forms a region of high concentration of the solute in the solution. Right: after a few hours, the solute is evenly spread in the water as a result of diffusion.

- Visking tubing is an artificial partially permeable membrane that can be used to model diffusion across cell membranes. You can create a small bag shape by knotting one end of some tubing. If you place a solution of glucose and starch into the bag, and suspend it in a beaker of water for a few hours, you can then test the water in the beaker for reducing sugar (glucose) and starch. The tests will show that glucose has diffused through the membrane, but the starch has not, because glucose molecules are small enough to pass through the holes but the starch molecules are too large.

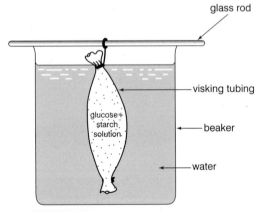

glass rod

visking tubing

glucose + starch solution

beaker

water

Δ Fig 3.7 Visking tubing can act as a model for the cell membrane.

Diffusion in cells may be investigated by looking at coloured cells such as red onion or beetroot cells. If slices of tissue from these are left in water, after a while the colour will start to diffuse out of the cells into the water.

QUESTIONS

1. In your own words, define the terms *net movement* and *diffusion*.

2. Is diffusion across a cell membrane a passive or active process? Explain your answer.

3. Explain why some particles can diffuse through cell membranes but not others.

OSMOSIS

Water molecules are small enough to diffuse through partially permeable membranes, such as cell membranes. However, because water molecules are so important to cells, and may be diffusing in a different direction to other molecules, this kind of diffusion has a special name – **osmosis**. Like diffusion, osmosis is a passive process and is a result of the random movement of particles.

Water molecules diffuse from a place where there is a high concentration of water molecules (such as a dilute sucrose sugar solution) to where there is a low concentration of water molecules (such as a concentrated sucrose sugar solution).

Osmosis is the diffusion (net movement) of water molecules from a region of their higher concentration to a region of their lower concentration through a partially permeable membrane.

Concentrations in solutions

Many people confuse the concentration of the solution with the concentration of the water. Remember, in osmosis it is the *water molecules* that we are considering, so you must think of the concentration of water molecules in the solution instead of the concentration of solutes dissolved in it.

- A low concentration of dissolved solutes means a high concentration of water molecules.
- A high concentration of dissolved solutes means a low concentration of water molecules.

So the water molecules are moving from a *high concentration* (*of water molecules*) to a *low concentration* (*of water molecules*), even though this is often described as water moving from a low-concentration solution to a high-concentration solution.

Osmosis in plant cells

If a cell is placed in a solution that has a higher concentration of solute (and so a lower concentration of water molecules) than the cytoplasm inside the cell, water will leave the cell by osmosis and the cytoplasm will shrink.

If a cell is placed in a solution that has a lower concentration of solute (and so a higher concentration of water molecules) than the cytoplasm inside the cell, osmosis will result in water entering the cell.

Plant cells are surrounded by cell walls that are completely permeable. This means water and solute molecules pass easily through them.

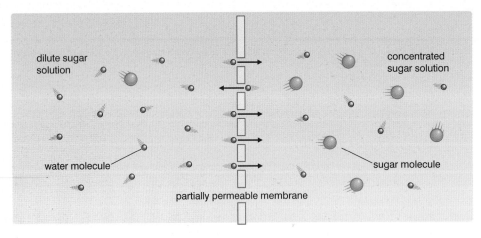

△ Fig 3.8 Water molecules diffuse from an area of higher concentration (of water molecules) into an area of lower concentration (of water molecules). This kind of diffusion is known as osmosis.

In a solution of high concentration of solute (low concentration of water), water will leave a plant cell by osmosis. This can be seen in plant cells as the cytoplasm shrinks inside the cell. However, the whole cell doesn't shrink, because the plant cell wall controls the structure of the cell. The plant as a whole will show wilting.

In a solution of low concentration of solute (high concentration of water), water will enter the plant cell by osmosis. However, the plant cell does not eventually burst. The strong cell wall provides strength when the cytoplasm is full of water, preventing the cell from expanding any further and bursting. The pressure of water in the cytoplasm against the cell wall also provides strength, making the plant stand upright with its leaves held out to catch the sunlight.

△ Fig 3.9 When the cells of the plant are not full of water, the cell walls are not strong enough to support the plant, and the plant collapses (wilts). When the cells are full of water, the plant stands upright.

Developing investigative skills

Strips of dandelion stem about 5 cm long and 3 mm wide were placed in sodium chloride solutions of different concentrations. After 10 minutes, the strips looked as shown in the diagram. (Note that the outer layer of a dandelion stalk is 'waterproofed' with a waxy layer to protect it from water loss to the environment.)

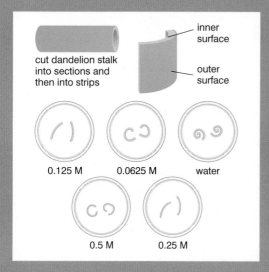

◁ Fig 3.10 Investigating osmosis.

Devise and plan investigations

❶ Write a plan for an experiment to carry out this investigation. Your plan should include:

   a) instructions on how to prepare the stem samples

   b) instructions on how to keep the stem samples until the experiment starts.

Make observations and measurements

❷ Using the diagram, describe the results of this investigation.

Analyse and interpret data

❸ Explain as fully as you can the results of this investigation.

❹ Use the results to suggest the normal concentration of cell cytoplasm. Explain your answer.

STOMATA

Stomata (single: stoma) are the holes in the surface of a leaf (usually the undersurface) that allow air to move into and out of the leaf. This provides the oxygen for respiring cells and carbon dioxide for photosynthesising cells, and allows water vapour that has evaporated from cell surfaces inside the leaf to diffuse out into the atmosphere.

Each stoma is surrounded by two guard cells. These control the opening and closing of the stoma. Usually stomata are open during the day, and close at night. The stoma opens and closes as the guard cells change shape. During the day the guard cells gain water from surrounding cells as a result of osmosis. This makes the cells turgid and, because the inner edge of the guard cell does not stretch, the cells curve and create a space between them – that is the stoma. During the night, the guard cells lose water by osmosis. The cells lose their turgidity and collapse a little, closing the stoma between them.

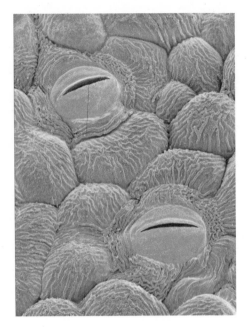

△ Fig 3.11 Each stoma is surrounded by two guard cells.

REMEMBER

You will need to explain diffusion and osmosis in terms of particles and their concentration gradients. Be clear that, even when diffusion and osmosis stop because there is no concentration gradient, the particles in the solution continue to move – there is just no longer any net movement.

QUESTIONS

1. **EXTENDED** In your own words, define the term osmosis.

2. Explain how osmosis is

    a) similar to

    b) different from, diffusion.

3. Describe the role of the plant cell wall in supporting a plant that has been well watered.

WATER POTENTIAL

The ability of a cell to draw water into itself is called its **water potential**. Pure water has a water potential of zero. As solutes are added to the water its water potential falls – it becomes more negative. So, a concentrated sugar solution has a lower water potential (more negative) than pure water.

When two regions of different water potential are separated by a partially permeable membrane, water moves from the region of higher water potential to lower water potential. Water molecules move *down* the **water potential gradient**.

Turgid and flaccid cells

A **turgid** plant cell is one that is full of water. The pressure of the water in the cytoplasm in a turgid cell against the cell wall is called **turgor pressure.** This pressure prevents any more water entering the cell by osmosis, even if it is in a solution that has a higher water concentration than the water concentration of the cytoplasm.

A plant cell that has lost water so that the cytoplasm has shrunk enough to start pulling away from the inside of the cell membrane is said to be **plasmolysed**. It may also be called a **flaccid** cell. A plant with many flaccid cells will show wilting.

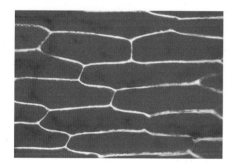 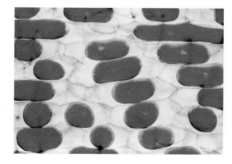

Δ Fig 3.12 Cells from a red onion. Left: fully turgid cells. Right: plasmolysed (flaccid) cells.

Osmosis and plant uptake of water

Plant roots are surrounded by soil water, and the cytoplasm inside root hair cells has a lower concentration of water molecules than the soil water. So water molecules will cross the cell membrane of root hair cells and enter the plant as a result of osmosis.

The water molecules that enter the root hair cells increases the cells' concentration of water molecules, so that it is higher than the concentration of water molecules in surrounding cells. So water molecules cross the cell membranes of the root hair cells into the other cells. This raises their concentration of water molecules, and makes it higher than the concentration in cells even further into the root tissue, so water molecules cross those cell membranes. Osmosis continues from the surface root hair cells, deeper and deeper into the root tissue until the water molecules reach the xylem vessels. Once they have entered the xylem vessels, the water molecules are transported away from the root towards the leaves. Transpiration from the leaves (see Topic 8) helps to draw the water up the xylem tubes from the roots, so maintaining the concentration gradient between the root cells and xylem vessels.

REMEMBER

Look for applications of diffusion and osmosis in the processes that you learn about in the rest of the course, and make sure you refer to them appropriately in exam answers. For example, the fact that osmosis causes a change in shape of cells is important in the opening and closing of stomata in plants.

We can explain the movement of water molecules into and through the root of a plant in terms of water potential gradient, because the soil water has the highest water potential and the cells nearest the xylem vessels have the lowest water potential. So water molecules move into the root hair cell, and across the cells of the root, down the water potential gradient. The water potential gradient is maintained as the xylem vessels remove water molecules from the root due to transpiration from the leaves.

END OF EXTENDED

The effect of osmosis on animal cells

Animal cells also gain and lose water as a result of osmosis. However, the effects of this can be more dramatic than in plant cells because animal cells do not have a supporting cell wall.

If you place an animal cell (such as a red blood cell) into a solution of lower water potential, it will lose water by osmosis and become crenated, like the cell shown in the photograph at the start of this Topic (Fig. 3.1).

If you place an animal cell into a solution of higher water potential, it will gain water by osmosis. Even when it is full of water, it will continue to take in water if the water potential is higher outside the cell than inside. The cell membrane is not strong, so if it is stretched too far it will burst.

OVERHYDRATION

It is possible (although not easy) to die as a result of drinking too much water. If you drink a large volume of water very quickly, the water moves into the blood – and from there into cells – by osmosis.

The cells in the brain are particularly at risk because the brain has a limited space within the skull. If the brain cells swell quickly as a result of osmosis, the increased brain volume can cut off the blood supply, and brain cells start to die. Fortunately, we have an effective mechanism for getting rid of extra water from the body in urine (Topic 13). So overhydration is rare.

QUESTIONS

1. **EXTENDED** Explain the meaning of the following terms:

   a) flaccid

   b) turgid

   c) plasmolysis

   d) turgor pressure.

2. **EXTENDED** Describe the uptake of water from the soil by plant roots in terms of water potential gradient.

3. **EXTENDED** Draw a labelled diagram to show what happens to the water molecules when a red blood cell is placed in a solution that has a higher concentration of solute than the cytoplasm of the cell. Your labels should include the terms *water potential* and *osmosis.*

ACTIVE TRANSPORT

Sometimes cells need to absorb molecules or ions from a region of their low concentration into a region of their higher concentration. For example, root hair cells take in nitrate ions from the soil even though the concentration of these ions is higher in the plant cells than in the soil. Also, glucose, which is needed for respiration, is absorbed from the digested food in the gut by the epithelial cells of villi.

The cells use energy to absorb these substances from a region of lower concentration to a region of higher concentration, so this is an *active* process and is called **active transport**. The energy comes from respiration.

Active transport is the absorption across a cell membrane of molecules or ions *against their concentration gradient*. Active transport occurs when special **carrier proteins** in the surface of a cell pick up particles from one side of the membrane and transport them to the other side. You can see this happening in Fig. 3.13.

The energy from respiration provides the kinetic energy needed for the carrier protein to change shape, and so move the molecule or ion through the cell membrane.

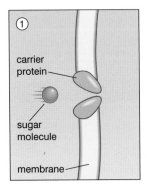 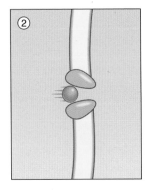 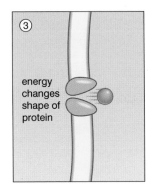

△ Fig 3.13 Active transport of a sugar molecule through a carrier protein in a membrane.

You will learn more about the process of active transport in Topic 8, which discusses ion uptake from soil water by root hairs in plants, in Topic 7, which discusses the uptake of glucose by villi in the human small intestine, and in Topic 13, which discusses the uptake of glucose in kidney tubules.

 SCIENCE IN CONTEXT **METABOLIC POISONS**

The energy for active transport comes from cell respiration. A simple test to show whether a substance is being absorbed by an active process or a passive process is to treat the cells with a metabolic poison that stops the cells respiring. For example, treating root hair cells with cyanide stops the uptake of nitrate ions but doesn't affect osmosis.

QUESTIONS

1. Explain what is meant by *active transport*.

2. EXTENDED Give one example of active transport in plant cells and one in animal cells, and explain why this is important for the organism.

3. EXTENDED Explain where the energy for active transport comes from, and how it makes the process possible.

End of topic checklist

Key words

active transport, concentration gradient, diffusion, flaccid, net movement, osmosis, partially permeable, passive, plasmolysed, turgid, water potential gradient

During your study of this topic you should have learned:

○ To define diffusion as the net movement of particles from a region of their higher concentration to a region of their lower concentration, and as a passive process

○ That water diffuses through partially permeable membranes by osmosis

○ EXTENDED To define osmosis as the net movement of water molecules across a partially permeable membrane from their higher concentration (a dilute solution) to their lower concentration (a more concentrated solution), and is a passive process.

○ How to investigate and describe osmosis in plant tissues.

○ EXTENDED To state that diffusion results from the random movement of particles in gases and liquids.

○ EXTENDED To investigate the factors that affect diffusion.

○ Plant and animal cells lose water when placed in solutions of lower water concentration, and gain water in solutions of higher water concentration.

○ EXTENDED That the cell wall surrounding plant cells prevents turgid cells from bursting, and so turgid cells support the plant.

○ EXTENDED That animal cells will burst if they take in too much water because they do not have a strong cell wall.

○ That active transport as the transfer of molecules across a cell membrane, from a region of their lower concentration to a region of their higher concentration using energy from respiration.

○ EXTENDED Active transport uses energy from cell respiration to transport molecules or ions across the cell membrane against their concentration gradient.

○ EXTENDED Active transport is important for the uptake of ions by root hairs in plants and of glucose by the epithelial cells of the villi and kidney tubules in humans.

End of topic questions

Note: The marks awarded for these questions indicate the level of detail required for the answers. In the examination, the number of marks awarded to questions like these may be different.

1. An old-fashioned way of killing slugs in the garden is to sprinkle salt on them. This kills the slugs by drying them out. Explain why this works. **(2 marks)**

2. Copy and complete the table to compare diffusion, osmosis and active transport.

	Diffusion	Osmosis	Active transport
Active or passive?			
Which molecules move?			
Requires special carrier proteins?			

(9 marks)

3. Which of the following are examples of diffusion, osmosis or neither?

   a) Carbon dioxide entering a leaf when it is photosynthesising. **(1 mark)**

   b) Food entering your stomach when you swallow. **(1 mark)**

   c) A dried-out piece of celery swelling up when placed in a bowl of water. **(1 mark)**

4. Explain why a large animal, such as a human, needs special adaptations to organs that exchange materials with the environment (such as the lungs, small intestine and kidney), but a single-celled organism does not. **(4 marks)**

5. There are many membranes within a cell, separating off organelles that produce substances such as hormones and enzymes, or where cell processes such as photosynthesis and respiration occur. Explain fully the importance of these membranes and why it is an advantage to the cell to have them. **(3 marks)**

6. EXTENDED **a)** If you measured the rate of respiration of plant root hair cells, would you expect it to be

   - the same as

   - more than or

   - less than

   the rate of respiration of other plant cells? **(1 mark)**

   b) Explain your answer to part **(a)**. **(1 mark)**

There are around 90 000 different proteins in the human body, and thousands more in other organisms. What is unique about proteins is that each one may be a different shape. The different shapes make it possible for proteins to carry out different roles in the body.

All these many thousands of proteins are made up of chains of smaller molecules, called amino acids, which join together in long chains. All proteins are made up from different combinations of just 20 amino acids. It is the order of these amino acids in the chain, and the way that the chain folds up into its 3D shape, that gives each protein its unique function.

CONTENTS

4
Biological molecules

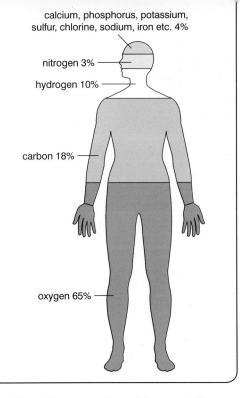

calcium, phosphorus, potassium, sulfur, chlorine, sodium, iron etc. 4%

nitrogen 3%

hydrogen 10%

carbon 18%

oxygen 65%

Δ Fig 4.1 The proportions of elements in the human body.

Biological molecules

INTRODUCTION

Around 65% of your body mass is oxygen, another 18% is carbon and 10% is hydrogen. The remainder of your mass is made up of a large range of other elements, including nitrogen, sulfur, calcium and iron. These elements are combined in different ways to form all the compounds in your body.

KNOWLEDGE CHECK

✓ Most of the foods that we eat can be grouped into carbohydrates, proteins and fats.
✓ Carbohydrates, proteins and fats are formed from smaller molecules.

LEARNING OBJECTIVES

✓ Name the elements in carbohydrates, fats and proteins.
✓ Name the basic units from which carbohydrates, fats and proteins are made.
✓ State that water is important as a solvent.
✓ **EXTENDED** Describe the roles of water in digestion and transport.
✓ **EXTENDED** Explain why proteins, such as enzymes and antibodies, have a specific shape, and how this relates to their function.
✓ **EXTENDED** Describe the structure of DNA.
✓ Describe tests for starch, reducing sugars, protein, fats and oils, and vitamin C.
✓ **EXTENDED** Explain that different sequences of amino acids give different shapes to protein molecules.

CARBOHYDRATES, PROTEINS AND LIPIDS

Most of the molecules found in living organisms fall into three main groups: carbohydrates, proteins, and lipids, which are commonly called fats and oils. All of these molecules contain carbon, hydrogen and oxygen. In addition, all proteins contain nitrogen and some also contain sulfur.

Carbohydrate molecules are made up of small basic units called **simple sugars**. These are formed from carbon, hydrogen and oxygen atoms, sometimes arranged in a ring-shaped molecule. One example of a simple sugar is glucose.

Simple sugar molecules can link together to form larger molecules. They can join in pairs, such as **sucrose** (the 'sugar' we use in our food). They can also form much larger molecules called polysaccharides, such as starch, glycogen and cellulose, which are long chains of glucose molecules.

Protein molecules are made up of long chains of **amino acids** linked together. There are 20 different kinds of amino acid in plant and animal cells, and they can join in any order, in long chains, to make all the different proteins within the plant or animal body. Examples include the structural proteins in muscle, as well as enzymes that help to control cell reactions.

A **lipid** is what we commonly call a fat or oil. At room temperature **fats** are solid and **oils** are liquid, but they have a similar structure. Both fats and oils are made from basic units called **fatty acids** and **glycerol**. There are three fatty acids in each lipid, and the fatty acids vary in different lipids. Lipids are important in forming cell membranes, and many other molecules in the body such as fats in storage cells.

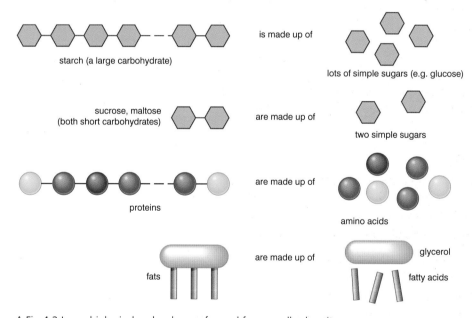

starch (a large carbohydrate)   is made up of   lots of simple sugars (e.g. glucose)

sucrose, maltose (both short carbohydrates)   are made up of   two simple sugars

proteins   are made up of   amino acids

fats   are made up of   glycerol   fatty acids

△ Fig 4.2 Large biological molecules are formed from small sub units.

QUESTIONS

1. What are the basic units of:

   a) lipids

   b) carbohydrates

   c) proteins.

2. Using the diagram of food molecules in Fig. 4.2, give two differences between the structure of a protein and a carbohydrate.

The structure of proteins

There are thousands of different proteins in the human body and in other organisms. Many of these are different shapes. The reason that different proteins have different shapes is that they are each formed from a different sequence of amino acids. The amino acids interact with other nearby amino acids and cause the amino acid chain to fold up in a particular way. This gives each protein a unique three-dimensional shape.

Enzymes are proteins that interact with other molecules during reactions. They have a small gap in them called the **active site**. During a reaction, another molecule is held in this site. (You will learn more about this in Topic 5.) The shape of the active site matches the shape of the other molecule closely, usually making it easier for the reaction to happen. There is a different enzyme for every different molecule that is involved in a reaction, because this matching of shapes is so important.

Protein shape is also important in protecting us against infection by pathogens. Proteins called **antibodies** are produced by the immune system to attack any pathogen that gets into the body. The shape of the antibody must match the **antigen** produced by the pathogen, so that the antibody can attack the pathogen and cause it to be destroyed. (There is more on this in Topic 10.)

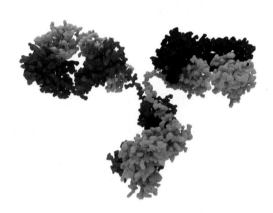

△ Fig 4.3 A model of the three-dimensional structure of an antibody.

QUESTIONS

1. Explain the importance of amino acid sequence for protein structure.

2. Give two examples in humans where structure is related to the function of a type of protein. Explain your answers.

WATER

Water is essential for living organisms, as many substances dissolve in it.

Dissolved substances can be transported around organisms, such as in the xylem and phloem of plants (see Topic 8). Dissolved food molecules in the alimentary canal easily diffuse into the body and dissolve in the blood for transport around the body (see Topics 7 and 9). The cell cytoplasm also has a high concentration of water, making it possible for many metabolic reactions to take place in the cytoplasm.

END OF EXTENDED

QUESTIONS

1. Why is water essential for living organisms?

2. EXTENDED Give two examples of why water is essential for transport inside living organisms.

EXTENDED

THE STRUCTURE OF DNA

Inside virtually every cell in the body is a **nucleus**, which contains long thread-like structures called **chromosomes**. The chromosomes are made of a chemical called **deoxyribonucleic acid (DNA)**. DNA is a very long molecule that is formed from two parallel strands ('backbones') joined together at regular spaces by pairs of **bases**, like the rungs of a ladder. The whole structure is twisted, forming a **double helix**.

The DNA strands contain four different bases, which are called A, T, C and G. (The letters stand for the name of each base, but you do not need to remember these.) The bases on each strand cross-link with the bases on the other strand to form pairs.

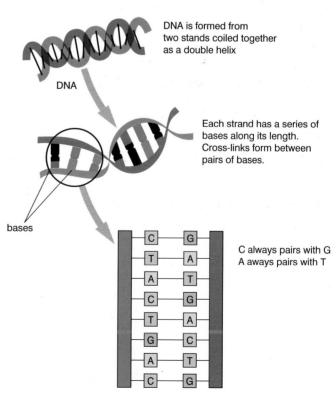

DNA is formed from two stands coiled together as a double helix

DNA

Each strand has a series of bases along its length. Cross-links form between pairs of bases.

bases

C always pairs with G
A aways pairs with T

△ Fig 4.4 The structure of a DNA molecule.

The bases always form the same pairs: A pairs with T and C pairs with G (see Fig. 4.4). So you can use the order of bases on one strand of DNA to identify the bases that will be on the opposite strand.

The bases can occur in any order along one strand of DNA, but their order forms the **genetic code**, which codes for particular proteins, as you will see in Topic 17.

QUESTIONS

1. The structure of DNA is called a double helix. Explain what this means.

2. Explain why we can work out the sequence of bases on one DNA strand from the sequence on the other strand.

END OF EXTENDED

TESTS FOR FOOD MOLECULES

We can use simple tests to indicate whether or not a food contains particular food molecules, such as starch, glucose, proteins or lipids.

Test for starch

Starch is the storage molecule of plants, and is found in many foods that are made from plant tissue. When iodine/potassium iodide solution is mixed with a solution of food containing starch, or dropped onto food containing starch, it changes from brown to dark blue. This happens when even small amounts of starch are present and can be used as a simple test for the presence of starch. The colour change is easiest to see if the test is examined against a white background, such as on a white spotting tile.

◁ Fig 4.5 The blue-black colour shows there is starch in the biscuit.

Test for glucose

Glucose is a 'reducing sugar' that is important in respiration and photosynthesis. So it is commonly found in plant and animal tissues, and therefore in our food. Its presence can be detected using **Benedict's reagent**. The pale blue Benedict's solution is added to a prepared sample that contains glucose and heated to 95 °C. If it changes colour or forms a precipitate, this indicates the presence of reducing sugars. A green colour means there is only a small amount of glucose in the solution. A medium amount of glucose produces a yellow colour. A significant amount of glucose produces a precipitate that is an orange-red colour.

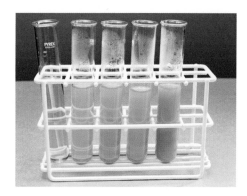

◁ Fig 4.6 Benedict's reagent with a range of concentrations of reducing sugars (very low in the tube on the left, getting more concentrated towards the right).

REMEMBER

The test using Benedict's reagent will produce an orange-red precipitate for any reducing sugar, such as the simple sugars fructose and galactose, and the disaccharides (made from two basic units: *di-* means 'two' or 'double') lactose and maltose. So it is not exclusively a test for glucose. But as glucose is the usually the most common sugar, this is the test usually used for it.

Test for protein

The **biuret test** is used to check for the presence of protein. A small sample of the food under test is placed in a test tube.

◁ Fig 4.7 A positive biuret test for protein.

An equal volume of biuret solution is carefully poured down the side of the tube. If the sample contains protein, a blue ring forms at the surface. If the sample is then shaken the blue ring disappears and the solution turns a light purple.

Test for fat

This test depends upon the fact that fats and oils do not dissolve in water but do dissolve in ethanol. The test sample is mixed with ethanol. If fat is present it will be dissolved in the ethanol to form a cloudy solution. The liquid formed is poured into a test tube of water, leaving behind any solid that has not dissolved. If there is any fat dissolved in the ethanol it will form a cloudy white precipitate when mixed with the water.

◁ Fig 4.8 Fats have dissolved in the top layer of ethanol, making it appear cloudy.

Test for vitamin C

Vitamin C is an essential nutrient that helps to keep skin and hair healthy. It is found in many fresh fruits and vegetables, especially citrus fruits (e.g. oranges and lemons), leafy green vegetables such as cabbage, and potatoes.

To test for vitamin C, add 1 cm³ of DCPIP dye solution to a test tube. Make a solution of the food sample and add a small amount to the dye solution. If there is vitamin C in the food sample, the blue colour of the dye will disappear.

QUESTIONS

1. Describe what you would see if you tested sample of the following with Benedict's solution and then iodine solution:

   a) glucose syrup

   b) a cake made with wheat flour, table sugar (sucrose), fat and eggs.

   Explain your answers.

2. Explain how you would test the seed from a walnut tree to see if it contained stores of:

   a) fat

   b) protein

   c) vitamin C.

End of topic checklist

Key words

amino acid, antibody, antigen, base, Benedict's reagent, biuret test, carbohydrate, chromosome, DNA, double helix, enzyme, fat, fatty acid, glycerol, lipid, oil, protein, simple sugar, starch

During your study of this topic you should have learned:

- ○ That carbohydrates, proteins, fats and oils all contain the elements carbon, hydrogen and oxygen.
- ○ That proteins also contain the element nitrogen and some may contain sulfur.
- ○ That large carbohydrates, such as starch and glycogen, are made up of smaller carbohydrates (reducing sugars) such as glucose.
- ○ Proteins are made of smaller molecules called amino acids.
- ○ **EXTENDED** How to explain that the specific three-dimensional structure of proteins is caused by the sequence of amino acids that form them.
- ○ **EXTENDED** How to explain that the three-dimensional structure of an enzyme produces an active site that matches the shape of the molecule that it joins with during a reaction.
- ○ **EXTENDED** How to explain that the three-dimensional structure of an antibody matches the shape of an antigen produced by a pathogen and helps the body to destroy the pathogen.
- ○ **EXTENDED** To explain that DNA has a double helix structure formed from two strands that are joined by the bases on the two parallel strands cross-linking with each other.
- ○ **EXTENDED** To describe that in DNA base A always pairs with base T, and base C always pairs with base G.
- ○ To state that water is an essential solvent for living organisms, and forms the basis of cell cytoplasm in which many metabolic reactions occur.
- ○ **EXTENDED** How to describe the roles of water in digestion and transport.
- ○ To state that fats and oils are made of smaller molecules called fatty acids and glycerol.
- ○ Describe the use of the iodine test to identify the presence of starch.
- ○ Describe the use of Benedict's reagent to test for the presence of simple reducing sugars such as glucose.
- ○ Describe the use of the biuret test to identify the presence of proteins.
- ○ Describe the use of the ethanol emulsion to identify the presence of fats and oils.
- ○ Describe the use of the DCPIP test to test for the presence of vitamin C.

End of topic questions

Note: The marks awarded for these questions indicate the level of detail required in the answers. In the examination, the number of marks awarded to questions like these may be different.

1. a) Explain why carbon, hydrogen and oxygen are the most common elements found in the human body. **(1 mark)**

   b) Why does the body need other elements, in addition to those mentioned in part **(a)**? **(1 mark)**

2. A sample of bread was ground up. Some of the breadcrumbs were tested with Benedict's reagent and some with iodine solution. The rest of the crumbs were mixed with Substance A. After 20 minutes, some of the mixture was tested with Benedict's reagent and some with iodine solution. The results of the tests are shown in the table.

	Test with Benedict's solution	**Test with iodine solution**
Before adding Substance A	no precipitate	change to blue-black colour
After 20 min with Substance A	orange-red precipitate	no colour change

   a) Describe what the results show. **(2 marks)**

   b) What was Substance A? Explain your answer. **(4 marks)**

3. EXTENDED The diagram shows the three-dimensional shape of an enzyme molecule (blue). The molecule that it joins with in a reaction is shown in yellow.

   a) Name the gap labelled A. **(1 mark)**

   b) Explain fully how the shape of the enzyme is produced. **(2 marks)**

   c) Explain the importance of this three-dimensional shape of an enzyme molecule. **(2 marks)**

4. a) EXTENDED In relation to DNA, explain what we mean by:

   i) a double helix **(2 marks)**
   ii) paired bases. **(2 marks)**

   b) The sequence of bases on one strand of DNA is AATGCAGCT. Write down the sequence of bases on the parallel strand, and explain why you were able to identify this sequence. **(2 marks)**

Many useful enzymes come from bacteria and other microorganisms, and these organisms are harnessed both in industry and in the home, for uses as wide-ranging as washing detergents, to baking leavened bread. Yeast is a single-celled organism that produces enzymes that break down the sugars in flour, and in the process tiny bubbles of carbon dioxide gas are released, which cause the bread to rise.

The first enzyme used commercially in washing products was introduced in the 1960s. It was a protease that broke down protein-based stains such as blood, and it was extracted from a bacterium. Since then a much wider range of enzymes has been added to washing products, to digest fats, starches and other molecules.

CONTENTS

5
Enzymes

△ Enzymes released into the gut, and attached to the gut surface (shown here), digest food so that nutrients can be absorbed.

Enzymes

Δ Fig 5.1 Enzymes in the mouth, stomach and small intestine will break down this food into much smaller molecules.

INTRODUCTION

Many of our staple foods, such as rice, potato, pasta or bread, contain large quantities of starch. Take a mouthful of one of these, without anything else, and you won't taste a lot to start with. But continue chewing on it for a few minutes, to mix it with saliva and reduce it to a slush, and you will find it starts to taste sweeter. This is because there are enzymes in saliva that start to break down the starch into smaller sugar molecules that taste sweet. Enzymes are essential in digestion, to break down the large molecules in our food into molecules small enough for diffusion through the cells of the gut wall and into our bodies.

KNOWLEDGE CHECK

✓ Food is digested in the gut into smaller molecules.

LEARNING OBJECTIVES

✓ Define the term *catalyst*.
✓ Describe enzymes as proteins that are biological catalysts.
✓ Describe the importance of enzymes to life.
✓ Describe enzyme action.
✓ Describe the effect of temperature and pH on the rate of an enzyme-controlled reaction.
✓ Investigate the effect of temperature and pH on enzyme activity.
✓ **EXTENDED** State that enzymes catalyse reactions in which substrates are converted to products.
✓ **EXTENDED** Describe the importance of the shape of the active site.
✓ **EXTENDED** Explain the effect of temperature and pH on enzyme activity.
✓ **EXTENDED** Explain the specificity of enzymes.

ENZYMES AS CATALYSTS

A **catalyst** is a substance that changes the speed of a reaction, often speeding it up. Catalysts are used in many industrial processes, such as making ammonia. Living cells also use catalysts to change the rate of reactions that happen inside them. These are known as *metabolic reactions* because they are the reactions of the metabolism (all the processes that keep a living organism alive). This makes enzymes very important to all living organisms.

Catalysts that control metabolic reactions are **enzymes,** and because they work in living cells they are called **biological catalysts**. Enzymes are proteins. They help cells carry out all the life processes quickly. Without them, most metabolic reactions would happen too slowly for life to carry on.

Some enzymes help two or more small molecules join together, such as when the polysaccharides starch and glycogen are built from glucose. Other enzymes help large molecules break down into smaller ones, such as when proteins are broken down into separate amino acids.

A molecule that an enzyme joins with at the start of a reaction is called a **substrate**, and the molecule that is formed by the end of the reaction is called a **product**. So, during a reaction, substrate molecules are changed to product molecules.

QUESTIONS

1. Define the term *catalyst*.

2. Explain what is meant by *biological catalyst*.

3. Explain why cells need enzymes.

4. Define the terms *substrate* and *product*.

ENZYME ACTION

Enzymes are proteins and, like all proteins, they have a three-dimensional (3D) shape produced by the way the molecule folds up. Enzymes are unusual proteins in that they have a space in the molecule with a particular 3D shape. This space matches the shape of the substrate molecule. We say the shapes are **complementary**, because the substrate fits neatly into the space in the enzyme, like fitting two jigsaw pieces together.

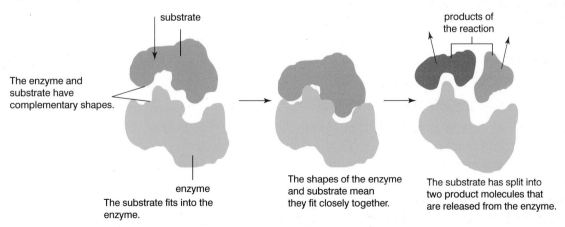

substrate

products of the reaction

The enzyme and substrate have complementary shapes.

enzyme
The substrate fits into the enzyme.

The shapes of the enzyme and substrate mean they fit closely together.

The substrate has split into two product molecules that are released from the enzyme.

△ Fig 5.2 In this reaction, the enzyme helps a substrate molecule split into two product molecules.

The space in the enzyme shape into which the substrate fits is called the enzyme's **active site**. The substrate fits tightly into the active site, forming an enzyme–substrate complex. This makes it easier for the bonds inside the substrate to be rearranged to form the products. Once the products are formed, they no longer fit the active site, so they are released, leaving the active site free and the enzyme unchanged. This means the enzyme molecule is able to bind with another substrate molecule.

Explaining enzyme action

Enzymes are **specific**, which means that each enzyme only works with one substrate or a group of similar-shaped substrates. For example:

- amylase is a type of carbohydrase enzyme produced in the mouth, which starts the digestion of starch in food into simple sugars
- proteases are digestive enzymes that break down proteins into smaller units
- lipases are digestive enzymes that break down lipids in foods.

The complementary shapes of the enzyme and substrate helps to explain the fact that enzymes are specific, because only a substrate with the correct shape can fit into the active site and so be affected by the enzyme.

QUESTIONS

1. Describe how an enzyme causes a substrate molecule to change into product molecules.

2. EXTENDED Explain what is meant by the active site of an enzyme.

3. EXTENDED Explain how shape of the active site is related to the specificity of an enzyme.

ENZYMES AND TEMPERATURE

Enzymes work best at a particular temperature, called their **optimum temperature**. For many enzymes in the human body, particularly those that work in the organs in the core (centre) of the body, such as the heart, liver, kidneys and lungs, the optimum temperature is around 37 °C.

At lower temperatures, enzymes in the human body work more slowly. At temperatures that are much higher than the optimum, the structure of an enzyme will be changed so that it will not work. This is a permanent change, and when it happens the enzyme is said to be **denatured**.

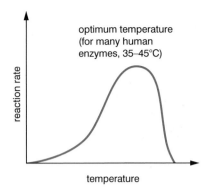

△ Fig 5.3 Many enzymes work best at an optimum temperature.

REMEMBER

Remember the relationship between enzyme activity, temperature and pH, particularly when discussing excretion (Topic 13) and homeostasis (Topic 14), as this helps to explain why maintaining particular conditions in the body is so important for health.

Investigating the effect of temperature on enzymes

The effect of temperature on an enzyme can be tested by measuring the rate of action of the enzyme at different temperatures. One method is shown in the Developing investigative skills box. Alternatively, you could use the following method to investigate the optimum temperature of amylase.

Starch is broken down to glucose by the enzyme amylase. Starch reacts with iodine solution by turning it blue-black. Glucose does not react with iodine solution, leaving it bright orange. If you mix starch solution with amylase solution and place different tubes of the mixture in water baths of different temperature and take a sample for testing with iodine solution every minute or so, you can see at which temperature the amylase works fastest. The sample that is the first to stop reacting with iodine solution comes from the tube kept at the optimum temperature for amylase.

EXTENDED

The effect of temperature

Kinetic energy is the energy of moving particles. Particles that have a greater kinetic energy move more or move faster. The kinetic energy of molecules that are free to move will cause them to bump into surrounding molecules. The kinetic energy of atoms held within larger molecules by bonds will cause them to vibrate.

An enzyme molecule and substrate molecule can only form an enzyme–substrate complex when they bump into each other with sufficient energy, and the substrate fits into the active site.

- At a low temperature the enzyme and substrate molecules move slowly, so they may take a long time to bump into each other with enough force to join and start the reaction.

- As the temperature increases, the molecules gain more energy and move faster, so the chance of them bumping into each other and joining together increases. The rate of reaction increases up to the optimum temperature.
- Beyond the optimum temperature, the atoms in the enzyme molecule are vibrating so much that they start to change the shape of the active site. This means the substrate doesn't fit as well, so the chances of an enzyme–substrate molecule forming decreases. The rate of reaction decreases.
- If the temperature increases too much, the bonds between atoms in the enzyme molecule start to break, changing the shape of the active site permanently and denaturing the enzyme.

END OF EXTENDED

Developing investigative skills

Developed black-and-white negative film consists of a celluloid backing covered with a layer of gelatin. Where the film has been exposed the gelatin layer contains tiny particles of silver, which make that area black. Gelatin is a protein and is easily digested by proteases.

Strips of exposed film were soaked in protease solution at different temperatures. When the gelatin had been digested, the silver grains fell away from the celluloid backing, leaving transparent film. The table shows the results.

Tube	Temperature in °C	Time to clear
1	10	6 min 34 s
2	20	3 min 15 s
3	30	2 min 43 s
4	40	3 min 55 s
5	50	8 min 33 s

Devise and plan investigations

❶ Describe how you would set up this investigation to get results like those shown in the table.

Analyse and interpret data

❷ Draw a graph using the data in the table.

❸ Describe the shape of the graph.

❹ Explain the shape of the graph.

Evaluate data and methods

❺ How could you modify this experiment to get a more accurate estimate of the optimum temperature for this enzyme?

ENZYMES AND pH

Enzymes also often work best at a particular pH, called their **optimum pH**. Extremes of (very high or very low) pH can slow down the rate of action of the enzyme and even denature it.

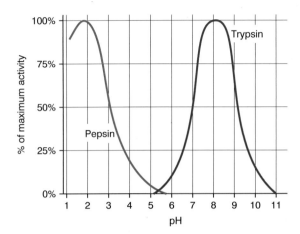

△ Fig 5.4 Pepsin (an enzyme found in the stomach) and trypsin (an enzyme released into the small intestine) have different optimum pHs.

Different enzymes have different optimum pHs, depending on where they are normally found in the body. Pepsin digests proteins in the stomach, which is a highly acidic environment. Trypsin digests proteins in the small intestine, where conditions are more alkaline.

Investigating the effect of pH on enzymes

You can investigate the effect of pH on amylase enzyme using a similar method to the one above for temperature.

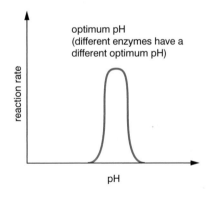

△ Fig 5.5 Many enzymes work best at an optimum temperature.

Set up one tube for each pH to be investigated and add buffer solution, which will keep the contents at a particular pH. Add starch solution to each tube, and then amylase solution. Take a sample from each tube every minute or so and test for starch using iodine solution. The sample that is the first to stop turning iodine solution blue-black comes from the tube where digestion of starch to glucose was fastest, and therefore from the tube kept at the optimum pH for that enzyme.

△ Fig 5.6 The tubes show the results of an experiment on the digestion of meat. Pepsin is a protease enzyme that is released in the stomach where it starts the digestion of proteins in food. Acid is also secreted into the stomach contents, reducing the pH and providing the optimum pH for pepsin. The left tube shows that acid has no effect on the meat. The middle tube shows that pepsin on its own digests the meat slowly. Only when the pepsin is mixed with acid can the enzyme work quickly to digest the protein.

QUESTIONS

1. Describe the effect of temperature on the rate of an enzyme-controlled reaction.

2. Compare the optimum pHs for pepsin and trypsin, shown in the graph in Fig. 5.4, and explain the differences.

EXTENDED

The effect of pH

Proteins are made of amino acids, joined together in a chain. The amino acids then interact with nearby amino acids, which causes the chain to fold up into the 3D shape of the enzyme.

Some of the interactions between amino acids in the enzyme molecule depend on the pH of the surrounding solvent. So the shape of the enzyme will depend on the surrounding pH. If the pH changes too much from the optimum pH, the shape of the enzyme, and particularly its active site, will change. So the substrate will not fit as well and the rate of reaction will decrease.

QUESTIONS

1. Explain the effect of temperature on enzyme activity:

   a) at temperatures below the optimum

   b) at temperatures above the optimum.

2. Explain the effect of pH on pepsin (see graph in Fig. 5.4) in terms of the active site of the enzyme.

END OF EXTENDED

End of topic checklist

Key terms

active site, biological catalyst, catalyst, denature, enzyme, optimum pH, optimum temperature, product, specific, substrate

During your study of this topic you should have learned:

○ How to define the term catalyst.

○ How to define enzymes as proteins that are biological catalysts, which control the rate of metabolic reactions.

○ How to describe enzymes and substrates have complementary shapes so that they fit closely together.

○ How to investigate the optimum temperature of enzymes at which the rate of reaction occurs most rapidly; the rate is slower at lower temperatures, and also at higher temperatures when the enzyme molecule starts to denature.

○ That enzymes may have an optimum pH at which the rate of reaction happens most rapidly.

○ How to describe the importance of enzymes in all living organisms.

○ EXTENDED How to explain the active site as the space in the enzyme into which the substrate fits neatly during a reaction.

○ EXTENDED Explain that a temperature lower than the optimum causes a slower rate of an enzyme-controlled reaction because the molecules move around more slowly and so don't come into contact with each other as often.

○ EXTENDED How to explain that a temperature higher than the optimum causes a slower rate of an enzyme-controlled reaction because the vibration of atoms in the enzyme slightly changes the shape of the active site so that the substrate does not fit as easily into it.

○ EXTENDED How to explain that a very high temperature denatures the enzyme as interactions between amino acids break and change the shape of the active site completely.

○ EXTENDED How to explain that pH affects the interactions between amino acids in the enzyme molecule and so the ability of the substrate to fit into the active site.

○ EXTENDED That enzymes catalyse reactions in which substrates are converted to products.

○ EXTENDED How to describe enzyme action with reference to the active site, substrate and product.

End of topic questions

Note: The marks awarded for these questions indicate the level of detail required in the answers. In the examination, the number of marks awarded to questions like these may be different.

1. There are around 75 000 different enzymes in the human body. Explain why we need so many. **(2 marks)**

2. Describe how you would investigate the optimum temperature for a particular enzyme. **(4 marks)**

3. Sketch a graph to show the effect of temperature on the rate of reaction for an enzyme from humans. Label the value of the optimum temperature on your graph. **(2 marks)**

4. The body has many mechanisms for keeping internal conditions within limits. One of the internal conditions that is controlled is the concentration of carbon dioxide in the blood. Carbon dioxide gas is acidic and highly soluble.

   a) Which process in cells produces carbon dioxide? **(1 mark)**

   b) How is this gas removed from the body? **(1 mark)**

   c) What would you expect to happen to the amount of carbon dioxide in the body during exercise? Explain your answer. **(2 marks)**

   d) What effect would this have on conditions inside cells if the carbon dioxide was not removed? **(1 mark)**

   e) What problem would this cause for enzymes and the cell processes that they control? **(2 marks)**

5. EXTENDED Explain fully the shape of the graph you drew for Question 3. **(5 marks)**

The world's tallest known living tree, which has been named Hyperion, is a coast redwood tree growing in Northern California in the US. When it was measured in 2006 it was found to be 115.61 m tall (379.3 ft). Like all plants, from the smallest seedling to the tallest redwood giant, Hyperion makes its own food from three simple ingredients, sunlight, water and carbon dioxide. This process is known as photosynthesis, and is one of the features of plants that distinguish them from animals.

CONTENTS

6

Plant nutrition

△ Saplings growing towards a controlled light source.

Plant nutrition

INTRODUCTION

From space we can see where plants do or do not grow. We can distinguish different environments by looking at where the land is green, brown or white. The green areas are a result of chlorophyll in photosynthesising plants. We can also see where land use is changing, by looking at how the green areas of rainforests are slowly becoming brown as a result of deforestation.

Δ Fig 6.1 The green on this satellite image shows plant growth on Earth.

KNOWLEDGE CHECK

✓ Plants make their own food in their leaves using photosynthesis.
✓ Plant structures, such as the leaf and root cells, are adapted for their functions in nutrition.

LEARNING OBJECTIVES

✓ State the word equation for photosynthesis.
✓ Define the term *photosynthesis* and write the word equation for the reaction.
✓ Investigate the need for chlorophyll, light and carbon dioxide for photosynthesis.

✓ EXTENDED Write the balanced symbol equation for photosynthesis.

✓ EXTENDED Explain the importance of photosynthesis for plant nutrition.

✓ EXTENDED Investigate the effect of varying light intensity, carbon dioxide concentration and temperature on the rate of photosynthesis.

✓ EXTENDED Define the term *limiting factor*, and explain it in terms of the environmental conditions that affect the rate of photosynthesis.

✓ EXTENDED Explain the use of changing conditions on plant growth in glasshouse systems.

✓ Identify structures in a leaf.
✓ EXTENDED Explain how a leaf is adapted for photosynthesis.
✓ Describe the importance of some mineral ions in plant growth.
✓ EXTENDED Explain the effect of the deficiency of some minerals on a plant.

PHOTOSYNTHESIS

Plant tissue contains the same types of chemical molecules (carbohydrates, proteins and lipids) as animal tissue. However, whereas animals eat other organisms to get the nutrients they need to make these molecules, plants make these molecules from basic building blocks, beginning with the process of **photosynthesis**.

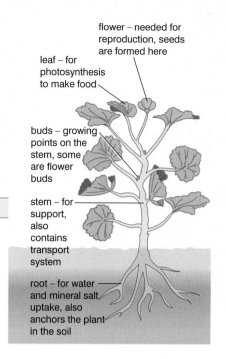

flower – needed for reproduction, seeds are formed here

leaf – for photosynthesis to make food

buds – growing points on the stem, some are flower buds

stem – for support, also contains transport system

root – for water and mineral salt uptake, also anchors the plant in the soil

△ Fig 6.2 Anatomy of a plant.

EXTENDED

In photosynthesis, plants combine the raw materials carbon dioxide (from the air) and water (from the soil) to form glucose, a simple sugar and also a carbohydrate. This process transfers energy from light (usually from sunlight) into chemical energy in the bonds of the glucose. The light is absorbed by the green pigment **chlorophyll** in plants.

END OF EXTENDED

Photosynthesis is fundamental to almost all life on Earth, because most organisms other than plants get their energy from the chemical energy in the food that they eat, whether that is herbivores getting energy directly from plants or carnivores consuming the herbivores.

Oxygen is also produced in photosynthesis. Although some is used inside the plant for respiration (releasing energy from food), most is not needed and is given out as a **waste product**.

The process of photosynthesis can be summarised in a word equation:

$$\text{carbon dioxide} + \text{water} \xrightarrow[\text{light energy}]{\text{chlorophyll}} \text{glucose} + \text{oxygen}$$

EXTENDED

Photosynthesis can also be summarised as a balanced symbol equation:

$$6CO_2 + 6H_2O \xrightarrow[\text{light energy}]{\text{chlorophyll}} C_6H_{12}O_6 + 6O_2$$

END OF EXTENDED

REMEMBER

For higher marks you will need to know, and be able to balance, the chemical equation for photosynthesis.

Much of the glucose formed by photosynthesis is converted into other substances, including **starch**. Starch molecules are large carbohydrates made of lots of glucose molecules joined together. Starch is insoluble and so can be stored in cells without affecting water movement into and out of the cells by **osmosis**. Some plants, such as potato and rice plants, store large amounts of starch in particular parts of the plant (tubers or seeds). We use these parts as sources of starch in our food.

Some glucose is converted to **sucrose** (a type of sugar formed from two glucose molecules joined together). This is still soluble, but not as reactive as glucose, so can easily be carried around the plant in solution.

The energy needed to join simple sugars to make larger carbohydrates comes from respiration.

QUESTIONS

1. Write the word equation for photosynthesis.

2. Explain the importance of light in photosynthesis.

3. EXTENDED **a)** Write the balanced symbol equation for photosynthesis.

   b) Annotate your equation to show where each of the reactants come from, and each of the products go to.

4. EXTENDED Explain why the transfer of energy from light to chemical energy in plant cells is essential for life on Earth.

Investigating photosynthesis

We can use the iodine test to show that photosynthesising parts of a plant produce starch. Before carrying out this test, though, we must start by leaving the plant in a dark place for 24 hours. This will make sure that the plant uses up its stores of starch (this is known as de-starching) and means that any starch identified by the test is the result of photosynthesis during the investigation.

- The production of starch after photosynthesis can be shown simply by placing a de-starched plant in light for an hour. Remove one leaf and place it in boiling water for a few minutes to soften it. Then place the leaf in boiling ethanol heated in a beaker of boiling water, not over a Bunsen because ethanol fumes are flammable. This removes the chlorophyll in the leaf. When the leaf has lost its green, wash it in cold water before placing it in a dish and adding a few drops of iodine solution. The leaf should turn blue/black, indicating the presence of starch.

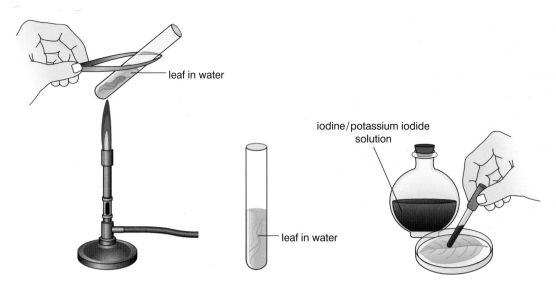

△ Fig 6.3 Preparing and testing a leaf for starch.

- The investigation above can be adjusted to show the need for light by covering part of the leaf before the de-starched plant is brought into the light. Only the part of the leaf that received light should test positive for the presence of starch, showing that photosynthesis is linked to the production of starch.

- This investigation can also be adjusted to show the need for chlorophyll by using variegated leaves. Variegated leaves are partly green (where the cells contain chlorophyll) and partly white (where there is no chlorophyll). A variegated leaf after this investigation will show the presence of starch where there was chlorophyll but not in the parts of the leaf that had no chlorophyll.

△ Fig 6.4 Light was excluded from all of the lower leaf except an L-shaped window. After exposure to light, only the L shape tests positive for starch.

- A simple test to show the need for carbon dioxide can be carried out by setting up two bell jars on glass sheets. Sodium or potassium hydroxide reacts with the carbon dioxide, removing it from the air. So a dish of one of the hydroxides is placed in one bell jar. Carbon dioxide is added to the other bell jar by burning a candle in it, which also removes some of the oxygen. Similar de-starched plants are placed in each bell jar, and the base of the jar sealed to the glass sheet, for example with petroleum jelly. After a few hours in light, a leaf from each plant is tested for starch, which should show that the plant with the least carbon dioxide produces little starch.

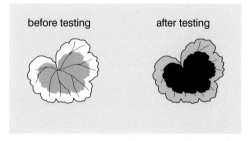

△ Fig 6.5 Only the green parts of a variegated leaf can photosynthesise, as shown by the leaf on the right, which has been tested for starch.

1. Describe a test that would show the need for chlorophyll in photosynthesis.

2. What precautions should be taken when boiling ethanol to remove chlorophyll in a leaf? Explain your answer.

3. How could you show that plants need carbon dioxide for photosynthesis?

EXTENDED

Factors affecting the rate of photosynthesis

The rate at which a process can occur depends on how quickly the required materials can be supplied. Photosynthesis needs light energy. As light levels fall as night approaches, or on a very cloudy day, the rate at which energy is absorbed by chlorophyll decreases and the rate at which the photosynthesis proceeds slows down. Light has become a limiting factor for the process. A **limiting factor** is a factor in the environment that is limiting the rate of the reaction.

If there is plenty of light, such as on a sunny day, then light will not be a limiting factor. Instead the rate of photosynthesis may be dependent on the rate of diffusion into the photosynthesising cells in the leaf from the air. In this case, carbon dioxide has become the limiting factor.

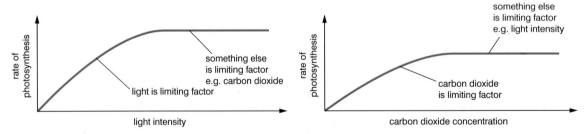

Δ Fig 6.6 The rate of photosynthesis is affected by (left) light intensity and (right) carbon dioxide concentration, up to a point when something else becomes a limiting factor.

We can test whether this is true by adding more carbon dioxide. Farmers sometimes do this in glasshouses to increase the growth rate of crops. If the rate of photosynthesis increases, then carbon dioxide was the limiting factor.

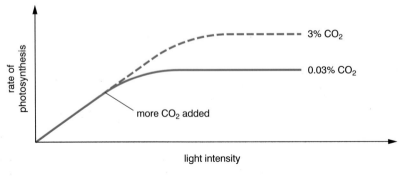

Δ Fig 6.7 The effect on rate of photosynthesis of adding more carbon dioxide to a leaf with increasing light intensity.

The process of photosynthesis involves several chemical reactions. Like all chemical reactions, the rate of reaction is affected by temperature because it affects the energy of the reacting particles and how quickly and how hard they bump into each other. So, on a cool day, or in the early morning when the air hasn't yet heated up, temperature may be the factor that limits the rate of photosynthesis. If temperature rises too high, however, the enzymes that control the rate of reactions start to become denatured and so the reactions go more slowly.

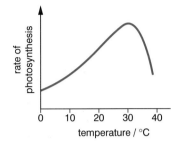

◁ Fig 6.8 The effect of temperature on the rate of photosynthesis.

Changing glasshouse conditions

Farmers and plant growers want their crops to grow well, but in open fields it is not usually possible to control the amount of carbon dioxide or light the plants receive, or the temperature at which they are growing. However, if the plants are grown in sheltered conditions, such as in glasshouses, then it can be possible to change conditions, for example by:

Δ Fig 6.9 Plants can be kept under the best conditions for growth in a greenhouse.

- using artificial lighting so that the plants can continue growing at a maximum when conditions are cloudy or even at night
- enriching the atmosphere around the plants with carbon dioxide by burning coal or oil
- using a heating system to increase the temperature to an optimum for photosynthesis.

Remember that enzymes have an optimum temperature at which they work, so glasshouses and polytunnels may also need to be ventilated to release hot air if the temperature rises too high, otherwise the rate of photosynthesis will decrease.

Investigating the rate of photosynthesis

Measuring starch production is an indirect measurement of photosynthesis, because starch is made from the glucose produced in photosynthesis. You can investigate photosynthesis more directly by measuring the amount of oxygen produced by a plant. The oxygen is usually collected over water, and these investigations are most simply done using aquatic plants (plants that grow in water), such as pondweed, using the apparatus shown in the Developing investigative skills box on the following page.

- To prove that photosynthesis produces oxygen, simply use the glowing splint test on the gas collected. The splint should re-ignite, showing that the gas is oxygen.
- The investigation can be adjusted to test for the effect of light intensity on the rate of photosynthesis as described in the Developing investigative skills 1 box below.
- The investigation can be adjusted to test for the effect of carbon dioxide concentration by adding different amounts of sodium bicarbonate to the water and measuring the rate at which bubbles of oxygen are produced.
- The investigation can be adjusted to test for the effect of temperature by placing the beaker of pondweed in water baths of different temperatures and measuring the rate at which bubbles of oxygen are produced.

In each of these investigations, all other factors that may affect the rate of photosynthesis must be controlled and kept constant as far as possible.

Developing investigative skills

You can investigate the effect of light on photosynthesis by shining a light on a water plant and measuring how quickly bubbles are given off, as shown in Fig. 6.10.

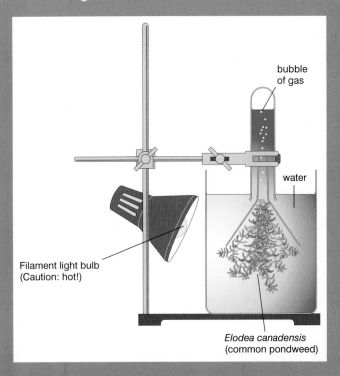

bubble of gas

water

Filament light bulb
(Caution: hot!)

Elodea canadensis
(common pondweed)

△ Fig 6.10 Apparatus for the investigation into the effect of light on photosynthesis.

The results below were gathered using this apparatus.

	Distance to lamp/cm				
	5	10	15	20	25
Number of gas bubbles given off in 5 minutes	67	57	40	20	4

Devise and plan investigations

❶ a) Explain why the rate of producing bubbles can be used as a measure of the rate of photosynthesis.

b) Explain how you would identify the gas produced by the plant.

Analyse and interpret data

❷ a) Use the data in the table to draw a suitable graph.

b) Describe and explain the shape of the graph.

Evaluate data and methods

❸ Light is not the only factor that can affect the rate of photosynthesis.

a) Which other factor might have had an effect on these measurements.

b) Suggest how the method could be changed to avoid this problem.

QUESTIONS

1. Explain what is meant by a *limiting factor*.

2. Describe how each of the following factors affects the rate of photosynthesis.

    a) light intensity

    b) carbon dioxide concentration

    c) temperature.

3. Explain why the factors have the effect you described in Question 2.

Gas exchange in plants

All organisms use cellular respiration to release the chemical energy in food molecules such as glucose. Cellular (usually aerobic) respiration must take place all the time because organisms need energy continually for other life processes. So animal and plant cells are always taking in oxygen and releasing carbon dioxide for respiration.

Plants photosynthesise as well as respire. For photosynthesis, plant cells need to take in carbon dioxide and release oxygen. However, photosynthesis can only take place when there is sufficient light.

At night, plants do not photosynthesise, but they do continue respiring. So plants give out carbon dioxide and take in oxygen. At daybreak, as light intensity increases, the rate of photosynthesis increases. At a particular light intensity, the amount of oxygen produced by photosynthesis will balance the amount used by the plant in respiration, and the *net production of oxygen* will be zero. This is known as a compensation point.

During daylight, oxygen production from photosynthesis exceeds its use in respiration, and the opposite is true for the use (by photosynthesis) and production (by respiration) of carbon dioxide. This continues until light intensity decreases, when the sun sets and a second compensation point is reached.

You can investigate the effect of light on net gas exchange in a plant using a pH indicator, because carbon dioxide is acidic when dissolved in water. Hydrogencarbonate solution is often used because it is non-toxic and can be used with living organisms. Before use in an investigation it needs to be *equilibrated*, so that the concentration of carbon dioxide in the solution is the same as the concentration of carbon dioxide in the surrounding air. This is done by drawing air through the solution using a vacuum pump for a few minutes.

Discs can be cut from leaves using a core borer of large diameter. The discs are placed in Petri dishes containing equilibrated hydrogencarbonate indicator. Placing one dish in bright light and covering the other with dark paper shows a difference in colour of the indicator after 10–15 minutes as a result of the net release or net uptake of carbon dioxide. A similar investigation using an aquatic plant is shown in the Developing investigative skills box on the next page.

Developing investigative skills

Hydrogencarbonate indicator can be used to indicate the acidity or alkalinity of a solution. At neutral pH it is a red-orange colour. In acidic solutions it is yellow, and in alklane solutions it is purple.

Devise and plan investigations

❶ Using the information above, write a plan for testing the effect of light on the net gas exchange from an aquatic plant such as *Elodea* (pondweed), as used in the investigation box on page 119.

Analyse and interpret data

The following results were obtained in a similar experiment to the one you have described after 10 minutes of setting up the experiment.

Time in minutes	Light dish	Dark dish
0	red-orange	red-orange
2	red	light orange
4	reddish-purple	yellowish-orange
6	purple	yellow
8	purple	yellow
10	purple	yellow

❷ Describe the results shown in the table for:

   a) the light dish
   b) the dark dish.

❸ What caused the colour change in the dark dish? What does this suggest is happening in the plant cells?

❹ What caused the colour change in the light dish? What does this suggest is happening in the plant cells?

❺ What other process is happening in the plant cells in the light dish that we cannot see because its effects are masked? Explain your answer as fully as possible.

Evaluate data and methods

❻ What would no change in the colour of the indicator mean?

❼ Explain how you would adapt your method to find the compensation point for this plant.

QUESTION

1. Explain why a pH indicator can be used to investigate the net exchange of gases in a leaf.

LEAF STRUCTURE

Photosynthesis takes place mainly in the leaves, although it can occur in any cells that contain green chlorophyll. Leaves are adapted to make them very efficient as sites for photosynthesis, gas exchange, transport and support.

◁ Fig 6.11 The leaves of trees are often arranged so that they do not overlap each other, which makes it possible for the tree to capture as much light energy as possible.

Fig. 6.12 shows the arrangement of cells and tissues inside a leaf.

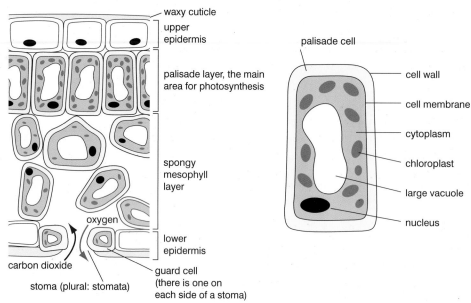

△ Fig 6.12 Cells in a section of a leaf (left), and a palisade cell (right), which contains many chloroplasts, for photosynthesis.

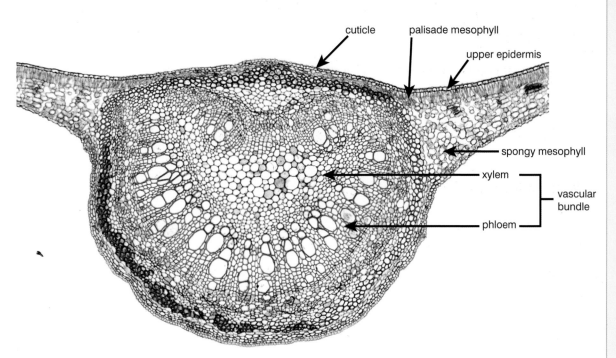

cuticle palisade mesophyll

upper epidermis

spongy mesophyll

xylem

vascular bundle

phloem

△ Fig 6.13 Photomicrograph of a section of a dicotyledonous plant leaf. Stomata are not easily seen in this section.

EXTENDED

Adaptations for photosynthesis

Many structures in a leaf are adapted so that photosynthesis can be carried out as efficiently as possible.

- The waxy **cuticle** that covers the leaf, particularly the upper surface, prevents the loss of water from epidermal cells and helps to stop the plant from drying out too quickly.
- The transparent upper **epidermis** allows as much light as possible to reach the photosynthesising cells within the leaf.
- The **palisade cells**, where most photosynthesis takes place, are tightly packed together in the uppermost half of the leaf so that as many as possible can receive sunlight.
- **Chloroplasts** containing chlorophyll are concentrated in the palisade cells in the uppermost half of the leaf to absorb as much sunlight as possible.
- The **spongy mesophyll cells** and air spaces in the lower part of the leaf provide a large internal surface area to volume ratio to allow the efficient exchange of the gases carbon dioxide and oxygen between the cells and the air in the leaf.
- Many pores or **stomata** (singular: stoma) allow the movement of gases into and out of the leaf, to allow efficient gas exchange between the leaf and the air surrounding it.
- The **vascular bundles** form the veins in the stem and leaf. The thick cell walls of the tissue in the bundles help to support the stem and leaf.
- **Phloem** tissue transports sucrose, formed from glucose in photosynthesising cells, away from the leaf. **Xylem** tissue transports water and minerals to the leaf from the roots.

END OF EXTENDED

1. Name four tissues in a leaf.

2. **EXTENDED** List as many adaptations of a plant leaf for photosynthesis as you can.

3. **EXTENDED** Explain why a large surface area inside the leaf is essential for photosynthesis.

4. **EXTENDED** Explain why a transparent epidermis is an adaptation for photosynthesis.

MINERAL REQUIREMENTS OF PLANTS

Photosynthesis produces carbohydrates, but plants contain many other types of chemical. Carbohydrates contain just the elements carbon, hydrogen and oxygen, but the amino acids that make up proteins also contain nitrogen. So plants need a source of nitrogen. Other chemicals in plants contain different elements; for example, chlorophyll molecules contain magnesium and nitrogen. Without a source of magnesium and nitrogen, a plant cannot produce chlorophyll and so cannot photosynthesise.

These additional elements are dissolved in water in the soil as **mineral ions**. The plant absorbs the mineral ions through their roots, using active transport because the concentration of the ions in the soil is lower than in the plant cells.

EXTENDED

Mineral deficiencies

Plants that are not absorbing enough mineral ions show particular symptoms of deficiency. For example:

• a plant with a nitrate ion deficiency has stunted growth
• a plant with magnesium ion deficiency has leaves that are yellow between the veins, particularly in older leaves as the magnesium is transported in the plant to the new leaves.

△ Fig 6.14 A plant showing symptoms of nitrate ion deficiency.

△ Fig 6.15 A plant showing symptoms of magnesium ion deficiency.

END OF EXTENDED

QUESTIONS

1. Explain why plants need a supply of mineral ions.

2. Explain what plants use the following mineral ions for:

   a) nitrogen ions

   b) magnesium ions.

3. EXTENDED Describe and explain the deficiency symptoms in a plant for the following mineral ions:

   a) nitrate ions

   b) magnesium ions.

End of topic checklist

Key terms

chlorophyll, chloroplast, epidermis, limiting factor, mineral ion, palisade cell, phloem, photosynthesis, spongy mesophyll cell, starch, stomata, xylem

During your study of this topic you should have learned:

○ How to define photosynthesis as the process by which plants make carbohydrates (glucose) from raw materials using light.

○ How to investigate the necessity of chlorophyll, light and carbon dioxide for photosynthesis, using appropriate controls.

○ EXTENDED That photosynthesis takes place in chloroplasts in plant cells, using chlorophyll, and converts light energy into chemical energy.

○ The word equation for photosynthesis:

$$\text{carbon dioxide} + \text{water} \xrightarrow[\text{light energy}]{\text{chloroplast}} \text{glucose} + \text{oxygen}$$

○ EXTENDED The balanced symbol equation for photosynthesis:

$$6CO_2 + 6H_2O \xrightarrow[\text{light energy}]{\text{chloroplast}} C_6H_{12}O_6 + 6O_2$$

○ EXTENDED How to outline the use and storage of the carbohydrates made in photosynthesis.

○ EXTENDED How to investigate the rate of photosynthesis increases as carbon dioxide concentration increases, as light intensity increases, and as temperature increases up to an optimum temperature, after which it decreases as enzymes denature.

○ That chloroplasts are found mainly in cells in the upper part of a leaf.

○ To identify the tissues that can be seen in leaves, including: cuticle, upper epidermis, lower epidermis including stomata and guard cells, palisade mesophyll, spongy mesophyll, phloem and xylem.

○ **EXTENDED** To explain how the leaf is adapted to maximise the rate of photosynthesis by:

- being broad and thin
- the cells where most photosynthesis takes place are in the palisade mesophyll near the upper surface of the leaf
- the transparent upper epidermis lets lots of light through
- the spongy mesophyll maximises the internal surface area of the leaf for diffusion
- stomata allow gases to diffuse into and out of the leaf and are opened and closed by guard cells
- xylem transports water to the leaf
- phloem transports sugars away from the leaf.

○ To describe how plants use mineral ions to convert the sugars from photosynthesis into other essential substances, such as chlorophyll, which contains magnesium, and amino acids, which contain nitrogen.

○ **EXTENDED** The deficiency of nitrate ions causes stunted growth with yellowing leaves because the plant cannot make proteins for growth and chlorophyll.

○ **EXTENDED** The deficiency of magnesium ions causes yellowing leaves as the plant cannot make chlorophyll.

○ **EXTENDED** How to explain a limiting factor as something in the environment that is in short supply and restricts life processes such as photosynthesis.

○ **EXTENDED** How to explain that an understanding of limiting factors in photosynthesis is used to maximise plant growth in glasshouse systems.

○ **EXTENDED** How to explain the use of changing conditions on plant growth in glasshouse systems.

End of topic questions

Note: The marks awarded for these questions indicate the level of detail required in the answers. In the examination, the number of marks awarded to questions like these may be different.

1. Some students used an oxygen sensor to measure the amount of dissolved oxygen there was in pond water containing pondweed, when a light was on and when it was switched off. The graph shows their results.

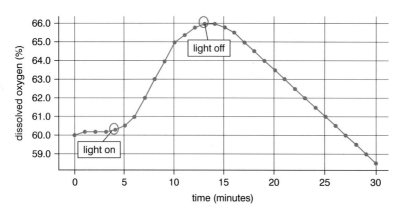

a) The light was switched on after 4 minutes. Describe and explain what happened until the light was switched off again. **(2 marks)**

b) Describe and explain what happened after the light was switched off. **(2 marks)**

2. **EXTENDED** Explain why gardeners may add a liquid feed containing nitrogen and magnesium ions to the water for the plants that they are growing. **(2 marks)**

3. **EXTENDED** Using what have you learnt about the effect of concentration gradient and surface area to volume ratio, explain the adaptations of a leaf for photosynthesis. **(4 marks)**

4. **EXTENDED** Sketch the axes of a graph with time of day along the x-axis and rate of photosynthesis on the y-axis. The units on the x-axis should start at midnight on one day and end at midnight on the following day. Add an arrowhead at the top of the y-axis to show that the units are arbitrary (have no values) but increase as you go up the axis.

a) Draw a line on your graph to show how the rate of photosynthesis might change during the day for a large tree. **(1 mark)**

b) Annotate your graph to explain which factor (or factors) may be limiting the rate of photosynthesis at different times of day. **(3 marks)**

5. In a greenhouse a grower is growing tomato plants. Explain as fully as you can why she might do the following:

    a) leave lights on in the greenhouse all night   **(2 marks)**

    b) close the greenhouse windows at night but open them during the day.   **(4 marks)**

6. It is commonly stated that 'Plants produce oxygen during the day and carbon dioxide at night.' Explain fully the limits of this statement.   **(5 marks)**

Nutrition is one of the seven characteristics of living organisms. For humans and other animals, nutrition is the taking in of nutrients (including organic substances and minerals) that contain the raw materials needed by the body to make essential molecules, such as proteins, which are used as the building blocks to maintain healthy growth and tissue repair.

We think of malnutrition as not having enough food, but many people may be malnourished because they don't eat enough of the kinds of foods that contain all the nutrients that their bodies need, or they eat too much of the types of foods that will supply more energy than the body needs, so the excess is stored as fat.

CONTENTS

7

Human nutrition

△ Green beans contain vital nutrients essential to maintaining growth and tissue repair.

Human nutrition

△ Fig 7.1 Honey is still a highly prized source of sugar today.

INTRODUCTION

Human taste buds have evolved to give us useful information about what we are putting into our mouth. Sour or bitter tastes can indicate food that is decaying or poisonous, and so is dangerous to eat. Sweet (presence of sugars), salty and savoury (presence of proteins) tastes indicate nutrients that are essential for healthy growth. These were particularly important in our hunter-gatherer past, when it could be difficult to find foods containing these nutrients. They are not so useful to us now because, for many of us, foods containing large quantities of these are easily available. The urge to eat foods containing high levels of sugars and salt has led to problems of obesity and disease, particularly heart disease in people who have increasingly sedentary lifestyles.

KNOWLEDGE CHECK

✓ Animals eat other organisms to get the food they need for their life processes.
✓ The organs, tissues and cells of the digestive system are adapted to digest and absorb nutrients from food.
✓ Food may be chemically or mechanically digested before absorption.
✓ Different groups of people need different diets.

LEARNING OBJECTIVES

✓ Describe what is meant by a *balanced diet* and how it varies in different groups of people.
✓ Describe the sources and functions of nutrients in human nutrition.
✓ EXTENDED Describe the deficiency symptoms for some nutrients in the human diet.
✓ Describe some effects of malnutrition in humans.
✓ Explain the causes and effects of protein malnutrition.
✓ Describe the structures and functions of organs in the human alimentary canal and related organs of the digestive system.
✓ Describe the processes involved in human nutrition, including *ingestion*, *digestion*, *absorption*, *assimilation* and *egestion*.
✓ Identify and describe the functions of the main regions of the alimentary canal.
✓ State the functions of enzymes and hydrochloric acid in chemical digestion.
✓ Describe how to treat diarrhoea.
✓ Describe cholera.
✓ EXTENDED Explain the effects of cholera.
✓ Describe the structure and function of different types of human teeth.
✓ Describe the care of teeth.
✓ Outline the role of enzymes in digestion.
✓ EXTENDED Describe the functions of hydrochloric acid and bile in digestion.
✓ EXTENDED Describe the role of pepsin, trypsin and starch in the alimentary canal.
✓ Identify the small intestine as the region of absorption of digested food.

✓ **EXTENDED** Describe the importance of surface area of the villus in absorption.

✓ **EXTENDED** Explain the importance of the structure of a villus.

✓ **EXTENDED** Describe the roles of capillaries and lacteals in villi.

✓ Describe how water is absorbed in the small intestine and colon.

DIET

Essential nutrients

To keep healthy, humans need a diet that includes all the nutrients that our cells and tissues use, such as:

- **proteins** – these are broken down to make amino acids. The amino acids are used to form other proteins needed by cells, including enzymes. Protein sources include eggs, milk and milk products (cheese, yoghurt, etc.), meat, fish, legumes (peas and beans), nuts and seeds.
- **carbohydrates** – which are broken down to simple sugars for use in respiration. This releases energy in our cells and enables all the life processes to take place. Good sources of carbohydrate include rice, bread, potatoes, pasta and yams.
- **fats** – these are deposited in many parts of the body, including just below the skin. Some fat helps to maintain body temperature. Fat is also a store of energy to supply molecules for respiration if the diet does not contain enough energy for daily needs. Fat is present in meat and can also come in the form of oils, milk products (butter, cheese), nuts, avocados and oily fish.
- **vitamins** and **minerals** – these substances are needed in tiny amounts for the correct functioning of the body. Vitamins and minerals cannot be produced by the body, and cooking food destroys some vitamins. For example, vitamin C is best supplied by eating raw fruit and vegetables.

Essential vitamins and minerals	Job	Good food source	EXTENDED Deficiency disease
vitamin C	for healthy skin, teeth and gums, and keeps lining of blood vessels healthy	citrus fruit, green vegetables, potatoes	scurvy (bleeding gums and wounds do not heal properly)
vitamin D	for strong bones and teeth	fish, eggs, liver, cheese and milk	rickets (softening of the bones)
calcium	needed for strong teeth and bones, and involved in the clotting of blood	milk and eggs	rickets (softening of the bones)
iron	needed to make haemoglobin in red blood cells	red meats, liver and kidneys, leafy green vegetables such as spinach	anaemia (reduction in number of red blood cells, person soon becomes tired and short of breath)

Δ Table 7.1 Vitamins and minerals, their roles, sources and effects of deficiency.

- **fibre (roughage)** – which is made up of the cell walls of plants. Good sources are leafy vegetables, such as cabbage, and unrefined grains such as brown rice and wholegrain wheat. It adds bulk to food so that it can be easily moved along the digestive system by peristalsis. This is important in preventing constipation. Fibre is thought to help prevent bowel cancer.
- **water** – which is the major constituent of the body of living organisms and is necessary for all life processes. Water is continually being lost through excretion and sweating, and must be replaced regularly through food and drink in order to maintain health. Most foods contain some water, but most fruit and vegetables contain a lot of water.

Δ Fig 7.2 A healthy meal contains a good balance of the foods your body needs and nothing in too large an amount.

Kwashiorkor

Kwashiorkor is a condition found in young children in areas where the diet contains very little protein. The condition typically occurs in children who had been breast-fed but then are weaned after the birth of another baby. Breast milk contains proteins, but after weaning the child may get a carbohydrate-rich diet that includes few proteins that is often lacking in some vitamins and minerals. So kwashiorkor is often referred to as **protein energy malnutrition**. Typical symptoms include swelling of the feet and abdomen, wasting muscles, thinning hair and loss of teeth. The liver is often damaged, and treatment requires careful adjustment of the diet so as not to damage the liver even more.

Δ Fig 7.3 A child suffering from kwashiorkor, a protein deficiency.

QUESTIONS

1. Which three groups of food molecules do we need most of in a healthy diet?

2. Give examples of foods that are good sources of each group of food molecules.

3. Which other substances are needed in our diet?

4. Explain the role of each of these substances in our diet.

5. EXTENDED Describe the causes and effects of kwashiorkor.

The right balance

A **balanced diet** contains all of these nutrients in the right proportions to stay healthy because we need more of some nutrients than of others. As most foods contain more than one kind of nutrient, trying to work out what a balanced diet looks like can be difficult. Governments use images like the ones in Figs. 7.4 and 7.5, of food on a plate, to guide people on what proportions of food to eat.

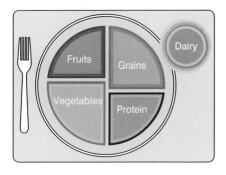

△ Fig 7.4 Guidance from the USDA (United States Department of Agriculture) on the proportions of different nutrients in a balanced diet.

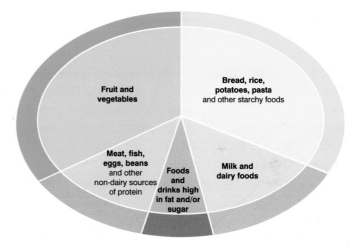

△ Fig 7.5 Guidance from the UK Government on the proportions of different nutrients in a balanced diet.

Different groups of people may have different needs for nutrients at different times in their lives, so this balance can change. For example, children need a higher proportion of protein than adults because they are still growing rapidly. Also, some groups of people have a greater need for a specific nutrient. During pregnancy, for example, a woman needs more iron than usual, to supply what the growing baby needs for making blood cells.

Even with the right proportions of nutrients in our foods, we can still be eating an unhealthy diet. This is because many of our foods, particularly carbohydrates but also fats and proteins, can contribute to the energy our bodies need. If we eat food that supplies more energy than we use, the extra will be deposited as energy stores of fat. This can lead to **obesity**, which is related to many health problems, such as heart disease and diabetes. Controlling the portion size at each meal, keeping between-meal snacks to a minimum, and increasing levels of exercise can help to reduce the risk of becoming overweight.

Energy requirements depend on body size, stage of development and level of exercise, as shown in Table 7.2.

	Energy used in a day (kJ)	
	Male	**Female**
6-year-old child	7 500	7 500
12–15-year-old teenager	12 500	9 700
adult manual worker	15 000	12 500
adult office worker	11 000	9 800
pregnant woman		10 000
breastfeeding		11 000

Δ Table 7.2 Daily energy requirements for different people.

Malnutrition

The term **malnutrition** literally means 'bad nutrition' and applies to any diet that will lead to health problems. A diet that is too high in energy content, and leads to obesity, is one form of malnutrition, because obesity increases the risk of several diseases.

Malnutrition can occur if one or more nutrients is in too high a proportion in the diet. For example, a high proportion of saturated fats in the diet can lead to deposits of cholesterol forming on the inside of arteries, increasing blood pressure and also increasing the risk of coronary heart disease (see Topic 9).

Malnutrition also occurs if any of the substances needed for a healthy body are in too low a proportion in the diet. For example, a lack of a vitamin or a mineral can cause deficiency diseases, as shown in Table 7.1. Too little fibre in the diet can lead to **constipation**, in which food moves too slowly through the **alimentary canal**, increasing the risk of diseases such as diverticulitis and bowel cancer.

Δ Fig 7.6 Starvation is most commonly seen in places where crops have failed due to drought (**famine**) or people are displaced as a result of war. However, it can also happen in people who choose to starve themselves, in crash diets or as a result of conditions such as anorexia.

Developing investigative skills

Combustion (burning) of foods releases heat energy. The word equation for combustion is:

food + oxygen → carbon dioxide + water (+ heat energy)

This reaction is similar to respiration inside cells, so we can use a combustion experiment to model the energy that is released from foods during respiration.

A crisp/potato chip and a plant leaf were tested in an investigation to see which released the most energy by combustion. Here are the results.

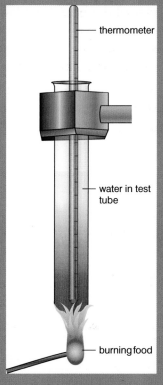

Δ Fig 7.7 Apparatus for burning food.

	Sample	
	Crisp	Leaf
mass of sample in grams	22	12
temperature of water after burning in °C	27	16
temperature of water before burning in °C	15	15
temperature rise in °C	12	1
energy released by the sample in joules	1260	105

Demonstrate and describe techniques

❶ a) Look at the diagram and describe what happens during the experiment.

b) Identify any areas of safety that should have been considered and suggest how risks could be controlled.

Analyse and interpret data

❷ a) Use the results to calculate the energy released per gram of each sample.

b) Explain why you need to do this.

❸ Which part of the sample released the most energy per gram?

❹ A plant seed contains a similar amount of energy as a crisp. Suggest why some animals that eat the leaves of plants for most of the year change to eating seeds (nuts) when they are available.

Evaluate data and methods

❺ The apparatus shown does not give accurate results for the amount of energy in the burning material. Explain why, and suggest a method that would increase the accuracy of the results.

Starvation occurs when there is too little energy provided by the diet. In this state, the body will start to break down its energy stores. Initially this uses the fat stores but, when those have run out, the body will start to break down muscle tissue to produce substances that can be used in respiration. This can damage the muscle tissue of the heart, and also the immune system, increasing the risk of many diseases.

QUESTIONS

1. Explain why different groups of people need different amounts of nutrients. Give examples in your answer.

2. Explain why a healthy diet needs to consider energy as well as nutrients.

3. Explain why the following are considered to be a result of *malnutrition*:

   a) obesity

   b) starvation

   c) constipation.

THE HUMAN ALIMENTARY CANAL

Eating food involves several different processes:

- **ingestion** – taking food and drink into the body (through the mouth in humans)
- **digestion** – breaking down of large food molecules into smaller water-soluble molecules
- **absorption** of digested food molecules from the intestine into the blood and lymph
- **assimilation** – moving absorbed food molecules into cells where they can be used to produce other molecules or in respiration
- **egestion** – removal of substances through the anus that were ingested but not absorbed by the body (faeces).

All these different processes take place in different parts of the alimentary canal.

The alimentary canal is a continuous tube through the body, from the mouth where food is ingested, through the oesophagus, stomach, small intestine and large intestine, to the anus where faeces are egested. You could say that materials in the alimentary canal aren't truly in the body. Not until food molecules are absorbed do they cross cell membranes into body tissue. Then they can be assimilated and **waste products** *excreted* through other organs.

The digestive system includes the alimentary canal and the other organs that contribute to digestion, such as the liver, pancreas and gall bladder. Table 7.3 describes the functions of each of the organs in the digestive system.

Part of digestive system	What happens there
mouth	teeth and tongue break down food into smaller pieces
salivary glands	produce liquid saliva, which moistens food so it is easily swallowed and contains the enzyme amylase to begin breakdown of starch
oesophagus	each lump of swallowed and chewed food, called a bolus, is moved from the mouth to the stomach by waves of muscle contraction called peristalsis
stomach	acid and protease enzymes are secreted to start protein digestion; movements of the muscular wall churn up food into a liquid
liver	cells in the liver make bile; amino acids not used for making proteins are broken down to form **urea**, which passes to the kidneys for excretion; excess glucose is removed from the blood and stored as **glycogen** in liver cells
gall bladder	stores bile from the liver; the bile is passed along the bile duct into the small intestine, where it neutralises the stomach acid in the chyme
pancreas	secretes digestive enzymes in an alkaline fluid into the duodenum
small intestine (duodenum and ileum)	secretions from the gall bladder and pancreas enter the first part of the small intestine (duodenum) to complete the process of digestion; digested food molecules and water are absorbed in the ileum
large intestine (colon)	water is absorbed from the remaining material
rectum	the remaining, unabsorbed, material (**faeces**), plus dead cells from the lining of the alimentary canal and bacteria, are compacted and stored
anus	faeces is egested through a sphincter

△ Table 7.3 The functions of parts of the human digestive system.

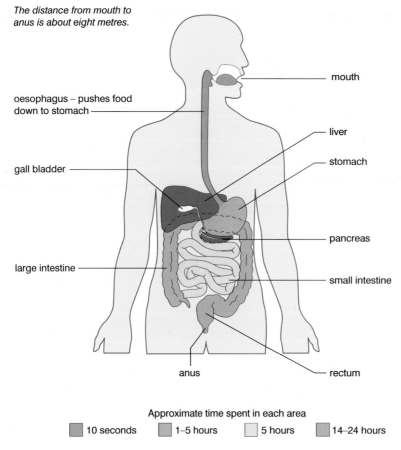

The distance from mouth to anus is about eight metres.

mouth

oesophagus – pushes food down to stomach

liver

gall bladder

stomach

pancreas

large intestine

small intestine

anus

rectum

Approximate time spent in each area

| 10 seconds | 1–5 hours | 5 hours | 14–24 hours |

Δ Fig. 7.8 The human digestive system.

Food moves along the alimentary canal because of the contractions of the muscles in the walls of the alimentary canal. This is called **peristalsis**. Fibre in the food keeps the bolus bulky and soft, making peristalsis easier.

Peristalsis moves food along the digestive system.

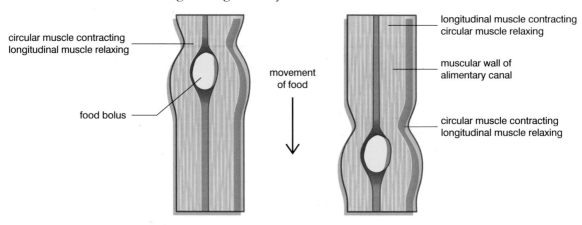

circular muscle contracting
longitudinal muscle relaxing

food bolus

movement of food

longitudinal muscle contracting
circular muscle relaxing

muscular wall of alimentary canal

circular muscle contracting
longitudinal muscle relaxing

Δ Fig 7.9 Peristalsis moves food along the digestive system.

QUESTIONS

1. Sketch the diagram of the digestive system shown in Fig. 7.8. Label the organs, and add notes to each organ to explain its function in the system.

2. Explain the difference between egestion and excretion.

3. Explain how the muscles of the alimentary canal wall move food.

Diarrhoea

Sometimes the small and large intestines fail to absorb water as normal. This is usually the result of infection, such as in food poisoning. It may also be caused by a bacterium found in contaminated drinking water that causes a disease called **cholera**. The result is that large amounts of watery faeces are produced, which we call **diarrhoea**.

If diarrhoea continues for any length of time it can be very harmful, because the body not only loses water but also essential nutrients in the faeces that would normally have been absorbed. It is important to treat diarrhoea not just by drinking water, but also by taking in some of these nutrients in a simple form. **Oral rehydration salts** contain the right balance of simple nutrients for mixing with water for drinking. It is essential that the water used to make up the rehydration solution is clean and not contaminated. If rehydration salts are not available, a simple replacement is a solution produced using about 15 g table sugar and 5 g salt dissolved in a litre of clean water.

△ Fig 7.10 Cholera is a disease that frequently occurs after major disasters, which allow drinking water to be contaminated with infected water.

Cholera

Cholera is caused by the bacterium *Vibrio cholerae*, which is found in the brackish water of estuaries and the faeces of infected people. Flooding of low-lying areas can make it possible for the bacterium to get into drinking water supplies.

Many people infected with the cholera-causing bacterium do not become ill, so it is easy to pass the microorganism on without knowing it. Some people get mild diarrhoea, but others get severe diarrhoea, which is what we call cholera.

The bacterium produces a toxin that affects the lining of the small intestine. In extreme cases the toxin causes the small intestine to secrete chloride ions from the body into the alimentary canal. This draws water out of the body by osmosis (Topic 3), resulting in rapid **dehydration** of the body as well as loss of mineral salts and diarrhoea. Rehydration is essential to prevent death. Antibiotics may also be given in these cases, to kill the bacteria.

END OF EXTENDED

QUESTIONS

1. Describe the condition of *diarrhoea*.

2. Explain how diarrhoea can be treated.

3. EXTENDED Explain how cholera can lead to severe dehydration and loss of salts from the body.

Different types of digestion

If food is to be of any use to us the food molecules must enter the blood so that they can travel to every part of the body. Many of the foods we eat are made up of large, **insoluble** molecules that cannot cross the wall of the alimentary canal and the cell membranes of cells lining in the blood vessels. This means the food molecules have to be broken down into small, **soluble** molecules that can easily cross cell membranes and enter the blood. Breaking down the molecules is called digestion.

There are two types of digestion.

- **Mechanical and physical digestion** occurs mainly in the mouth, where food is broken down physically into smaller pieces by the biting and chewing action of the teeth. It also happens in the small intestine, where **bile** helps to emulsify fats, which means breaking them into small droplets (see Topic 7).
- **Chemical digestion** is the breakdown of large food molecules into smaller ones using chemicals such as enzymes (see Topic 6).

Some molecules, such as glucose, vitamins, minerals and water, are already small enough to pass through the alimentary canal wall and do not need to be digested.

MECHANICAL AND PHYSICAL DIGESTION

Human teeth

Teeth cause the mechanical digestion of food in the mouth. Humans are omnivores that eat a varied diet of plant and animal material. So we have a range of tooth type to help us bite off and chew these different materials:

- **incisors** at the front of the mouth are chisel-shaped, for biting off food (particularly good with plant material)
- four pointed **canines** pierce and hold food, particularly meat, so that it can be chewed
- **premolars** help with the cutting off of tough foods, such as meat, and grinding of plant material on a small grinding surface
- **molars** at the back of the mouth have large grinding surfaces for chewing, particularly plant material.

In each adult jaw, we have four incisors, two canines, four premolars and between four and six molars.

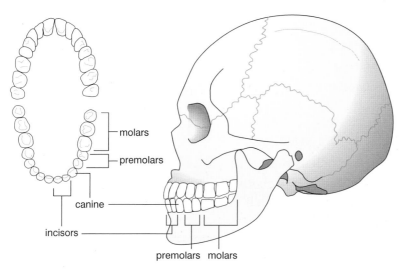

△ Fig 7.11 Plan and side view of teeth in a human skull.

Like other mammals, humans have two sets of teeth: the 'milk' teeth of childhood are replaced by permanent (adult) teeth from the age of about 6 years. The molars at the far back of the mouth, sometimes called the 'wisdom teeth' may not grow until adulthood, if at all.

Dental decay and tooth care

Although **enamel** is very hard, it is vulnerable to attack by acids. Acids are naturally present in fruits and other foods. Bacteria living in the spaces between teeth, in crevices on the tooth surface, and at the edges of the gums also make acids. Food particles get lodged in these crevices and bacteria grow on them, forming plaque. Plaque makes it even easier for bacteria to grow and produce acids right against the surface of the teeth. These acids corrode the tooth enamel and expose the softer **dentine** underneath. This can cause pain (or toothache) because the nerves in the **pulp cavity** are affected by acid, heat or cold more easily. The enamel on teeth does not extend far below the gum edge, so when plaque forms there the dentine can quickly be attacked. The links between the tooth and its socket can be weakened and the tooth might fall out.

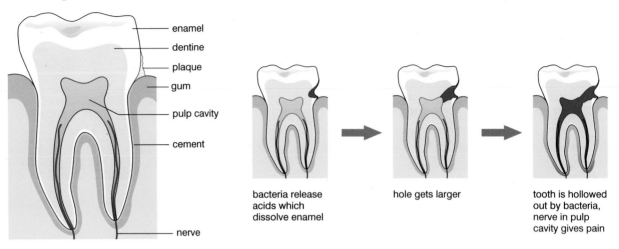

enamel
dentine
plaque
gum
pulp cavity
cement
nerve

bacteria release acids which dissolve enamel

hole gets larger

tooth is hollowed out by bacteria, nerve in pulp cavity gives pain

△ Fig 7.12 The structure of a molar tooth, and how tooth decay happens.

Brushing your teeth regularly helps to remove any build-up of plaque, and also any bits of food stuck between the teeth or at the edge of the gum. This reduces the risk of bacteria producing acid that damages the enamel. Using toothpaste helps because:

- it is alkaline and so neutralises acids near the teeth
- it contains antibacterial substances such as mint
- it usually contains a mild abrasive that helps to remove plaque
- it may contain **fluoride**, which helps to strengthen enamel and reduce acidic damage.

EXTENDED

Bile in digestion

Bile is a substance produced by cells in the liver. It is stored in the gall bladder until it is needed and then passes along the bile duct into the small intestine.

Bile is important in the physical digestion of fats. Fats do not mix well with aqueous (water-based) mixtures such as the digesting food, and so remain as large droplets. This produces a small surface area for lipase enzymes to work on, which slows down the rate of digestion. Bile **emulsifies** fats, breaking them up into much smaller droplets, so that the rate of digestion is much faster.

 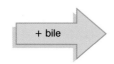 

large fat droplet   small fat droplets

△ Fig 7.13 Bile lowers the surface tension of large droplets of fat so that they break up.
This part of the digestive process is called emulsification.

END OF EXTENDED

QUESTIONS

1. Explain the difference between chemical and mechanical/physical digestion.

2. Describe the different tooth types in a human mouth and explain how their structure is related to their function.

3. Explain why regular brushing of teeth helps prevent tooth decay.

4. EXTENDED Explain the role of bile in digestion.

CHEMICAL DIGESTION

Chemical digestion in the alimentary canal is the result of enzymes. **Digestive enzymes** are a group of enzymes that are produced in the cells lining parts of the digestive system and are **secreted** (produced) into the alimentary canal to mix with the food.

The digestive enzymes include:

- carbohydrases that break down carbohydrates, one example of which is **amylase**
- **proteases**
- **lipases**.

REMEMBER

The -ase at the end of the name means it is an enzyme, and the first part usually names the substrate that the enzyme works on.

Each of the food groups (carbohydrates, proteins and fats) contains many different molecules. As each enzyme is specific to its substrate, this means that in each group of digestive enzymes there are many different enzymes.

Different enzymes are made in different parts of the digestive system, as shown in Table 7.4.

Enzyme	Where produced	Substrate	Final products*
amylase	salivary glands (mouth) pancreas	starch	glucose
protease (many types)	stomach wall pancreas	proteins	amino acids
lipase (many types)	pancreas	fats and oils (lipids)	fatty acids and glycerol

△ Table 7.4 Digestive enzymes.

*These are the soluble substances produced at the end of digestion. The substances in food and drink may go through many stages of digestion by different enzymes as they pass through the alimentary canal.

SCIENCE IN CONTEXT **LACTOSE**

Lactose is the disaccharide sugar in milk (from *lactis,* meaning 'milk'), which is broken down in the alimentary canal by the enzyme lactase to the simple sugars glucose and galactose.

Like all young mammals, human babies produce lactase, which helps them to digest the lactose in breast milk. In most mammals the production of lactase decreases as the young mature, because the adult diet does not include milk. This also happens in adults from many human cultures in which adults generally do not drink milk, such as in South-East Asia. However, there are human cultures in Europe, India and parts of East Africa, where mammals such as sheep, goats or cattle are kept to supply meat and milk for food. In these human groups the adults continue to produce lactase and are able to digest the lactose in milk. Adults who cannot do this are *lactose intolerant*. In these people bacteria in the alimentary canal break down the lactose, producing gas, which causes great discomfort.

EXTENDED

Details of digestion

Amylase only partly digests starch, to the disaccharide (two simple sugars) maltose. Digestion to the monosaccharide glucose is completed by the enzyme maltase, which is attached to the epithelial cell membranes of the small intestine.

Similarly, there are several proteases involved in the breakdown of proteins to amino acids. Pepsin is found in the stomach, whereas trypsin is produced in the pancreas and released into the small intestine. Both of these proteases digest proteins into smaller molecules, and then other proteases complete the digestion to amino acids in the small intestine. As pepsin functions in the stomach, it has an optimum pH of about pH 2 (see Topic 5). By contrast, trypsin has an optimum pH of about 8, which is the pH created in the small intestine by the neutralisation of the acid chyme from the stomach by bile.

END OF EXTENDED

The right conditions

Remember that different enzymes work better in different conditions (see Topic 5). Those enzymes that digest food in the stomach work best in acid conditions. Special cells in the lining of the stomach secrete hydrochloric acid into the stomach to create the right conditions for the enzymes. The acid is also helpful in killing microorganisms taken in with the food (see Topic 10).

EXTENDED

This happens because the low pH denatures enzymes in the microorganisms so that they cannot function properly.

END OF EXTENDED

In the duodenum, the enzymes from the pancreas work best at slightly alkaline conditions. So the acidic food mix that enters the duodenum from the stomach has to be neutralised. Bile is highly alkaline, so when it is added to the contents of the duodenum, it neutralises the acid from the stomach and makes the digesting food slightly alkaline.

QUESTIONS

1. Explain why enzymes are needed in the digestive system.

2. a) Which enzyme has starch as its substrate?

  b) Which product is formed by the digestion of starch by this enzyme?

3. EXTENDED Describe the roles of

  a) stomach acid

  b) bile in digestion.

ABSORPTION OF FOOD

After food has been digested in the duodenum (first part of the small intestine), small food molecules can diffuse across the wall of the ileum (the rest of the length of the small intestine) and be absorbed into the body.

About 80% of water in the contents of the small intestine is also absorbed into the blood. This includes water in the food and drink plus water in all the secretions that have been added as they have moved from the mouth to the ileum. This amounts to between 5–10 dm^3 of water absorbed every day. Another 0.3–0.5 dm^3 of water is absorbed as the remaining gut contents pass through the **colon** (large intestine). The relatively dry faeces that pass into the rectum are egested through the anus.

EXTENDED

Structure of villi

The intestine is over 6 m long in an adult human, but to increase the rate of transport of food molecules across the ileum wall, its surface area is increased by millions of finger-like projections called villi (singular: **villus**). The surface area of the cells lining the villi is increased even further by tiny **microvilli**. The combination of all these factors means that the surface area for absorption in the small intestine of an adult human is about 250 m^2, about the size of a tennis court.

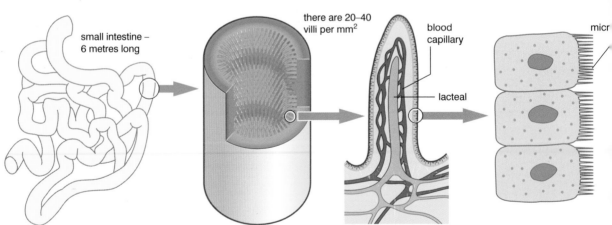

small intestine – 6 metres long

there are 20–40 villi per mm^2

blood capillary

lacteal

micr

Δ Fig 7.14 The structure of the small intestine (ileum).

The villi have other adaptations that help to increase the rate of diffusion.

- They are covered in a thin layer of cells, so that digested food molecules do not have to travel far to be absorbed into the body and into the blood in the capillaries in the villi.

- They are well supplied with blood capillaries, taking absorbed food molecules from the small intestine to the rest of the body and supplying fresh blood – this keeps the concentration gradient between the digested food in the intestine and the cells in the body as high as possible.
- Villi also contain **lacteals** (part of the lymphatic system), which carry fat droplets separate from the rest of the food molecules because fat does not dissolve well in blood.

END OF EXTENDED

QUESTIONS

1. Define *absorption*.

2. Where in the alimentary canal does absorption of water take place?

3. EXTENDED Explain why a large surface area is needed in the small intestine.

4. EXTENDED Describe how villi maximise the surface area of the small intestine wall.

5. EXTENDED Describe the role of capillaries and the lacteal in a villus.

End of topic checklist

Key words

absorption, alimentary canal, amylase, assimilation, balanced diet, bile, canine, carbohydrate, chemical digestion, cholera, colon, constipation, diarrhoea, digestion, digestive enzyme, egestion, enamel, enzyme, faeces, fat, fibre, incisor, ingestion, kwashiorkor, lacteal, lipase, malnutrition, mechanical digestion, microvilli, mineral, molar, obesity, peristalsis, physical digestion, premolar, protease, protein, soluble, starvation, villus, vitamin

During your study of this topic you should have learned:

○ How to describe the roles of the main components of a healthy human diet are: carbohydrates, proteins, lipids, vitamins (e.g. A, C and D), minerals (e.g. calcium and iron), water and dietary fibre.

○ That a balanced diet includes all the components needed for health in the right proportions.

○ How to describe the effects of malnutrition.

○ EXTENDED How to explain the causes and effects of malnutrition.

○ That diet provides energy as well as nutrients, and different groups of people have different requirements.

○ That the human alimentary canal is made up of the mouth, oesophagus, stomach, small intestine and large intestine.

○ That ingestion takes place in the mouth, digestion is the breakdown of large food molecules into smaller ones by mechanical and chemical digestion, absorption is the taking of nutrients from the small intestine, and egestion is the removal of waste food from the body.

○ How to define assimilation as the movement of digested food molecules into cells.

○ To describe diarrhoea as the production of large amounts of watery faeces that can be treated by oral rehydration solution to replace lost water and salts.

○ To describe cholera is a bacterial disease.

○ EXTENDED How to explain how cholera results in severe diarrhoea and loss of salts from the body.

○ To describe the different types of teeth, including their structure and different functions.

○ That teeth can be cared for by diet and by proper brushing.

○ That chemical digestion breaks down large food molecules into small molecules that can be absorbed.

○ To state the functions of digestive enzymes including amylase (digests starch to simpler sugars), lipases (digest fats to fatty acids and glycerol) and proteases (digest proteins to amino acids).

○ **EXTENDED** How to describe the digestion of starch, and the role of pepsin and trypsin in the alimentary canal.

○ That amylase is secreted in the mouth, stomach and by the pancreas; lipases are secreted by the pancreas; proteases are secreted in the stomach and by the pancreas: enzymes secreted by the pancreas pass into the small intestine.

○ **EXTENDED** That bile from the liver, stored in the gall bladder until needed, is added to the small intestine to neutralise the acid from the stomach and emulsify fats.

○ **EXTENDED** How to explain that hydrochloric acid in the stomach denatures harmful microorganisms and provides the right pH for gastric enzymes.

○ To state that digested food molecules are absorbed in the small intestine.

○ **EXTENDED** To explain the importance of the villi and microvilli on the surface of the small intestine in providing an enormous surface area for absorption of digested food molecules into blood capillaries and lacteals.

○ That water is absorbed in both the small intestine and the colon but that most absorption of water happens in the small intestine.

End of topic questions

Note: The marks awarded for these questions indicate the level of detail required in the answers. In the examination, the number of marks awarded to questions like these may be different.

1. Describe the importance of the following in a healthy diet:

   a) vitamins C and D   (2 marks)

   b) the minerals calcium and iron   (2 marks)

   c) water   (1 mark)

   d) dietary fibre   (2 marks)

2. There is an old saying that you should chew your food 100 times before swallowing to help look after your stomach. Explain why chewing food well helps digestion.   (3 marks)

3. Identify the organs of the digestive system involved, and their role, in each of the following processes:

   a) ingestion   (2 marks)

   b) digestion   (5 marks)

   c) absorption   (2 marks)

4. This is the diet schedule for a male Olympic athlete training for a competition, not including drinks during training.

breakfast	large bowl of cereal, such as porridge or muesli
	half pint semi-skimmed milk plus chopped banana
	1–2 thick slices wholegrain bread with olive oil or sunflower spread and honey or jam
	glass of fruit juice + 1 litre fruit squash
post-training 2nd breakfast	portion of scrambled eggs
	portion of baked beans
	1–2 pieces of grilled tofu
	portion of grilled mushrooms or tomatoes
	2 thick slices wholegrain bread with olive oil spread
	1 litre fruit squash
lunch	pasta with Bolognese or chicken and mushroom sauce
	mixed side salad
	fruit
	1 litre fruit squash

post-training snack	4 slices toast with olive oil or sunflower spread and jam
	large glass of semi-skimmed milk
	fruit
	500 ml water
dinner	grilled lean meat or fish
	6–7 boiled new potatoes, large sweet potato or boiled rice
	large portion of vegetables, e.g. broccoli, carrots, corn or peas
	1 bagel
	1 low-fat yoghurt and 1 banana or other fruit
	750 ml water and squash
bedtime snack	low-fat hot chocolate with 1 cereal bar

a) Identify the foods that contribute to each of these food types:

   i) carbohydrates   **(5 marks)**

   ii) proteins   **(3 marks)**

   iii) lipids   **(2 marks)**

   iv) vitamins and minerals   **(2 marks)**

   v) dietary fibre.   **(1 mark)**

b) Which food type is most represented in this diet?   **(1 mark)**

c) Explain why this food type is so important in this diet.   **(1 mark)**

d) Which food group would you expect to be more represented in an athlete's diet in the early stages of training? Explain your answer.   **(2 marks)**

e) Explain why this diet is not suitable for everyone.   **(2 marks)**

Plants live in many different environments on Earth, from the hot, humid rainforests, to the high, cold mountains. Just like animals, plants need to be well adapted to the conditions in which they live to enable them to survive. In deserts, for example, water is usually very limited, and the air temperature may range from above 40 °C during the day to below zero at night. Most plants would not be able to survive in these conditions, but those that do live in the desert have developed some very special adaptations that allow them to store water, reduce the loss of water from their leaves, and even help to insulate them against the very cold desert nights.

CONTENTS

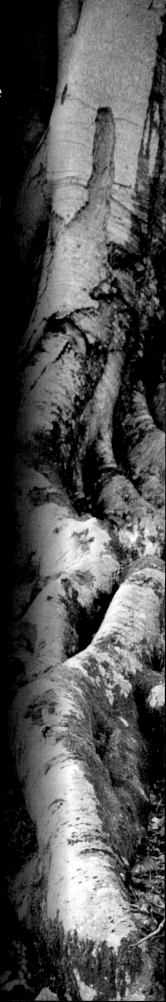

8
Transport in plants

△ The roots of this tree have grown away from the trunk in order to access the highest quantities of nutrients, which are most plentiful in the top layers of soil.

Transport in plants

INTRODUCTION

In one day, hundreds of litres of water will be absorbed from the soil and transpired through a fully grown tree in the Amazonian rainforest. This has a major impact on the environment in the rainforests. It reduces the amount of water in the soil. It also cools the air around the trees as the water evaporates into the air. The increase in water vapour in the air also affects where rainfall occurs. So the trees are effectively controlling the climate.

△ Fig 8.1 These fine clouds over the Amazon rainforest are formed from water transpired by trees earlier in the day.

KNOWLEDGE CHECK

✓ Cells in a plant leaf make glucose by photosynthesis, which is converted to sucrose and transported to other parts of the plant in phloem cells.

✓ Xylem vessels transport water and mineral ions from the roots of a plant through the stem to the leaves.

LEARNING OBJECTIVES

✓ State the functions of xylem tissue and identify xylem in sections of plant structures.

✓ State the functions of phloem tissue and identify phloem in sections of plant structures.

✓ Identify root hair cells and state their functions.

✓ Describe and investigate the pathway taken by water through a plant.

✓ EXTENDED Explain the importance of the large surface area of root hairs.

✓ EXTENDED Describe the roles of osmosis and active transport in the uptake of water and ions by a plant.

✓ Define the term *transpiration*.

✓ Describe and investigate the effect of temperature, humidity and light intensity on transpiration rate.

✓ EXTENDED Explain the relationship between leaf structure and transpiration.

✓ EXTENDED Explain the effects of variation of temperature and humidity on transpiration rate.

✓ EXTENDED Explain water movement through a plant in terms of tension and cohesion of water molecules.

✓ EXTENDED Explain wilting in a plant.

✓ EXTENDED Describe the translocation of sucrose and amino acids in a plant.

✓ EXTENDED Explain that different parts of a plant may act as source or sink at different times.

TRANSPORT IN PLANTS

In plants, water and dissolved substances are transported throughout the plant in a series of tubes or vessels. There are two types of transport vessel in plants, called **xylem** and **phloem**.

- Xylem tissue contains long, hollow xylem cells that form long tubes through the plant. The tubes are the hollow remains of dead cells. The thick strong cell walls help to support the plant. Xylem tubes are important for carrying water and dissolved mineral ions, which have entered the plant through the roots, to all the parts of the plant that need them. They are particularly important for supplying the water that the leaf cells need for photosynthesis.

- Phloem cells are living cells that are linked together to form continuous phloem tissue. Dissolved food materials, particularly sucrose and amino acids that have been formed in the leaf, are transported all over the plant from the leaves. For example, sucrose will be carried to any cell that needs glucose for respiration. Sucrose is less reactive than glucose and therefore is easier to transport without causing problems for other cells. Sucrose may also be carried to parts of the plants where it will be stored, often as another carbohydrate such as starch which is stored in seeds and root tubers. This transport of sucrose and other materials is called **translocation**.

In roots the xylem and phloem vessels are usually grouped together separately, but in the stem and leaves they are found together as **vascular bundles** or **veins**.

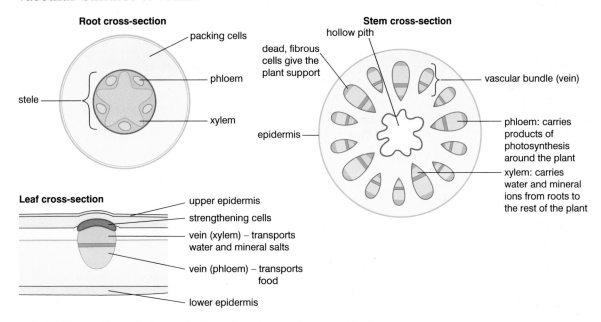

△ Fig 8.2 The positions of xylem and phloem tissue in a root, stem and leaf.

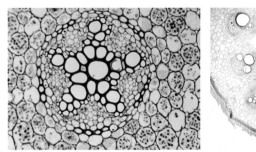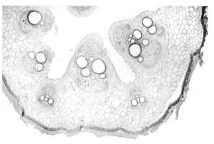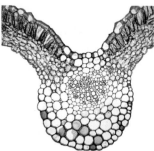

△ Fig 8.3 Photomicrographs of (left) a cross-section of the middle of a buttercup root, (middle) a cross-section of part of a pumpkin stem, (right) a cross-section of a vein in a meadow-beauty leaf.

TREE RINGS

The wood of a tree is mostly xylem tissue. Every year, new xylem cells are produced from a ring of cells just inside the bark of the tree. When the tree is growing rapidly, the new xylem cells are large. In temperate regions, such as the UK, the rate of growth and the size of new cells decrease as autumn approaches, and growth stops during winter. The difference in size of cells produced over one year gives the tree its 'rings' and makes it possible to estimate the age of the tree.

△ Fig. 8.4 Growth rings occur in temperate climates when new xylem cells alternately grow (in spring and summer) and stop growing (in winter).

QUESTIONS

1. Where would you find xylem and phloem tissue in a plant?

2. Describe the structure and function of xylem tissue.

3. Describe the structure and function of phloem tissue.

WATER UPTAKE

Plants absorb water and dissolved mineral ions from the soil through **root hair cells**. Root hair cells are found in a short region just behind the growing tip of every root. They are very delicate, and easily damaged. As the root grows, the hairs of the cells are lost, and new root hair cells are produced near the tip of the root.

△ Fig 8.5 The root of this germinating seed has many fine root hair cells that greatly increase its surface area.

EXTENDED

Root hair cells are specially adapted for absorption of substances, because they have a fine extension that sticks out into the soil. This greatly increases their surface area for absorption. Water enters the root hair cell by **osmosis**, because the concentration of water molecules is higher outside the root, in the soil water, than inside the cytoplasm of the root hair cells. This means that the **water potential** outside the root is higher than inside, so water molecules move down their **water potential gradient**.

Soil water contains minute amounts of dissolved mineral ions. So dissolved mineral ions are usually in higher concentration inside root cells than in the soil water. This means that essential mineral ions cannot usually enter the root by **diffusion**, because that would be against their concentration gradient. Instead, the cell membranes of root hair cells are adapted to take in mineral ions such as nitrates and magnesium ions by **active transport**.

END OF EXTENDED

Water enters the root hair cells, then passes across the root from cortex cell to cortex cell by osmosis. It then enters the xylem tissue in the root and can move from there to all other parts of the plant, including the leaves.

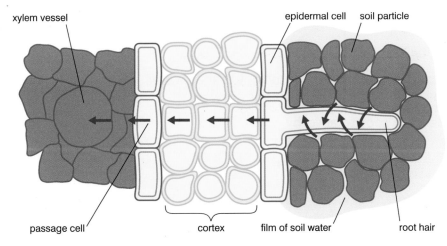

△ Fig 8.6 The passage of water across a root.

In the leaves, water moves out of the xylem cells in the vascular bundle, into the cells of the spongy mesophyll by osmosis.

Investigating water movement through a plant

The movement of water through the above-ground parts of a plant can be investigated by adding food colouring to the water given to the plant. Food colouring is soluble and is carried through the plant with the water in the xylem. After a day or two in coloured water, the veins of the leaves and flowers of a plant will show the colour.

△ Fig 8.7 A section across a celery stalk that has been standing in coloured water for a day will show colour mainly within the veins (vascular bundles) of the stalk.

△ Fig 8.8 A carnation flower that has been standing in coloured water shows the colour in its petals.

QUESTIONS

1. Describe the route that water takes as it moves through a plant.

2. How could you investigate the above-ground route that water takes as it moves through a plant? Explain your answer.

3. Which process is used in a root to absorb

   a) water

   b) mineral ions from soil water?

4. EXTENDED Copy the diagram of water movement across a root in Fig. 8.6 and annotate it to explain how water potential controls the movement of water in a root.

TRANSPIRATION

Water is a small molecule that easily crosses cell membranes. Inside the leaf, water molecules cross the cell membranes of the spongy mesophyll cells into the air spaces. This process is called **evaporation** because the liquid water in the cells becomes water vapour in the air spaces. Whenever the **stomata** in a leaf are open, water molecules diffuse from the air spaces out into the air (where there are usually fewer water molecules). So, in addition to using water in the process of photosynthesis, plants lose water by evaporation from the leaf. This loss of water from the leaves is called **transpiration**.

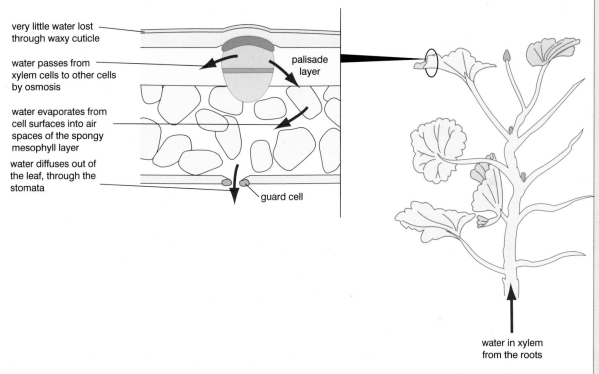

very little water lost through waxy cuticle

water passes from xylem cells to other cells by osmosis

water evaporates from cell surfaces into air spaces of the spongy mesophyll layer

water diffuses out of the leaf, through the stomata

palisade layer

guard cell

water in xylem from the roots

△ Fig 8.9 How water leaves a plant.

EXTENDED

Evaporation takes place from the surfaces of spongy mesophyll cells. The many interconnecting air spaces between these cells and the stomata creates a large surface area. So evaporation can happen rapidly when stomata are open. If the rate of transpiration of water from the leaves of a plant is greater than the rate at which water is supplied to the plant through absorption from soil water by root hair cells, the plant will start to wilt. This is when all the cells of the plant are not full of water, so the strength of the cell walls cannot support the plant and it starts to collapse (see Topic 3).

END OF EXTENDED

Factors that affect the rate of transpiration

Several factors affect the rate of transpiration. Transpiration is faster when:

- the temperature is higher
- the air is moving faster (windier)
- the air is dry (low humidity).

EXTENDED

The rate of transpiration from a leaf will be affected by anything that changes the concentration gradient of water molecules between the leaf and the air. The steeper the concentration gradient, the faster the rate of transpiration.

END OF EXTENDED

Several factors can affect the rate of transpiration.

- **Temperature** – Increased temperature means particles have more energy, which results in faster movement of the particle. The faster particles move, the easier it is for them to evaporate from cell surfaces into the air spaces, diffuse out of the leaf and move away. So increased temperature increases the rate of transpiration.
- **Humidity** – This is a measure of the concentration of water vapour in the air. When the air is very **humid**, it feels damp because there is a high concentration of water vapour in the air. When the air feels dry, the humidity is low. The concentration of water molecules inside the air spaces in the leaf is high. The higher the humidity of the air, the lower the concentration gradient between the air outside and inside the leaf, and so the lower the rate of transpiration.
- **Light intensity** – At higher light intensities there will be a greater amount of photosynthesis taking place in the palisade cells. So the stomata are usually opened at their widest in order to exchange carbon dioxide and oxygen as quickly as possible with the cells inside the leaf. Open stomata also make it possible for water molecules to diffuse out of the air spaces into the air more quickly. So a higher light intensity increases the rate of transpiration, up to a maximum when the stomata are fully open.

Developing investigative skills

The diagram shows apparatus called a potometer that can be used to investigate the effect of a range of factors on the rate of transpiration. As water evaporates from the leaf surface, the bubble of air in the potometer moves nearer to the leafy twig.

Devise and plan investigations

❶ Suggest how you could use a potometer to measure the effect of the following factors on transpiration: (a) temperature, (b) light intensity, (c) wind speed, (d) humidity.

Analyse and interpret data

The table below shows the results of an investigation, using a potometer in five different sets of conditions.

Conditions	Time for water bubble to move 5 cm, in seconds
still air, sunlight	135
moving air, sunlight	75
still air, dark cupboard	257
moving air, dark cupboard	122
hot, moving air, sunlight	54

❷ For each of the following factors, identify which data in the table should be compared to show the effect of the factor, and explain why those are the right data to compare.

a) temperature

b) light intensity

c) wind speed

❸ Using the data you have identified, draw a conclusion about the effect of the following on the rate of transpiration.

a) temperature

b) light intensity

c) wind speed

Evaluate data and methods

❹ Explain why the time taken for the bubble to move 5 cm is a measure of transpiration.

❺ What else could make the bubble move?

❻ Explain how could you improve the reliability of the conclusions you drew in Question 3.

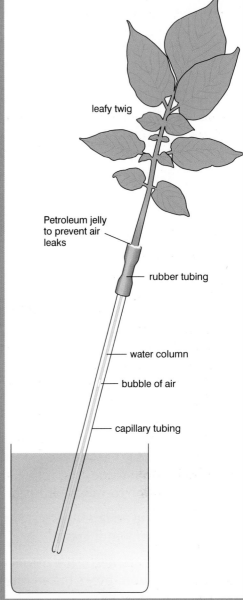

leafy twig

Petroleum jelly to prevent air leaks

rubber tubing

water column

bubble of air

capillary tubing

△ Fig 8.10 A potometer.

Transpiration and water potential

The loss of water from spongy mesophyll cells to the air spaces in a leaf increases the water potential of the cell cytoplasm. So water molecules will move from surrounding cells into these mesophyll cells by osmosis. This movement creates a water potential gradient between those cells and the ones further into the leaf, so water molecules move into them by osmosis, and so on all the way back to the xylem in the vascular bundles. Water molecules will move out of the xylem into surrounding cells by osmosis.

Water molecules show **cohesion**, meaning that they have a tendency to stick together. So, as water molecules move out of the xylem cells in a leaf vascular bundle, they create a **tension** (or 'pull') at the top of a xylem tube that connects all the way through the plant to a root (rather like when you suck on a straw). This tension pulls water molecules up the xylem into the leaf, which pulls water molecules out of the root cortical cells into xylem tubes in a root. The water potential gradient is continued through the root cortical cells to the root hair cells and into the soil water.

END OF EXTENDED

QUESTIONS

1. Define the word *transpiration*.

2. Copy the diagram of the plant and leaf section in Fig. 8.9 and add your own annotations to explain how water moves through the plant. Includes the following words in your labels: evaporation, osmosis, diffusion, transpiration.

3. Explain the advantage to plants of closing their stomata at night in terms of water loss.

4. Explain, in terms of the movement of water molecules, why transpiration rate is faster when:

   a) the temperature is higher

   b) the humidity of the air is lower.

5. EXTENDED Explain the relationship between cohesion of water molecules and a continual water potential gradient between leaf and root cells.

TRANSLOCATION

Translocation is the transport or movement of materials, including sucrose and amino acids, in the phloem of a plant. Sucrose is made directly from glucose that is produced in photosynthesis. Sucrose is a less active molecule than glucose, and so is more straightforward to transport around the plant. Amino acids are produced by cells using glucose from photosynthesis and nitrogen ions taken from the soil.

Sucrose is transported in the phloem to other parts of the plant:

- for conversion back to glucose and use in respiration
- for conversion back to glucose and production of other molecules in the cell for cell growth
- for conversion to starch to be stored until needed.

Amino acids are used to produce proteins for the formation of new plant tissue during growth, and to produce enzymes needed to control cell reactions.

Sources and sinks

We can describe transpiration in terms of sources and sinks.

- A **source** is where a substance is produced or is supplied to the plant.
- A **sink** is where the substance is used or converted to another substance.

In transpiration, the soil water is the *source* of water and dissolved mineral ions such as nitrogen ions, which enter the plant through root hair cells. The air is the source of carbon dioxide. The photosynthesising cells are the *sink* for carbon dioxide and water, when they use them to produce glucose.

In translocation, the *source* of glucose is the photosynthesising cells of the leaf. The main *sink* for glucose may differ at different times of the year. Early in the year, when the plant is growing rapidly, the root and shoot tips will be the main sinks for glucose, for use in producing new plant tissue. Later in the year, a plant may direct more glucose to flowers for reproduction, and then to producing seeds. Some plants may also direct glucose to storage organs, such as root and stem tubers (e.g. potato), where it is used to starch that can be used at the start of the next growing season for rapid new growth.

QUESTIONS

1. In which tissue does translocation occur in a plant?

2. Give two examples of substances that are translocated.

3. Explain what is meant by a source and a sink in terms of take back

    a) transpiration

    b) translocation.

End of topic checklist

Key words

active transport, cohesion, diffusion, evaporation, humidity, osmosis, phloem, root hair cell, sink, source, stomata, tension, translocation, transpiration, vascular bundle, water potential gradient, xylem

During your study of this topic you should have learned:

○ That xylem tissue transports water and mineral ions from plant roots to other parts of the plant.

○ That phloem tissue carries sucrose and amino acids from where they are made in the leaves to other parts of the plant.

○ That root hair cells are the site of absorption of water and mineral ions into a plant.

○ EXTENDED How to explain the importance of the large surface area of root hair cells.

○ To explain how water is absorbed from the soil through root hair cells and crosses the root cells to the xylem. It then passes up the stem in the xylem to the leaf and moves through the spongy mesophyll cells to the air spaces.

○ To explain that transpiration is the evaporation of water from the surfaces of a plant, mostly through the stomata.

○ To explain that the rate of transpiration increases with increased temperature, increased wind speed, increased light intensity and decreased humidity.

○ EXTENDED To describe the roles of osmosis and active transport in the uptake of water and ions by a plant.

○ EXTENDED To explain that a plant wilts when it loses more water by transpiration than it gains through root hair cells, so plant cells are not full of water.

○ EXTENDED That the transpiration of water from the leaf causes a water potential gradient to be set up through the plant, across the leaf and through the xylem in the stem to the root, and cohesion of water molecules is important in this.

○ EXTENDED To define translocation as the transport of substances such as sucrose and amino acids from the cells in which they are made, through the phloem to the parts of the plant where they are used to produce energy or other molecules for growth or are stored for later use.

○ EXTENDED That the *source* of a substance in a plant is where it was made or entered the plant; the *sink* is where the substance is used or leaves the plant. Plants may have different sinks for sucrose at different times of year.

End of topic questions

Note: The marks awarded for these questions indicate the level of detail required in the answers. In the examination, the number of marks awarded to questions like these may be different.

1. Look at the photos in Fig. 8.3 of sections through a plant leaf, stem and root.

   a) Using a sharp pencil, make careful diagrams that show the positions of all the main tissues in the sections. (Only draw a few cells in each tissue, to show their form. It will take too long to draw all the cells.) **(3 marks)**

   b) Use the labelled diagrams in Fig 8.3 to help you to clearly label your drawings to show the position of xylem. **(3 marks)**

   c) Clearly label the position of phloem in each of your drawings. **(3 marks)**

2. Flower sellers sometimes produce flowers of unusual colours for sale, starting with white flowers. Explain how they may do this, and why it is possible. **(4 marks)**

3. EXTENDED A potted plant sitting on a sunny windowsill wilts more quickly than an identical plant placed on a shaded shelf in the room. Explain why. **(4 marks)**

4. EXTENDED Cactus plants have many adaptations to help them survive in a dry desert. One of these adaptations is that they close their stomata during the day and open them at night. Explain fully the advantage of this adaptation. **(4 marks)**

5. EXTENDED Explain how and why different parts of a plant are sinks for the translocation of sucrose at different times of the year in a country where there are seasons, such as Russia. **(7 marks)**

An average-sized human adult carries about 4.5–5.0 litres of blood. Blood is pumped around the bodies of mammals by the heart to carry oxygen, nutrients and water to every organ, tissue and cell, and transport waste products away from cells. The human heart is about the size of an adult fist, located just about in the centre of the chest. It beats over 100,000 times a day, and the characteristic double sound of a beat corresponds to the two sets of heart valves opening and closing in order.

CONTENTS

9

Transport in animals

△ Polar bears, like humans, have a double circulatory system.

Transport in animals

Δ Fig 9.1 This photograph shows the larger blood vessels that are found in a lung. The millions of capillaries are not visible.

INTRODUCTION

Almost no cell in your body is more than 20 μm (0.02 mm) from a blood vessel. This is because the blood delivers a constant supply of oxygen and glucose, for respiration, without which the cells will rapidly die. So it's not surprising that, no matter where you cut yourself, you will bleed. Many of the blood vessels that penetrate the tissues are extremely narrow – about 5 to 10 μm wide, which is about the width of one red blood cell. It has been calculated that if you placed the blood vessels of an adult in a line it would wrap four times around the equator of the Earth.

KNOWLEDGE CHECK

✓ The heart and blood vessels form the human circulatory system.
✓ Cells need a continuous supply of oxygen and glucose for respiration, which are supplied by the blood in a human body.

LEARNING OBJECTIVES

✓ Describe the circulatory system as a system of continuous blood vessels, with a pump and valves to ensure one-way flow of blood.

✓ EXTENDED Describe the single circulation of a fish.

✓ EXTENDED Describe the double circulatory system of mammals and explain its advantages.

✓ Describe the structure of the heart and how its activity can be monitored.

✓ EXTENDED Explain how the structure of the heart is linked to its function.

✓ Investigate the effect of exercise on heart rate.

✓ Describe coronary heart disease and how it is linked to diet, stress, smoking, genetic factors, age and gender.

✓ EXTENDED Describe ways in which coronary heart disease may be prevented and how it may be treated.

✓ Describe the structure of arteries, veins and capillaries and identify some of the main arteries and veins in the human body.

✓ EXTENDED Explain how the structure of different blood vessels is related to their different roles in transporting blood.

✓ EXTENDED Outline the structure of the lymphatic system and describe its role in the circulation of body fluids and the production of lymphocytes.

✓ List the main components of human blood, and describe their functions.

✓ Identify red and white blood cells in diagrams and photomicrographs.

✓ EXTENDED Identify lymphocytes and phagocytes and describe their functions.

TRANSPORT IN ANIMALS

Transport in animals usually takes place inside a **circulatory system**. A circulatory system is formed from a system of continuous tubes (blood vessels) that carry blood around the body. The tubes are connected to a pump, the heart, which forces the blood through the circulation. Valves in the heart and in some of the blood vessels make sure that blood circulates in only one direction.

EXTENDED

Different circulatory systems

Fish have a single circulatory system, which means that blood passes all parts of the body in one circuit before returning to the heart.

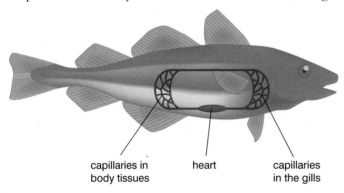

capillaries in   heart   capillaries
body tissues   in the gills

Δ Fig 9.2 A fish has a single circulatory system.

Oxygen from the water is absorbed into the blood flowing through the gills. The oxygenated blood passes through the heart and is pumped to the body tissues. Here oxygen is taken from the blood for respiration in cells, and carbon dioxide is added to the blood and carried to the gills, where it diffuses out into the water.

The mammalian circulatory system (as in humans) is more complex than that of a fish. It is described as a **double circulation** because the blood passes through the heart twice for each time that it passes through the body tissues. When blood leaves the right side of the heart it passes through the tissues of the lungs before returning to the left side of the heart for pumping around the rest of the body.

Separating the circulation to the lungs from the circulation to the body means that the blood in the two circulations can be at different pressures.

- Blood leaving the right side of the heart is normally below 4 kPa. Blood does not travel far to the lung tissue, so there is little loss of pressure before it reaches the capillaries surrounding the alveoli. This lower pressure prevents damage to the delicate capillaries that pass through lung tissue.

- Blood leaving the left side of the heart has to travel all round the body and back to the heart. So it needs to start at a much higher pressure, at about 16 kPa as it leaves the heart. By the time it reaches the capillaries within body tissues, the pressure has dropped to below 3 kPa and so will not damage them.

END OF EXTENDED

QUESTIONS

1. What is the role of the heart in the circulatory system?
2. What prevents blood flowing the wrong way round through the circulatory system?
3. EXTENDED Explain what is meant by a *double circulatory system*.
4. EXTENDED Explain the advantages of a double circulatory system compared with the single circulatory system of a fish.

HEART

The **heart** is a muscular organ that pumps blood by expanding in size as it fills with blood, and then contracting, forcing the blood on its way through the blood vessels. Blood is pumped away from the heart in arteries and returns to the heart through veins.

EXTENDED

The heart is two pumps in one. The right side and left side are separated by a layer of tissue called the septum. The right side pumps blood to the lungs to collect oxygen. The left side then pumps the **oxygenated** blood around the rest of the body. The **deoxygenated** (without oxygen) blood then returns to the right side to be sent to the lungs again.

END OF EXTENDED

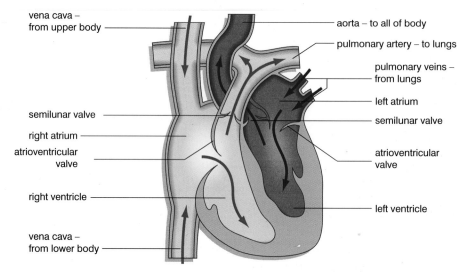

◁ Fig 9.3 Structure of the human heart. Oxygenated blood is shown in red and deoxygenated blood is shown blue. (Knowledge of the names of heart valves is required at Extended level only.)

We always draw diagrams of the circulatory system and heart as if looking in a mirror, or at another person. So in the diagram the 'left' side of the heart/circulation in a body is drawn on the right side of the diagram.

The heart consists of four chambers: two **atria** (single: atrium) and two **ventricles**. The walls of the chambers are formed from thick muscle. Blood that flows towards the heart passes through blood vessels called **veins**. Blood that leaves the heart passes through blood vessels called **arteries.** To make sure that blood only flows in one direction through the heart, there are **valves** at the points where blood vessels enter and leave the heart, and between the atria and ventricles. These close when the heart contracts, to prevent backflow of blood.

The heart has its own separate blood supply, to provide the muscle tissue with oxygen and glucose for respiration so that it can contract. These blood vessels are called the coronary arteries and coronary veins. You can see some of these on the outside of a whole heart.

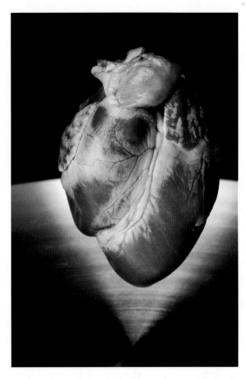

Δ Fig 9.4 Whole human heart.

Structure and function

The valves of the heart have particular names:

- the tricuspid valve is the atrioventircular valve that sits between the right atrium and right ventricle
- the bicuspid valve is the atrioventricular valve that sits between the left atrium and left ventricle
- the semilunar valves are found at the base of the pulmonary vein and aorta, where they join the heart.

The bicuspid and tricuspid valves have strong tendinous cords that attach the outer edge of the valve to the ventricle wall. These prevent valves turning inside out when the heart is contracting forcefully.

The walls of the heart are formed from thick muscular tissue. The ventricle walls are thicker than the walls of the atria, as their contractions provide the force that carries blood over a longer distance. The wall of the left ventricle is noticeably thicker than the wall of the right ventricle for a similar reason – the right ventricle only has to push blood to the nearby lungs, whereas the left ventricle has to push blood over a greater distance to the extremities of the body.

Blood flow through the heart

Blood passes through the chambers of the heart in a particular sequence as the walls of the chambers contract. First the atria contract at the same time, then the ventricles both contract at the same time, to move the blood through the heart.

- Blood from the body arrives at the heart via the vena cava, and enters the right atrium.
- Contraction of the right atrium passes blood through the tricuspid valve to the right ventricle.
- Contraction of the right ventricle forces blood out through the pulmonary artery to the lungs. The tricuspid valve closes to prevent backflow of blood into the right atrium, and the semilunar valve then closes to prevent backflow of blood into the ventricle.
- Blood enters the left atrium from the lungs through the pulmonary vein.
- Contraction of the left atrium passes blood to the left ventricle through the bicuspid valve.
- Contraction of the left ventricle forces blood out through the aorta towards the rest of the body. The bicuspid valve closes to prevent backflow of blood into the left atrium, and then the semilunar valve closes to prevent backflow of blood into the ventricle.

END OF EXTENDED

QUESTIONS

1. Name the four chambers of the mammalian heart.

2. Distinguish between *arteries* and *veins*.

3. EXTENDED Starting in the vena cava, list the chambers and blood vessels in the order that blood passes through them until it reaches the aorta.

Heart rate

Heart rate is the measure of how frequently the heart beats, generally given as beats per minute. We can take measurements of heart rate by feeling for a pulse point, where the blood flows through an artery near to the skin, such as in the wrist or at the temple.

Taking the pulse rate is actually measuring the expansion and relaxation of the artery wall as the blood passes through it. However, as each pulse of blood is created by one contraction of the ventricles, we say that we are measuring *heart beats*.

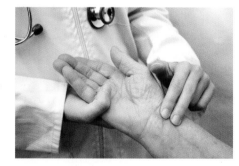

△ Fig 9.5 Taking the pulse at the wrist.

Heart rate can also be measured by listening to the heart. The 'lub, dup' sounds of one complete contraction are the sounds of the valves inside the heart as they open and shut.

The contraction of the heart is regulated by electrical activity in nerves in the heart. We can measure this electrical activity by attaching sensors to the skin. A normal heart beat produces a particular pattern of activity, which can be recorded as an **electrocardiogram (ECG)**.

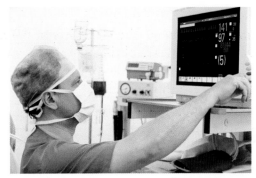

△ Fig 9.6 During an operation, a doctor continually checks the patients ECG trace to make sure all is well.

Resting heart rate is the rate at which the heart beats when the person is at rest. On average it is between 60 and 80 beats per minute for an adult human, but this range is very variable. Resting heart rate may vary as a result of:

- age – children usually have a faster average than adults
- fitness – a trained athlete may have a resting rate as low as 40 beats per minute because their heart contains more muscle and can pump out more blood with each contraction
- illness – infection can raise resting heart rate, but some diseases of the circulatory system can slow resting heart rate.
- drugs – some drugs can change heart rate (see Topic 15).

Changing heart rate

Heart rate increases during activity. The harder you exercise, the faster the heart beats.

EXTENDED

The increase in heart rate increases the amount of blood that is pumped around the body, and the speed with which it reaches body tissues. This supplies oxygen and glucose more rapidly to respiring cells, particularly in the muscles, and removes waste products more rapidly.

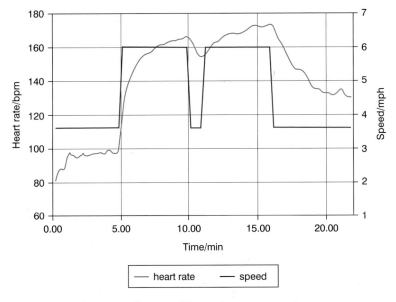

△ Fig 9.7 How heart rate changes with exercise.

END OF EXTENDED

Developing investigative skills

The effect of exercise on heart rate can be measured by taking pulse measurements after different levels of exercise.

Devise and plan investigations

In an investigation of the effect of exercise on the heart rate, a student was asked to exercise at different levels for 2 minutes, at which point the pulse rate was measured. The student was then allowed to rest for 5 minutes and then continue to exercise at the next level of activity.

❶ a) Explain why the pulse rate was taken after 2 minutes of exercise and not sooner.

b) Explain why the student rested for 5 minutes before starting the next level of exercise.

Analyse and interpret data

Table 9.1 shows the results of an investigation into the effect of exercise on heart rate of one student.

	Resting	Walking	Jogging	Running
heart rate beats per minute)	72	81	96	122

△ Table 9.1 Heart rate with activity.

❷ Describe the pattern shown in the data.

❸ Use the data to draw a conclusion for the investigation.

❹ Explain why heart rate responds like this to different levels of exercise.

Evaluate data and methods

❺ How reliable is this conclusion, and what could have been done during the investigation to improve the reliability?

QUESTIONS

1. Describe three ways of monitoring heart rate.

2. Explain why resting heart rate in an adult is given as a range of values and not a single value.

3. Describe the effect of activity on heart rate.

4. EXTENDED Explain the effect of activity on heart rate.

Coronary heart disease

The muscle of the heart needs its own blood supply to provide the oxygen and sugars it needs for respiration. It cannot get these materials from the blood that flows through it, so there are coronary arteries and veins that pass through heart muscle. If the blood flow through these coronary blood vessels is reduced, it can reduce the amount of oxygen and sugars getting to the muscle cells, and so reduce the amount of energy that they can release through respiration.

Blockage of the coronary arteries can occur when layers of cholesterol are deposited on the inner lining of the blood vessel. This causes **coronary heart disease**. Even partial blockage can cause a health problem, such as angina (heart pains) or high blood pressure. A full blockage will cause a heart attack, which may result in death.

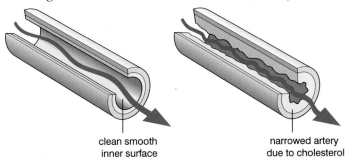

clean smooth
inner surface

narrowed artery
due to cholesterol

△ Fig 9.8 Deposits of cholesterol inside arteries makes it more difficult for blood to flow through freely, increasing the risk of diseases of the circulatory system.

Some factors can increase the risk of a blockage of the coronary arteries:

- **diet**: high levels of saturated fats in the diet (particularly from red meats) may cause increased deposits of cholesterol
- **smoking**: chemicals in tobacco smoke that pass into the blood can damage the delicate lining of arteries, which increases the chance that deposits of cholesterol are laid down at these points.

Stress is not a direct cause of coronary heart disease, but response to stress, such as smoking, drinking alcohol or eating for comfort, particularly over a long time, can increase the risk of heart disease.

Genes can give some people a tendency towards developing coronary heart disease. As this tendency can be inherited, the disease may appear more commonly in some families than in others, and more frequently in some particular ethnic groups than others. For example, African-Americans are at greater risk of developing coronary heart disease than white Americans.

EXTENDED

Preventing coronary heart disease

Medical advice for preventing coronary heart disease includes changing the diet and amount of exercise taken.

Many studies of the relationship between saturated fat and heart disease have concluded that reducing the amount of saturated fat in the diet should reduce the risk of heart disease. However, it is difficult to prove this relationship because people don't just change their diet when they are advised to live more healthily. For example, they may also change how much they exercise.

The amount of exercise taken each day does seem to affect the risk of heart disease. Someone who has a sedentary lifestyle (mainly sitting) can significantly reduce their risk of an early death by just a little exercise every day. This exercise seems to strengthen the heart muscle and make it able to cope with sudden increases in heart rate more easily, such as when you run.

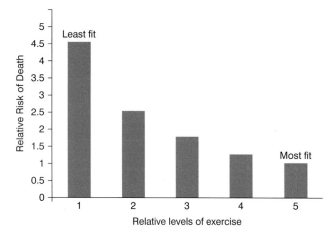

△ Fig 9.9 The relationship between risk of death and level of exercise.

Treating coronary heart disease

Coronary heart disease often shows first as a **heart attack**. This can cause the heart to stop working. Immediate treatment to get the heart beating again is essential because cells will die if they don't receive oxygen. This treatment can be done by hand by pressing on the chest to stimulate the heart, or more intensively with an electrical shock. Rapid transfer to a hospital is then essential.

If the cause of heart disease is a blocked coronary artery, or a blocked blood vessel nearby, surgery can be used to widen the blood vessel. A short, wire mesh tube, called a **stent**, is inserted into the artery at its narrrowest part to hold it open and increase blood flow. If the artery is so damaged that it cannot function properly, then an artery bypass operation is done. This involves inserting a piece of blood vessel between the aorta and the part of the coronary artery just beyond the blockage, so that the tissue can receive oxygenated blood. If the heart has been very badly damaged, then a **heart transplant** may be done. This is when the damaged heart is replaced by a fully functioning heart from someone who has just died, for example from a car accident.

After a transplant, the patient will need to take drugs for life to suppress their immune system, otherwise their body will reject the transplanted heart (see Topic 10). Any patient with coronary heart disease may also be treated with drugs to help thin the blood and reduce the risk of a blood clot that could cause a heart attack. Patients will also be advised to live a more healthy lifestyle.

QUESTIONS

1. Explain why the heart needs its own blood supply.

2. Identify four possible risk factors for coronary heart disease.

3. EXTENDED Explain how a person can reduce their risk of coronary heart disease.

4. EXTENDED Name two different kinds of treatment for coronary heart disease.

BLOOD VESSELS AND LYMPHATIC VESSELS

Blood vessels

Fig. 9.10 shows a simplified layout of the human circulatory system, including the major blood vessels. The name of a major blood vessel is

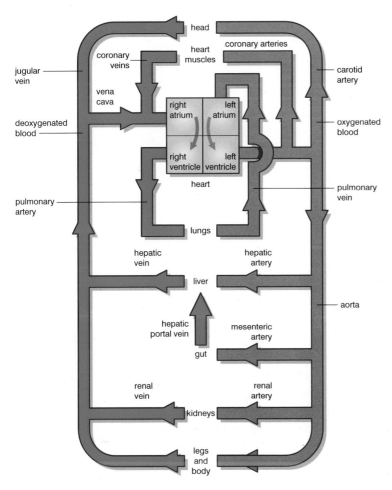

△ Fig 9.10 Plan of the human circulatory system.

often related to the organ it supplies: *coronary* for heart (from the Latin *corona* for 'crown' because the blood vessels surround the top of the heart like a crown), *renal* for kidneys (from the Latin *renes* meaning 'the kidneys'), *pulmonary* for lungs (from the Latin *pulmonis* meaning 'lungs'). Learn the names of the blood vessels that are associated with the heart, the lungs and kidneys.

The largest vein and the largest artery in the body have special names. The **vena cava** is the vein that carries blood to the heart, and the **aorta** is the artery that receives blood from the heart.

REMEMBER

Remember, **a** for arteries that travel **a**way from the heart. **V**eins carry blood into the heart and contain **v**alves.

The blood vessels are grouped into three different types: arteries, capillaries and veins.

vein:

thin walled, carrying blood at low pressure

capillary:

very small; the walls may be just one cell thick

△ Fig 9.11 Veins vary in diameter from about 5 to 15 mm. Capillaries are very small, with a diameter of around 0.01 mm.

artery:

thick walled, carrying blood at high pressure

△ Fig 9.12 Arteries vary in diameter from about 10 to 25 mm.

- **Arteries** are large blood vessels that carry blood that is flowing away from the heart. Arteries have thick muscular and elastic walls, with a narrow central space (lumen) through which the blood flows.
- **Capillaries** are the tiny blood vessels that form a network throughout every tissue and connect arteries to veins. Capillaries have very thin walls. All the exchange of substances between the blood and tissues happens in the capillaries.
- **Veins** are large blood vessels that carry blood that is flowing back towards the heart. Veins have a large lumen through which blood flows. Valves in the veins prevent backflow.
- As arteries divide more as they get further from the heart, they get narrower. These narrow vessels that connect arteries to capillaries are called **arterioles**.

Similarly, veins become narrower as they get further from the heart, and the narrow vessels that connect capillaries to veins are called venules. **Shunt vessels** are small blood vessels that connect an arteriole to a venule directly, so that blood bypasses the capillaries. These are important in the control of blood flow through the skin in temperature regulation (see Topic 14).

Structure related to function

The structure of different blood vessels enables them to carry out their function most efficiently.

- Blood carried in the arteries is at higher pressure than in the other vessels. The highest pressure is in the aorta, the blood vessel that leaves the left ventricle. The thick walls of arteries help to protect them from bursting when the pressure increases as the pulse of blood enters them. The recoil of the elastic wall after the pulse of blood has passed through helps to maintain the blood pressure and even out the pulses. By the time the blood enters the fine capillaries, the change in pressure during and after a pulse has been greatly reduced.

Blood vessels	Blood pressure (kPa)
aorta	>13
arteries	13–5.3
capillaries	3.3–1.6
veins	1.3–0.7
vena cava	0.3

Δ Table 9.2 Blood pressure in different blood vessels.

- The thin walls of capillaries helps to increase the rate of **diffusion** of substances by keeping the distance for diffusion between the blood and cell cytoplasm to a minimum.
- By the time blood leaves the capillaries and enters the veins, there is no pulse and the blood pressure is very low. The large lumen (centre) of the veins allows blood to flow easily back to the heart. The contraction of body muscles, such as in the legs, helps to push the blood back toward the heart against the force of gravity. The valves make sure that blood can flow only in the right direction, back towards the heart.

normal blood flow

veins have valves to stop
the blood flowing backwards

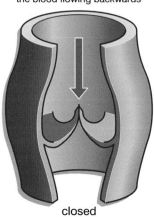

open

closed

Δ Fig 9.13 Valves in the veins make sure that blood can only move in one direction, towards the heart.

END OF EXTENDED

QUESTIONS

1. Name the following blood vessels:

   a) the vessels that carry blood to the kidneys

   b) the vessel that carries blood from the heart towards the body

   c) the vessels that carry blood from the lungs back towards the heart.

2. Describe the differences in structure of arteries, capillaries and veins.

3. EXTENDED Explain how the structure of arteries helps to reduce and even out the blood pulses from the heart.

Lymphatic vessels

The walls of capillaries are so thin that water, dissolved solutes (e.g. glucose and mineral ions) and dissolved gases (e.g. oxygen) can easily pass through the wall from the plasma into the **tissue fluid** surrounding the cells. Cells exchange materials across their cell membrane with the tissue fluid.

More fluid is pushed out of the capillaries by the pressure of the blood inside them, but only some of this returns to the capillaries. The rest passes into the **lymphatic system** and becomes a fluid called **lymph**. The lymphatic system is formed from a series of connected tubes that flow from tissue back towards the heart. This system connects with the blood system near to the heart, where the lymph is returned to the blood plasma.

Lymph nodes are small clumps of lymphatic tissue that are found throughout the lymphatic system, particularly in the neck and armpits. Large numbers of lymphocytes are found in the lymph nodes.

Tissues associated with the lymphatic system, such as the bone marrow in the centre of long bones of the legs and arms, produce the lymphocytes.

QUESTIONS

1. Describe the relationship between blood, tissue fluid and lymph.

2. Describe the roles of the lymphatic system.

END OF EXTENDED

BLOOD

The human circulatory system carries substances around the body. The table shows some of the important substances transported around the human body. These substances are carried within the blood, in different forms.

Substance	Carried from	Carried to
molecules absorbed from digested food, e.g. glucose, amino acids, fatty acids	small intestine	all parts of the body
water	intestines	all parts of the body
oxygen	lungs	all parts of the body
carbon dioxide	all parts of the body	lungs
urea (waste)	liver	kidneys
hormones	glands	all parts of the body (different hormones affect different parts)

Δ Table 9.3 Substances carried by the blood around the body.

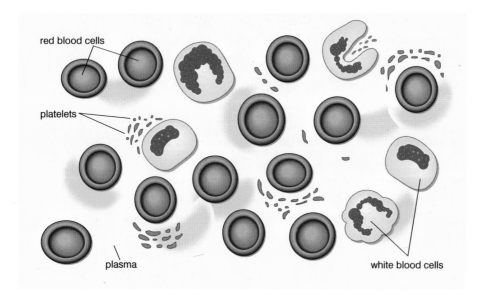

△ Fig 9.14 Blood is mostly water, containing cells and many dissolved substances.

Blood is made from plasma, red blood cells, white blood cells and platelets. Each of these has a particular function in the body.

Plasma

Plasma is the straw-coloured, liquid part of blood. It mainly consists of water, which makes it a good solvent for many substances. Digested food molecules, such as glucose and amino acids, easily dissolve in plasma. Urea, which is formed by the liver from excess amino acids, is also soluble in plasma. Many hormones (see Topic 14) are also soluble and are carried around the body dissolved in plasma. Carbon dioxide dissolves in water to form carbonic acid (H_2CO_3), and most carbon dioxide is carried in the blood in this form.

Red blood cells

Red blood cells are the most common cell in blood. Their main function is to carry oxygen around the body. The oxygen is attached to molecules of **haemoglobin** inside the cells, which give red blood cells their colour.

White blood cells

There are several different types of white blood cell, but they all play an important role in defending the body against disease. They are part of the **immune system** that responds to infection by trying to kill the **pathogen** (the disease-causing organism). Some kinds of white blood cell kill pathogens by engulfing (flowing around the pathogen until it is

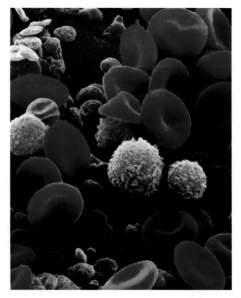

△ Fig 9.15 Red blood cells (shown in red), white blood cells (yellow) and platelets (pink).

completely enclosed), which is known as **phagocytosis**. Other kinds of white blood cell produce chemicals called **antibodies** that attack pathogens. (There is more on diseases and the immune system in Topic 10.)

EXTENDED

- **Phagocytes:** Several types of white blood cell belong to this group, but they all kill pathogens by phagocytosis (flowing round the pathogen and engulfing it). The phagocytes then digest the pathogens inside them. Different types of phagocytes target different pathogens, such as bacteria, fungi and protoctist parasites.

1 A phagocyte moves towards a bacterium

2 The phagocyte pushes a sleeve of cytoplasm outwards to surround the bacterium

3 The bacterium is now enclosed in a vacuole inside the cell. It is then killed and digested by enzymes

△ Fig 9.16 Phagocytosis of a bacterium by a phagocyte, a type of white blood cell.

- **Lymphocytes:** This type of white blood cell has a very large nucleus, and is responsible for producing antibodies.

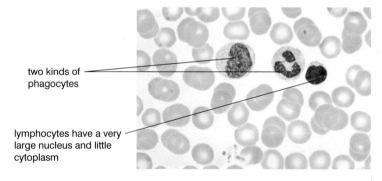

two kinds of phagocytes

lymphocytes have a very large nucleus and little cytoplasm

△ Fig 9.17 Photomicrographs of (left) phagocytes and (right) a lymphocyte.

END OF EXTENDED

Platelets

Platelets are small fragments of much larger cells that are also important in protecting us from infection by causing blood to clot where there is damage to a blood vessel.

Clotting helps to seal the cut and prevent blood from leaking out and pathogens from getting in. The formation of a clot takes several steps. The liver makes a protein called **fibrinogen**, which is released into the plasma. When there is damage to a blood vessel, the platelets respond by releasing an enzyme that causes the soluble fibrinogen to change and become a fibrous protein called **fibrin**. The fibres of this protein trap blood cells to produce the clot.

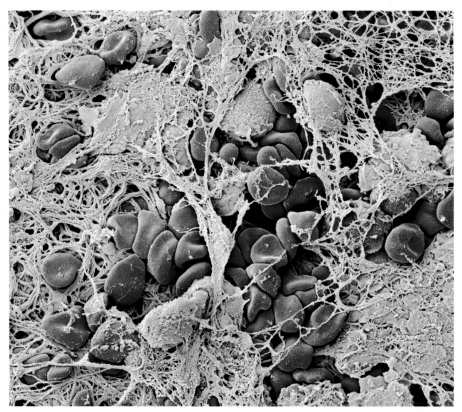

△ Fig 9.18 A blood clot is made of protein fibres that trap blood cells to block leaks from a damaged blood vessel.

SCIENCE IN CONTEXT · BLOOD TESTS

Doctors often send blood off to be tested when a patient is unwell. These tests not only check the concentrations of different substances in the blood, such as glucose, they also count the number of different kinds of cells. Taking a blood sample can be quick and easy for a doctor to do, and the tests can help in diagnosing what is wrong with the patient.

- An abnormal concentration of glucose may indicate diabetes.
- Too few white blood cells may indicate liver or bone marrow disease.
- Too few red blood cells can make the blood look paler than normal. Low numbers of red blood cells cause anaemia, which usually results in the patient feeling more easily exhausted than usual.

Any abnormal results need following up with other tests to confirm diagnosis.

QUESTIONS

1. Draw up a table to show the components of blood and the roles that they play in the body.

2. **EXTENDED** Explain how the structure of a red blood cell is adapted to its function.

3. **EXTENDED** Describe the role of white blood cells in the immune system.

4. **EXTENDED** Explain how platelets can protect us from infection.

End of topic checklist

Key words

aorta, artery, atrium, capillary, circulatory system, coronary heart disease, deoxygenated, double circulation, electrocardiogram (ECG), haemoglobin, heart, heart attack, heart rate, heart transplant, lymph, lymphatic system, lymphocyte, oxygenated, pathogen, phagocyte, phagocytosis, plasma, platelet, red blood cell, stent, tissue fluid, valve, vein, vena cava, ventricle

During your study of this topic you should have learned:

○ To describe a circulatory system as consisting of tubes that carry blood around the body, where the blood is pushed by a pump called the heart.

○ EXTENDED To describe the single circulation of blood through the body of fish.

○ EXTENDED To describe the double circulatory system of humans in which blood from the right side of the heart is pumped through the lungs, then back to the left side of the heart and to the rest of the body.

○ The heart pumps blood through arteries, then through capillaries, and finally through the veins back to the heart.

○ The heart is formed from four chambers, two atria and two ventricles, which have muscular walls to push blood through the heart. Valves prevent backflow of blood so that it only flows in one direction.

○ The activity of the heart can be measured by taking a pulse, listening to the sounds produced when heart valves close, or monitoring the electrical activity with an ECG.

○ EXTENDED The heart pumps blood by the contraction of the atria followed by the ventricles, with one-way valves preventing the backflow of blood. The septum separates oxygenated from deoxygenated blood.

○ Heart rate increases during exercise.

○ EXTENDED Increase in heart rate during exercise supplies oxygen and glucose more rapidly to active muscle cells and removes carbon dioxide more rapidly.

○ To describe coronary heart disease as caused by the blockage of a coronary artery.

○ Diet, smoking, stress and genetic tendency are all risk factors for coronary heart disease.

○ EXTENDED A more healthy diet, with less saturated fat, and more exercise can help to reduce the risk of coronary heart disease.

End of topic checklist continued

○ **EXTENDED** Coronary heart disease may be treated with surgery, e.g. inserting a stent into the blocked artery, or a heart transplant, or with drugs, or a combination of these methods.

○ To describe the structure of arteries including the thick muscular walls and thin central lumen.

○ **EXTENDED** The muscular walls of arteries resist the pressure of blood as it enters and even out the change in pressure as blood flows through.

○ How to describe the structure of veins and capillaries.

○ **EXTENDED** The thin capillary walls make it easier for substances such as carbon dioxide, oxygen and glucose to be exchanged with cells.

○ **EXTENDED** The large lumen in veins helps blood to flow easily through them, and the valves prevent the blood flowing in the wrong direction.

○ **EXTENDED** Arterioles carry blood from arteries to capillaries, venules carry blood from capillaries to the veins and shunt vessels directly link arteries to veins so that blood can bypass capillaries in particular areas.

○ **EXTENDED** The lymphatic system is formed from lymph vessels and lymph nodes and its function is to circulate body fluids and produce lymphocytes.

○ Human blood is formed from liquid plasma that carries red blood cells, white blood cells and platelets around the body.

○ Plasma is mostly water in which many substances dissolve, such as glucose, urea and hormones.

○ **EXTENDED** How to identify red and white blood cells in diagrams and photomicrographs.

○ Red blood cells have a biconcave disc shape, contain large amounts of haemoglobin, and are small and flexible so that they can carry oxygen efficiently to all the cells in the body.

○ White blood cells protect aginst infection, by the phagocytosis of pathogens and by producing antibodies.

○ **EXTENDED** White blood cells include phagocytes that engulf pathogens, and lymphocytes which produce antibodies specific to a pathogen.

○ Platelets cause blood to clot.

○ **EXTENDED** Clotting occurs where there is damage to a blood vessel, preventing further blood loss and entry by pathogens.

○ **EXTENDED** Fluid leaving the capillaries in tissues becomes tissue fluid. This fluid enters the lymphatic system and is returned to the blood system near to the heart.

End of topic questions

Note: The marks awarded for these questions indicate the level of detail required in the answers. In the examination, the number of marks awarded to questions like these may be different.

1. The diagram on the left shows a normal ECG, whereas the one on the right shows an ECG of a patient soon after a heart attack.

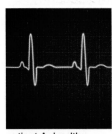 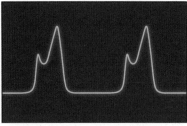

patient A: healthy   patient B: just after a heart attack

△ Fig 9.19 ECGs from two patients.

    a) Explain what an ECG measures. **(1 mark)**

    b) Explain why the two ECGs look different. **(1 mark)**

    c) Describe how the ECG for patient A would change after 5 minutes of moderate exercise. Explain your answer. **(2 marks)**

    d) Describe one possible cause of patient B's heart attack. **(3 marks)**

2. People who suffer from anaemia often have a low red blood cell count (fewer blood cells per mm^3 blood) than usual. One of the symptoms of anaemia is becoming tired more easily than usual. Explain why this symptom occurs. **(4 marks)**

3. People who have suffered a thrombosis, in which the blood unnecessarily clots and blocks a blood vessel, may be given aspirin every day to help to protect them from it happening again. Aspirin interferes with the way platelets function.

    a) Describe the role of platelets in the blood. **(2 marks)**

    b) Explain why this normal function helps us to remain healthy. **(2 marks)**

    c) What damage might be caused if a blood vessel that supplies heart muscle is blocked by a blood clot? **(3 marks)**

    d) Explain why aspirin is effective in reducing the risk of another thrombosis. **(1 mark)**

4. Doctors look for risk factors in a person's lifestyle to help advise their patients on how to live more healthily.

a) Describe four risk factors for coronary heart disease. **(4 marks)**

b) EXTENDED For each of your answers to part (a), explain what the patient can or cannot do about them. **(4 marks)**

5. EXTENDED The blood pressure of blood leaving the right ventricle of the human heart is 3 kPa, and from the left ventricle is around 16 kPa. Explain how the heart can produce these different pressures, and why this difference is important for the body. **(4 marks)**

6. EXTENDED Explain why inserting a stent into a coronary artery is a treatment for coronary heart disease. **(3 marks)**

7. EXTENDED The graph shows the death rate from coronary heart disease (CHD) in some European countries compared with the proportion of the energy in the average diet in those countries that is provided by saturated fat.

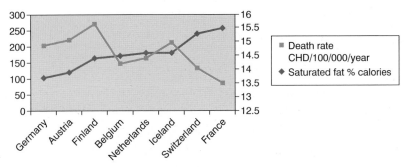

△ Fig 9.20 Death rates and saturated fat intake for some European countries.

a) Saturated fat consumption is a risk factor for coronary heart disease. Explain what we mean by a *risk factor*. **(1 mark)**

b) Explain why saturated fat consumption is a risk factor for coronary heart disease. **(1 mark)**

c) Analyse the shape of the graph. **(3 marks)**

d) Some people think this graph indicates that there is no correlation between saturated fat consumption and CHD. Evaluate this idea. **(4 marks)**

Vaccination is a way of making the body prepare in advance for a potential disease-causing micro organism (a pathogen), so that if that micro organism does invade at some point in the future, the body is ready to fight it. Vaccines are prepared from small amounts of material derived from the pathogen, which is either dead or weakened so that it cannot cause disease. The vaccine triggers the body to develop killer cells and other defences that will fight off the active pathogen in the event of an infection.

CONTENTS

10
Diseases and immunity

Δ Vaccinations are used to prevent the contraction of a disease.

Diseases and immunity

INTRODUCTION

△ Fig 10.1 After the 2010 earthquake in Haiti many water sources were contaminated leading to a serious outbreak of cholera.

Cholera is a disease that causes people to produce large amounts of watery diarrhoea, which can result in death through dehydration. In the 1800s it killed millions of people across the world. In 1854 John Snow, a doctor in London UK, identified a link between cholera and drinking water contaminated with human faeces. This led to massive efforts in cities to make sure that drinking water was kept separate from sewage. Today, good hygiene protects us from disease such as cholera. Although cholera is now a much rarer disease, it still occurs in disaster areas and refugee camps where the drinking water is not well protected.

KNOWLEDGE CHECK

✓ Disease may be caused by infection that can be passed from person to person.
✓ Good hygiene, such as washing hands, can prevent the spread of disease.
✓ Different infectious diseases may be spread in different ways.

LEARNING OBJECTIVES

✓ State that a pathogen is an organism that causes disease.
✓ Describe a transmissible disease as a disease that can be passed from one host to another.
✓ Describe ways in which pathogens are spread.
✓ Describe the defences of the body to infection.
✓ Explain ways that control the spread of disease.

✓ EXTENDED Describe how antibodies attack pathogens.

✓ EXTENDED Describe and explain active immunity.

✓ EXTENDED Describe and explain immunisation.

✓ EXTENDED Describe and explain passive immunity.

✓ EXTENDED Describe the role of the immune system in Type 1 diabetes.

TRANSMISSIBLE DISEASES

Many factors can cause disease, such as bad diet, smoking and genetic tendency, but diseases that can be passed (transmitted) from one individual to another are called **transmissible diseases**, or infectious diseases. Common infectious diseases in humans include not only colds and flu, but also diseases such as food poisoning or sexually transmitted infections (STIs).

Transmissible diseases are caused by **pathogens**, which are disease-causing organisms. Many of these organisms are microscopic, so it is only since the development of the microscope that we have been able to study them in detail and find out how to prevent them. For example, before cholera bacteria were seen in water, many people thought that the disease was transmitted through the air. However, treatment to clean the air, such as fumigation, had no effect on cholera.

The organism that is infected by the pathogen is called the **host**. Many groups of organisms include pathogens, such as bacteria, fungi and protoctists. Viruses that cause disease are also called pathogens, even though many scientists do not recognise them as being living organisms (see Topic 1). All living organisms may be a host to an infection.

Disease	Pathogen	Host
cholera	*Vibrio cholerae* (bacterium)	human
tobacco mosaic disease	TMV virus	many plants including tobacco
malaria	*Plasmodium* spp. (protoctist)	human
athlete's foot	*Trichophyton* (fungus)	human
–	bacteriophage (virus)	*E. coli* bacteria

△ Table 10.1 Transmissible diseases occur in every kind of living organism.

QUESTIONS

1. Define the term *transmissible disease* in your own words.

2. Human immunodeficiency virus (HIV) causes a transmissible disease in humans. Identify the host and the pathogen in this disease.

3. Name three groups of organisms that include pathogens.

Methods of transmission

Transmission is the passing of a disease from an infected person to an uninfected person. Inside the new host, the pathogen will reproduce rapidly to produce hundreds or thousands of new pathogens. These leave the host so that they can infect others.

There are many different ways that pathogens can be transmitted.

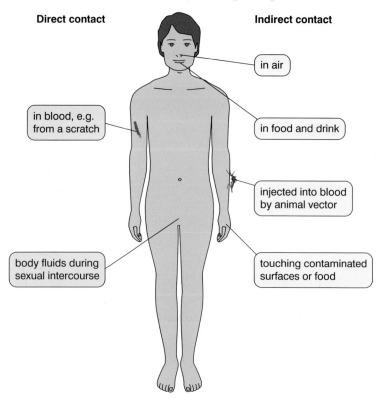

△ Fig 10.2 Methods of transmission of disease.

Direct contact methods are those where the pathogen is transmitted by the transfer of body fluids from a host to an uninfected person. These fluids include blood, semen and other fluids made in the body. Body fluids are exchanged during sexual intercourse, and this is the method of transmission of STIs such as syphilis, HIV and gonorrhoea. Blood is not usually exchanged between people, except by accident, during blood transfusions and when drug users share used hypodermic needles. Diseases transmitted this way include HIV, hepatitis B and hepatitis C. Blood for transfusion is usually checked to make sure it is clear of pathogens before it is given to another person.

Indirect methods of transmission are where the pathogen leaves the host and is carried in some way to an uninfected individual. Examples include:

- transmission in water droplets in air – for example, colds and flu when the host coughs or sneezes
- transmission in infected drinking water – for example, cholera, typhoid and dysentery
- transmission by touching contaminated surfaces – for example, athlete's foot fungus can be transmitted by walking on damp floors, and many food poisoning pathogens (e.g. *Salmonella* and *Clostridium*) are carried to food on the feet of flies that have recently been feeding on contaminated food or faeces
- transmission in insect bites – for example, insects, such as mosquitoes, that feed on human blood carry the pathogens in their body and inject them into the blood when they feed, causing diseases such as malaria and dengue fever.

Animals that help to transfer pathogens from one host to another, such as mosquitoes and flies, are known as **vectors**. Vector organisms do not suffer from the disease that a pathogen causes in its host.

△ Fig 10.3 A mosquito sucking blood from a human. The mosquito is a vector that carries pathogens from an infected person to other people.

Controlling the spread of disease

We can control the spread of transmissible diseases by preventing pathogens in a host reaching uninfected individuals.

Good **hygiene** means keeping things clean, which also reduces the numbers of pathogens on surfaces and on parts of the body. Good personal hygiene includes:

- washing hands thoroughly with warm water and detergent (soap) after going to the toilet; this removes pathogens that are found in faeces and makes it less likely that the pathogens can be transmitted by touch
- covering the mouth and nose with a tissue when coughing or sneezing; this will trap the pathogens and stop them passing into the air; disposing of the tissue properly and washing the hands afterwards will help reduce the risk of transmission by touch

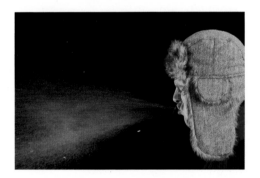

△ Fig 10.4 Large numbers of pathogens can be spread over a large area from a single sneeze.

Hygienic food preparation is important in preventing the transmission of pathogens that cause food poisoning. Food should be kept away from flies, and stored appropriately until it is prepared for eating. Meat, fish and dairy products provide good growing environments for pathogens, so they should be kept in a fridge before use, and should be used within a limited time period after purchase. Foods that are cooked should be prepared separately from those that are uncooked, including using different utensils such as knives for chopping. The heat of cooking kills many pathogens, but uncooked food can easily transmit microorganisms.

Waste food and human waste (faeces) are attractive food sources for many insects that can act as vectors for transmissible diseases. The risk of transmission in this way can be reduced by:

- placing waste food into covered containers and then disposing of the waste away from human habitation in landfill tips, by burning or by composting it in sealed containers

- collecting human waste in sewage systems and keeping it completely separate from drinking water supplies until it has been treated to kill the pathogens and is safe to release into the environment.

QUESTIONS

1. Give one example of a direct method of transmission of disease, and one example of an indirect method. In each case identify a disease transmitted between humans in this way.

2. Define the term *vector* in your own words.

3. Using a particular example, suggest one way to reduce the risk of transmission of a disease. Explain why your suggestion would work.

METHODS OF DEFENCE

We are not completely at risk of infection by pathogens. In fact, the body has many defences that help to prevent us becoming infected.

Mechanical barriers, such as the skin or hairs in the nose, physically prevent pathogens from getting into the body. Chemical barriers, such as lysozyme enzymes in mucus in the nose and acid in the stomach, are chemicals that kill pathogens and prevent them getting into body tissues.

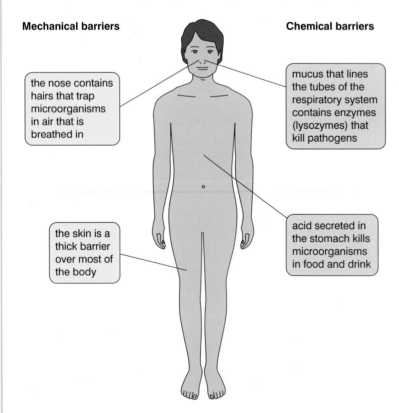

Mechanical barriers

the nose contains hairs that trap microorganisms in air that is breathed in

the skin is a thick barrier over most of the body

Chemical barriers

mucus that lines the tubes of the respiratory system contains enzymes (lysozymes) that kill pathogens

acid secreted in the stomach kills microorganisms in food and drink

△ Fig 10.5 Barriers to infection.

Even if a pathogen gets past these defences, the body has another way of protection. White blood cells in the **immune system** will attack pathogens in one of two ways:

- **phagocytosis** – where the white blood cell engulfs and surrounds the pathogen (see Topic 9) and then breaks it down
- they produce chemicals called **antibodies** that attack and destroy the pathogens.

We can prepare the immune system to attack a particular disease by giving a person a **vaccination**. This helps to prevent the person ever becoming ill with the disease.

The response of the immune system can be improved by vaccination, where the body is exposed to a safe version of the pathogen so that the immune system learns how to attack it.

QUESTIONS

1. Using an example, explain the meaning of a *mechanical barrier* of the body to infection.

2. Using an example, explain the meaning of a *chemical barrier* in the body to infection.

3. Explain how white blood cells protect us from infection.

THE IMMUNE SYSTEM AND ACTIVE IMMUNITY

The immune system coordinates the response of the body to infection. This includes the production of phagocyte cells that directly attack the invading pathogen, and lymphocyte cells that produce antibodies.

Antibodies are a group of chemicals that work by shape. Molecules called **antigens** on the surface of a pathogen have a particular shape, which differs depending on the pathogen. An antibody for a particular pathogen has a shape that matches this, so that it can attach to the surface of the pathogen and either attract phagocytes to engulf the pathogen or cause the pathogen to break open and die.

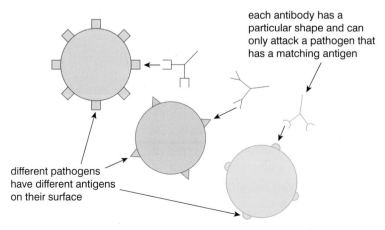

each antibody has a particular shape and can only attack a pathogen that has a matching antigen

different pathogens have different antigens on their surface

△ Fig 10.6 The shape of an antibody must match the shape of the antigen so that it can attach.

Lymphocytes also produce **memory cells**, which remain in the blood after the pathogen has been destroyed. If you are attacked by the same pathogen another time, the memory cells rapidly respond, causing a rapid increase in the production of antibodies. These antibodies attack and destroy the pathogen, often before you are even aware of another infection. For most infections, it is usually not possible for you to become ill with the infection a second time. We say that you have become **immune** to that kind of infection.

This kind of immunity is called **active immunity** because infection has actively produced the immunity.

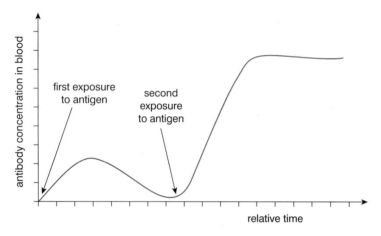

△ Fig 10.7 Antibody production is much greater the second time you are infected with a pathogen.

SCIENCE IN CONTEXT — MUTATING PATHOGENS

Antigens on the surface of pathogen cells are proteins, as are the antibodies that are made by the body to attack the pathogens. The order of amino acids in these proteins produces their particular shape (see Topic 4).

Proteins are coded for by genes (Topic 17), so a particular gene will make a particular protein. Sometimes there is a change in a gene, called a mutation, which changes one or more of the amino acids in the chain. This changes the shape of protein that is formed. If an antibody no longer matches the shape of the antigen, then it can no longer protect the body from infection by that pathogen.

Mutations are usually relatively rare events. However, in some pathogens, such as the viruses that cause the common cold, flu or HIV, the genes for the antigen proteins mutate more frequently. So, even if you are affected by the same kind of pathogen again, your immune system won't recognise it and you will suffer from the disease again.

VACCINATION

Active immunity can be induced by making the body respond as if it has been infected. A **vaccine** is prepared from small amounts of material from the pathogen, which is either dead or weakened so that it is harmless and cannot cause infection. However, it still has the antigens on its surface.

The vaccine is put into the body, either through the mouth (for polio vaccination) or by injection. This is known as vaccination. Lymphocytes in the immune system respond by making antibodies to the antigens on the pathogen, and also by producing memory cells. These memory cells remain in the blood after the pathogen has been destroyed. Some memory cells may last for the rest of your life; others may need a booster vaccination after a few years.

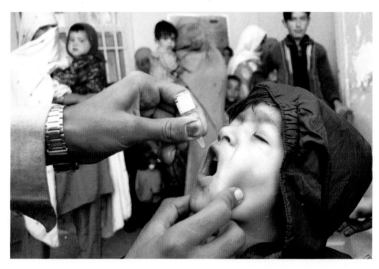

Δ Fig 10.8 A health worker is administering an oral polio vaccine in Pakistan as part of an anti-polio campaign.

If you are ever infected by the live pathogen, the memory cells recognise it very rapidly and stimulate lymphocytes to produce huge quantities of antibodies very quickly. This response kills off the pathogen rapidly, often before you develop symptoms and realise you have been infected. This rapid response makes you immune to that pathogen.

Most countries have immunisation programmes in which particular vaccinations are offered to all individuals of a specific age. Young children may receive vaccinations against a wide range of infections, including measles, mumps, rubella, whooping cough, diphtheria and polio. Teenage girls may receive vaccinations for human papillomavirus (HPV). Many of these infectious diseases are so rarely seen now that nobody really remembers how dangerous they were and how badly people were affected by them.

Parents are usually given the choice whether or not to vaccinate a child. This can cause concern because very rarely a vaccination may cause a reaction and harm the child. However, if someone who has not been immunised catches the disease, the risk of permanent damage or even death is far greater.

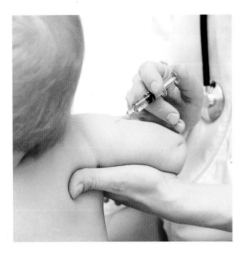

△ Fig 10.9 An injection of vaccine can be a painful experience, but childhood vaccinations can give life-long protection from dangerous infections.

A very few people, particularly those with damaged immune systems, are at risk of harm from vaccination. However, if most people have been immunised, the risk that anyone will come into contact with the pathogen is so small that everyone is protected. This is known as herd immunity.

SCIENCE IN CONTEXT **SMALLPOX ERADICATION**

Smallpox was a devastating disease that killed up to 60% of adults and over 80% of children who became infected with the smallpox virus. It produced large, fluid-filled blisters all over the body. The virus was transmitted between people either through the air or through touching the blisters.

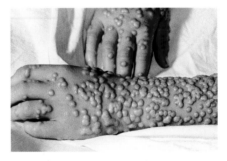

△ Fig 10.10 Smallpox covered the body in fluid-filled blisters.

In 1796 Edward Jenner produced the first vaccine against the disease, using a similar but much weaker virus that caused cowpox. Over the next 100 years, in areas such as Europe and the US, there were great efforts to immunise every person using smallpox vaccine. In 1897 in the US, and around 1900 in Europe, the disease was almost completely eradicated.

In 1958 the World Health Organisation (WHO) started a campaign of worldwide immunisation against smallpox. Where an outbreak of the disease occurred, everyone in the area was vaccinated and people with smallpox were isolated until they were no longer infectious. In 1980, WHO confirmed that the disease had been completely eradicated.

PASSIVE IMMUNITY

You can also be made immune by being given antibodies against the pathogen that causes a disease. For example, someone who has a bad scratch and is at risk of infection from tetanus will be given antibodies to attack any tetanus bacteria that have got into the body.

In **passive immunity**, the body does not produce its own antibodies, and the immune system does not respond. So no memory cells are produced which means that the protection is only short term, and the body has no long-term protection against the disease.

Passive immunity also happens naturally when antibodies in the mother's blood pass through the placenta to her developing fetus before birth. Antibodies will also be transferred from a mother to her baby in breast milk. These antibodies help the very young to fight off infections until they are older and stronger.

QUESTIONS

1. Write your own definitions of

   a) antigen

   b) immunity.

2. Explain why you become immune after being infected with a disease.

3. Compare active and passive immunity to show how they are produced and how long they last.

DISEASES CAUSED BY THE IMMUNE SYSTEM

Very rarely, the immune system of the body starts to attack cells within the body. This is rare because usually lymphocytes recognise cells from their own body by their antigens, and they don't respond to them. Scientists are not sure why this system sometimes goes wrong, although occasionally a viral infection might trigger the reaction. As a result the lymphocytes produce antibodies that attack and destroy particular body cells.

One example of this kind of disease is **Type 1 diabetes**. People who suffer from this disease no longer produce a hormone called **insulin** to help regulate their blood glucose concentration (see Topic 14). Insulin is normally produced by particular cells in the **pancreas** when blood glucose concentration increases, such as after a meal. In a few young people, the immune system starts to attack and destroy these pancreatic cells, which reduces the amount of insulin they can produce. When a large number of these cells have been destroyed, the blood glucose concentration can increase to a dangerous level, demonstrating the presence of Type 1 diabetes.

QUESTIONS

1. Give one example of a disease caused by the immune system.

2. Explain how the immune system can cause disease.

END OF EXTENDED

End of topic checklist

Key words

active immunity, antibody, antigen, host, hygiene, immune, immune system, insulin, memory cell, pancreas, passive immunity, pathogen, phagocytosis, transmissible disease, Type 1 diabetes, vaccination, vector

During your study of this topic you should have learned:

◯ A pathogen is a disease-causing organism.

◯ A transmissible disease can be passed from one host to another.

◯ Pathogens that cause transmissible diseases may be transmitted through direct contact or indirectly.

◯ The human body has mechanical and chemical defences against infection.

◯ Hygienic food preparation, good personal hygiene, effective waste disposal and sewage treatment all help to control the spread of disease.

◯ **EXTENDED** The immune system protects the body by producing antibodies that attack pathogens.

◯ **EXTENDED** Each pathogen has its own antigens on the cell surface, which are recognised by a specific antibody.

◯ **EXTENDED** Active immunity occurs when the body produces its own antibodies, as well as memory cells that protect the body from future infections.

◯ **EXTENDED** Immunisation causes the body to respond as if to an infection; when a harmless form of the pathogen is introduced to the body it triggers an immune reaction and the formation of antibodies and memory cells by lymphocytes.

◯ **EXTENDED** Immunisation can control the spread of a disease because most individuals in the population cannot be infected by it.

◯ **EXTENDED** Passive immunity provides short-term protection against a disease through injection of antibodies into the body, or through transmission of antibodies from mother to fetus through the placenta, or mother to baby through breast milk.

◯ **EXTENDED** Some diseases, such as Type 1 diabetes, are caused by the immune system attacking cells within the body.

End of topic questions

Note: The marks awarded for these questions indicate the level of detail required in the answers. In the examination, the number of marks awarded to questions like these may be different.

1. The kitchen of a restaurant displays a list of hygiene rules that everyone must follow.

   a) State the meaning of *hygiene*. **(1 mark)**

   b) Explain why the restaurant has these rules. **(2 marks)**

   c) For each of the rules, explain how it helps to maintain good hygiene. **(5 marks)**

> *Hygiene rules*
>
> 1. *Wash hands before any food preparation.*
>
> 2. *Only use clean equipment for food preparation.*
>
> 3. *Keep cooked and uncooked food separate – use separate preparation surfaces and utensils.*
>
> 4. *Clean any cuts immediately and cover with a waterproof plaster before continuing work.*

2. Many pathogens are microscopic.

   a) Explain the meaning of the words *pathogen* and *microscopic*. **(2 marks)**

   b) Explain the importance of the development of the microscope in helping us to understand the cause of transmissible diseases. **(2 marks)**

3. EXTENDED Explain why the immune response to an infection of the pathogen that causes measles:

   a) will protect you from a future infection by the measles pathogen **(2 marks)**

   b) will not protect you against infection by the pathogen that causes chickenpox. **(2 marks)**

4. EXTENDED One of the diseases that health organisations are now trying to eradicate from the world is polio. Polio is a highly infectious disease caused by a virus that is transmitted usually in contaminated food or water. Severe cases may result in paralysis or even death. Many parts of the world are free from polio as a result of immunisation, but around 1000 cases occur each year in a few countries.

   a) Immunisation for polio is with drops placed in the mouth. Explain how this leads to immunity. **(4 marks)**

   b) Polio immunisation and boosters give life-long protection against the disease Name this type of immunity and explain why it has this name. **(2 marks)**

   c) A newborn baby is immune to the disease if its mother is immune. Explain why, and why the baby will later need immunisation. **(3 marks)**

   d) Suggest how eradication of polio could be carried out, and explain why your suggestion would work. **(2 marks)**

5. EXTENDED In many countries parents of young children may choose whether or not to have their child immunised against diseases that used to be common. In some countries, immunisation is compulsory for particular diseases.

a) Explain why some parents might not want their child immunised. **(1 mark)**

b) Describe an argument that a doctor would give to parents to explain why immunisation is in the best interests of the child. Explain your answer. **(2 marks)**

c) Give arguments for and against compulsory immunisation, and use them to decide whether compulsory immunisation should be carried out. **(4 marks)**

Our lungs are the organs that allow the body to take in oxygen from the air and expel carbon dioxide that is produced in cells. We breathe in and out about 500 ml of air during every breath. Oxygen from this air passes into tiny air sacs in the lungs, which are called alveoli, and diffuses into the capillaries that lie just underneath them. From here, the oxygen-rich blood is passed to the heart, where it is pumped around the rest of the body, before being passed back to the lungs to offload carbon dioxide and pick up a fresh supply of oxygen.

CONTENTS

11
Gas exchange
in humans

▲ Gas exchange takes place in the alveoli, located in the lungs.

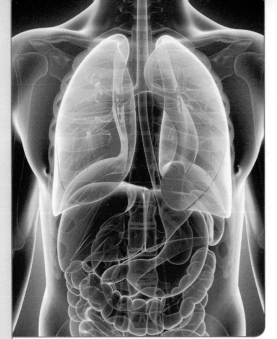

△ Fig 11.1 The lungs are the site of gas exchange in humans.

Gas exchange in humans

INTRODUCTION

Respiration needs substances that are gases in air and produces gases that need to be returned to the environment. These gases must get into and out of the body fast enough to support the rate at which body processes need to work. For single-celled organisms this isn't a problem. They have a large surface area to volume ratio, and diffusion across the cell membrane can supply and remove the gases at a fast enough rate. Larger organisms cannot do this. Not only do they have a much smaller surface area to volume ratio, which slows the rate of diffusion, many of them also live on land, where the delicate surface required for gas exchange would dry out. Different groups of organisms have different solutions to these problems. Plants exchange gases inside the leaf; insects have internal tubes (a tracheal system) inside the body where they exchange gases; fish have gills; and many vertebrates, including humans, have lungs.

KNOWLEDGE CHECK

✓ Animals breathe in oxygen from the air and breathe out carbon dioxide.
✓ Humans use lungs for breathing.

LEARNING OBJECTIVES

✓ Describe how the gas exchange surfaces of the lung are adapted for diffusion.
✓ Identify on a diagram the larynx, trachea, bronchi, bronchioles, alveoli and associated capillaries.

✓ **EXTENDED** State the function of cartilage in the trachea.

✓ **EXTENDED** Describe the role of the diaphragm, ribs and intercostal muscles in the ventilation of the lungs.
✓ Describe the differences in composition of gases in inspired air and expired air.

✓ **EXTENDED** Explain the differences in composition of gases in inspired air and expired air.
✓ Describe how you would investigate the effect of physical activity on the rate and depth of breathing.

✓ **EXTENDED** Explain why the rate and depth of breathing increase with increasing activity.

✓ **EXTENDED** Explain the role of mucus and cilia in the lungs in protecting against damage and infection.

GAS EXCHANGE

Animals need to exchange gases with the environment, to supply oxygen for respiration in cells and to remove the waste product of respiration – carbon dioxide. These gases are exchanged at surfaces by diffusion. So gas exchange surfaces, such as in the human lungs, need adaptations to maximise the rate at which diffusion occurs.

An effective gas exchange surface has:

- a large surface area
- a short distance over which substances have to diffuse, so cells across which diffusion occurs are usually thin
- a good blood supply
- good ventilation to deliver more oxygen and remove carbon dioxide from the body rapidly.

THE HUMAN RESPIRATORY SYSTEM

Breathing is the way that oxygen is taken into our bodies and carbon dioxide is removed. When we breathe, air is moved into and out of our lungs. This involves different parts of the respiratory system within the thorax (the chest cavity).

When we breathe in, air enters though the nose and mouth. In the nose the air is moistened and warmed. The air passes over the **larynx**, where it may be used to make sounds, for example when we talk. The air travels down the **trachea** (windpipe) to the **lungs**. The air enters the lungs through the **bronchi** (singular: bronchus), which branch and divide to form a network of **bronchioles**.

EXTENDED

Bands of cartilage surround the trachea and bronchi. These support the tubes and keep them open during breathing, as otherwise they might collapse when air pressure inside them is reduced.

Cells called goblet cells in the lining of the trachea, bronchi and bronchioles secrete **mucus,** which is a slimy liquid. This traps microorganisms and dust particles that are breathed in. The lining of the trachea and bronchi are covered in tiny hairs called **cilia**, which are found on the surface of ciliated cells. The cilia sweep in a combined motion to move the mucus up from the lungs, up the trachea to the back of the mouth, where it can be swallowed. The combined action of mucus and cilia helps to prevent dirt and microorganisms entering the lungs and causing damage and infection.

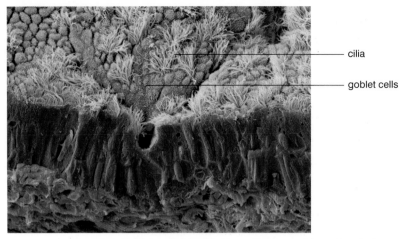

△ Fig 11.2 Section through the tracheal epithelium, showing goblet cells, which secrete mucus, and cilia, which sweep the mucus along the epithelial surface.

END OF EXTENDED

At the end of the bronchioles are air sacs. The bulges on an air sac are called **alveoli** (singular: alveolus). The alveoli are covered in tiny blood capillaries. This is where oxygen and carbon dioxide are exchanged between the blood and the air in the lungs. This is called **gas exchange**. The movement of air across the alveolar surface is called **ventilation**.

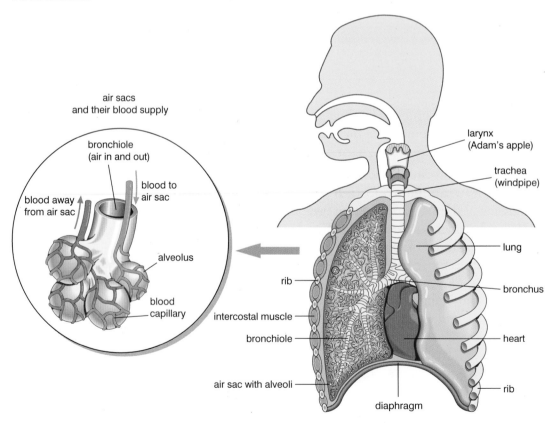

△ Fig 11.3 The human respiratory system.

The alveoli are where oxygen and carbon dioxide diffuse into and out of the blood. For this reason the alveoli are described as the *site of gas exchange*, or the *respiratory surface*.

The alveoli are adapted for efficiency in exchanging gases by diffusion. They have:

- thin permeable walls, which keep the distance over which diffusion of gases takes place between the air and blood to a minimum
- a moist lining, in which the gases dissolve before they diffuse across the cell membranes
- a large surface area – there are hundreds of millions of alveoli in a human lung, giving a surface area of around 70 m² for diffusion
- high concentration gradients for the gases, because the blood is continually flowing past the air sacs, delivering excess carbon dioxide and taking on additional oxygen, and because of ventilation of the lungs, which refreshes the air in the air sacs.

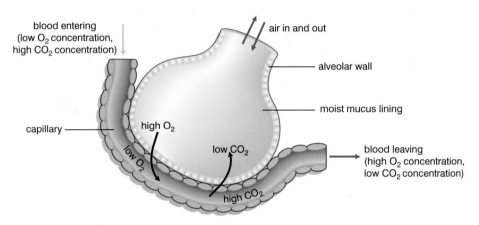

△ Fig 11.4 Gas exchange in an air-filled alveolus.

REMEMBER

For the highest marks, be careful how you describe the process of gas exchange between the air in the lungs and the blood. Remember that diffusion is a passive process, so that it only occurs while there is a concentration gradient. Avoid answering in simple terms, which imply that the movement of oxygen is only from the air to the blood, and that the movement of carbon dioxide is only from the blood to the air.

1. Explain as fully as you can why the lungs show adaptations for a rapid rate of diffusion.

2. List the structures of the human respiratory system and, for each structure, explain its role in breathing.

3. Sketch a diagram of an alveolus and annotate it to show how it is adapted for efficient gas exchange. (Hint: remember to refer to diffusion.)

4. EXTENDED What is the role of the cilia and mucus in the human respiratory system?

EXTENDED

BREATHING IN AND OUT

Breathing in is known as *inhalation* or **inspiration**, and breathing out as *exhalation* or **expiration**. Both happen because of changes in the volume of the thorax. The change in volume causes pressure changes, which in turn cause air to enter or leave the lungs.

The ribs surrounding the thorax are joined together by **intercostal muscles**, and below the lungs is the **diaphragm**. The diaphragm is a domed sheet of tough tissue surrounded by muscle that attaches to the thorax. There are two sets of intercostals: the internal intercostal muscles and the external intercostal muscles. The ribs, intercostal muscles and diaphragm work together to bring about breathing or ventilation of the lungs.

In gentle breathing, only the diaphragm may be involved. In deeper breathing, such as during exercise, or if we think about it, the ribs and intercostal muscles become involved.

Breathing in

Air is breathed into the lungs in a large breath as follows.

1. The muscle around the diaphragm *contracts* so the diaphragm *flattens* in shape.

2. The external intercostal muscles *contract*, making the ribs move upwards and outwards.

3. These changes cause the *volume* of the thorax to *increase*.

4. This causes the *air pressure* in the thorax to *decrease*.

5. This decrease in pressure draws air into the lungs.

Rings of cartilage in the trachea and bronchi keep the air passages open and prevent them from collapsing when the air pressure decreases and from bursting when air pressure increases.

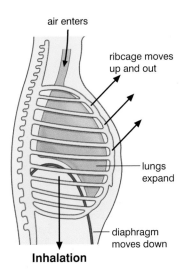
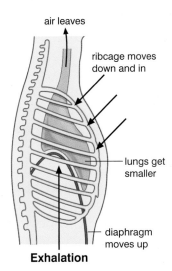

air enters

ribcage moves
up and out

lungs
expand

diaphragm
moves down

Inhalation

air leaves

ribcage moves
down and in

lungs get
smaller

diaphragm
moves up

Exhalation

△ Fig 11.5 Left: breathing in. Right: breathing out.

Breathing out

Air is breathed out from the lungs as follows.

1. The muscle of the diaphragm *relaxes* so the diaphragm returns to its domed shape, pushed up by the liver and stomach. This means it pushes up on the lungs.

2. The external intercostal muscles *relax*, allowing the ribs to drop back down. This also presses on the lungs. If you are breathing hard the internal intercostal muscles also contract, helping the ribs to move down.

3. These changes cause the *volume* of the thorax to *decrease*.

4. This causes the *air pressure* in the thorax to *increase*.

5. This causes air to *leave* the lungs.

REMEMBER

Be prepared to answer questions on breathing in terms of comparing the pressure inside the lungs and external air pressure. Air moves from an area of higher pressure to an area of lower pressure.

- During inhalation air enters because the air pressure inside the lungs is lower than the air pressure outside the body.
- During exhalation air leaves the lungs because the air pressure inside is higher than the air pressure outside the body.

VENTILATION BY MACHINE

Sometimes accident or illness can damage a person's ability to breathe. As exchange of gases is essential for respiration, and so for life, it is crucial that this process is continued artificially until the patient is sufficiently recovered to be able to do it independently again.

In the past, the patient was placed inside a large machine, sometimes called an *iron lung*. The machine was sealed from the air, and changes in pressure inside the machine caused changes in thoracic volume, which resulted in air being drawn in or forced out of the patient's lungs. Today, a sealed mask is placed over the patient's mouth and nose, and air is forced into the lungs by increasing the air pressure. The air is naturally breathed out again as the stretched muscles relax.

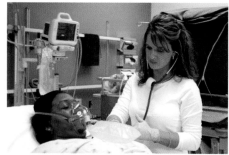

△ Fig 11.6 A ventilator mask forces air into the patient's lungs by increasing air pressure, and allows air out of the patient's lungs by decreasing the air pressure in the mask.

QUESTIONS

1. Describe what happens during inhalation in terms of

   a) movement of structures in the respiratory system and

   b) pressure and volume changes in the thoracic cavity.

2. Describe what happens during exhalation in terms of

   a) movement of structures in the respiratory system and

   b) pressure and volume changes in the thoracic cavity.

END OF EXTENDED

INSPIRED AIR AND EXPIRED AIR

The air we breathe in and out contains many gases. Oxygen is taken into the blood from the air we breathe in. Carbon dioxide and water vapour are added to the air we breathe out. The other gases in the air we breathe in are breathed out almost unchanged, except for being warmer.

	In inspired air	**In expired air**
oxygen	21%	16%
carbon dioxide	0.04%	4.5%
water	variable	high

△ Table 11.1 Differences in composition of inspired and expired air.

We can compare the carbon dioxide in inspired air and expired air using the apparatus shown in Fig. 11.7. Limewater reacts with carbon dioxide and turns cloudy, so this is a test for carbon dioxide.

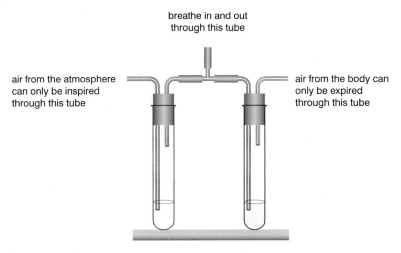

△ Fig 11.7 Limewater in the tubes show that expired air contains much more carbon dioxide than inspired air. Note: one-way valves must be used when setting up this apparatus.

EXTENDED

The composition of inspired and expired air changes because:

- oxygen is removed from blood by respiring cells and used for cellular respiration (see Topic 12), so blood returning to the lungs has a lower concentration of oxygen than blood leaving the lungs
- carbon dioxide is produced by respiration (see Topic 12) and diffuses into the blood from respiring cells; the blood transports the carbon dioxide to the lungs, where it diffuses into the alveoli
- water vapour concentration increases because water evaporates from the moist linings of the alveoli into the expired air as a result of the warmth of the body.

Other gases remain unaffected because they are not used or produced by the body.

END OF EXTENDED

INVESTIGATING THE EFFECT OF EXERCISE ON BREATHING

There are two aspects of breathing that can change during exercise – the rate of breathing and the volume of breath.

- Rate of breathing is usually counted as number of breaths per minute.
- The volume of a breath can be measured in dm³ using a spirometer. A simple spirometer can be made using a 2-litre plastic bottle that has been marked down the side with volumes of water. (This can be done by adding 500 cm³ of water at a time, and marking the volume on the side of the bottle with a waterproof marker.) When the bottle is full of water, turn it upside-down into a water trough without allowing

any air into the bottle. Insert a flexible plastic tube into the neck of the bottle and secure the bottle and tube in position. Clean the other end of the tubing with antiseptic solution. (Alternatively, add a mouthpiece to the end of the tubing that can easily be removed and sterilised after each test.) To measure the volume of a breath, ask the person to wear a noseclip and then to breathe out a normal breath into the tube. The scale on the bottle can be used to measure the volume of air breathed out.

(Safety note: this apparatus must only be used for measuring one breath. The bottle must be set up again before measuring another breath. This is because carbon dioxide build-up in the air in the bottle over several breaths can be dangerous.)

Developing investigative skills

Devise and plan investigations

❶ Design an investigation into the effect of exercise on breathing. (Hint: think carefully about how many people to test, and how to test them, in order to get reliable results.)

Demonstrate and describe techniques

❷ This investigation could involve vigorous exercise. What risks will you need to prepare for, and how should they be minimised?

Analyse and interpret data

The data in the table are the results from an investigation into the effect of exercise on breathing in 4 people. They were first tested at rest and then after 2 minutes of running on a treadmill set at the same speed.

Person	A		B		C		D	
	Rate (breaths/ minute	Breath volume (dm³)	Rate (breaths/ minute	Breath volume (dm³)	Rate (breaths/ minute	Breath volume (dm³)	Rate (breaths/ minute	Breath volume (dm³)
at rest	13	0.5	15	0.4	12	1.2	18	0.6
after exercise	19	1.3	23	0.9	18	1.3	26	1.5

❸ Explain how these data should be adjusted before they can give a reliable answer to the question 'How does exercise affect breathing?'

The results of an investigation like the one in the Developing investigative skills box should show that both the rate of breathing and depth of breathing increase with the level of activity. However, a trained athlete will change in rate and depth of breathing less than an untrained person.

EXTENDED

The rate and depth of breathing increase with level of activity because as the muscles contract faster they respire faster and so make carbon dioxide more quickly. Carbon dioxide is an acidic gas that dissolves easily in water-based solutions, such as the cytoplasm of a cell and blood plasma. The more carbon dioxide there is in solution the more acidic the solution. A change in pH can affect the activity of many cell enzymes (see Topic 5), so it is important that carbon dioxide is removed from the cells and the body as quickly as possible.

The increase in carbon dioxide concentration as a result of increased physical activity is detected as the blood flows past receptors in part of the brain. The receptors send impulses to the lungs, causing an increase in the rate and depth of breathing, which helps to remove the extra carbon dioxide as quickly as possible.

SCIENCE IN CONTEXT **HOW BREATHING RATE IS CONTROLLED**

Rate of breathing is controlled by part of the brain that measures not the oxygen concentration of the blood but the carbon dioxide concentration. This is because a small increase in carbon dioxide concentration in body fluids could have a much more damaging effect on the body than a small decrease in oxygen concentration.

END OF EXTENDED

QUESTIONS

1. Describe the differences in composition between inspired air and expired air.

2. Describe the effects of exercise on the rate and depth of breathing.

3. EXTENDED Explain the differences in composition between inspired air and expired air.

4. EXTENDED Explain what would happen to cells if rate and depth of breathing did not change during exercise.

End of topic checklist

Key words

alveoli, bronchus, bronchiole, cilia, diaphragm, gas exchange, intercostal muscles, larynx, lungs, mucus, trachea, ventilation

During your study of this topic you should have learned:

○ That humans exchange gases with the environment by diffusion, so the lungs need a large surface area, a short distance for diffusion to the blood, and continual ventilation of the inside of the lungs.

○ To describe ventilation as the breathing in and out of air to the lungs, through the larynx, where sound may be produced, down the trachea to the two bronchi, and through the bronchioles to the alveoli, where the gases are exchanged with the many capillaries that lie next to the alveoli.

○ EXTENDED How to state the function of cartilage in the trachea

○ EXTENDED Breathing in is caused by the diaphragm moving down and the intercostal muscles contracting to lift the ribcage up and out, causing an increase in volume and decrease in pressure inside the thoracic cavity, which draws air into the lungs.

○ EXTENDED Breathing out is caused by the diaphragm relaxing and pushing up, and the intercostal muscles relaxing so the ribcage falls and moves in again. This reduces the volume and increases the pressure inside the thoracic cavity, so pushing air out of the lungs.

○ Expired air contains more carbon dioxide, less oxygen and more water vapour than inspired air.

○ EXTENDED The differences in gas concentration in inspired air and expired air are the result of respiration in cells using oxygen and producing carbon dioxide, and the evaporation of water vapour from surfaces inside the lungs.

○ An increased level of activity increases the rate and depth of breathing.

○ EXTENDED The increased rate of depth of breathing during activity removes the increased amount of carbon dioxide produced by respiration and so stops the pH of body tissues and blood falling.

○ Goblet cells in the linings of the lungs secrete mucus that trap pathogens and particles. The mucus is swept out of the lungs by cilia, which protects the lungs from damage and infection.

End of topic questions

Note: The marks awarded for these questions indicate the level of detail required in the answers. In the examination, the number of marks awarded to questions like these may be different.

1. **a)** Define the terms *diffusion* and *gas exchange* **(2 marks)**

   b) Describe the role of diffusion in gas exchange in humans. **(2 marks)**

   c) EXTENDED Explain how the tissues and organs of the lungs are adapted to maximise the rate of gas exchange. **(4 marks)**

2. EXTENDED Fig. 11.8 shows a model that can be used to demonstrate the role of the diaphragm in breathing.

   a) Describe and explain what will happen to the balloon 'lungs' when the rubber diaphragm is:

   i) pulled down **(4 marks)**

   ii) pushed up. **(4 marks)**

   b) Which parts of the body that can be involved in breathing are not included in this model? Explain their role in breathing. **(5 marks)**

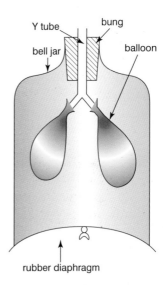

△ Fig 11.8 Model for demonstrating breathing.

3. EXTENDED Fig. 11.9 shows a few cells of the epithelium lining the trachea.

   a) State where the trachea is found and explain its role in the body. **(2 marks)**

   b) Name the type of cell shown by cell A and describe its function. **(2 marks)**

   c) Name the type of cell shown by cell B and describe its function. **(2 marks)**

   d) Explain the role of these cells in protecting the body. **(3 marks)**

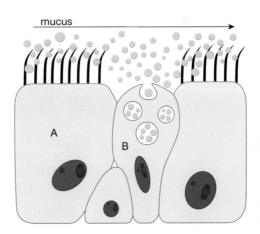

△ Fig 11.9. Cells of the trachea epithelium

Blood delivers oxygen from the lungs, and nutrients from the digestive system, to all cells so that they can respire and carry out all the processes needed for life. When we talk about respiration we often think of the process of breathing, but cellular respiration is a series of chemical reactions that take place in cells to generate the energy that they need to carry out their specific functions.

CONTENTS

12
Respiration

Δ During vigorous exercise, anaerobic respiration takes place in the muscle cells.

△ Fig 12.1 Sperm whales have been recorded around 3 km below the surface of the water and may remain submerged for about 90 minutes, although a normal dive is about 35 minutes long.

Respiration

INTRODUCTION

The current record for a human holding their breath under water is about 11.5 minutes, although this can be extended by starting with a breath of pure oxygen. For most people, this length of time would be impossible, and the urge to breath would become overwhelming after 2 or 3 minutes. Even people who are well trained for this risk damage to cells – particularly brain cells, which need a constant supply of oxygen to function properly. These records are small in comparison with those for diving whales, some of which may be underwater for over an hour.

KNOWLEDGE CHECK

✓ Organisms need energy for all the life processes that keep them alive.
✓ Plants get this energy from the sugars they make in photosynthesis.
✓ Animals get this energy from their food.
✓ Plants take in oxygen and give out carbon dioxide as a result of photosynthesis.

LEARNING OBJECTIVES

✓ State that respiration releases energy in living organisms, and involves the action of enzymes in cells.
✓ Give examples of how energy released from respiration is used in the human body.
✓ Define aerobic and anaerobic respiration.
✓ Describe aerobic respiration as the release of energy from glucose using oxygen from the air.
✓ Give the word equation for aerobic respiration as:
glucose + oxygen → carbon dioxide + water
✓ **EXTENDED** Give the balanced symbol equation for aerobic respiration as:
$C_6H_{12}O_6 + 6O_2 \rightarrow 6CO_2 + 6H_2O$
✓ Investigate the uptake of oxygen by respiring organisms.
✓ **EXTENDED** Investigate the effect of temperature on the rate of respiration in seeds.
✓ Describe anaerobic respiration as the release of energy from glucose without using oxygen.
✓ Give the word equation for anaerobic respiration during hard exercise in animal cells as:
glucose → lactic acid
✓ Give the word equation for anaerobic respiration in yeast as:
glucose → alcohol + carbon dioxide

✓ State that much less energy is released from glucose in anaerobic than in aerobic respiration.

✓ **EXTENDED** Give the balanced symbol equation for anaerobic respiration in yeast as:

$$C_6H_{12}O_6 \rightarrow 2C_2H_5OH + 2CO_2$$

✓ **EXTENDED** Describe how lactic acid concentration increases in muscles and in blood during vigorous exercise.

✓ **EXTENDED** Explain how the oxygen debt after exercise is removed.

RESPIRATION

When we talk about respiration generally, we usually mean breathing (or ventilation, see Topic 11), when gases are exchanged across a respiratory surface. This topic focuses specifically on **cellular respiration**, which is the release of energy from the chemical bonds in food molecules such as glucose. This only takes place inside cells, and every living cell carries out cellular respiration.

REMEMBER

Be clear in your answers that you are using the term *respiration* to mean *cellular respiration*, and to use *ventilation* not *respiration* when talking about breathing.

Every cell in a living organism requires energy, and this energy comes from respiration, which is the breakdown of chemical bonds in food molecules such as glucose to release energy in a form that can be used in cells.

In human cells, this energy is used:

- to produce the contraction of muscle cells
- to produce new chemical bonds during the **synthesis** (formation) of new protein molecules
- to produce new chemicals needed for cell division and for the growth of cells
- for the active transport of molecules across cell membranes
- to produce the movement of nerve impulses along nerve cells
- for the maintenance of a constant core body temperature.

Note that we usually refer to glucose as the *nutrient molecule* or *food molecule* that is broken down in respiration. This is because it is the molecule most commonly used in this reaction in the body. If glucose is in short supply, then other molecules may be used instead from the breakdown of fats or proteins.

Respiration is a series of reactions and, like other reactions in cells, these are controlled by enzymes. So any change in a cell that affects enzymes (such as a change in temperature or pH) will affect the rate of respiration (see Topic 5).

AEROBIC RESPIRATION

Most plant and animal cells use oxygen during cellular respiration. Respiration that uses oxygen to release energy from glucose is called **aerobic respiration**. Water and carbon dioxide are produced as waste products. This is very similar to burning fuel except that in our bodies enzymes control the process.

Aerobic respiration can be summarised by a word equation:

glucose + oxygen → water + carbon dioxide (+ energy)

EXTENDED

It can also be written as a symbol equation:

$$C_6H_{12}O_6 + 6O_2 \rightarrow 6H_2O + 6CO_2 \text{ (+ energy)}$$

END OF EXTENDED

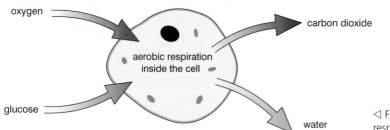

◁ Fig 12.2 Aerobic respiration in a cell.

The oxygen needed for respiration comes from the air (except for a small proportion in photosynthesising plants, which comes from photosynthesis). The carbon dioxide from cellular respiration is released to the air, and the water is either used in the body or excreted through the kidneys.

SCIENCE IN CONTEXT   WATER FROM RESPIRATION

A camel can survive for many days without drinking liquid water, which means it survives well in desert conditions. The camel's hump is not a store of water, but a store of fat. Over a long period without food, the fat is broken down to release substances for aerobic respiration. As water is one of the products of aerobic respiration, this also helps the camel to survive longer without drinking water.

△ Fig 12.3 Wild camels live in dry areas and so must go many days without drinking water.

A complete lack of food and drinking water are conditions that would kill a human in a few days, because we don't metabolise fat as well as the camel does, or retain water as well. So, before setting out into the desert for a long trip, make sure your camel has a large hump (and you have plenty of food and water).

During aerobic respiration, many of the chemical bonds in the glucose molecule are broken down. This releases a lot of energy: around 2900 kJ of energy are released for each mole of glucose molecules used in aerobic respiration.

Investigating aerobic respiration

We can investigate aerobic respiration in living organisms by measuring the amount of oxygen that they take from the air. This is done by measuring the change in volume in an enclosed flask containing the organisms. However, as they respire the organisms release carbon dioxide, which increases the gas volume. So this must be removed from the air using soda lime, otherwise it will mask the effect of oxygen uptake on gas volume in the flask.

Any small organisms can be used in the apparatus, such as germinating seeds or woodlice, but they must be handled with care. Any animals must be kept in suitable conditions and returned to their natural environment as soon as possible after the experiment.

Developing investigative skills

We can use this apparatus to investigate what happens to seeds as they germinate. When the apparatus is set up, the rubber tubing above is left open for a short while. Then it is sealed with the screw-clip. An initial reading is taken on the 1 cm³ pipette. After 5–10 minutes the glass tube is lifted until the levels of coloured liquid in the two tubes are equal, and another reading of the level in the 1 cm³ pipette is taken. The difference between the initial and final readings is the volume of oxygen taken up by the seeds.

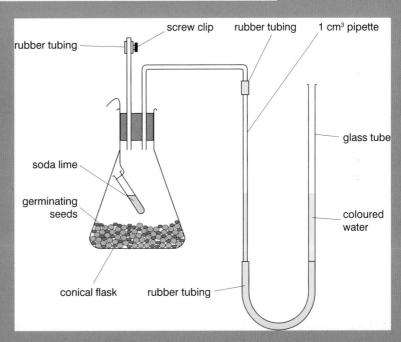

△ Fig 12.4 Investigating oxygen uptake in germinating seeds.

Analyse and interpret data

❶ The results from this investigation are shown in the table.

	First experiment	Second experiment
initial reading on pipette/cm³	0.41	0.48
reading on pipette after 10 min/cm³	0.72	0.81

Developing investigative skills continued

❶ a) Calculate the difference between the initial reading and final reading in each experiment.

b) Calculate the average of the two results and convert the value to cm³ per hour.

❷ Explain why the rubber tubing was left open for a short while before the experiment began, and was then closed completely.

❸ Explain, as fully as you can, what was happening in the apparatus during the experiment.

❹ Explain why the large tube was lifted until the top of the liquid in that tube was equal to the top of the liquid in the pipette before the pipette reading was taken at the end of the experiment.

Evaluate data and methods

❺ Describe a control that you could use to show that it was the seeds that caused these changes. Explain your answer.

EXTENDED

The effect of temperature on the rate of respiration can be investigated by placing identical sets of apparatus in water baths of different temperatures. However, as many living organisms are killed at above 40 °C, care must be taken not to harm the organisms. A temperature range of between 5 and 25 °C is sufficient to produce a measurable effect.

END OF EXTENDED

QUESTIONS

1. a) Write out the word equation for aerobic respiration.

b) Annotate your equation to show where the reactants come from.

c) Annotate your equation to show what happens to the products of the reaction in a human.

d) Describe how your answer to part (c) might differ for a camel on a long journey without water, and explain your answer.

2. Where does respiration take place in the body?

3. Give three examples of the use of energy from respiration in the human body.

4. EXTENDED Write the balanced symbol equation for aerobic respiration.

ANAEROBIC RESPIRATION

Aerobic respiration supplies most of the energy that plant cells and animal cells need most of the time. However, there are times when not enough oxygen is available for aerobic respiration to be carried out fast enough to deliver all the energy that is needed – for example:

- in diving animals, such as whales and seals
- in muscle cells, when vigorous exercise requires more energy than can be provided by an increased supply of oxygen from deeper faster breathing and a faster heart rate.

In these cases, the additional energy needed is supplied by **anaerobic respiration** (sometimes called *fermentation*). This kind of respiration also releases energy from glucose molecules, but without the need for oxygen.

Some organisms, such as yeast (a unicellular fungus) and some bacteria may respire anaerobically in preference to aerobically even when oxygen is present.

In anaerobic respiration, the glucose molecule is only partly broken down, so far less energy is released from each glucose molecule in anaerobic respiration compared with aerobic respiration. Only about 150 kJ is produced from every mole of glucose molecules respired anaerobically in a muscle cell.

Anaerobic respiration in muscle cells

When animal cells respire anaerobically, such as muscle cells during vigorous exercise, the glucose is broken down to lactic acid:

glucose $\rightarrow$ lactic acid (+ energy)

EXTENDED

The balanced symbol equation for this reaction is:

$C_6H_{12}O_6 \rightarrow 2C_3H_6O_3$

END OF EXTENDED

Note that, even when a muscle cell is respiring anaerobically, aerobic respiration is also taking place and using all the oxygen that is available. Where aerobic respiration cannot supply all the energy needed, only the additional energy needed comes from anaerobic respiration.

RESPIRATION IN ATHLETICS

If you watch carefully, you will not see a sprint athlete breathe during a race. At the start of the race there will be some oxygen in their muscle cells, but this is rapidly used up as they start running. Anaerobic respiration provides virtually all of the energy used in a 100 m sprint by a well-trained athlete.

Sprinting cannot be maintained for long, because the muscle cells also need a rapid supply of glucose for respiration. So longer distance races are managed using a combination of aerobic and anaerobic respiration. In marathons, most of the race is run aerobically, with only the last stretch being managed as a sprint using anaerobic respiration.

△ Fig 12.5 A fit athlete in the middle of a sprint is using almost entirely anaerobic respiration.

During anaerobic respiration, the concentration of lactic acid builds up in the cells and in the blood. When exercise has finished and sufficient oxygen is available again, a fast heart rate is maintained for a while to help transport lactic acid to muscle and liver cells. Fast breathing also continues to supply the additional oxygen for breaking down the lactic acid. The lactic acid is converted in muscle and liver cells back to glucose, for use in aerobic respiration later, or broken down fully, using oxygen, to carbon dioxide and water.

The additional oxygen needed after exercise used to be called the **oxygen debt**, but it is now known that additional oxygen is needed after any prolonged exercise, even if completely aerobic, to return many processes in the body back to their resting state. This need, which you can feel when you breathe more deeply after exercise, is now called *excess post-exercise oxygen consumption* (EPOC).

Anaerobic respiration in yeast cells

Yeast cells break down glucose without using oxygen, even if oxygen is present. The word equation for this reaction is:

glucose → ethanol + carbon dioxide (+ energy)

The balanced symbol equation for anaerobic respiration in yeast cells is:

$$C_6H_{12}O_6 \rightarrow 2C_2H_5OH + 2CO_2 \text{ (+ energy)}$$

We make use of this reaction when we use yeast in brewing to make beer and wine. The ethanol is formed when sugars in the barley or grapes is broken down. Ethanol causes the alcoholic effects that occur when we drink these drinks. We also use yeast in bread-making, because the carbon dioxide released forms bubbles in the dough, making the bread light and spongy.

Δ Fig 12.6 The froth on top of this yeast culture is carbon dioxide from anaerobic respiration escaping from the mixture.

QUESTIONS

1. Explain why muscle cells sometimes need to respire anaerobically.

2. Describe the similarities and differences between anaerobic respiration in yeast cells and in animal cells.

3. Compare the amount of energy released during aerobic respiration and anaerobic respiration of glucose in a muscle cell.

4. Explain why bread dough rises and becomes soft and spongy if it is kept warm.

End of topic checklist

Key words

aerobic respiration, anaerobic respiration, cellular respiration, oxygen debt, synthesis

During your study of this topic you should have learned:

○ To define respiration as the process in which energy is released from nutrient molecules in the cells of living organisms, and is controlled by enzymes.

○ How to define anaerobic and aerobic respiration.

○ That in aerobic respiration, glucose is broken down using oxygen from the air:
glucose + oxygen → carbon dioxide + water (+ energy)
EXTENDED $C_6H_{12}O_6 + 6O_2 \rightarrow 6CO_2 + 6H_2O$ (+ energy)

○ The uptake of oxygen can be investigated in respiring organisms such as arthropods and germinating seeds.

○ EXTENDED The effect of temperature on the rate of respiration can be investigated using germinating seeds.

○ Anaerobic respiration occurs in muscle cells when not enough oxygen is available to supply the energy needed for contraction during vigorous exercise.

○ That in anaerobic respiration in animal cells, glucose is broken down to lactic acid which is often called the oxygen debt: glucose → lactic acid (+ energy)
EXTENDED $C_6H_{12}O_6 \rightarrow 2C_3H_6O_3$ (+ energy)

○ EXTENDED The lactic acid produced needs to be broken down in muscle and liver cells after anaerobic respiration ends, and this needs additional oxygen.

○ That in anaerobic respiration in yeast cells, glucose is broken down to ethanol:
glucose → ethanol + carbon dioxide (+ energy)
EXTENDED $C_6H_{12}O_6 \rightarrow 2C_2H_5OH + 2CO_2$ (+ energy)

○ Aerobic respiration releases much more energy from each glucose molecule than anaerobic respiration.

○ That in humans, energy from respiration is used in muscle contraction, protein synthesis, cell division, active transport, growth, the passage of nerve impulses and the maintenance of a constant body temperature.

End of topic questions

Note: The marks awarded for these questions indicate the level of detail required in the answers. In the examination, the number of marks awarded to questions like these may be different.

1. a) List the body systems in a human that are involved in supplying the reactants of cellular respiration. **(3 marks)**

b) List the body systems in a human that are involved in removing the products of cellular respiration. **(3 marks)**

2. Draw up a table to summarise the similarities and differences between aerobic and anaerobic respiration. **(8 marks)**

3. Students were studying the results of respiration in some woodlice. They set up two identical sets of apparatus: a boiling tube fitted with a bung and linked to a tube of limewater through a delivery tube. They placed some woodlice in one boiling tube, and no woodlice in the other tube. The boiling tubes were fitted with their bungs so that no additional air could enter the apparatus and then were left overnight.

a) What was the role of the second set of apparatus? Explain your answer. **(2 marks)**

b) Suggest what happened to the limewater in the two sets of apparatus. **(2 marks)**

c) Explain as fully as you can your answer to part (b). **(3 marks)**

4. A whale takes a deep breath of air and then dives for half an hour. Suggest how energy would be generated in the whale's muscles over the period of the dive. **(4 marks)**

5. In bread-making, the yeast is first mixed with a solution containing sugar and kept in a warm place until a froth forms on the surface. The yeast mixture is then added to flour and any additional constituents, and mixed thoroughly. The dough is placed in a warm place for a while, until it has doubled in size. It is then baked as a loaf.

a) Explain why a sugar solution is added to the yeast at the start. **(2 marks)**

b) 'A warm place' means around 25–30 °C.

i) Explain what would happen if the temperature was lower than this. **(3 marks)**

ii) Explain what would happen if the temperature was higher than this. **(3 marks)**

Excretion in humans is the process by which the body gets rid of waste products generated by cells, and unwanted or harmful substances. The process of excretion involves a number of body organs, including the skin, lungs and kidneys. We have two, bean-shaped kidneys, which are located on either side of the spine in the middle of the back. Their main job is to filter blood passing through them, retaining any useful substances, and allowing excess water, waste products and harmful substances to be passed to the bladder, where they are subsequently removed in urine.

CONTENTS

△ A urine test strip being checked against the color on the side of the canister.

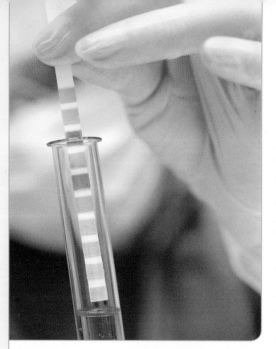

△ Fig 13.1 A dipstick test like this can quickly test urine for a number of excreted substances.

Excretion in humans

INTRODUCTION

More blood flows through the kidneys every hour than through the blood vessels of any other organ in the body. This helps to filter out waste and toxic substances as quickly as possible from the blood, and excrete them in urine. In the past doctors used to check the colour of urine, smell it and even taste it, to help diagnose what was wrong with a patient. Today, doctors and nurses use diagnostic urine tests as a quick way to identify if a patient is healthy or not.

KNOWLEDGE CHECK

✓ Humans breathe out carbon dioxide produced from respiration.
✓ Excess amino acids from digestion are broken down to form urea in the liver.

LEARNING OBJECTIVES

✓ State that the kidneys are major organs of excretion in humans, and that they excrete urea, water and salts in urine.
✓ State that the lungs excrete carbon dioxide.
✓ **EXTENDED** Define deamination.
✓ **EXTENDED** Describe the role of the liver.
✓ Identify the kidneys, ureters, bladder and urethra in the urinary system.
✓ Explain why volume and concentration of urine varies in different conditions.
✓ State that urea is formed from the breakdown of excess amino acids in the liver.
✓ **EXTENDED** Describe the structure of a kidney including the cortex, medulla and ureter.
✓ **EXTENDED** Describe the structure of a kidney tubule.
✓ **EXTENDED** Describe the role of the glomerulus in filtration.
✓ **EXTENDED** Describe the reabsorption of glucose, water and salts in the kidney tubule, which concentrates urea in urine.
✓ **EXTENDED** Explain how dialysis can be used to treat patients with kidney failure, by cleaning the blood on a regular basis using a dialysis machine.
✓ **EXTENDED** Compare the advantages and disadvantages of using kidney transplants instead of dialysis to treat kidney failure.

EXCRETION

Excretion is defined as the process or processes by which an organism eliminates the waste products of its chemical activities, and any substances that are in **excess** (more than is needed by the body). (Remember that this excretion is different from *egestion*.)

The activities in human cells produce many substances that need to be excreted.

- Carbon dioxide is the waste product from respiration. It diffuses from respiring cells into the plasma of the blood, and is carried around the body until it reaches the lungs. Here it diffuses through the capillary and alveoli walls and is breathed out.

EXTENDED

Carbon dioxide must be excreted from the body because it dissolves in water, reducing its pH. This can reduce the activity of enzymes that are essential for controlling reactions in the body. Too much carbon dioxide in the body is therefore **toxic**.

END OF EXTENDED

- Waste products of many cell processes dissolve in the blood and are carried to the kidneys, where they are excreted.
- Food and drink can add more water and salts to the body than the cells need. So the excess is excreted by the kidneys.

The liver plays an important role in preparing some substances for excretion. For example, **urea** is produced in liver cells from the breakdown of excess amino acids. The urea is then carried in the blood to the kidneys, where it is excreted in urine.

EXTENDED

The role of the liver in excretion

Many of the digested food molecules that are absorbed into the blood from the small intestine are transported in the blood to the liver for **assimilation**. This is when the food molecules are converted to other molecules that the body needs. For example, amino acids absorbed after the digestion of proteins in the alimentary canal are used to build new proteins, such as **enzymes**, **hormones**, and **plasma proteins** such as antibodies that are found in the blood and fibrinogen which is important in blood clotting (see Topic 9).

Glucose absorbed from digestion may be used in respiration. Any glucose that is not needed may be converted to glycogen for storage in liver cells. If more amino acids are absorbed in digestion than are needed to make proteins, the excess cannot be stored. Any excess amino acids are broken down in a process called **deamination**, which removes the nitrogen-containing part of the molecule. This part is converted to urea in liver cells. The rest of the molecule is broken down in respiration.

Urea is toxic to the body when in high concentration, which is why it must be excreted.

QUESTIONS

1. Define the term *excretion* in your own words.

2. Describe the role of the lungs in excretion in humans.

3. Describe the role of the kidneys in excretion in humans.

4. EXTENDED Explain why urea and carbon dioxide must be excreted from the body.

THE HUMAN URINARY SYSTEM

Humans have two **kidneys** situated just inside the ribcage at the back of the body, about halfway down the spine in the abdomen. The kidneys are well supplied with blood via the renal arteries and veins. The kidneys produce **urine**, which contains urea, water and mineral salts that the body doesn't need.

Urine flows out of the kidneys, down the **ureters**, and into the **bladder**. The urine is stored in the bladder until a ring of muscle at the base is released (usually when you go to the toilet). The urine then flows out of the bladder, through the **urethra** to the environment.

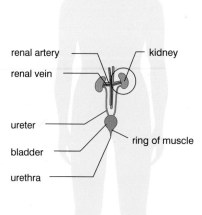

Δ Fig 13.2 The human urinary system.

QUESTIONS

1. Draw up a table to list the main structures of the urinary system and their functions.

2. State three substances found in urine.

STRUCTURE OF THE KIDNEY

Each kidney consists of around one million tiny **kidney tubules**. Each tubule is associated with a blood capillary. The exchange of substances between the tubule and capillary forms urine, which passes into the ureter.

All the tubules pass between the outer area of the kidney, called the **cortex**, and the inner area, called the **medulla**. The cortex is brighter red than the medulla because of the large number of capillaries flowing through this region. The innermost part of the kidney is the pelvis, into which the tubules drain and the urine collects before it flows down the ureter.

Each tubule begins with a small cup-shaped structure called a **renal capsule**. This surrounds a knot of tiny capillaries called a **glomerulus**. Several tubules open into a collecting duct. All the collecting ducts empty into the pelvis of the kidney, which leads to the ureter.

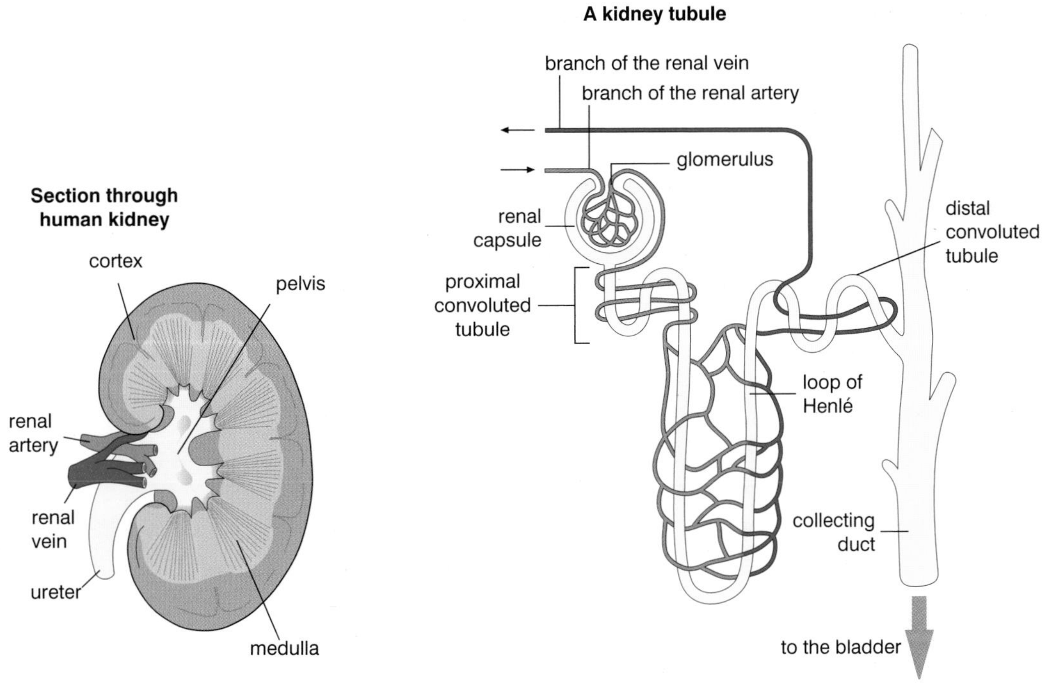

△ Fig 13.3 The structure of the kidney (left) and one tubule (right).

EXCRETION BY THE KIDNEYS

The formation and excretion of urine by the kidneys involves two separate processes: **filtration** and **reabsorption**.

Filtration

Filtration of the blood by the kidney tubules is at the level of molecules. The walls of the renal capsule are only one cell thick, and there are tiny gaps between the cells. The pressure of the blood in the glomerulus squeezes many small molecules out from the blood and into the capsule. These molecules include water, glucose, mineral ions (such as sodium and chloride), hormones, vitamins and urea, which together form the **filtrate**. Large molecules such as plasma proteins and blood cells are too large to be filtered through into the capsule, so they remain in the blood.

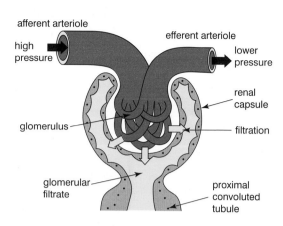

△ Fig 13.4 The glomerulus and renal capsule.

REMEMBER

Remember to describe the movement of molecules in terms of their concentration gradients, in order to get the best marks.

Reabsorption

As the filtrate passes through the kidney tubule, some substances are reabsorbed from the filtrate back into the blood in the capillary that runs close by. Most of the sodium ions, and all of the glucose, that were filtered into the tubule are reabsorbed. These substances are very important in the body, so it is essential that they are not lost. A lot of water is also reabsorbed from the kidney tubule into the blood.

SCIENCE IN CONTEXT

SURVIVING WITHOUT WATER

Australian hopping mice live in the deserts of Australia. These mice can survive without ever drinking liquid water. This is because most of the water that is released from food molecules during respiration is reabsorbed in their kidneys and kept within the body. The mice produce very small amounts of thick, syrupy urine.

△ Fig 13.5 The Australian hopping mouse cannot find drinking water in the desert.

END OF EXTENDED

CHANGES IN URINE

The colour and quantity of urine produced can change quite quickly.

- Urine that is pale yellow in colour is usually produced in large quantities. This is because it contains a lot of water.
- Urine that is a darker orange in colour is usually produced in small quantities. This is because it contains only a little water.

Anything that changes the amount of water in your body will affect the colour and volume of urine you produce.

- **Water intake**: The more water, or water-based drinks, that you drink, the more urine you produce of a pale colour. Drinking very little will result in small quantities of dark urine.
- **Temperature**: The hotter the temperature, the more water you lose in sweat. This leaves less water in the body, so you will produce less urine of a darker colour.
- **Exercise**: During moderate and vigorous exercise, you will also lose more water in sweat. So you will produce less urine of a darker colour afterwards.

QUESTIONS

1. Name three factors that can affect the colour and volume of urine.

2. Describe the colour and volume of urine you would expect a person to produce (a) a little while after drinking a large bottle of cola, (b) after half-an-hour of vigorous exercise. Explain your answers.

3. EXTENDED Name the two processes that take place in a kidney tubule that result in producing urine.

4. EXTENDED Name one substance that is taken back into the blood from the kidney filtrate, and one substance that is not taken back.

KIDNEY FAILURE

You have two kidneys but you can survive with just one. However, if both kidneys become damaged through accident or disease then some means of replacing them must be found. There are two possible courses of action: kidney dialysis and kidney transplant.

Kidney dialysis

If the kidneys stop functioning, it will take only a few days before the concentration of urea and excess substances in the body increase to a level that damages the functioning of cells. It is essential that these substances are removed from the blood to keep them at a level that reduces the risk of cell damage. This is done using an artificial method of cleaning the blood, called **dialysis**.

During dialysis, blood from an artery in the patient's arm is pumped through the dialysis machine, checked for bubbles and then returned to the body through a vein.

The dialysis machine mimics the effect of the kidney by passing the blood through a tube that is separated from the dialysis fluid by a partially permeable membrane. The dialysis fluid contains a balance of solutes that cause waste products such as urea and excess ions, protein and water to diffuse out of the blood into the fluid. The fluid in the machine is continually refreshed so that the concentration gradient is maintained between the dialysis fluid and the blood, and to make sure that the blood is restored to the correct balance of substances needed in the body.

Dialysis may take three or four hours to complete and needs to be done several times a week, to prevent damage to the body by the build-up of substances in the blood.

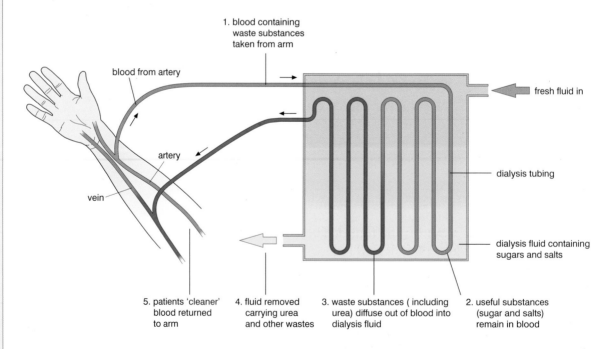

Δ Fig 13.6 How dialysis works.

Kidney transplant

A better long-term solution to kidney failure is to **transplant** a healthy kidney into the patient. This is because a healthy kidney works continually to maintain the right concentration of substances in the blood. The failed kidneys are only removed if they are diseased, and the new kidney is attached to the blood system lower in the body. The healthy kidney may come from someone who has just died, such as in a car accident, or from a living person who has two healthy kidneys.

Successful transplants of organs are difficult because of the immune system, which attacks any cells in the body that it does not recognise as being part of the body. This is useful in infection, but a problem for transplants. If the immune system attacks the transplanted organ, the tissue will be destroyed – this is known as **tissue rejection**.

The immune system identifies cells by molecules on their surfaces. Different people have different markers on their cell surfaces, and people who are closely related have markers that are usually more alike than those of people who are not related. The risk of rejection can be minimised by matching the markers on the tissue of the patient and the new kidney, so that they are as similar as possible. This is why a kidney from a close relative is more likely to be successful in a transplant than a kidney from a stranger.

Even with a close tissue match, the patient will have to take drugs continually to suppress the immune system and prevent rejection. This increases the risk that the patient may suffer more from other infections because the immune system does not tackle them as well as usual. A transplanted kidney may last many years, or just a short time, depending on how well the body accepts the new tissue.

Until a kidney that is a close tissue match becomes available, the patient will have to continue with dialysis every few days.

QUESTIONS

1. Describe two treatments for kidney failure.

2. Explain why treatment for kidney failure is only needed if both kidneys fail.

3. Compare dialysis with normal kidney function to show its similarities and its differences.

4. Explain why one patient with kidney failure may need to wait years before they can have a kidney transplant, but a second patient may get a transplant much sooner.

5. Write down two disadvantages of kidney transplants.

END OF EXTENDED

End of topic checklist

Key words

bladder, cortex, dialysis, excess, excretion, filtrate, filtration, glomerulus, kidney, medulla, reabsorption, renal capsule, tissue rejection, transplant, urea, ureter, urethra, urine

During your study of this topic you should have learned:

○ That excretion is the removal from the body of waste and toxic substances, such as urea and carbon dioxide, and of substances that are in excess of the body's needs, including water and salts.

○ That carbon dioxide is excreted through the lungs.

○ EXTENDED How to define deamination.

○ How to explain that liquid that flows out of the kidneys is urine, which contains water, urea and excess salts that the body does not need.

○ Urea is formed in liver cells from the breakdown of excess amino acids to remove the nitrogen-containing part of the amino acid.

○ EXTENDED How to describe the role of the liver.

○ EXTENDED That each kidney contains millions of kidney tubules that carry out the processes of filtration and reabsorption.

○ EXTENDED That filtration of the blood occurs in the renal capsule, where small molecules in the blood are forced through the walls from the blood into the tubule to form the filtrate.

○ EXTENDED That all the glucose in the filtrate is reabsorbed from the kidney tubule back into the blood.

○ EXTENDED That water and mineral salts needed by the body are also reabsorbed from the kidney tubule into the blood, and the excess remains in the urine.

○ EXTENDED That urea is not reabsorbed from the filtrate, and is excreted in the urine.

○ EXTENDED That kidney failure can be treated by dialysis or kidney transplant.

○ EXTENDED That dialysis passes blood through a dialysis machine to remove waste products and substances in excess in the blood by diffusion into the dialysis fluid.

○ EXTENDED That in a kidney transplant, a healthy kidney is placed in the body of the patient and connected to the blood supply to carry out the functions of filtration and reabsorption.

○ EXTENDED That kidney transplants give better control of substances in the blood than dialysis, but a successful transplant depends on a good tissue match and the patient needs to be on drugs to suppress the immune system for life.

End of topic questions

Note: The marks awarded for these questions indicate the level of detail required in the answers. In the examination, the number of marks awarded to questions like these may be different.

1. a) Give two examples of organs of excretion in humans. **(2 marks)**

   b) For each organ name one substance that is excreted. **(2 marks)**

2. Doctors often test urine to help identify what is wrong with a patient. Explain what the doctor can tell about the patient just by looking at the volume and colour of the urine. **(2 marks)**

3. EXTENDED One of the tests for a condition called diabetes is for glucose in the urine. Explain where the glucose has come from in the urine and why this condition is not normal. **(2 marks)**

4. EXTENDED Describe the role of the liver in controlling the concentration of amino acids in the body. **(4 marks)**

5. EXTENDED **a)** Describe the role of filtration in the formation of urine in a kidney tubule. **(2 marks)**

   b) Describe the role of reabsorption in the formation of urine in a kidney tubule. **(2 marks)**

6. EXTENDED Explain why some substances are reabsorbed from the kidney tubule, some are reabsorbed in limited amounts and others are not reabsorbed at all. **(4 marks)**

7. EXTENDED Explain why kidney failure must be treated rapidly and continually. **(2 marks)**

8. EXTENDED Draw up a table to compare the processes of kidney dialysis and kidney transplant, and to identify their advantages and disadvantages. **(9 marks)**

△ Fig 13.7 A urine sample can show a lot about a person's health.

The human nervous system is the body's control and communications network that uses chemicals and electrically conducting nerve cells to detect, interpret and respond to changes within the body and in the environment. The nervous system tells the body how to react to these changes by sending electrochemical impulses to organs such as the muscles, blood system and skin. The longest nerve cell in the body is the sciatic nerve, which stretches from the base of the spine to the big toe in each foot!

CONTENTS

14
Coordination and response

Δ A micrograph showing a motor nerve from a pig.

Coordination and response

△ Fig 14.1 Professional tennis players serve so fast that a radar gun is used to measure the speed of their serves.

INTRODUCTION

US tennis star Andy Roddick can hit a tennis ball so hard that it travels at 250 km per hour – only a little less than the top speed of a Ferrari. In order to return the ball successfully, his opponents have only a fraction of a second to work out where to stand and how best to return the ball. Their response is built on years of training, so that they can respond without thinking.

KNOWLEDGE CHECK

✓ Plants and animals detect the environment with specialised sense organs.
✓ Animals respond to changes in the environment using nervous and hormonal systems.
✓ Plants respond to changes in the environment, such as by growth.
✓ Nerve cells are specialised cells adapted to the function of carrying electrical impulses.

LEARNING OBJECTIVES

✓ Describe a nerve impulse as an electrical impulse that passes along neurones (nerve cells).
✓ Describe the structure of the human nervous system, including the central nervous system, the peripheral nervous system and the sense organs of the body.
✓ Describe the role of human nervous systems in the coordination and control of body functions.
✓ Distinguish between sensory, relay and motor neurones.
✓ Describe a simple reflex arc in terms of neurones.
✓ Describe a reflex action.
✓ Identify muscles and glands as effector organs.
✓ **EXTENDED** Distinguish between actions that are voluntary or involuntary.
✓ **EXTENDED** Describe the structure and action of a synapse.
✓ **EXTENDED** Link the shape of neurotransmitter chemicals and their receptors to the action of some drugs.
✓ Describe sense organs as a group of cells adapted to respond to a specific stimulus in the environment.
✓ Describe the function and structure of the eye.
✓ Explain the pupil reflex.
✓ **EXTENDED** Explain accommodation in the eye to near and distant objects.

✓ **EXTENDED** Describe the distribution of rods and cones in the retina and outline their function.

✓ **EXTENDED** Identify the position of the fovea.

✓ Describe a hormone as a chemical substance produced by a gland that changes the activity of one or more target organs.

✓ Identify some endocrine glands in the body and describe the functions of the hormones that they produce.

✓ Describe some of the effects of adrenaline, which is produced at times of increased action or stress.

✓ **EXTENDED** Compare the reaction of the nervous and hormonal control systems.

✓ Describe homeostasis as the maintenance of a constant internal environment.

✓ Identify the structures of the skin that respond to changes in body temperature.

✓ Describe how a constant internal body temperature is maintained in humans.

✓ **EXTENDED** Explain control by *negative feedback*.

✓ **EXTENDED** Describe how the hormones insulin and glucagon control blood glucose concentration.

✓ **EXTENDED** Outline the symptoms and treatment of Type 1 diabetes.

✓ Define gravitropism as the response of plants to the force of gravity, and phototropism as the response of plants to light intensity.

✓ Describe investigations of gravitropism and phototropism.

✓ **EXTENDED** Explain phototropism and gravitropism as a result of the plant hormone auxin.

✓ **EXTENDED** Explain how plant hormones are used in synthetic weedkillers.

Sensitivity

Sensitivity is the ability to recognise and respond to changes in external and internal conditions, and is one of the characteristics of living organisms.

A change in conditions is called a **stimulus**. For a coordinated response to occur to that stimulus there must be a **receptor organ,** which recognises the stimulus, and an **effector**, which is a mechanism to carry out the response.

There are two systems involved in coordination and response in humans.

- One is the *nervous system*, which includes the brain, the spinal cord, the peripheral **nerves** and specialist sense organs such as the eye and the ear.
- The other is the *hormonal* (or endocrine) *system*, which uses chemical communication by means of **hormones**.

REMEMBER

Try to identify the stimulus, receptor, effector and response in any example of the nervous or hormonal system.

NERVOUS CONTROL IN HUMANS

The human nervous system consists of:

- the **central nervous system** (CNS; the brain and spinal cord), which processes nervous impulses from the body and coordinates any response
- specialised receptor organs (**sense organs** such as the eye and ear) that contain receptor cells, and which sense stimuli (changes in conditions)
- nerves (large bundles of many neurones) of the **peripheral nervous system** that connect the central nervous system to other parts of the body
- specialised effectors, which produce the response to the stimulus, such as the contraction of muscles and the secretion of hormones from glands.

The nervous system coordinates and regulates many functions in the body.

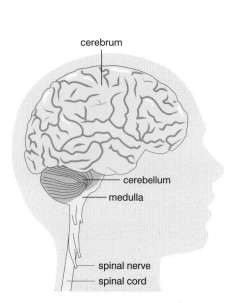

△ Fig 14.2 The human central nervous system (CNS).

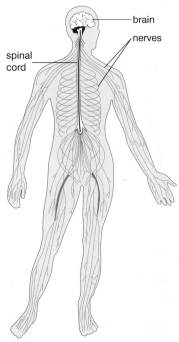

△ Fig 14.3 The human nervous system.

Neurones

Nerves connect the sense organs to the central nervous system. Nerves, and the brain and spinal cord are made of specialised nerve cells called **neurones**. These cells are specially adapted for their function because they have many endings that connect with other neurones, for passing electrical impulses, and cell extensions, called axons and dendrons, that carry the electrical impulses.

- Neurones that link sense organs to the central nervous system are called **sensory neurones**.
- Neurones within the central nervous system may be very short, and are called **relay neurones** (or sometimes *intermediate* or *connector* neurones).
- Neurones that connect the central nervous system to an effector, such as a muscle, are called **motor neurones** (or *effector* neurones).

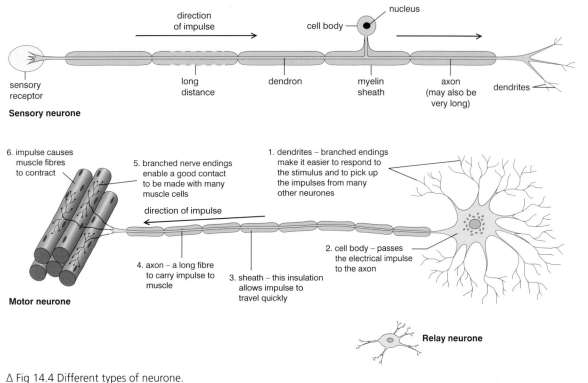

△ Fig 14.4 Different types of neurone.

QUESTIONS

1. Explain what is meant by the term *sensitivity*.

2. Use the following words in one or two sentences to explain how the body responds to change: *effector, receptor, response, stimulus.*

3. Describe two different kinds of effector organ in the human body.

4. Name three different types of neurone and describe the function of each in the nervous system.

EXTENDED

SYNAPSES

Neurones do not directly touch each other, so it is not possible for an electrical impulse in one neurone to pass directly to the next neurone. This is because the junction between two neurones, called a **synapse**, contains a tiny gap across which the electrical impulse cannot pass. Instead, when an impulse reaches the end of the axon of one neurone, it triggers the release of small amounts of a chemical, called a **neurotransmitter**, into the synaptic gap between the neurones. The neurotransmitter diffuses across the gap and binds with receptor molecules in the membrane of the next neurone (often called the post-synaptic neurone, as it is the neurone after the synapse – *post* means 'after'). The binding of the neurotransmitter molecules in the membrane receptors triggers a new electrical impulse in the post-synaptic neurone. As an impulse can only cross a synapse in one direction, this ensures that impulses only travel along neurones in one direction, such as from a receptor to the brain, and from the brain to an effector.

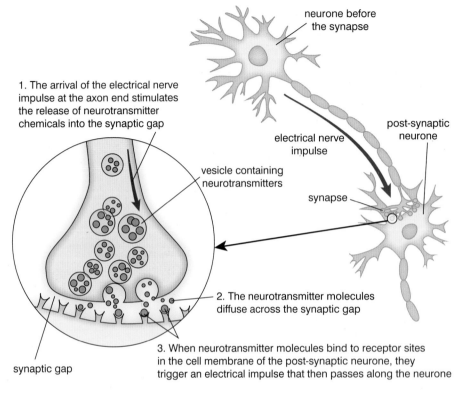

1. The arrival of the electrical nerve impulse at the axon end stimulates the release of neurotransmitter chemicals into the synaptic gap

neurone before the synapse

electrical nerve impulse

post-synaptic neurone

vesicle containing neurotransmitters

synapse

2. The neurotransmitter molecules diffuse across the synaptic gap

synaptic gap

3. When neurotransmitter molecules bind to receptor sites in the cell membrane of the post-synaptic neurone, they trigger an electrical impulse that then passes along the neurone

△ Fig 14.5 The role of neurotransmitters in crossing a synapse.

Different kinds of neurotransmitter chemicals are found in different parts of the human nervous system, but they share one thing in common. They bind to the receptors in the post-synaptic membrane as a result of their shape. Different neurotransmitter molecules are different shapes, and each type will bind only to the receptor of the right shape. Some of the drugs that people use have an effect because they have molecules of a similar shape to a particular neurotransmitter, and so can bind to the receptor molecule for that neurotransmitter. In this way they affect the action of the nervous system. For example, heroin and morphine have a similar shape to a neurotransmitter that is found mostly in the brain. So they can bind to the post-synaptic neurones and cause the same response as the neurotransmitter, in this case to change the way a person experiences feelings, resulting in a sudden feeling of pleasure.

QUESTIONS

1. Explain what is meant by a *neurotransmitter*.

2. Explain why drugs such as morphine and heroin affect the brain.

END OF EXTENDED

Reflex response

The simplest type of response to a stimulus is a **reflex**. Reflexes are rapid, automatic responses to a specific stimulus that often act to protect you in some way – for example, blinking if something gets in your eye or sneezing if you breathe in dust.

The pathway that impulses travel along during a reflex is called a **reflex arc**:

stimulus → receptor → sensory neurone → relay neurone in CNS → motor neurone → effector → response

Simple reflexes are usually spinal reflexes, which means that the impulses are processed by the spinal cord, not the brain. The spinal cord sends an impulse back to the effector. Effectors are the parts of the body that respond, either muscles or glands. Examples of spinal reflexes include standing on a pin or touching a hot object.

stand on pin → nerve endings → sensory neurone → spinal cord → motor neurone → leg muscles → leg moves

When the spinal cord sends an impulse to an effector, other impulses are sent on to the brain so that it is aware of what is happening. It also allows the brain to over-ride the reflex response. For example, if you were holding a large bowl of hot food that you were looking forward to eating, you might look around quickly for somewhere to put it down rather than drop it immediately and risk breaking the bowl.

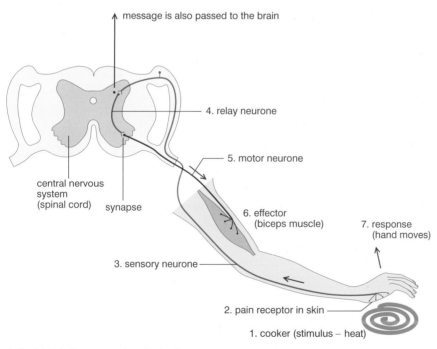

△ Fig 14.6 A diagrammatic spinal reflex.

For higher marks you will need to understand the structure and functioning of the reflex arc, and be able to interpret diagrams and describe what happens at each step.

EXTENDED

The synapses between the neurones in a simple reflex arc ensure that impulses travel only in the direction from the receptor via the central nervous system to the effector.

Reactions that happen automatically, such as those caused by a reflex response, are usually **involuntary**, meaning that the body responds without the conscious control of the central nervous system. Many more of our responses are **voluntary**, meaning that we make a conscious decision, using the brain, to make that response and not a different one. Involuntary actions are usually ones essential to basic survival and are rapid, whereas voluntary responses often take longer.

END OF EXTENDED

QUESTIONS

1. Explain what is meant by the term *reflex response*.

2. Explain why reflex responses are important for survival.

3. EXTENDED With examples, distinguish between a voluntary and an involuntary reaction.

SENSE ORGANS

Different sense organs contain different specialised receptor cells that respond to different stimuli. Table 14.1 shows the different sense organs in humans.

Sense organ	Sense	Stimulus
skin	touch	pressure, pain, hot/cold temperatures
tongue	taste (chemicals)	chemicals in food and drink
nose	smell (chemicals)	chemicals in the air
eyes	sight	light
ears	hearing	sound
	balance	movement/position of head

Δ Table 14.1 Human sense organs and their responses.

The eye

In humans, the eye is the sense organ that responds to changes in light. The specialised light-sensitive receptor cells are the cells of the **retina** at the back of the eye. Different light receptors are sensitive to different wavelengths of light, which is why we can see in colour.

Light passing through the eye and reaching the light-sensitive cells causes changes in these cells, which result in electrical impulses being sent to the brain along the optic nerve. Other structures of the eye have adaptations that support this process.

- The **cornea** and **lens** are transparent, to let light pass through without interference. Both structures also focus the light as it enters the eye, so that a focused image falls on the retina.
- The **pupil** is a hole that lets light through into the eye.
- The jelly inside the eye maintains the shape of the eyeball, so that the distance from front to back of the eye (the focusing distance) does not change.
- The **retina** is very dark, to absorb as much of the light that enters the eyes as possible.

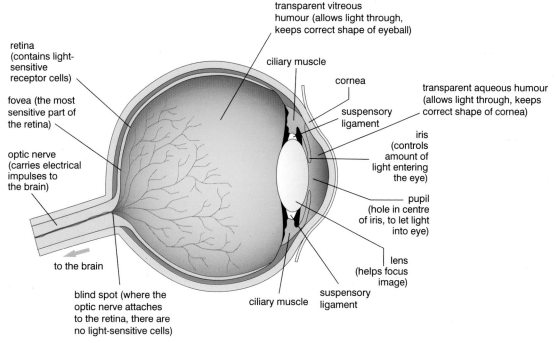

△ Fig 14.7 Structure of the human eye.

There are two different kinds of light-sensitive cells in the retina.

- **Cone** cells respond to light of a certain wavelength, and therefore colour. They only work well in bright light, so we only see colour images when the light is bright enough. The cone cells are mostly clustered around the fovea on the retina, where most light falls in bright conditions. There are three different types of cone. Each type responds best to a different colour of light (red, blue and green). Impulses from each type of cone cell are interpreted in the brain as colour.
- **Rod** cells respond to differences in light intensity, not wavelength. They are more sensitive at low light intensities than cone cells, so we use these mostly in low light conditions. The responses of rod cells give us images that are mainly black and white. Rod cells are found all over the retina.

Where the neurones of the optic nerve connect with the light-sensitive cells, there is an area on the retina where there are no light-sensitive cells. This area cannot respond to light and is known as the blind spot.

END OF EXTENDED

The pupil reflex

The light-sensitive cells in the retina will only respond to the stimulus of light above a certain light intensity. When it is so dark that the cells are not stimulated, we cannot see. As vision is an important sense to us, at low light intensities our eyes need to gather as much light as possible. So the pupil opens wider to allow more light to reach the retina.

However, the light-sensitive cells in the retina are easily and permanently damaged by high light intensity (which is why you should *never* look directly at a bright light source such as the Sun). So, to help protect the cells in the retina, the pupil responds in bright light by becoming smaller. This automatic response is called the pupil reflex.

EXTENDED

The iris (the ring-shaped, coloured part of the eye) controls the amount of light entering the eye by adjusting the size of the hole in the centre, the pupil. The iris contains circular and radial muscles, which have an antagonistic action. This means the contraction of one set of muscles causes the relaxation and extension of the other set of muscles. In bright light the circular muscles contract and the radial muscles relax, making the pupil smaller. This reduces the amount of light entering the eye, to avoid damage to the light-sensitive cells of the retina. The reverse happens in dim light, when the eye has to collect as much light as possible to see clearly.

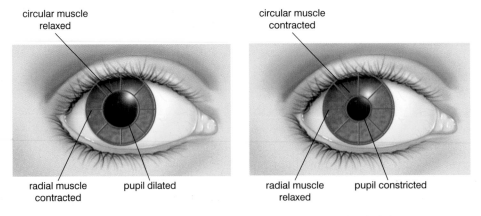

circular muscle relaxed | circular muscle contracted

radial muscle contracted | pupil dilated | radial muscle relaxed | pupil constricted

Δ Fig 14.8 The pupil reflex response to light. Left: in dim light. Right: in bright light.

QUESTIONS

1. Explain how the following structures are adapted to support the role of the eye in sensing light:

   a) cornea

   b) pupil

   c) retina.

2. Explain how the eye responds to changing light intensity.

3. Explain the difference in distribution and role of rod and cone cells in the eye.

Accommodation

In order to see clear images of our surroundings, the light that enters our eyes needs to be focused properly on the retina. The thick clear cornea bends light rays as they enter the eye in order to bring them to a focus on the retina. The lens provides fine focus to sharpen the image.

Adjustment of the fine focusing is needed to focus clearly on objects that are far away or near to us. This adjustment is called **accommodation**. Rays of light from distant objects are almost parallel when they enter the eye. They require less refraction (bending) to come to a focus on the retina and the cornea can manage most of it without help from the lens. The ciliary muscles relax and the lens is pulled into a thinner shape by the suspensory ligaments. This helps to focus the image clearly on the retina.

Rays of light from near objects are diverging when they enter the eye. They need much more powerful refraction to bend them to a focus on

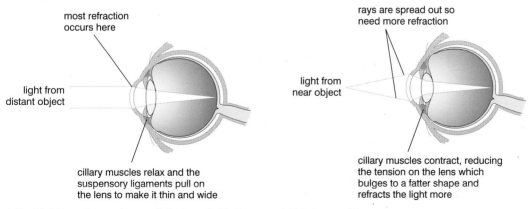

△ Fig 14.9 How the eye focuses light from (left) distant and (right) near objects.

the retina. The ciliary muscles contract, which means they pull less on the suspensory ligaments. This allows the lens to form a more rounded shape. This refracts light more to achieve a focused image on the retina.

QUESTIONS

1. Describe how the eye produces a focused image of an object that is near to the observer.

2. Explain how the eye adjusts to produce a focused image of an object that is distant to the observer.

END OF EXTENDED

HORMONES IN HUMANS

Hormones are chemical messengers used in the **hormonal system**. They are produced in **endocrine glands**. Endocrine glands do not have ducts (tubes) to carry away the hormones they make: the hormones are secreted directly into the blood to be carried around the body dissolved in the blood plasma. Hormones change the activity of other specific parts of the body, called the **target organs**. Most hormones affect several target organs; others may only affect one target organ.

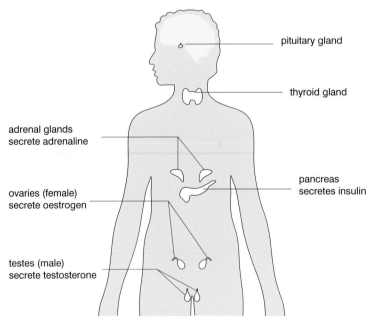

△ Fig 14.10 The position of some endocrine glands in the human body and the hormones they secrete.

Different hormones produce different responses by the body:

- Insulin, produced by the pancreas, causes muscle cells and liver cells to take glucose out of the blood (such as after a meal – see Topic 7), and so reduce blood glucose concentration.
- **Oestrogen**, produced in the ovaries, helps to produce the female secondary sexual characteristics and control the menstrual cycle in women (see Topic 16).
- **Testosterone**, produced in the testes, controls the development of the male secondary sexual characteristics (see Topic 16).
- **Adrenaline**, produced by the adrenal glands, prepares the body for 'flight or fight' in times of excitement, anger, fright or stress.

Adrenaline

Adrenaline is a hormone that is produced in the adrenal glands just above the kidneys. This hormone is released in the crucial moments when an animal must instantly decide whether to attack or run for its life.

Some of the effects of adrenaline are:

- increased pulse (heart) rate to circulate blood more rapidly around the body and deliver glucose and oxygen to muscle cells to allow more rapid contraction
- increased depth of breathing and breathing rate to take more oxygen into the body and remove carbon dioxide more rapidly from the body
- dilated pupils for better vision.

All these changes prepare the body for action.

EXTENDED

Adrenaline also causes liver and muscle cells to release glucose, which increases blood glucose concentration. This means that there is more glucose available for increased muscle cell respiration, which will release more energy for muscle contraction.

Comparison of the nervous and hormonal systems

Changes in the body caused by the nervous system are usually produced rapidly, such as in a reflex response, and only last for a short time. This enables the body to respond quickly to rapid changes in the environment, such as when hunting for food.

The changes in the body that happen due to the secretion of hormones are usually slower and longer lasting than the changes brought about by the nervous system, and may continue until the hormone is broken down by liver cells.

END OF EXTENDED

QUESTIONS

1. Explain the meaning of the following terms:

   a) hormone

   b) endocrine gland

   c) target organ.

2. In what conditions might adrenaline be released in the body?

3. Explain the advantages of adrenaline in preparing the body for action.

4. EXTENDED Compare the actions and effects of the nervous system and hormonal system in terms of the way that they are brought about, the speed of response and their duration.

HOMEOSTASIS

For our cells to carry out all the life processes properly they need the conditions in and around them, such as the temperature and amount of water and other substances, to stay relatively constant. Keeping the internal environment constant is called **homeostasis**.

Temperature control

Homeostasis is the control of internal conditions within set limits. Staying within these limits helps the processes in the body to work most effectively. For example, as you saw in Topic 5, enzymes and the processes they control work best at an optimum temperature.

The temperature in the core (middle) of your body is about 37 °C, regardless of how hot or cold you may feel on the outside. This **core temperature** may naturally vary a little, but it never varies a lot unless you are ill.

Energy is constantly being released by cells as a result of respiration and other chemical reactions in the body, and is transferred to the surroundings outside the body. To maintain a constant body temperature these two processes have to balance. The temperature of the blood from the core of the body is monitored by the hypothalamus in the brain. If the temperature varies too much from 37 °C, the hypothalamus causes changes to happen that result in the temperature returning to about 37 °C. The hypothalamus also receives electrical impulses from heat receptor cells in the skin surface.

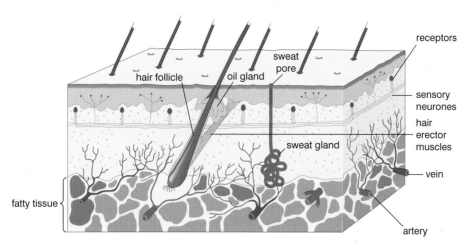

△ Fig 14.11 The structure of skin.

If core temperature rises too far, the following events occur.

- Sweat is released on to the surface of the skin from glands. Sweat is mostly water, and this water evaporates. Evaporation needs energy, so energy is removed from the skin surface as the sweat evaporates, cooling the skin.

EXTENDED

- Arterioles carrying blood near the surface of the skin dilate (get wider) so more blood flows through the capillaries in the skin. This is known as **vasodilation**, and is what makes you look pink when you are hot. This makes it easier for heat energy to be transferred to the skin surface and from there to the environment by radiation and conduction.

END OF EXTENDED

If core temperature falls too far, the following events occur.

- Body hair may be raised by muscles in the skin. This has little effect in humans (often called 'goose bumps') but is more effective in mammals with fur and in birds, because the fur or feather trap air next to the skin. Air is not a good conductor of heat energy, so this still layer of air acts as insulation.
- Muscles may start to 'shiver'. This means that they produce rapid, small contractions. Cellular respiration is used to produce these contractions, releasing energy at the same time, which warms the blood flowing through the muscles.

- Arterioles carrying blood near the surface of the skin constrict (get narrower), which reduces the amount of blood flowing through the surface capillaries. This is known as **vasoconstriction**. As the warm blood is kept deeper in the skin, this reduces the rate of heat transfer by conduction to the skin surface and from there to the environment.

A cold day

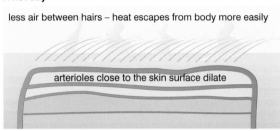

A hot day

Δ Fig 14.12 Arterioles respond to outside temperature.

Developing investigative skills

We can use a test tube of warm water wrapped in wet paper towel as a model to investigate whether sweating really does cool the body, measuring how the temperature of the water changes over time.

Devise and plan investigations

❶ Explain how the tube models sweating in a human.

❷ How would you set up the control for this investigation? Explain your answer.

Make observations and measurements

The table shows the results of an investigation like the one described above.

	Time (min)	0	2	4	6	8	10	12	14	16
Temperature of water in tube (°C)	wet towel	56	50	46	42	39	36	34	32	31
	dry towel	56	52	49	46	44	44	41	40	39

❸ Use the results to draw a suitable graph.

Analyse and interpret data

❹ Draw a conclusion from the graph, and explain the conclusion using your scientific knowledge.

Negative feedback

The control of core body temperature is an example of **negative feedback**. This is where a change in a stimulus causes a response that produces the opposite change. It depends on a monitoring control centre that detects changes and initiates responses, such as the hypothalamus in the brain. We can summarise a negative feedback response in a diagram like that shown in Fig. 14.13.

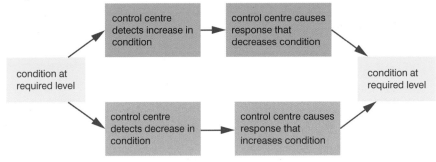

△ Fig 14.13 Negative feedback response.

The effect of a negative feedback response is to prevent large increases or decreases from the best condition for the body. This is how the temperature and pH of the tissues is controlled so that enzymes work most effectively.

Control of blood glucose concentration

It is important that the blood glucose concentration remains within a small range. If it rises or falls too much you can become very ill very quickly.

After a meal, the blood glucose concentration rises rapidly as glucose from digested food is absorbed from the small intestine. Cells in the pancreas detect this increase and respond by releasing the hormone **insulin**, which travels in the blood to the liver. Here it causes any excess glucose to be converted to another carbohydrate, glycogen, which is insoluble and is stored in the liver.

Between meals, glucose in the blood is constantly diffusing into cells for use in cellular respiration. So the blood glucose concentration falls. When a low level of glucose is detected by the pancreas, the insulin-secreting cells stop secreting insulin and other cells start to secrete the hormone glucagon instead. Glucagon converts some of the stored glycogen back into glucose, which is released into the blood to raise the blood glucose concentration again.

Type 1 diabetes

Some people are unable to control their blood glucose concentration because the insulin-secreting cells in their pancreas are not able to produce insulin. This condition is known as **Type 1 diabetes** (see Topic 10). It is important that this condition is treated properly because the concentration of blood glucose after a meal can rise to very high levels, and at other times may fall to a very low level. These changes have large effects on the body.

Symptoms of diabetes include extreme thirst, weakness or tiredness, blurred vision and loss of weight. In extreme cases, a person with Type 1 diabetes may become unconscious. Over a long time, wide ranges in blood glucose concentration can damage cells and cause problems in the eyes and kidneys.

Treatment of Type 1 diabetes is by injection of insulin into the fat beneath the skin. This has to be done regularly, often just before meals to prepare the body for removing the glucose from the blood as it would in a person without the condition.

END OF EXTENDED

QUESTIONS

1. Define the term *homeostasis* in your own words.

2. Give one example of homeostasis in the human body.

3. Explain the role of skin blood vessels in maintaining core body temperature.

4. EXTENDED Define the term *negative feedback*.

5. EXTENDED Use a negative feedback diagram like the one in Fig. 14.13 to show how blood glucose concentration is kept within a safe range.

6. EXTENDED Describe the symptoms and treatment of Type 1 diabetes.

TROPIC RESPONSES

Plants generally respond to changes in the environment by a change in the way that they are growing. For example, a shoot will grow towards light, and in the opposite direction to the force of gravity, whereas a root will grow away from light, but towards moisture and in the direction of the force of gravity. These growth responses to a stimulus in plants are called **tropisms**. They help the plant to produce leaves where there is the most light, and roots that can supply the water that the plant needs.

△ Fig 14.14 Growing towards light helps a plant get more light for photosynthesis.

- Growth in response to the direction of light is called **phototropism**. If the growth is towards light, it is called *positive* phototropism, as occurs in shoots. If the growth is away from light, it is called *negative* phototropism, as occurs in roots.
- Growth in response to gravity is called **gravitropism** (sometimes also called *geotropism*). Plant shoots show negative gravitropism, and plant roots show positive gravitropism.

Developing investigative skills

Fig. 14.15 shows apparatus that can be used to investigate the effect of light on the growth of seedlings.

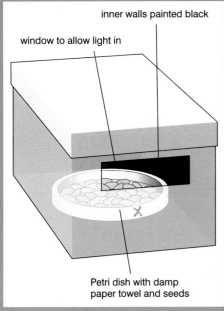

inner walls painted black

window to allow light in

Petri dish with damp paper towel and seeds

△ Fig 14.15 Apparatus for investigating the effect of light on the growth of seedlings.

Devise and plan investigations

❶ Explain how the apparatus could be used for this investigation.

❷ Explain how you would set up a control for this investigation.

Make observations and measurements

❸ If this investigation were set up correctly, what result would you expect to see in the seedlings from the windowed box, compared with your control? Explain your answer.

Evaluate data and methods

❹ Suggest how this investigation could be extended to investigate whether roots also show a phototropic response.

Control of tropic responses

Tropisms are controlled by plant hormones called **auxins**. Auxin is made in the tips of shoots and roots. It dissolves in water in the cells and diffuses away from the tip. Further back along a shoot, auxin *stimulates* cells to elongate so that the shoot or root grows longer.

SCIENCE IN CONTEXT

GARDENER'S TIP

One effect of auxin is to inhibit the growth of side shoots. This is why a gardener who wants a plant to stop growing taller and encourage it to become more bushy will take off the shoot tip, so removing a source of auxin.

The growth of shoots towards light can be explained by the response of auxin to light.

- When all sides of a shoot receive the same amount of light, equal amounts of auxin diffuse down all sides of the shoot. So cells all around the shoot are stimulated equally to grow longer. This means the shoot will grow straight up.
- When the light on the shoot comes mainly from the side, auxin on that side of the shoot appears to move across the shoot to the shaded side. The cells on the shaded side of the shoot will receive more auxin, and so grow longer, than those on the bright side. This causes the shoot to curve as it grows, so that it grows towards the light.

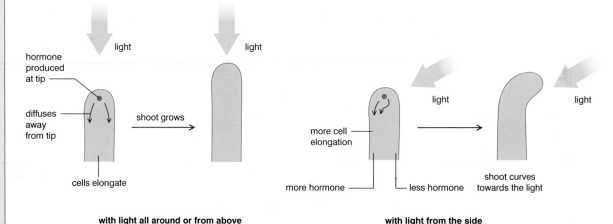

△ Fig 14.16 The effect of light on the growth of shoots.

In roots, auxin has the opposite effect on cells, so that it *reduces* how much the cells elongate.

- When roots are pointing straight downwards, all sides of the root receive the same amount of auxin, so all cells elongate by the same amount.
- When the root is growing at an angle to the force of gravity, gravity causes the auxin to collect on the lower side. This reduces the amount of elongation of cells on the lower side of the root, so that the root starts to curve as it grows until it is in line with the force of gravity.

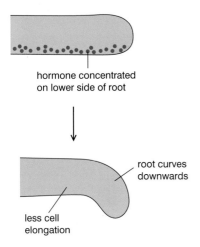

hormone concentrated on lower side of root

root curves downwards

less cell elongation

Δ Fig 14.17 The effect of gravity on the growth of roots.

REMEMBER

- A full understanding of the phototropic responses in stems is needed to gain higher marks.
- Auxin causes curvature in shoots by the elongation of existing cells, not by the production of more cells.

Using auxins

Auxins are now used to make synthetic weedkillers, or **herbicides**. One example that is commonly used is 2,4-D. When it is sprayed on plants, the chemical is absorbed into the plant through its leaves. Inside the plant it encourages the stems and leaves to grow very rapidly. Such large concentrations of auxin are used that growth is too fast, and the plant is unable to supply all the nutrients that the new cells need for healthy growth. Eventually the plant dies.

The advantage of using synthetic weedkillers like this is that grasses are unaffected by the herbicide, and only broad-leaved plants are killed. This is useful as many of our crop plants, such as wheat and maize, are grasses, and many of the weed plants that we want to clear from fields so they don't complete with the crop plants are broad-leaved plants.

END OF EXTENDED

QUESTIONS

1. Define the term *tropism* in your own words.

2. Give one example of:

   a) positive phototropism

   b) positive gravitropism.

3. EXTENDED Describe the action of auxin in a shoot growing in one-sided light.

4. EXTENDED Explain why auxins may be used as weedkillers.

End of topic checklist

Key words

accommodation, adrenaline, auxin, central nervous system, cone, cornea, core temperature, effector, endocrine gland, gravitropism, homeostasis, hormonal system, hormone, insulin, involuntary, lens, motor neurone, negative feedback, nerve, neurone, neurotransmitter, peripheral nervous system, phototropism, pupil, reflex, reflex arc, relay neurone, retina, rod, sense organ, sensory neurone, stimulus, synapse, target organ, tropism, Type 1 diabetes, vasoconstriction, vasodilation, voluntary

During your study of this topic you should have learned:

◯ Plants and animals detect stimuli (changes in their surroundings) and respond to them.

◯ A coordinated response requires a stimulus that is sensed by receptor cells, which results in a change in the organism brought about by an effector (usually muscles or glands in an animal).

◯ The central nervous system consists of the brain and spinal cord, which coordinate and control responses.

◯ Stimulation of receptor cells in sense organs causes electrical impulses to travel along nerves to the central nervous system.

◯ The simple reflex arc is the connection of sensory neurone, relay neurone and motor neurone, which allows rapid responses without thinking.

◯ EXTENDED Voluntary reactions are ones that we think about and can change; involuntary reactions are automatic responses, and often involve a reflex arc.

◯ EXTENDED A synapse is the junction between two neurones.

◯ EXTENDED An electrical nerve impulse that reaches a synapse causes neurotransmitter chemicals to be released into the synaptic gap.

◯ EXTENDED Neurotransmitters diffuse across the synaptic gap, bind with receptors in the cell membrane of the post-synaptic neurone, and trigger a new electrical impulse in that neurone.

◯ EXTENDED Drugs such as morphine and heroin affect the brain because they are similar in shape to a neurotransmitter and so can bind with receptors on the cell membrane of post-synaptic neurones.

◯ The eye has many adaptations for its function in receiving light, including the light-sensitive cells in the retina, and the cornea and lens for focusing light.

End of topic checklist continued

○ **EXTENDED** Cone cells, mainly in the centre of the retina, respond to red, green or blue colours of light; rod cells, mainly around the periphery of the retina, respond to light intensity and are mainly used to see in dim light conditions.

○ Constriction or dilation of the pupil in response to changes in light intensity controls the amount of light entering the eye.

○ **EXTENDED** Contraction or relaxation of muscles supporting ligaments attached to the lens change the shape of the lens to aid fine focusing of images on the retina.

○ A hormone is a chemical that is made in an endocrine gland, secreted into the blood so that it can move around the body, and controls the activity of cells in one or more target organs.

○ Examples of hormones include insulin produced in the pancreas, oestrogen produced in the ovaries of women, testosterone produced in the testes of men, and adrenaline produced in the adrenal glands.

○ Adrenaline is the hormone that prepares the body for action or flight at times of stress, by increasing pulse rate and breathing and dilating the pupils.

○ **EXTENDED** Adrenaline also causes muscle and liver cells to release glucose, and so increase blood glucose concentration.

○ **EXTENDED** Rapid responses in humans are coordinated through nervous impulses in the nervous system, and longer-term responses are coordinated through chemicals (hormones) in the hormonal system.

○ Homeostasis is the control of the internal environment of the body within narrow limits so that cells can function properly.

○ Core body temperature is monitored and regulated by the hypothalamus in the brain.

○ If the body is too hot, sweating helps to reduce body temperature. If the body is too cold, shivering helps to increase core temperature.

○ **EXTENDED** Vasodilation is the widening of blood vessels near the skin surface, which increases blood flow near the surface and increases the rate of loss of heat energy from the skin.

○ **EXTENDED** Vasoconstriction is the narrowing of blood vessels near the skin surface, which reduces blood flow and reduces the rate of heat loss from the skin.

○ **EXTENDED** Negative feedback occurs when a change in a stimulus results in a response that causes the opposite change to occur, and so maintain a steady state for a condition, such as core body temperature.

○ **EXTENDED** Insulin is the hormone made in the pancreas that reduces blood glucose concentration when it is too high by making muscle and liver cells take up glucose from the blood and convert it to glycogen.

○ **EXTENDED** Glucagon is the hormone made in the pancreas that increases blood glucose concentration by making liver cells break down glycogen to glucose and release it into the blood.

○ **EXTENDED** Type 1 diabetes is the inability to control blood glucose concentration because insulin is not secreted from the pancreas.

○ **EXTENDED** The symptoms of Type 1 diabetes include extreme thirst, fatigue, weight loss and in extreme cases, unconsciousness. It is treated with injections of insulin into the fat below the skin on a regular basis.

○ Plants respond to stimuli often by growth responses called tropisms.

○ Plant shoots show positive phototropism when they grow towards light, and negative gravitropism as they grow away from gravity.

○ Plant roots show positive gravitropism when they grow towards the force of gravity, and negative phototropism when they grow away from light.

○ **EXTENDED** Auxins are plant growth hormones that control the responses of shoots and roots to light and gravity.

○ **EXTENDED** Auxins may be used in synthetic weedkillers to selectively kill broad-leaved weeds in fields where grass-like crops are grown.

End of topic questions

Note: The marks awarded for these questions indicate the level of detail required in the answers. In the examination, the number of marks awarded to questions like these may be different.

1. Using the terms *stimulus*, *neurone*, *reflex arc*, *effector* and *response*, describe the response of someone who touches something very hot. **(5 marks)**

2. a) Describe the sequence of sensing and response in the nervous system of one of Andy Roddick's opponents who returns a serve successfully. **(4 marks)**

   b) Is this a reflex action? Explain your answer. **(2 marks)**

3. Explain the following.

   a) A student visiting an underground mine couldn't see anything in the mine when the lights were turned off. **(1 mark)**

   b) A cataract is a clouded lens in the eye, caused by many conditions. A patient with cataracts cannot see clear images. **(2 marks)**

   c) EXTENDED A person who is long-sighted needs to wear spectacles with converging lenses in order to read something near to them. **(2 marks)**

4. Explain the survival advantage to plants of having:

   a) shoots that are positively phototropic **(2 marks)**

   b) roots that are positively gravitropic. **(2 marks)**

5. One example of homeostasis in humans is the control of core body temperature.

   a) Identify the receptors, monitoring area, and effectors in the response to a change in external temperature. **(3 marks)**

   b) Describe the changes in the effectors if core body temperature is too high. **(1 mark)**

   c) Describe the changes in the effectors if core body temperature is too low. **(2 marks)**

   d) EXTENDED Explain why the changes that occur in the body when it is too hot help to return the core body temperature to normal. **(2 marks)**

6. EXTENDED Using the example of blood glucose concentration, explain why negative feedback control is an essential feature of homeostasis. **(3 marks)**

7. EXTENDED A simple test that is done to test for Type 1 diabetes is the glucose tolerance test. The person being tested is given a glucose drink, and their blood glucose concentration is measured for a while afterwards.

The graph in Fig. 14.18 shows the results of a glucose tolerance test on two people.

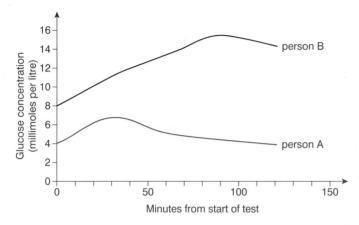

△ Fig 14.18 Results of a glucose tolerance test on two people.

a) Describe the shape of the curves on the graph. (2 marks)

b) Explain the shape of the curve for person A. (2 marks)

c) Explain why the curve for person B is a different shape to the one for person A. (2 marks)

Many of the medicinal drugs that we can take to help treat, prevent or cure illnesses are chemical compounds that scientists can make in the laboratory. A number of these were originally discovered in plants, animals and microorganisms, and have been found to help treat human diseases. The anticancer drug Taxol, for example, was originally discovered back in the 1960s in the bark of a particular species of yew tree. Some very poisonous chemicals have also led to the development of life-saving drugs. An example is a drug known as Lisinopril, which is used to treat high blood pressure and heart failure. This drug was originally developed from the venom of a poisonous snake in Brazil.

CONTENTS

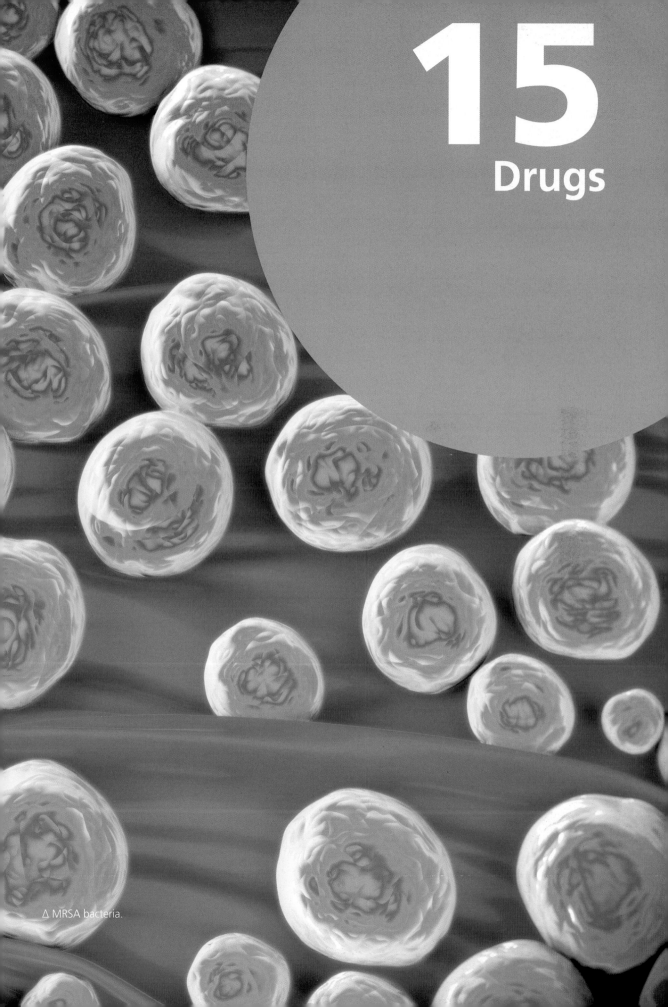

15
Drugs

△ MRSA bacteria.

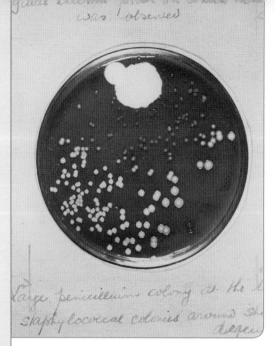

△ Fig 15.1 Alexander Fleming's record of his discovery of penicillin. The large blob at the top of the plate is the mould, and the smaller blobs on the rest of the plate are bacterial colonies. This shows how the bacteria nearest to the mould have been killed.

Drugs

INTRODUCTION

The first antibiotic was developed from an accidental discovery. In 1928, Alexander Fleming was studying the properties of some kinds of bacteria. After returning from a holiday he noticed that one of the bacterial plates he had made earlier was contaminated with a common mould fungus. What was strange was that bacteria near the mould had been killed, whereas those further away were still growing. Fleming grew the mould separately and extracted a chemical that killed many kinds of bacteria. This chemical was then developed as the first antibiotic, penicillin.

KNOWLEDGE CHECK

✓ Bacteria are single-celled organisms with a simple cell structure.
✓ Viruses infect the cells of organisms and reproduce within those cells.
✓ Some microorganisms are pathogenic and can cause disease.
✓ Some drugs can be used to treat disease.

LEARNING OBJECTIVES

✓ Define the term *drug*.
✓ Describe the use of antibiotics for controlling bacterial infections.
✓ Describe some of the limitations of using antibiotics, including that they do not kill viruses.
✓ EXTENDED Explain how antibiotic resistance evolves and what should be done to minimise this.
✓ EXTENDED Explain why antibiotics do not kill viruses.
✓ Describe the effects of the abuse of the drug heroin.
✓ EXTENDED Explain some of the effects of heroin.
✓ Describe the effects of excessive alcohol consumption.
✓ Identify that alcohol and other toxins are broken down by the liver.
✓ Describe the effects of tobacco smoke on the gas exchange system.
✓ EXTENDED Discuss evidence for the link between smoking and cancer.
✓ EXTENDED Discuss the use of hormones to promote sporting performance.

DRUGS

A **drug** is any substance that, when taken into the body, influences the way the body works by modifying or affecting chemical reactions.

MEDICINAL DRUGS

Some drugs are **medicinal drugs** that are used to treat the symptoms or causes of disease. Many medicinal drugs can only be prescribed by a doctor because they are potentially harmful, or because their use should be restricted. For example, **antibiotics** are drugs that kill bacteria in the body or stop them from reproducing. This can protect us from harmful bacterial diseases such as tetanus, pneumonia and some kinds of meningitis.

Antibiotics

Antibiotics are drugs that are used to control many kinds of infection. Different antibiotics are used to kill different kinds of organism – some kill fungi, some kill protoctists and some kill bacteria. However, when we talk about antibiotics generally, we usually mean those that are used against bacterial infections. Examples of antibiotics used to treat bacteria include penicillin, methicillin and erythromycin.

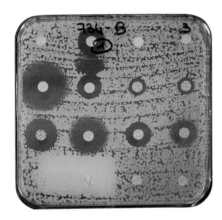

△ Fig 15.2 There are many different kinds of antibiotic.
Each one is most effective against a different type of pathogen.

Antibiotics *do not* kill viruses and so cannot be used to treat viral infections such as a cold or flu. The way antibiotics work against living organisms is not effective against viruses.

EXTENDED

Antibiotics are specific to the type of bacteria they attack because of the way they work. Some cause the bacterial cell membrane to break open, so killing the bacterial cell. Other antibiotics prevent some bacteria from making new cell walls and so prevent them from dividing and producing more bacteria. The advantage is that bacterial cells and human cells are different in structure, so antibiotics don't harm human cells.

Antibiotics cannot be used to attack viruses because viruses don't have cell membranes or carry out the usual processes and chemical reactions that happen inside bacterial cells. This means that antibiotics cannot be used to treat viral diseases such as flu, colds and human immunodeficiency virus (**HIV**). There are some antiviral drugs that can interfere with the way viruses behave in the cell, but these are not antibiotics.

Antibiotic resistance

As the use of antibiotics has increased, so there has also been an increase in the development of antibiotic-resistant bacteria. MRSA is one kind of antibiotic-resistant bacterium. The initials 'MRSA' mean 'methicillin-resistant *Staphylococcus aureus*', which refers to a strain of a common bacterium found in and on the human body that has become resistant not just to methicillin but also to other kinds of antibiotic. Normally *Staphylococcus aureus* grows on human skin and in the nose and throat without causing problems. In people who are not healthy for other reasons, it may cause skin infections, nose and throat infections, even pneumonia (infection of the lungs) and death.

The development of antibiotic resistance in bacteria such as MRSA is an example of evolution through natural selection (see Topic 18).

As bacteria develop resistance to more and more antibiotics, doctors have fewer ways to treat a person with a bacterial infection. Many people are becoming worried that we may get to a point when antibiotics are no longer useful. This could lead to many more deaths from simple bacterial infections, as there were before antibiotics were developed.

It is important that we try to minimise the development of antibiotic-resistant bacteria, such as MRSA, so that the drugs are effective when they are most needed. Minimising the development of resistance can be achieved in two ways.

- **Using antibiotics only when essential** – If bacteria are not exposed to an antibiotic there will be no development of resistance. So, only using the most suitable antibiotic to treat an infection, and not using antibiotics generally, will help to minimise the rate of development of resistance.

- **Making sure that the course of antibiotics prescribed by a doctor is completed** – When you take a course of antibiotics, you can feel better before you finish the treatment. However, it is important to complete the treatment because you need to kill as many of the pathogenic bacteria as possible with the drugs and your immune system. If you stop too soon, those bacteria that are partly resistant to the antibiotic will still be alive in your body. They may be able to reproduce and escape from you to infect someone else. As those bacteria are more resistant to the antibiotic, this infection will be more difficult to treat.

END OF EXTENDED

1. Define the following terms in your own words:

   a) drug

   b) antibiotic

   c) antibiotic resistance.

2. Identify which of the following infections can be treated with antibiotics, and explain your answers:

   i) tetanus

   ii) flu

   iii) viral meningitis

   iv) bacterial meningitis.

3. EXTENDED Describe two ways of minimising the development of antibiotic resistance and explain why they work.

MISUSED DRUGS

Some drugs are misused, which means that they are used in a way that harms the body. These drugs include **illegal** drugs, which cannot be owned, sold or used without legal permission such as prescription by a doctor. Someone who is caught in possession of, or using, illegal drugs can be punished by a fine or by being sent to jail. These drugs are illegal because they have a very powerful effect on the body. Other misused drugs are legal, such as alcohol and tobacco.

Heroin

Heroin is a powerful drug that is prescribed by doctors to control high levels of pain in patients. This is because it is a **depressant**, which means it reduces the normal responses of the body. Depressants can reduce feelings of pain, fear or panic and so make the user feel better. However, heroin is also used illegally by some people for its powerful effects on the brain.

EXTENDED

Heroin has its effect because it binds with receptors in the post-synaptic membrane of neurones in parts of the brain that control pain and emotions (see Topic 14). This can result in a sudden feeling of pleasure, commonly called a 'high'.

END OF EXTENDED

The problem with heroin is that the body rapidly gets used to it, so the user needs increasingly large doses to have the same effect. This is called **addiction**. It also means that if the user stops taking heroin, their body will suffer severe **withdrawal symptoms**, such as nausea, muscle cramps, sweating, anxiety and difficulty sleeping.

People who have become addicted to the drug will need more and more money to pay for increased amounts of the drug. As the drug makes them less able to cope with everyday life, they may lose their job and therefore get their money from crime, such as by burglary or theft.

◁ Fig 15.3 A heroin addict may need to steal around £45 000 worth of money or goods each year to buy the heroin they need to avoid withdrawal symptoms.

Heroin can be taken into the body in different ways, one of which is injection with a syringe. As syringe needles cost money, heroin users may share needles for injection. This increases the risk of transmission of blood-borne infections such as HIV, which causes the disease acquired immunodeficiency syndrome (**AIDS**).

QUESTIONS

1. Explain what is meant by *heroin is an illegal drug*.

2. Give two reasons why heroin is a dangerous drug.

3. EXTENDED Explain why heroin acts as a depressant in humans.

Alcohol misuse

Alcohol also has a depressant effect on the body, which is why it is commonly used as a **recreational drug**. In limited amounts, it can produce a warm relaxing effect, although this can be dangerous as it slows reaction time, and so it takes longer to react to a situation. This is why most countries have laws about the amount of alcohol that can be drunk before driving a vehicle or operating machinery.

In larger quantities alcohol can have many bad effects. In the short-term, large quantities of alcohol may cause:

△ Fig 15.4 Thousands of people are killed or injured each year as a result of car accidents in which the driver had drunk enough alcohol to affect their reaction time.

- vomiting, because alcohol is toxic in large amounts and this is the quickest way for the body to get rid of it
- violent behaviour because the user has reduced self-control – alcohol is a common factor in fights and domestic abuse
- unconsciousness – which increases the risk of death through choking on vomit.

Alcohol and other toxic substances are carried in the blood to the liver, where they are broken down into substances that are not as poisonous to the body. Large quantities of alcohol on a regular basis can cause liver damage (**cirrhosis**), which can eventually lead to liver failure. Many liver transplants are carried out on patients who were regular heavy drinkers of alcohol. Transplants are expensive operations and depend on the donation of a healthy organ, such as from someone who has just died in a car accident.

QUESTIONS

1. Alcohol is a commonly used drug. Explain why.

2. Describe three short-term effects of alcohol misuse.

3. Describe one long-term effect of alcohol misuse and explain why it has this effect.

The effects of smoking

When a person smokes tobacco, the chemicals in the smoke are taken into the lungs. Those chemicals that are small enough molecules can then diffuse into the blood and be carried around the body. Many of the chemicals in tobacco smoke have damaging effects, not only on the respiratory system, but also on other systems in the body.

Smoking tobacco can cause chronic pulmonary obstructive diseases (**COPD**), such as bronchitis and emphysema.

- The tar in tobacco smoke is a mixture of chemicals that form a black sticky substance in the lungs. This sticky layer can coat the tiny hair-like cilia lining the tubes of the lungs, making it more difficult for them to clear out dust and microorganisms. This can result in many lung infections and a thick cough as the smoker tries to clear sticky mucus from the lungs. The irritation and infection can cause a disease called **bronchitis**.

- Continued coughing, in order to clear tar and smoke particles from lungs, over a long time damages the alveoli, breaking down the divisions between them and so reducing their surface area. This causes a disease called **emphysema**, in which the patient has difficulty getting enough oxygen into their blood for any kind of activity. They may have to breathe pure oxygen to make sure their damaged lungs can absorb enough oxygen into their body.

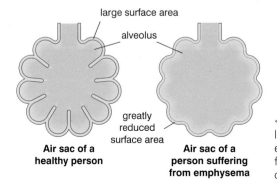

large surface area

alveolus

greatly reduced surface area

Air sac of a healthy person

Air sac of a person suffering from emphysema

◁ Fig 15.5 Repeated coughing over a long period breaks down the surface of each alveolus, reducing the surface area for exchange of gases. This condition is called emphysema.

◁ Fig 15.6 People with emphysema may have to breathe air containing a high concentration of oxygen, to make sure that their damaged lungs can absorb enough oxygen into their bodies. Breathing masks such as the one shown attached to oxygen tanks can provide this for patients.

Many other gases in tobacco smoke are **carcinogenic**, meaning they cause cells to become cancerous and take over tissue. Smoking is the greatest cause of lung cancer. Smoking is also linked to many other kinds of cancer in the body, and to heart disease. People who smoke are more likely to suffer a heart attack or heart pains (angina) than people who do not smoke.

Tobacco smoke also contains carbon monoxide, which is a toxic gas. It combines with haemoglobin in red blood cells and so prevents the cells from carrying oxygen. This reduces the amount of oxygen that gets to tissues, which in extreme cases can lead to cell death. In lower amounts carbon monoxide can result in breathlessness, when the body cannot get sufficient oxygen to cells for activity. During pregnancy, smoking passes through the placenta to the developing fetus. This can reduce the rate of growth of the fetus, resulting in a low birth weight, which can cause complications during the birth and health problems through life.

Nicotine in tobacco smoke alters people's moods – smokers often say they feel more relaxed but alert after smoking. Nicotine is also highly addictive, which makes it difficult for smokers to give up.

EXTENDED

The link between smoking and lung cancer

The graph in Fig. 15.7 shows one example of evidence for a link between tobacco smoking and lung cancer.

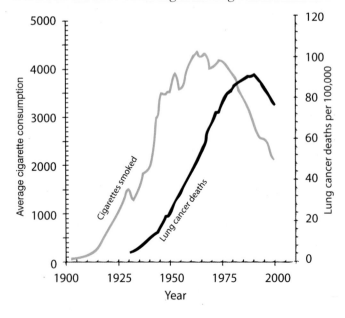

◁ Fig 15.7 Average number of cigarettes smoked in a year by men in the US and deaths from lung cancer between 1900 and 2002.

The graph clearly shows that the shapes of the curves for number of cigarettes smoked and number of death from lung cancer are similar. There appears to be a link between the two factors – we say they show a **correlation**. There are many examples now of graphs like this that show a correlation between smoking and lung cancer.

Although there has been evidence of a correlation between smoking and lung cancer for many decades, it has taken a long while for people to accept that smoking can *cause* lung cancer. The reason for this is:

- it takes time for cancer to develop, and during that time each person is affected by many factors, not just whether or not they smoke tobacco, so it is difficult to prove which factor was the cause of the cancer
- not everyone who smokes is equally affected, so some people who smoke are more likely to develop cancer than others (often a result of differences in genes; see Topic 17)
- much of the early research on the effects of smoking was carried out by tobacco companies, and they kept quiet about their results because it would have reduced sales of tobacco
- it needed research on other animals, such as mice and monkeys, to prove that contact with smoke directly affected cells in a way that produced cancers.

END OF EXTENDED

QUESTIONS

1. Give two examples of COPD, and describe the symptoms of each.

2. Describe the effects of carbon monoxide and nicotine on the body.

3. EXTENDED Look at Fig. 15.7, which shows cigarettes smoked and deaths from lung cancer. Describe the shape of the two curves and explain why they show a link between these factors.

EXTENDED

Hormone use in sport

Hormones produced in the body help to control the way that the body develops and responds to changes (see Topic 14). However, sometimes people take additional hormones to increase these effects. This is most commonly done to improve sporting performance and increase the chance of winning in a competition.

Testosterone is the hormone produced in the testes that affects the development of male secondary sexual characteristics (see Topic 17). It is also produced in small amounts in women.

Testosterone is one of a group of chemicals called **anabolic steroids**. *Anabolic* means they cause new large molecules to be built from smaller ones – testosterone stimulates the production of bone and muscle, particularly during puberty in boys. Steroids are a group of chemicals with a particular structure and are found in plants, animals and fungi.

People who want to improve their sporting performance may take testosterone or other anabolic steroids to help build stronger bones and larger muscles. This is commonly known as 'doping'.

Taking anabolic steroids can have many negative effects on the body. For example:

- it can increase the risk of heart disease due to higher cholesterol in the blood
- it can increase the risk of liver damage
- in women, it can have a damaging effect on the menstrual cycle (see Topic 16)
- in young people, it can limit bone growth, which causes problems for life.

△ Fig 15.8 This man has taken anabolic steroids to help develop his muscles for lifting weights.

Although the use of anabolic steroids by athletes was considered acceptable for a while, it was made illegal in competitive sports (such as the Olympics) when the damaging effects were realised. Today, any competitive athlete will be banned from their sport if they test positive for this group of drugs.

QUESTIONS

1. Explain what is meant by an *anabolic steroid*.

2. Explain why testosterone and other anabolic steroids may be misused by athletes.

3. Identify the disadvantages of using anabolic steroids.

END OF EXTENDED

End of topic checklist

Key words

addiction, anabolic steroids, antibiotics, bronchitis, carcinogenic, cirrhosis, COPD, correlation, depressant, drug, emphysema, heroin, HIV, illegal, medicinal drug, nicotine, recreational drug, withdrawal symptoms

During your study of this topic you should have learned:

○ A drug is a chemical that affects the way the body works.

○ Medicinal drugs are prescribed by doctors and include antibiotics that are used to treat bacterial infections.

○ Some bacteria are resistant to antibiotics, which means the drugs can no longer be effective in killing those bacteria.

○ Antibiotics do not work against viruses.

○ EXTENDED Antibiotics do not affect viruses because viruses do not have the same structures or processes as bacteria, on which the antibiotics work.

○ EXTENDED How to explain how antibiotic resistance evolves and what should be done to minimise this.

○ Heroin is a dangerous drug that is a powerful depressant, which causes addiction, the risk of withdrawal symptoms, and may lead to crime and infection with diseases such as HIV through the use of shared needles.

○ EXTENDED Heroin affects feelings because of the way it binds to neurones in the brain.

○ Alcohol is a depressant that increases reaction times and may cause loss of self-control, leading to violence.

○ Excessive quantities of alcohol over a long period of time can cause liver disease, because alcohol is broken down in the liver.

○ Smoking tobacco can cause chronic pulmonary obstructive diseases (COPD) such as bronchitis and emphysema.

○ Tar, nicotine and carbon monoxide in tobacco smoke all have toxic effects on the body.

○ EXTENDED Although there has been evidence of a link between tobacco smoking and lung cancer for a long time, it has been difficult for many people to accept that smoking can cause lung cancer.

○ EXTENDED Hormones such as testosterone and other anabolic steroids are often misused to improve sporting performance, even though they also damage the body.

End of topic questions

Note: The marks awarded for these questions indicate the level of detail required in the answers. In the examination, the number of marks awarded to questions like these may be different.

1. a) Distinguish between a medicinal drug and a recreational drug. **(2 marks)**

b) Heroin can be used medicinally. Explain why it is used this way. **(1 mark)**

c) Heroin is also used recreationally. Explain why it is used this way. **(1 mark)**

d) Describe the risks and dangers of using heroin recreationally. **(2 marks)**

2. The following shows advice from a medical website about the treatment of some conditions.

Influenza	**Strep throat**
Cause: influenza virus	Cause: *Streptococcus* bacterium
Treatment: bed rest for 24–48 hours, drink plenty of fluids. Contact a doctor after this time if symptoms have not improved.	Treatment: usually requires antibiotics, so see a doctor for a prescription.

a) Explain the difference in the advice for treatment of these two diseases. **(4 marks)**

b) Some medicines, such as paracetamol taken to ease pain or headache, are available to buy in shops. Suggest why you can't buy antibiotics like this. **(3 marks)**

3. The graph in Fig. 15.9 shows the relative risk of causing a car crash in relation to the blood alcohol concentration of the driver.

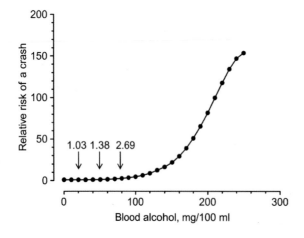

a) Describe the shape of the graph. **(2 marks)**

b) Use the graph to help you explain why alcohol is classified as a drug. **(2 marks)**

c) Alcohol is not an illegal drug. Explain as fully as you can why not. **(2 marks)**

d) Suggest the level above which blood alcohol concentration should be considered illegal while driving. Explain your answer. **(2 marks)**

4. EXTENDED The graph in Fig. 15.10 shows the results of a study in France of the risk of developing lung cancer in relation to the number of cigarettes smoked each day.

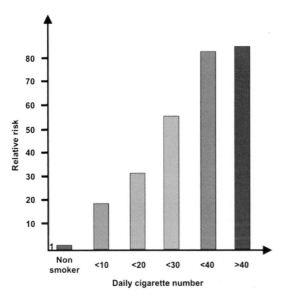

△ Fig 15.9 The bar graph shows the relationship between the number of cigarettes smoked and the risk of developing lung cancer.

a) Describe what the graph shows. **(2 marks)**

b) Explain the shape of the graph. **(4 marks)**

5. Many people who know that cigarette smoking is a risk to their health continue to smoke. Explain why the find it difficult to give up. **(2 marks)**

6. a) EXTENDED Explain as fully as you can why an athlete might be tempted to take anabolic steroids. **(2 marks)**

b) Blood tests are taken from athletes before competitions. If an athlete has anabolic steroids in their blood, they are disqualified from the competition. Explain why. **(2 marks)**

Scientists believe that there has been life on Earth for over 3500 million years. Nobody knows yet what triggered non-living molecules to become organised into living things that can reproduce themselves, but scientists have found traces of bacteria-like structures that may represent the earliest forms of life, in very ancient rocks.

Reproduction leads to different combinations of characteristics in offspring, and mutation produces new characteristics. The environment in which early organisms lived determined which of these combinations of characteristics would be the most successful, and so which individuals were likely to survive and pass on those characteristics to their offspring through reproduction. This process led to the evolution of new species and eventually to the millions of species that are alive on Earth today.

CONTENTS

△ Each poppy plant can produce up to 60 000 seeds, as a result of sexual reproduction.

Reproduction

INTRODUCTION

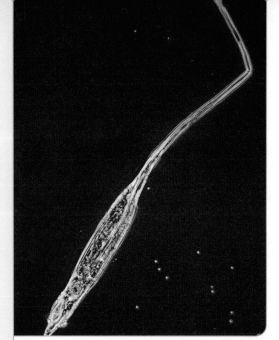

△ Fig 16.1 Scientists think that this species of rotifer has not reproduced sexually for over 40 million years.

Most multicellular organisms reproduce sexually, requiring the transfer of gametes from the male to the female for fertilisation. Some flowering plants and a very few animals can reproduce asexually, where there is no transfer of gametes and females produce new individuals (more females) without fertilisation. Until recently, it was thought that asexual reproduction in animals was something that only happened as an addition to sexual reproduction. However, DNA evidence suggests that some species of stick insect have not reproduced sexually for over 1 million years. Males of these species don't exist.

KNOWLEDGE CHECK

✓ The flower is the reproductive structure in flowering plants.
✓ The human reproductive system consists of organs, tissues and cells that are specially adapted for their role in reproduction.
✓ Sexual reproduction is the production of new individuals as a result of fertilisation; asexual reproduction is the production of new individuals without fertilisation.

LEARNING OBJECTIVES

✓ Describe the differences between sexual and asexual reproduction.
✓ Identify asexual reproduction in a range of organisms.
✓ **EXTENDED** Describe the advantages and disadvantages of asexual and sexual reproduction.
✓ Describe fertilisation as the fusion of gamete (sex cell) nuclei in sexual reproduction to produce a zygote.
✓ **EXTENDED** Describe a gamete cell as containing a haploid nucleus, and a zygote as containing a diploid nucleus.
✓ Identify the structures in wind-pollinated and insect-pollinated flowers and describe how they are adapted to their functions in reproduction.
✓ Define pollination of a flower as the transfer of pollen from an anther to a stigma.
✓ State that fertilisation occurs when a pollen nucleus fuses with a nucleus in an ovule.
✓ **EXTENDED** Compare cross pollination and self pollination.
✓ Investigate the conditions required for germination.
✓ Identify the organs, tissues and cells in the male and female human reproductive systems and describe their functions in reproduction.

✓ **EXTENDED** Relate the size, structure, motility and number of sperm and egg cells to their role in reproduction.

✓ Describe how the embryo implants into the uterus wall and how structures in the uterus and the placenta support the developing embryo.

✓ **EXTENDED** Describe the functions of the placenta and umbilical cord.

✓ Outline the growth and development of the human fetus.

✓ Describe the ante-natal care of pregnant women.

✓ Describe the processes involved in labour and birth.

✓ **EXTENDED** Compare the advantages and disadvantages of breast-feeding and feeding babies with formula milk.

✓ Describe the roles of oestrogen and testosterone in the development of secondary sexual characteristics.

✓ Describe the changes in the uterus and ovaries during the menstrual cycle.

✓ **EXTENDED** Explain the role of hormones in controlling the menstrual cycle.

✓ Outline how different birth control methods prevent fertilisation.

✓ **EXTENDED** Outline the process of artificial insemination (AI) and in vitro fertilisation (IVF).

✓ **EXTENDED** Explain the use of hormones in controlling fertility and discuss the social implications of this.

✓ Describe how some diseases, including HIV/AIDS, are transmitted during sexual intercourse, and explain how their spread can be controlled.

✓ **EXTENDED** Outline how HIV affects the immune system.

ASEXUAL REPRODUCTION

Some organisms increase in number by **asexual reproduction**. For this type of reproduction it is not necessary to have two parents. During asexual reproduction, cells from an adult organism divide to produce the offspring. This means that offspring produced by asexual reproduction are genetically identical to their parent and to each other.

Asexual reproduction is used by many different organisms. Bacteria reproduce asexually using binary fission. When they are large enough their genetic material copies itself exactly and then the cell splits in

Δ Fig 16.2 The toadstools we see growing are specialised spore-producing bodies of fungi.

half. The process then begins all over again. This can occur very rapidly to produce large numbers of identical bacteria.

Almost all fungi can reproduce asexually. Different types of fungi use different means of asexual reproduction but by far the most important type is that of spore formation. This can be seen in *Mucor*, the common pin mould, which often grows on bread. When this fungus has a plentiful supply of nutrients a hypha grows up vertically and the tip swells with cytoplasm containing many nuclei. This tip releases many spores into the atmosphere. If they find the right conditions for growth, each spore can develop into a new mycelium.

Another form of asexual reproduction is seen in plants such as potatoes that produce tubers. Tubers form from the end of stems that grow underneath the soil surface. The stems swell into storage organs filled with starch. When the leaves and stems of the plant die back at the end of the growing season the tubers stay dormant until the next season. Each tuber then produces several potato plants from the buds on the side of the tuber. Each potato plant gives rise to several tubers and each tuber produces a number of plants, so several new plants are formed from one parent.

△ Fig 16.3 Each of the potato tubers formed by this plant could produce a new plant in the next growing season.

EXTENDED

Advantages and disadvantages
Asexual reproduction has advantages and disadvantages.

Advantages:
- Only one parent is required; there is no need for a parent animal to find a mate or for pollination in plants.
- Often large numbers of organisms can be produced in a relatively short time.
- All the offspring produced are identical so should survive well in the conditions in which the parent grows.

Disadvantages:
- The lack of variation in the offspring means that any adverse change in conditions will affect all equally.
- Because the offspring do not vary they are not suited to moving away and exploiting environments with different conditions.

There are some crop plant species that we use for food that do not reproduce sexually very easily. For example, new banana plants are produced from offshoots of older plants. When the offshoot has well-developed roots, it is removed from the parent plant and planted separately. Like the production of tubers by potato plants, this is an example of asexual reproduction.

parent plant

offshoots produced by asexual reproduction of parent plant

△ Fig 16.4 Banana plants reproduce asexually by growing offshoots from the base of the plant.

The advantages of producing new crop plants using asexual reproduction is that you know they will grow as well as the parent plant has done in the local conditions. You also know how well the plant will produce the crop that you are harvesting. This is because the plants are genetically identical. However, the disadvantage is that if the parent plant is susceptible to a disease, then all the offshoots will be as well. The Black Sigatoka virus reduced banana production by over 40% when it arrived in East Africa towards the end of the 20th century.

END OF EXTENDED

REMEMBER

For the highest marks, you must be able to describe as many differences between asexual and sexual reproduction as you can.

QUESTIONS

1. Define the term *asexual reproduction* in your own words.

2. Explain why binary fission of bacteria is an example of asexual reproduction.

3. EXTENDED Explain the advantages and disadvantages to the banana species of reproducing asexually.

SEXUAL REPRODUCTION

Sexual reproduction is the most common method of reproduction for the majority of larger organisms, including almost all animals and plants. It occurs when there is **fertilisation**, which is when the nucleus of a male **gamete** (sex cell) fuses with the nucleus of a female gamete to form a **zygote**. The zygote will contain some of the genetic information of each of its parents. So it will be genetically different from each of the parents. It will also be genetically different from all other offspring produced by those parents (unless it has an identical twin).

EXTENDED

Sexual reproduction involves **haploid** cells, which have just one set of genetic information, and **diploid** cells that have two sets of genetic information (see Topic 17). The gametes are the haploid cells, and when they fuse they produce a diploid cell, which is the zygote. The cell of the zygote will divide repeatedly to produce all the cells of the new organism, and all these cells will be diploid.

Advantages and disadvantages

There are advantages and disadvantages to sexual reproduction.

Advantages:

- Fusion of gametes brings genetic information from two parents, which results in variety in the offspring. This produces individuals that may be better adapted to different conditions than the parents and each other, which makes the chance of survival of the species in changing conditions more likely.

Disadvantages:

- Sexual reproduction usually requires a second parent for fertilisation. Finding a mate can take time and energy for the individual, and failure to mate means that the individual produces no offspring.
- The need to find a mate also means that sexual reproduction takes longer to produce offspring than asexual reproduction.

Most crop plants can only reproduce sexually. For example, rice, wheat and other grain crops can only be grown from seed produced through the sexual reproduction of a previous crop. This has advantages because there is always a chance through reproduction that a new combination of genetic material will produce plants that grow faster and produce more harvest than the parent plants. We use the fact that sexual reproduction results in genetic diversity in plant breeding (see Topic 21). This is particularly important for breeding new crops that can cope with the different conditions that may arise as a result of environmental change, such as climate change.

△ Fig 16.5 Rice will only grow from seed. So new seeds must be planted each year.

The disadvantage is that new combinations of genetic material may result in offspring that are less successful than the parent plants in terms of growing well and producing a good harvest. This is why seeds from different breeding programmes are continually tested to make sure that they are producing plants that will give a good harvest.

END OF EXTENDED

QUESTIONS

1. Define the following terms in your own words:

   a) *fertilisation*

   b) *sexual reproduction.*

2. EXTENDED Give an example of

   a) a haploid cell

   b) a diploid cell.

3. EXTENDED Describe an advantage and a disadvantage of producing crops by sexual reproduction.

SEXUAL REPRODUCTION IN PLANTS

The most successful group of plants is the flowering plants. These are the only plants to have true flowers and produce **seeds** with a tough protective coat. During sexual reproduction, flowering plants:

- produce male and female gametes – some species may produce male and female gametes in the same flowers; other species may have male-only flowers and female-only flowers on the same plant; and in other species male flowers and female flowers are produced on different plants
- male pollen is transferred to the female part of the flower so that **pollination** can take place

- the male gamete and female gamete fuse during fertilisation to form a zygote
- the zygote develops to form an embryo within a seed, which protects the embryo and provides food during germination of the seed
- seeds are dispersed, so that they germinate and grow away from the parent.

Structure of flowers

All flowers have a similar basic arrangement. They have structures stacked one on top of each other along a short stem, arranged either in a spiral or in separate rings.

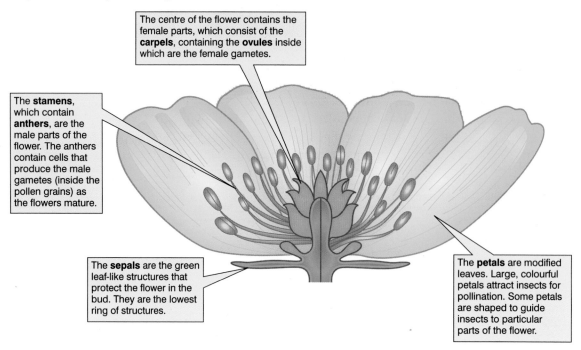

The centre of the flower contains the female parts, which consist of the **carpels**, containing the **ovules** inside which are the female gametes.

The **stamens**, which contain **anthers**, are the male parts of the flower. The anthers contain cells that produce the male gametes (inside the pollen grains) as the flowers mature.

The **sepals** are the green leaf-like structures that protect the flower in the bud. They are the lowest ring of structures.

The **petals** are modified leaves. Large, colourful petals attract insects for pollination. Some petals are shaped to guide insects to particular parts of the flower.

Δ Fig 16.6 Structure of an insect-pollinated flower.

The male part of a flower is the ring of **stamens**. There may be up to 100 stamens, or fewer than a dozen. Each stamen consists of two parts – the **anther** at the top and a stalk called the *filament*. Pollen grains develop inside the anthers. Inside each pollen grain is a male gamete. As a grain matures, it develops a thick outer wall to protect the delicate male gamete inside. When all the pollen grains in the anther are mature, the anther splits open to release them.

The female part of the flower is the **carpel**. A flower can contain more than one carpel, each with its own **style** and **stigma**. The **stigma** is the part of the carpel where the pollen lands during pollination. The **ovary** at the base of the carpel protects the female gamete from the dry air outside. The ovary contains one or more **ovules**, and each ovule contains an egg sac that surrounds the egg cell (female gamete).

Δ Fig 16.7 Alder catkins contain flowers that shed pollen into the air to be transported to other flowers.

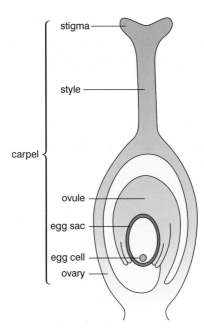

Δ Fig 16.8 The carpel.

◁ Fig 16.9 Even complex flowers like daisies, which contain thousands of male and female parts, have carpels surrounded by stamens.

QUESTIONS

1. Name the female parts of a flower, and describe the function of each part.

2. Name the male parts of a flower, and describe the function of each part.

Pollination

Before fertilisation can take place, the male gametes have to reach the female gametes. This involves transferring the pollen to the stigma, in a process known as *pollination*. In many plants this means transferring the pollen from one flower to another. Some plants use the wind to transfer their pollen between flowers; others use animals, especially insects, to carry the pollen. Flowers have different features depending on whether they are pollinated by wind or by insects.

Wind-pollinated plants	Insect-pollinated plants
small petals, which do not obstruct pollen dispersal	large petals for insects to land on
green or inconspicuous petals	brightly coloured petals to attract insects
no scent	often scented to attract insects
no nectaries	nectaries present at the base of the flower produce a sugary liquid to attract insects, e.g. bees and butterflies
many anthers, which are often large and hang outside the flower so that pollen is easily dispersed	a few small anthers, usually held inside the flower
pollen grains have smooth outer walls	pollen grains have sticky or spiky outer walls
stigmas are large and feathery, often hanging outside the flower to trap pollen	stigmas are small and held inside the flower
produce large amounts of pollen	produce smaller amounts of pollen
pollen is lightweight	pollen is heavier

△ Table 16.1 Comparison of wind-pollinated and insect-pollinated flowers.

△ Fig 16.10 In insect-pollinated plants, nectaries secrete a sugary liquid to attract insects.

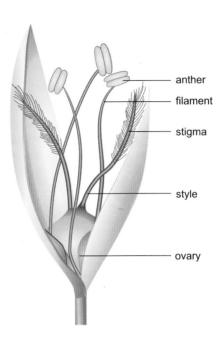

anther

filament

stigma

style

ovary

△ Fig 16.11 These grass plants have anthers that hang outside the flowers and release large amounts of pollen to the wind. The stigmas also hang outside the flower to collect pollen from other grass plants.

△ Fig 16.12 Pollen grains. Left: from a wind-pollinated plant (birch) with a simple smooth outer wall. Right: from an insect-pollinated flower (daisy), with a spiky coat that helps the grains stick to the hairs on an insect's body.

FLOWERS AND POLLINATORS

Different features of animal-pollinated flowers attract different pollinators. Tube-shaped flowers attract insects with a long tongue, such as butterflies, or birds with a long bill, such as hummingbirds. Blue and violet flowers are more attractive to bees, whereas butterflies often prefer red. Plants pollinated by moths or bats tend to open at night and may not be brightly coloured but instead produce a strong sweet scent. Plants that rely on flies to pollinate them often smell like rotting flesh.

One of the most bizarre partnerships between flower and insects occurs between a particular species of orchid and a wasp. Male wasps are attracted to the flowers to mate with what they think are female wasps. During the 'mating' the flowers deposit pollen on the insect, which then carries it to the next flower that it is attracted to.

△ Fig 16.13 A male wasp receiving pollen while 'mating' with an orchid flower.

REMEMBER

Be very careful not to confuse *pollination* with *fertilisation*.

EXTENDED

Self-pollination and cross-pollination

Cross-pollination occurs when the pollen from one plant transfers to the stigma of a different plant. However, plants can produce both male and female gametes, and it is possible for the pollen from one plant to pollinate its own stigma. This is called *self-pollination*.

Most flowering plants try to prevent self-pollination in one of several ways.

- Some plants produce only flowers of a single sex, which makes self-pollination impossible. For example, pistachio trees are single sex.
- Some plants have flowers that contain male and female parts, but the different parts mature at different times. For example, on a hemp plant the male flowers mature before the female. The female flowers mature before the male in the titan arum or bunga bangkai 'corpse flower' (*Amorphophallus titanum*).

- Even if pollen from one flower manages to reach its own stigma, the pollen grain will tend to grow more slowly than a foreign grain. This means that nuclei from foreign pollen grains are more likely to fertilise the egg cell in the ovule.

During the production of gametes it is random chance which chromosomes from the diploid parent cell move into each haploid gamete (see Topic 17). This means that there is some genetic variation between the gametes. However, in self-pollination all the gametes come from the same parent. This means that, when gametes in self-pollination fuse, there will be far more limited genetic variation in the offspring produced than there would be after cross-pollination.

Lack of variation in offspring is a disadvantage if environmental conditions change, because it is less likely that any offspring will have adaptations that suit the new conditions well. However, cross-pollination depends on the presence of suitable pollinators, which can be a problem if those pollinators are missing.

In just a few plant species, a flower will self-pollinate if cross-pollination doesn't occur. This means that seed will be produced so that new plants can grow.

END OF EXTENDED

SCIENCE IN CONTEXT

THE PROBLEM WITH BEES

About a third of all plants that we use for food or other uses depend on bees for pollination. This includes plants such as oilseed rape, cotton, coffee, apples and pears. If there are few bees, the crop harvest can be reduced by up to 75%. During the flowering season of crop plants, farmers and growers may place bee hives close to the crop to encourage successful pollination of most flowers. This helps to ensure a good harvest.

△ Fig. 16.14 By encouraging bees to build their hives in portable boxes, the farmer can move the hives to where the flowers of a crop are ready for pollination.

Recently people have become concerned about a large decrease in bee populations. There are many possible reasons for this. In some places, it has been suggested that the lack of a range of food plants, including weeds, has been the cause. An increase in the use of pesticides that also kill bees may be another cause of the fall in their numbers.

Without bees, food production will be greatly affected. So there are many studies being done to identify why bee numbers are decreasing and to work out how to improve the environment for bees.

Details of fertilisation

After pollination, the male gamete needs to get from the tip of the stigma to the ovule so that fertilisation (fusion with the female gamete) can take place. To do this, the pollen grain produces a thin tube called a **pollen tube**.

Fig. 16.15 shows how the pollen tube grows down through the style and into the ovule, and delivers the male gamete to the egg cell. Once fertilisation has taken place, the ovule and everything within it will develop into a seed.

A pollen grain lands on top of the stigma. If the egg cell is ready and the pollen grain is a suitable type, the grain starts to grow a pollen tube. The pollen tube grows down through the style and ovule wall.

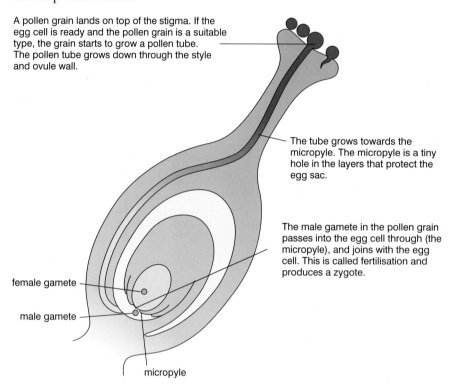

The tube grows towards the micropyle. The micropyle is a tiny hole in the layers that protect the egg sac.

The male gamete in the pollen grain passes into the egg cell through (the micropyle), and joins with the egg cell. This is called fertilisation and produces a zygote.

female gamete

male gamete

micropyle

△ Fig 16.15 Pollination leads to fertilisation.

QUESTIONS

1. Distinguish between *pollination* and *fertilisation* in a plant.

2. Describe *three* differences in structure between wind-pollinated and insect-pollinated flowers.

3. EXTENDED **a)** Explain the advantage to a flower of having adaptations for attracting insects rather than relying on wind for pollination.

   b) Describe one disadvantage for an insect-pollinated plant that relies on one or just a small number of insect species for pollination.

Germination

Germination is when the seed coat breaks open and the embryo starts to grow and develop into a new plant.

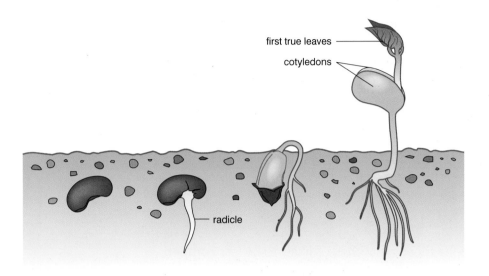

first true leaves

cotyledons

radicle

Δ Fig 16.16 Germination of a bean seed.

There are three environmental conditions that need to be right for seeds to germinate:

- temperature
- moisture
- oxygen.

The presence of light is not usually needed for germination. This is because most seeds germinate below ground, so they cannot get their food from photosynthesis.

Temperature

A seed will not start to germinate until the conditions around it reach a suitable temperature. Many seeds lie dormant for long a time during cold periods, such as winter, and start to grow as the earth warms. However, if the temperature becomes too hot the seed may be killed. This is why it is very important to store seeds in the correct conditions and to control the temperature in glasshouses carefully, e.g. through the use of ventilation and shading.

CONDITIONS FOR GERMINATION

Different plants are suited to different climates. Those that are adapted to colder climates will germinate at lower temperatures. They may also need a very cold period followed by an increase in temperature before they will germinate.

Other seeds will not germinate until they have been exposed to very high temperatures, such as the heat from a forest fire. The extreme heat weakens the seed coat so that water can enter the seed and germination can begin.

△ Fig 16.17 Fire clears the ground of competing plants, and stimulates these seeds to germinate in ideal conditions.

Germinating after a fire means that there is likely to be less competition with other species that usually cover the ground. Also, the ash left from the burning acts as a natural fertiliser for the new plants.

Water

Water is required to swell the seed and burst the seed coat. All seeds contain some moisture but during germination metabolic reactions are being carried out rapidly. More water is needed for:

- activation of hormones and enzymes
- hydrolysis of storage compounds, e.g. conversion of starch to glucose
- transport of materials to be used for respiration and growth
- metabolic reactions and enzyme actions that occur in solution.

Oxygen

Active living cells respire and the most useful form of respiration, aerobic respiration, requires oxygen. Seeds can use anaerobic respiration for a short while, but the rate at which energy is released is very slow (not useful in an actively growing organism) and the by-products are toxic. That is why most seeds will only germinate successfully if there is plenty of oxygen in the soil.

△ Fig 16.18 Waterlogged soil excludes oxygen, making it difficult for these seeds to germinate and grow.

Developing investigative skills

We can investigate the particular conditions for germination.

Devise and plan investigations

❶ Using the apparatus shown, write a plan to investigate the effect of (a) light, (b) water and (c) temperature on the germination of seeds. Think carefully about what controls to use in each case.

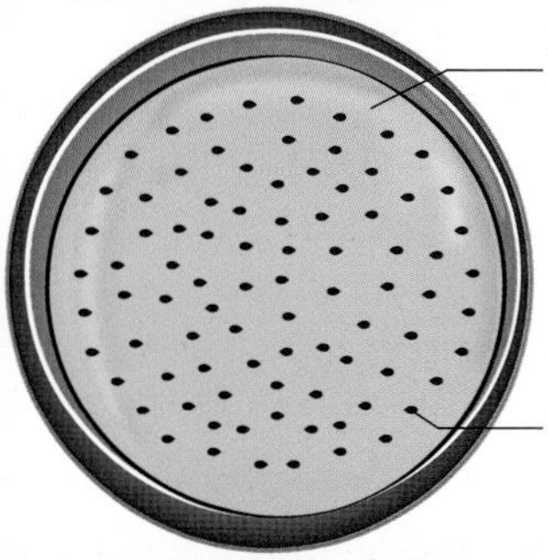

petri dish lined with damp paper towel

seed

△ Fig 16.19 A simple set-up for investigating seed germination.

Make observations and measurements

An investigation was carried out using two petri dishes containing 20 seeds of the same species. Both dishes received the same amount of light and moisture, but they were kept at different temperatures. The table shows the number of seeds that germinated over a period of 8 days.

Day	Total number germinated seedlings	
	Cool/10 °C	Warm/20 °C
1	0	0
2	0	0
3	0	5
4	1	11
5	6	15
6	16	17
7	18	17
8	18	17

❷ Display the results of this investigation in a suitable way.

Analyse and interpret data

❸ Describe the patterns shown by these results.

❹ Draw a conclusion from these results.

❺ Explain the results using your scientific knowledge.

1. What is *germination*?

2. What effect do the following conditions have on germination of seed? Explain why they have these effects.

   a) oxygen

   b) moisture

   c) warmth

SEXUAL REPRODUCTION IN HUMANS

Male reproductive system

A human male has two **testes** (singular: testis) in which **sperm** are produced. The testes are supported outside the body in the scrotum to keep them cooler, because at higher temperatures fewer sperm are produced.

Sperm ducts carry the sperm from the testes to the penis, through the prostate gland and seminal vesicles. The prostate gland and seminal vesicles together produce the liquid in which the sperm are able to swim. Semen is the mixture of sperm cells and fluids.

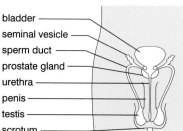

Semen passes along the sperm duct to the urethra to outside the body. The urethra also carries urine from the bladder to outside the body. When the man is sexually excited, large spaces in the penis fill with blood. This causes the penis to become larger and stiffer causing an erection. At the same time a muscle ring (sphincter) at the top of the urethra contracts, preventing urine entering the urethra from the bladder.

△ Fig 16.20 The male reproductive system. (Note that the bladder is not part of the reproductive system.)

The erection makes it possible for the man to insert his penis into the vagina of the woman for sexual intercourse. Rapid contractions of muscles in the penis during ejaculation send the sperm shooting out into the vagina.

Female reproductive system

The two **ovaries** are the organs in humans that produce the eggs. They are positioned within the abdominal cavity, either side of the **uterus** and joined to it by the **oviducts**.

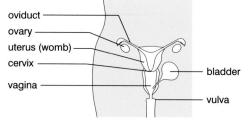

Every month from puberty until menopause, when a woman is around 50 years old, one ovary usually releases one egg, which travels down the oviduct to the uterus (womb). If it is not fertilised, the egg will be flushed from the uterus during the monthly period (bleed). At the lower end of the uterus is the **cervix**. This canal produces mucus which changes during the menstrual cycle, allowing sperm to pass through at some times (see page 303–304) and not

△ Fig 16.21 The female reproductive system. (Note that the bladder is not part of the reproductive system.)

others. It also keeps the developing baby secure in the uterus until birth. The cervix leads into the vagina. The **vagina** is an elastic muscular tube where sperm is received from the penis during sexual intercourse.

Human gametes

The human gametes are specialised for their roles in reproduction (see Topic 2). The adaptive features of the sperm include the flagellum and the presence of enzymes. The adaptive features of the egg cells include the jelly coating, which changes after fertilisation, and the energy stores. Fig. 16.22 shows the main adaptive features of the human sperm cell and egg cell.

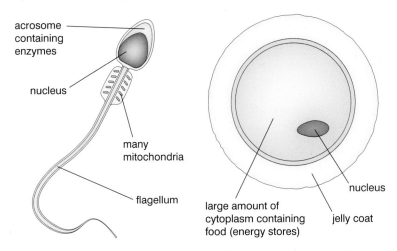

△ Fig 16.22 Left: human sperm. Right: human egg. (Not to scale: the egg cell is around five times larger than the length of a sperm cell.)

EXTENDED

Sperm are among the smallest cells in the human body, at about 45 micrometres long. Over 100 million sperm cells are produced each day. There are many mitochondria in the part of the sperm between the head and the flagellum (tail). The mitochondria provide energy from respiration that allows the flagellum to beat back and forth to move the sperm cell.

Most of the cell is formed by the flagellum, which propels the sperm through the female uterus to the egg for fertilisation. At the front tip of the sperm is a small sac of enzymes called the **acrosome**. When a sperm reaches an egg cell, the acrosome bursts open to release the enzymes. The enzymes digest through the jelly coat and cell membrane of the egg cell, allowing the male nucleus to enter the egg cell.

The egg cell is one of the largest human cells, at about 0.2 mm in diameter. It cannot move on its own, but is wafted along the oviduct by cilia on the inside of the tube. An ovary may contain thousands of egg cells, but only one is usually released from one ovary at **ovulation** each month. Within the egg cell is the nucleus and a large amount of cytoplasm. The cytoplasm provides nutrients for the dividing zygote after fertilisation. Surrounding the cell membrane is a jelly coat that protects the cell. Immediately after fertilisation by one sperm, the jelly coat changes to an impenetrable barrier. This prevents other sperm nuclei entering the egg cell.

END OF EXTENDED

QUESTIONS

1. a) Sketch a diagram of the human male reproductive system.

  b) Add labels to your sketch to name the main parts of the system.

  c) Describe the role of each of the main parts of the system in human reproduction.

2. a) Sketch a diagram of the human female reproductive system.

  b) Add labels to your sketch to name the main parts of the system.

  c) Describe the role of each of the main parts of the system in human reproduction.

3. EXTENDED Draw up a table to compare the size, numbers and mobility of human egg and sperm cells.

Fertilisation and development of the fetus

During sexual intercourse, sperm deposited near the cervix swim up into the uterus, and then along the oviduct to the egg. Many sperm fail to make the journey, but some will reach the oviducts at the top end of the uterus.

The egg will have been travelling along the oviduct while the sperm have been swimming up from the uterus. Fertilisation takes place in the oviduct. The nucleus of one sperm cell fuses with the nucleus of the egg cell, forming a fertilised egg, or zygote.

After fertilisation in the oviduct, the fertilised egg (zygote) travels on towards the uterus. The journey takes about 3 days, during which time the zygote will divide several times to form a ball of 64 cells, which is now called an **embryo**.

In the uterus, the embryo embeds in the thickened lining (**implantation**) and cell division and growth continue. For the first 3 months, the embryo gets nutrients from the mother by diffusion through the uterus lining.

By the end of 3 months, the placenta has developed, and the embryo has become a **fetus** in which all the main organs of the body can be identified.

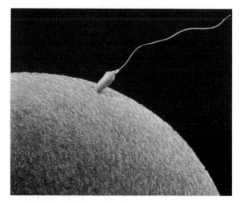

△ Fig 16.23 The moment just before fertilisation: sperm approaching an egg.

Over the next 28 weeks the fetus will increase its mass roughly 8 million times. At no other point in an individual's lifetime will growth occur at such a high rate. This period of development in the uterus is

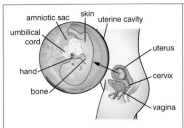	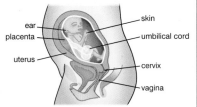	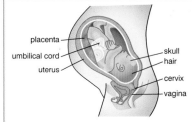
11 weeks: • fetus about 4 cm long • most of the main body structures have formed	**23 weeks:** • fetus about 29 cm long and weighs about 500 g • fetus hears sound from outside, and moves	**40 weeks:** • fetus is about 51 cm long and weighs about 3.4 kg • all organs fully developed ready for birth

Δ Fig 16.24 The fetus in the uterus at three time points during gestation.

SCIENCE IN CONTEXT

ULTRASOUND SCANS

Ultrasound is very high frequency sound, far above the frequency that can be heard. It is used in medical imaging for showing soft tissues inside the body. It is particularly useful for looking at the developing fetus in the uterus, because it does not harm either the fetus or the mother.

An ultrasound scan is commonly done about halfway through gestation, to make sure that the fetus is developing normally. At about this stage, if the fetus is lying at the right angle, it may even be possible to tell if it is a male fetus because the testes can be distinguished at this age.

Ultrasound scans may be done at other times during gestation if there is any concern about the development of the fetus.

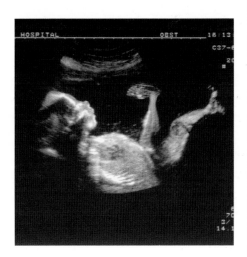

Δ Fig 16.25 This ultrasound scan was taken in the 20th week of gestation and shows that the fetus is developing normally.

---

known as *gestation*, and it lasts about 40 weeks in humans, measured from the time of the woman's last period. The rapid growth during gestation depends on a good supply of food and oxygen, provided by the mother.

The fetus develops inside a bag of fluid called **amniotic fluid.** This fluid is produced from the amniotic membrane that forms the outer layer of the bag (**amniotic sac**). The fluid protects the fetus from mechanical damage, for example if the mother moves suddenly. It also reduces the effect of large temperature variations that would affect the rate of development of the fetus. One of the signs that birth will happen soon is when this bag bursts shortly before labour. Once the placenta has formed, until birth, it is the only way that the developing fetus exchanges materials with the outside world. Birth occurs when all the organs of the fetus are fully developed and ready to carry out the life processes on their own.

The **placenta** is an organ that is produced by the growing fetus. The placenta allows a constant exchange of materials between the mother and fetus. The fetus is joined to the placenta by the umbilical cord, which carries the blood vessels of the fetus.

The placenta and the uterus wall have a large number of blood vessels that run very close to each other, but do not touch. So maternal and fetal blood do not mix. If they did, the higher blood pressure in the mother could damage the fetus. The structure of the placenta also helps to prevent many pathogens and some chemicals getting into the blood of the fetus. However, some pathogens (such as the rubella virus) and chemicals (such as nicotine from tobacco smoke) are small enough to cross through the placenta from the mother into the fetus and cause harm to the fetus.

Dissolved food molecules, oxygen and other nutrients that the fetus needs for growth diffuse from the mother's blood into the blood of the fetus. Waste products from metabolism, such as carbon dioxide and urea, in the fetus's blood diffuse across into the mother's blood.

QUESTIONS

1. Define the following terms in your own words: a) *zygote*, b) *embryo*, c) *fetus*.

2. Where in the human body does fertilisation of the egg cell occur?

3. Briefly describe how the fetus develops up to the point of birth.

4. EXTENDED Describe the role of the placenta during the development of a fetus.

Ante-natal care

Ante-natal care is the care that pregnant women get before their baby is born. During this time, they will receive checks from a doctor or midwife to make sure that they are healthy and to make sure that the fetus is developing well. Health checks include:

• encouraging the woman to give up smoking during pregnancy
• advice on how little alcohol should be drunk, and which drugs to avoid

- advice on food preparation to avoid food-borne infections such as from some types of cheese
- checks on the pregnant woman's blood for iron content, with a prescription for iron if this is low
- possible screening tests for some conditions in the fetus
- advice on a healthy diet, including taking folic acid to avoid development problems (such as spina bifida) in the fetus
- advice on what exercise is suitable and how to remain fit during pregnancy.

In addition, the mother-to-be will probably receive instruction on what to expect during labour and birth, and on breast-feeding after birth.

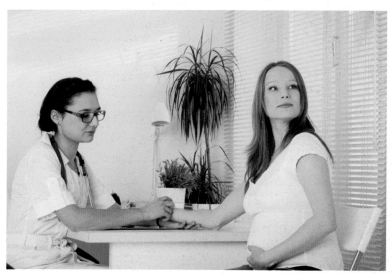

△ Fig 16.26 Urine and blood tests of pregnant women can show if the fetus is developing properly and check that the mother is healthy.

Labour and birth

Birth is the final part of a process called **labour**, which takes hours, sometimes days. Labour starts with contractions of the uterus wall, which goes hard during these contractions. As labour proceeds the contractions become longer, occur more often and become more painful. Another sign of labour starting may be a show of blood-tinged mucus, which is the plug at the entrance to the uterus. A flow of water from the vagina, often called the 'breaking of the waters', shows labour is near, as does unexpected diarrhoea or sickness.

At the hospital the mother-to-be will be checked to make sure all is progressing well. She may be linked to monitors that can follow her blood pressure and heart rate, as well as the heart rate of the fetus.

The next stage of labour can last some hours. During this stage the muscles of the uterus are opening up (dilation) the cervix so that the baby can pass through. Periodically a doctor or midwife will check to see how far the cervix has dilated. Contractions at this point can become quite painful and doctors can prescribe different kinds of pain relief.

When the cervix has fully dilated, the mother will feel an urge to push. In the final stage of labour contractions of the uterus wall and pushing by the mother push the baby through the vagina and the baby is born. In most cases the baby is born head first. A breech birth happens when the baby is born feet first. Breech births need to be very carefully managed by the midwife to prevent damage to the mother or baby due to tangling of, or damage to, the umbilical cord.

Birth of the baby is followed after 10 minutes or so by delivery of the afterbirth, which is mainly the placenta. The umbilical cord is clamped or tied off and cut to separate the baby from the placenta, which is no longer needed.

Feeding after birth

After birth, the first milk produced by the mother does not look like milk at all. This is the watery colostrum, which contains antibodies that protect the baby from infection in the first few days and months of life (see Topic 10). By about the third day after birth the normal milk begins to come through.

△ Fig 16.27 Mother breast-feeding her baby.

Human breast milk contains a mixture of chemicals that are different from the milk of any other animal. The levels of these chemicals can be measured and used to produce an artificial 'human' milk by modifying milk from other animals. These are called *formula milks*. However, it is impossible to produce a formula milk exactly like human milk. Doctors currently believe that breast milk is the best milk for growing babies if it is available and the mother is able to feed her baby.

	Breast milk	Formula (bottle) milk
Advantages	perfectly matched to baby's needs; contains antibodies that help to protect the baby from infection; always sterile and safe for baby	does not require a mother to provide it; can be more convenient in some circumstances
Disadvantages	nipples can become painful; some women find it difficult to produce enough milk at first	does not provide the antibodies of breast milk, so child is at greater risk of infection; sterile water and clean conditions are required to make up a feed; this can be difficult in certain areas

△ Table 16.2 Comparison of breast milk and formula milk.

END OF EXTENDED

QUESTIONS

1. Explain what is meant by *ante-natal care*.

2. Explain why a midwife will advise on what a woman should eat and drink during pregnancy, giving examples.

3. Give two signs that labour is beginning.

4. **EXTENDED** a) Why is breast-feeding a baby usually better for its health?

    b) Suggest one situation in which a baby might need to be bottle-fed.

SEX HORMONES IN HUMANS

Testosterone is the male sex hormone.

Testosterone is secreted from the testes.

At puberty, the increased secretion of testosterone causes the development of the following **secondary sexual characteristics** in boys:

- an increase in rate of growth until adult size
- hair growth on face and body, including pubic hair
- penis, testes and scrotum growth and development
- deepening of voice
- increased muscle development
- sperm production.

The female sex hormones are **progesterone** and **oestrogen**.

Progesterone and oestrogen are both produced in the ovaries.

At puberty, increased secretion of oestrogen causes the development of the following secondary sexual characteristics in girls:

- an increase in rate of growth until adult size
- breast development
- vagina, oviducts and uterus development
- start of menstrual cycle (periods)
- hips widening
- pubic hair and under-arm hair growth.

These hormones also control the changes that occur during the **menstrual cycle**.

The menstrual cycle

The menstrual cycle is a sequence of changes that occur in a woman's body every month. The average cycle is 28 days long, but it is normal for it to vary in different women.

The cycle begins with the monthly period, or bleeding, which is produced from the breakdown of the thickened lining of the uterus. After this, the uterus lining starts to thicken again. **Ovulation** occurs about halfway through the cycle, when an egg is released from one of the ovaries. The egg travels along the oviduct to the uterus.

If the egg is fertilised during this time, the egg will implant in the uterus lining and the lining will continue to develop for pregnancy. If the egg is not fertilised, the cell and the uterus lining are shed during the monthly period at the start of the next cycle.

The release of the egg from an ovary and the thickening of the uterus lining are controlled by the hormones oestrogen and progesterone from the ovaries, and luteinising hormone (**LH**) and follicle-stimulating hormone (**FSH**) produced by the pituitary gland in the brain.

- The first day of the cycle is taken to be the point when the lining of the uterus prepared for the previous egg starts to break down.
- At this point FSH is released from the pituitary gland and stimulates the development of an egg cell in the ovary.
- Cells surrounding the developing egg secrete increasing amounts of oestrogen.
- The oestrogen stimulates the lining of the uterus to repair and thicken.
- High levels of oestrogen in the body cause the pituitary gland to release more LH.
- About 2 weeks through the cycle (around day 14), high levels of LH cause an egg to be released from the ovary into the oviduct. This is

called ovulation. When this happens, cells in the ovary start to secrete progesterone, which reduces the amounts of LH and FSH released from the pituitary gland.

- Progesterone stimulates the uterus lining to thicken even more in preparation of receiving a fertilised egg.
- If the egg is not fertilised, the concentrations of oestrogen and progesterone start to fall.
- The fall in hormone concentration causes the uterus lining to break down – it is lost from the body during menstruation (a period).
- When the hormone concentrations are low enough, the pituitary gland starts to release more FSH and another egg starts to develop in one of the ovaries. The cycle begins again.

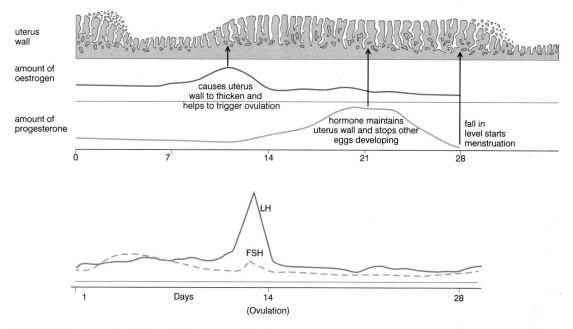

△ Fig 16.28 Hormone levels through the menstrual cycle.

If the egg is fertilised, then progesterone continues to be released from the ovary. This maintains the uterus lining during pregnancy and prevents further ovulation.

END OF EXTENDED

QUESTIONS

1. Name the male sex hormone.

2. Name two female sex hormones produced in the ovary.

3. Describe the role of secondary sexual characteristics in humans.

4. Define the following terms in your own words: **a)** *ovulation*, **b)** *menstrual cycle*.

5. EXTENDED Name four hormones that control the menstrual cycle and briefly explain the role of each hormone.

METHODS OF BIRTH CONTROL IN HUMANS

Sometimes people want to have sexual intercourse but not produce children. This is particularly important for couples who want to plan when, and how many, children they have. Using methods to prevent the formation of a baby is called **contraception**. The list below shows the most common methods of contraception.

Natural methods

Avoiding sexual intercourse completely is called **abstinence**. Without sexual intercourse, fertilisation and pregnancy cannot occur. However, many couples find abstinence difficult because of the emotional aspects of intercourse.

Another method is the **rhythm method**, which relies on the fact that the egg is only likely to be fertilised for a few days after ovulation. Avoidance of intercourse during this time, or withdrawing the penis before ejaculation, may reduce the chance of pregnancy but it is the least reliable method of birth control. Sperm can survive for up to 48 hours in the uterus, so if intercourse takes place one night and the ovulation occurs the next morning a pregnancy may result. A development of this method uses the woman's body temperature or quality of cervical mucus to monitor the moment of ovulation, but this only helps to predict ovulation more accurately.

Chemical methods

Use of a cream or foam containing a **spermicide** (chemical that kills sperm) can kill sperm in the vagina. This method is not considered very effective by itself and is usually used with other methods such as condoms or diaphragms (see below). Some women are allergic to the chemicals in the spermicides.

The **contraceptive pill** (commonly called 'the pill') may contain just progesterone, or a mixture of progesterone and oestrogen. The pill is very effective when taken regularly. However, if a pill is missed, other forms of contraception are needed for a while in case ovulation occurs at that point. These hormones can also be delivered from a small skin implant, or by injection, which lasts for several months and so increases the effectiveness of preventing fertilisation.

EXTENDED

The use of hormones in the contraceptive pill works because they mimic some of the hormone levels during pregnancy. By raising the concentration of progesterone and oestrogen in the body, the uterus lining is maintained. This stops the development of another egg cell even though the previous egg cell has not been fertilised, and it prevents ovulation.

END OF EXTENDED

An intrauterine system (**IUS**) is a small T-shaped object that is fitted inside the uterus by a doctor or nurse. The IUS releases sex hormone that thickens the mucus from the cervix, making it difficult for sperm to swim into the uterus. It also thins the lining of the uterus, making it more difficult for a fertilised egg to settle into the lining and develop into an embryo.

Mechanical methods

Mechanical methods work by preventing the sperm from reaching the egg. A **condom** is a thin sheath of rubber that is placed over the man's erect penis before intercourse. This prevents sperm getting into the vagina. There is also a female version, called a **femidom**, which the woman can insert in her vagina before intercourse to capture the sperm. A **diaphragm** or cap can be used by the woman in a similar way. This fits over the entrance to the cervix. Both condoms and diaphragms are used with spermicides that help to kill sperm in case of any leakage. Another advantage of condoms is that they offer some protection against sexually transmitted infections, including human immunodeficiency virus (**HIV**). These mechanical methods are fairly successful in preventing pregnancy unless they break or are not positioned correctly.

◁ Fig 16.29 The wide range of birth control methods available means that different couples can usually find something that fits their needs.

An intrauterine device (**IUD**) is similar to an IUS as it is a small T-shaped object that can be fitted inside the uterus by a doctor or nurse. However, it works in a different way from the IUS, in that it interferes with the passage of the sperm to the egg, and prevents a fertilised egg from implanting in the uterus wall. An IUD can be left in place for several years, during which time the contraceptive effect is 100%.

Both chemical and mechanical methods are temporary. When the couple decide they want children they can stop using them, and pregnancy should follow as normal.

Surgical methods

To prevent fertilisation from ever happening, surgery can be used to cut the tubes along which the sex cells travel. In men this means cutting the sperm ducts, which is called **vasectomy**. In women, **female sterilisation** involves cutting the oviducts. These operations are very difficult to reverse, so they are recommended only for couples who are certain that they want no more children.

Solving fertility problems

Not all those who wish to have children find it easy to conceive. In the past there was little that could be done about this and couples had to accept a childless life. Nowadays fertility treatment can help these people.

One method of fertility treatment is **artificial insemination** (**AI**). Here semen is introduced into the female reproductive tract by artificial means rather than through intercourse. Alternatively, **in vitro fertilisation** (**IVF**) may be used. *In vitro* literally means 'in glass' and refers to the fact that the gametes are taken out of the body and mixed together in a dish or tube to bring about fertilisation. A developing embryo (or two) is then placed in the woman's uterus to develop as normal.

There are greater risks of damaging the embryo in IVF than in AI, but the advantage is that the embryo can be tested to make sure it is fully healthy before placing it in the woman. And this can increase the chance of producing a healthy baby.

Fertility treatment might be carried out if the man is making only a few sperm or sperm that are not very strong. The sperm can be prepared to make them more effective before AI or IVF is completed. If the man makes no sperm at all, the semen may come from another man, called a sperm donor.

In some instances the woman in a couple may be unable to carry a baby to full term. In such a case artificial insemination of a surrogate mother using the father's sperm can be successful. If the woman is not releasing eggs properly from the ovaries, **fertility drugs** may be used to stimulate her ovaries to release eggs. Using drugs like this has a risk of releasing several eggs at once, and resulting in several fetuses developing at the same time, which can cause problems for the mother or for the babies after birth.

Fertility treatment has helped large numbers of people to have a family and thus improved the quality of their lives. However, many of the procedures are very expensive and the multiple births that sometimes occur following the use of fertility drugs can be a burden on family resources. Some women have used treatment to conceive at a later time in life than would be normal for childbearing and the advisability of this is questioned by some.

More recently there have been concerns about the legal rights of sperm donors and surrogate mothers, and about the right of a child to know who their 'natural' parent is.

END OF EXTENDED

QUESTIONS

1. Suggest why some couples may wish to use birth control methods.

2. Which methods of birth control produce 100% prevention of pregnancy if used correctly?

3. Explain why most natural methods of birth control are the least successful in preventing pregnancy.

4. Give one advantage of using mechanical methods of birth control apart from preventing pregnancy.

5. Explain why surgical methods of birth control prevent pregnancy.

6. EXTENDED Explain how artificial insemination may assist a couple to have a child.

7. EXTENDED Describe one advantage and disadvantage of using fertility drugs with a childless couple.

SEXUALLY TRANSMITTED INFECTIONS (STIs)

Unfortunately, sexual intercourse is a method by which infection can spread, because of the exchange of body fluids, which may contain pathogens (see Topic 10). There are many **sexually transmitted infections** (STIs), including HIV, which usually leads to acquired immunodeficiency disease (**AIDS**).

AIDS

AIDS is a disease of the immune system caused by a virus called HIV. The virus in an infected person is present in sexual fluids such as semen and vaginal fluids, and so can be transmitted during sexual intercourse. It may also be passed to another person in blood, either through a scratch, or through the sharing of needles for intravenous injection of drugs such as heroin (see Topic 15). Infection can also pass from a mother to her fetus, through the placenta, or to her baby through breast-feeding after birth.

There is no cure for AIDS, so prevention of infection is essential. This is most easily done by abstinence from sex, or by limiting sexual partners to those who do not carry the virus. As a person may have no obvious symptoms early in infection, barrier methods such as the condom or femidom are most effective in reducing the risk of infection during intercourse.

△ Fig 16.30 Advertising: the use of condoms during sexual intercourse can help prevent the spread of the HIV virus.

EXTENDED

Infection with HIV damages the immune system that protects the body against infection (see Topic 10). Normally lymphocytes seek out and destroy invading bacteria and viruses. HIV avoids being recognised and destroyed by lymphocytes by repeatedly changing its outer 'coat'. It multiplies within one type of lymphocyte. This reduces the number of lymphocytes, and so the amount of antibodies that can be made, which decreases the body's ability to fight off infection, eventually leading to AIDS.

END OF EXTENDED

QUESTIONS

1. Explain what we mean by a *sexually transmitted disease*.

2. Describe the methods of transmission of HIV.

3. EXTENDED Describe the effect of HIV on the body.

4. EXTENDED Describe two ways to prevent the transmission of HIV during sexual intercourse.

End of topic checklist

Key words

AIDS, amniotic fluid, ante-natal care, anther, artificial insemination, asexual reproduction, carpel, contraception, diploid, embryo, fertilisation, fertility drug, fetus, fruit, FSH, gamete, germination, haploid, HIV, in vitro fertilisation (IVF), labour, LH, menstrual cycle, oestrogen, ovary, ovulation, ovule, placenta, pollination, progesterone, secondary sexual characteristic, seed, sexual reproduction, sexually transmitted infection, sperm, stamen, stigma, style, testis, testosterone, uterus, zygote

During your study of this topic you should have learned:

○ How to define a sexual reproduction as the production of new individuals without fertilisation. It is the division of the body cells of one parent. It produces offspring that are genetically identical to the parent and to each other.

○ How to define sexual reproduction as the production of new individuals from the fusion of a male gamete and a female gamete during fertilisation. It requires two parents, and produces offspring that are genetically different to their parents and to each other.

○ That fertilisation of a male gamete and female gamete produces a zygote that develops into an embryo by cell division.

○ How to identify the male and female parts of a flower.

○ An insect-pollinated flower has features such as coloured petals, scent and nectaries to attract insects to feed at the flower. The insects pick up pollen, which they transfer to other flowers that they move on to.

○ A wind-pollinated flower is usually small, without colour, scent or nectaries. It produces a large amount of lightweight pollen, which is scattered over a large distance in the wind.

○ That some plant species self-pollinate and some only cross-pollinate.

○ EXTENDED After pollination, a pollen tube grows down inside the style to deliver the male gamete to the female gamete in the ovule.

○ EXTENDED How to define self-pollination and cross-pollination.

○ Seeds need moisture, oxygen and warmth for successful germination.

○ How to identify and name the human male reproductive system, including the testes where sperm are made; the sperm ducts, which carry the sperm to the urethra; the prostate gland and seminal vesicles, which produce liquid in which the sperm swim; the penis, which when erect delivers sperm into the vagina of the woman; and the urethra, which carries the sperm from the sperm ducts to the outside of the body.

End of topic checklist continued

○ How to identify and name the human female reproductive system, including the ovaries, where the egg cells are made; the oviducts, which carry the eggs to the uterus and where fertilisation takes place with sperm cells; the uterus, where the embryo embeds and develops into a fetus; the cervix, where sperm are deposited at the base of the uterus; and the vagina, where the penis is inserted during sexual intercourse.

○ Testosterone in men and oestrogen in women are the sex hormones that control the development of secondary sexual characteristics.

○ The menstrual cycle and egg is released from the ovary, and the uterus lining thickens. If fertilisation does not take place, the uterus lining and egg are shed at the start of the next cycle.

○ EXTENDED The hormones oestrogen and progesterone from the ovaries, and LH and FSH from the pituitary gland, control the menstrual cycle.

○ Once the embryo has embedded in the uterus wall, it develops the placenta. This is where nutrients and waste materials are exchanged between the blood of the mother and of the fetus.

○ During development, the embryo (and later the fetus) is protected from mechanical damage and temperature fluctuations by amniotic fluid that surrounds it in the amniotic sac.

○ EXTENDED That some toxins can pass across the placenta and affect the fetus.

○ How to describe ante-natal care as the care of the mother before the birth of her baby.

○ How to outline the processes involved in labour and birth.

○ EXTENDED Breast-feeding of a baby is usually better than bottle-feeding, because of the balance of nutrients and antibodies that are in the milk.

○ How to outline methods of birth control, including natural methods, chemical methods, mechanical methods or surgical methods.

○ EXTENDED That hormones may be used in contraception and fertility treatments, and these have social implications.

○ EXTENDED Artificial insemination (AI) or in vitro fertilisation (IVF) may be used to help a couple have a child.

○ AIDS is a disease caused by a virus that may be transmitted during sexual intercourse, or in blood, through the placenta or in breast milk.

○ EXTENDED HIV causes AIDS by damaging the immune system, so the person may be infected by other pathogens.

End of topic questions

1. The photograph in Fig. 16.31 shows a catkin on a goat willow tree. A catkin is formed from a group of flowers.

   △ Fig. 16.31 A goat willow catkin.

   a) What is the purpose of the flowers on a goat willow tree? **(1 mark)**

   b) Name the yellow parts of the flowers shown in this photograph. **(1 mark)**

   c) Describe their purpose in a flower. **(1 mark)**

   d) Are goat willow flowers pollinated by the wind or by insects? Explain your answer using clues from the photograph. **(3 marks)**

2. **a)** Explain the advantage to a flower of having adaptations for attracting insects rather than relying on wind for pollination. **(1 mark)**

   b) Describe one disadvantage for an insect-pollinated plant of relying on one or just a small number of insect species for pollination. **(1 marks)**

3. EXTENDED In many flowers that have stamens and stigmas, the stamens mature and shed their pollen before the stigma matures and accepts pollen.

   a) Describe and explain one advantage for the plant of doing this. **(2 marks)**

   b) Describe and explain one disadvantage for the plant of doing this. **(2 marks)**

4. EXTENDED Aphids are common pests of crop plants. In countries where the climate is seasonal, they reproduce in different ways at different times of the year. During the summer, when there is a lot of food about, female aphids reproduce asexually. As it gets cooler towards winter and plants start to die back, winged males and females reproduce sexually. Fertilised eggs are laid that survive through the winter, and hatch into females in the spring.

   a) Describe and explain two features of reproducing asexually that allow aphids to be successful during the summer. **(4 marks)**

   b) Describe one feature of sexual reproduction that helps aphids to be successful in the following year. **(4 marks)**

5. A gardener has some packets of seeds for planting. The packets explain how to plant the seeds to get the best germination.

   a) What is meant by *germination*? **(1 mark)**

   b) All the packets say that the seeds need to be planted in moist compost and kept warm. Explain why the seeds need these conditions. **(2 marks)**

c) Explain why the seeds will not germinate successfully in waterlogged soil.

(2 marks)

d) The larger seeds need to be planted deeper in the compost, and the tiniest seeds need to be scattered on the surface of the compost. Explain why different seeds need to be planted at different depths. (Hint: think about food reserves.) **(3 marks)**

e) Some seeds that come from plants in high-latitude regions (such as Canada or Russia) need to be placed in the freezer for a few weeks before they will germinate. This makes them respond as if they had been through a cold winter. Explain the survival advantage of this adaptation. **(2 marks)**

6. a) Where are sperm cells made in the human body? **(1 mark)**

b) Where are egg cells made in the human body? **(1 mark)**

c) Where is an egg cell fertilised by a sperm cell? **(1 mark)**

d) Starting from the point of their formation, explain how a sperm cell reaches the egg cell at fertilisation. **(4 marks)**

7. a) Draw the menstrual cycle as a circle of 28 days. On your diagram label:

i) ovulation **(1 mark)**

ii) menstruation **(1 mark)**

iii) EXTENDED increases and decreases in oestrogen secretion **(2 marks)**

iv) EXTENDED increases and decreases in progesterone secretion. **(2 marks)**

b) EXTENDED Describe the role of LH and FSH in the control of the menstrual cycle. **(2 marks)**

8. a) What is the *placenta*? **(1 mark)**

b) What role does the placenta play in supporting the fetus? **(1 mark)**

c) EXTENDED How are substances exchanged across the placenta? **(2 marks)**

d) EXTENDED What is the advantage of keeping the mother's blood separated from the blood of the fetus? **(1 mark)**

9. Explain as fully as you can why, during ante-natal care, a woman will be advised to give up smoking. **(5 marks)**

10. Draw up a table to show the advantages and disadvantages of different
methods of birth control. **(14 marks)**

11. a) Explain why HIV is classified as a sexually transmitted infection. **(1 mark)**

   b) Describe two ways that HIV can be transmitted from a mother
   to her baby. **(2 marks)**

   c) EXTENDED Explain why someone with HIV is unlikely to die from
   that virus, but may die from other infections. **(2 marks)**

In the 1990s an international group of scientists embarked on the Human Genome Project, an ambitious research effort to read the whole sequence of human DNA and identify all the genes that it contained. Completed in 2003, the project surprisingly found that the 3 billion or so base pairs of DNA that make up the human genome equate to only about 20 000 genes, far fewer than was originally thought.

CONTENTS

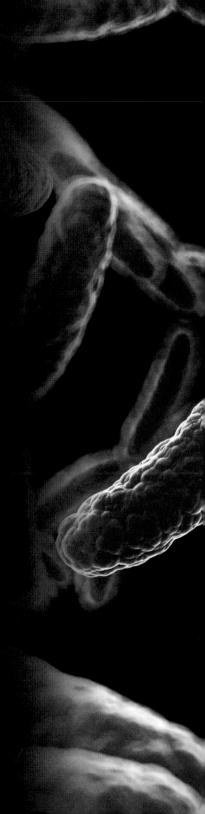

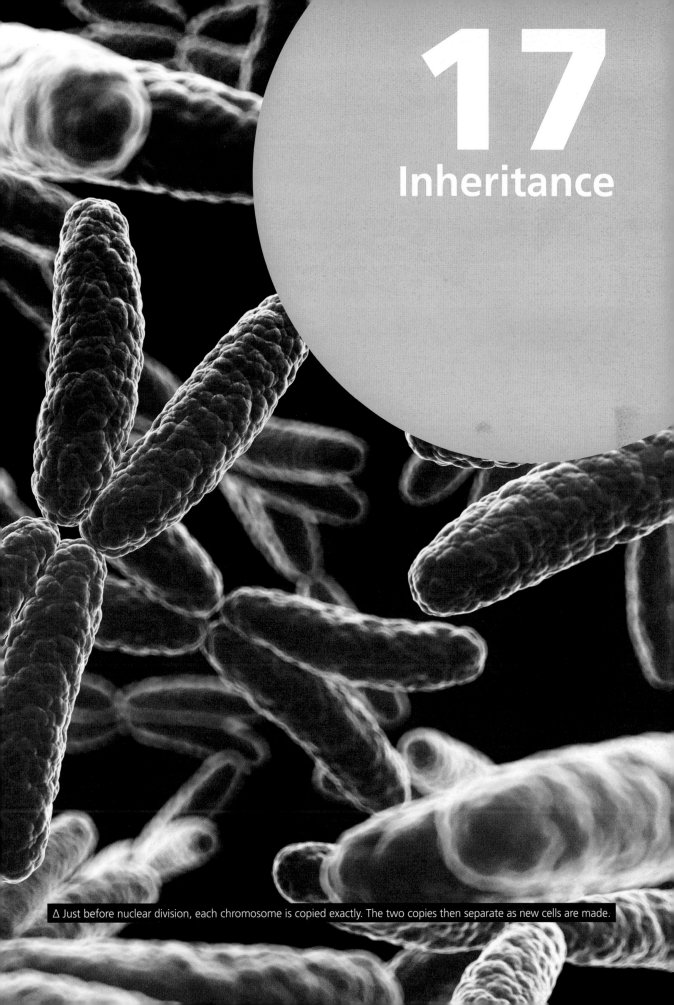

17
Inheritance

△ Just before nuclear division, each chromosome is copied exactly. The two copies then separate as new cells are made.

△ Fig 17.1 This baby will have inherited some characteristics from her mother and some from her father.

Inheritance

INTRODUCTION

Unless a zygote (fertilised egg) divides completely into two separate cells on its first division, and develops as two identical twins, the baby that develops from that zygote is genetically unique. Each cell in a zygote contains genetic information, half of which came from the father and half from the mother. And during gamete formation, some changes will have occurred in some of that genetic information. So the baby will have about 100 variations in its genes that neither of its parents has. Interestingly, although the baby is genetically unique, virtually all of the cells in its body are genetically identical.

KNOWLEDGE CHECK

✓ Organisms show variation in their features.
✓ Genes are small parts of the genetic information (DNA) found in the nucleus of a cell.

LEARNING OBJECTIVES

✓ Define inheritance as the transmission of genetic material from one generation to the next.
✓ Describe a chromosome as a thread of DNA made up of a string of genes.
✓ Define a gene as a small length of DNA that codes for a specific protein or characteristic.
✓ Describe alleles as different forms of the same gene that produce variations of the same protein or characteristic.
✓ Describe the inheritance of sex in humans.
✓ EXTENDED Explain the relationship between the sequence of bases in a gene and the order of amino acids in a protein.
✓ EXTENDED Explain how a protein is made using DNA from the nucleus, RNA and ribosomes.
✓ EXTENDED Explain that cells differ even though they contain the same genes because not all genes are expressed.
✓ EXTENDED Define *haploid nucleus* and *diploid nucleus* in terms of human cells.
✓ Define mitosis as the division of the nucleus of a cell giving rise to two genetically identical cells, during growth, repair of tissues or asexual reproduction.
✓ EXTENDED Describe how chromosomes duplicate and separate in mitosis to maintain the chromosome number.
✓ EXTENDED Describe the roles of embryonic and adult stem cells in humans.
✓ Define meiosis as division of the nucleus of a cell giving rise to genetically different cells, such as in the production of gametes.

✓ Describe meiosis as the division of a diploid cell to produce four haploid cells that show genetic variation, during the formation of gametes.

✓ Define important terms in genetics including: *dominant*, *recessive*, *homozygous*, *heterozygous*, *phenotype* and *genotype*.

✓ Use genetic diagrams and Punnett squares to predict the result of monohybrid crosses.

✓ EXTENDED Describe and explain the use of test crosses.

✓ EXTENDED Explain co-dominance in the inheritance of human blood groups, including the use of genetic diagrams to predict inheritance.

✓ EXTENDED Define and give examples of sex-linked inheritance, including the use of genetic diagrams to predict inheritance.

INHERITANCE

Inheritance is the passing on (transmission) of characteristics from one generation to the next, from parents to offspring. As characteristics are coded for by genetic information in the cell nucleus, inheritance is also the transmission of genes from the parents' gametes to the offspring.

CHROMOSOMES, GENES AND PROTEINS

Inside virtually every cell in the body is a nucleus, which contains long threads called **chromosomes**. These threads are usually stretched out and fill the nucleus but, when the chromosomes condense (gather into bundles) just before cell division, they can be seen through a microscope. The chromosomes are made of a chemical called deoxyribonucleic acid (**DNA**).

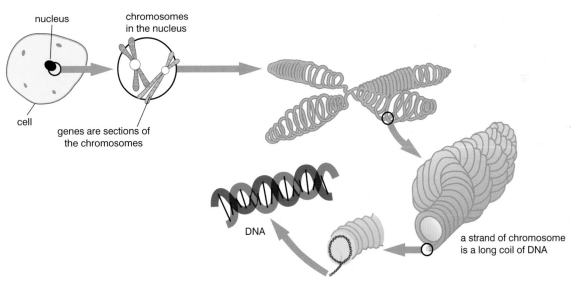

△ Fig 17.2 The relationship between cell, nucleus, chromosome and DNA.

DNA bases

DNA is formed from two parallel strands ('backbones') joined together at regular spaces by pairs of **bases**, like the rungs of a ladder. The whole structure is twisted, forming a shape called a double helix. There are four different bases in DNA: adenine (A), thymine (T), cytosine (C) and guanine (G).

The bases always form the same pairs: A pairs with T and C pairs with G (see Fig. 17.3). So you can use the order of bases on one strand of DNA to identify the bases that will be on the opposite strand. For example, AATGCAGCT on one strand is matched with TTACGTCGA on the opposite strand.

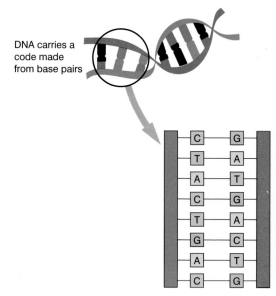

DNA carries a code made from base pairs

△ Fig 17.3 The bases on the DNA strands pair only as A with T and C with G.

To help you remember the base pairing:

- the straight letter A pairs with the straight letter T
- the round letter G pairs with the round letter C.

The bases can occur in any order along one strand of DNA, but their order forms the **genetic code**, which codes for particular proteins.

Genes and alleles

Small sections of the DNA code for different proteins. These small sections are called **genes**. During cell division the string of genes on each chromosome is copied and passed on to the new cells.

There are many different kinds of proteins, including enzymes (Topic 5), antibodies (Topic 9) and receptors for neurotransmitters (Topic 14). These kinds of proteins have important effects on the way cells and the body work:

- enzymes control the reactions that happen inside the cell
- antibodies help protect us from infections
- receptors for neurotransmitters in synapses control how nerve impulses pass along neurones.

Genes code for particular characteristics, such as eye colour. However, variations in a characteristic are caused by different forms of a gene, called **alleles**. For example, some people have alleles that code for brown eye colour; others have alleles that code for hazel eyes, or blue eyes or grey eyes.

In the identical pairs of chromosomes, both chromosomes have the same genes in the same order, but the genes on each chromosome may be in the form of the same allele or different alleles. This causes differences in inheritance (as you will see below).

QUESTIONS

1. Put the following in order of size, starting with the smallest: cell, chromosome, gene, nucleus.

2. Using an example, explain the difference between *gene* and allele.

3. Define the term *inheritance* as fully as you can.

4. EXTENDED Here is the order of bases on one DNA strand: ATTGCTAGGCT. Write down the order of bases on the matching DNA strand and explain your answer.

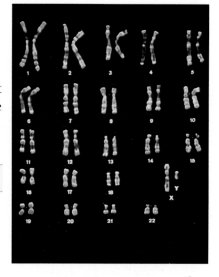

△ Fig. 17.4 The chromosomes from a man's body cell arranged in their pairs. The chromosomes in each pair look very similar except in the sex chromosome pair (marked X and Y).

Making proteins

Proteins are formed from a chain of amino acids (see Topic 4), and the order of amino acids in the chain defines which protein is produced. A gene produces a particular protein because the order of the bases on the DNA strand controls the order of amino acids that are joined together to form the protein.

The formation of a protein starts with the DNA in the nucleus. DNA always remains in the nucleus, but proteins are made on ribosomes in the cytoplasm. So there needs to be communication between the two. This communication is messenger RNA.

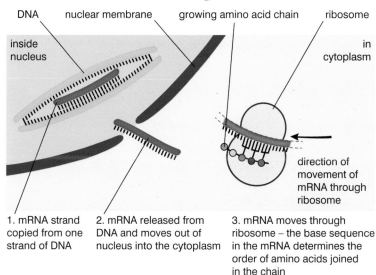

1. mRNA strand copied from one strand of DNA

2. mRNA released from DNA and moves out of nucleus into the cytoplasm

3. mRNA moves through ribosome – the base sequence in the mRNA determines the order of amino acids joined in the chain

△ Fig 17.5 The genetic code on DNA is transferred to mRNA, which carries the code to a ribosome where it is used to make an amino acid chain.

1. The two strands of DNA separate and one strand is used to make a strand of messenger RNA (**mRNA**). The order of bases on the DNA strand determines the order of bases on the mRNA strand – the DNA acts as a template for the mRNA strand.

2. When the mRNA strand is complete, it is released from the DNA. It passes out of the nucleus into the cytoplasm.

3. In the cytoplasm are many small structures called **ribosomes** (see Topic 2). One end of mRNA strand binds to a ribosome – the mRNA then moves through the ribosome and the base code is 'read' by the ribosome (imagine a bar code being passed across a scanner).

4. Different codes in the base sequence code for different amino acids. As the base code is read by the ribosome, the appropriate amino acid is attached to the growing chain of amino acids.

5. Eventually a 'stop' code is reached and the amino acid chain is released into the cytoplasm. The chain folds up depending on the order of the amino acids to form the complete protein (see Topic 4).

As the base sequence on the mRNA is determined by the original base sequence on the DNA, it is the DNA genetic code that controls which proteins are formed in the cell.

The nucleus of every body cell contains the same DNA (as the result of mitosis, which you will see later in this topic). However, not every body cell produces the same proteins. Cells are specialised for different roles in the body tissues (see Topic 2). For example, muscle cells make special proteins that bring about cell contraction, and particular gland cells in the pancreas produce the protein hormone insulin.

Muscle cells do contain the gene for producing insulin, and pancreatic gland cells do contain the genes for the contractile proteins. However, each cell only produces the particular proteins that it needs for its function because most genes in specialised cells are 'switched off'. Only the genes that are 'switched on' are expressed as proteins in the cell.

QUESTIONS

1. Describe the role of the following in the formation of a protein:

   a) DNA   **b)** mRNA   **c)** ribosome.

2. Explain why specialised cells do not produce all the proteins that their genes code for.

Chromosome sets

Most of the cells in the body contain two sets of chromosomes. This is because each individual that is produced by sexual reproduction receives one set of chromosomes from their mother and one set from their father. This means you will inherit some characteristics from each of your parents.

You only inherit one set of chromosomes from each parent because each gamete only contains one set.

If you remember from Topic 16, body cells are **diploid** – meaning that their nucleus contains two sets of chromosomes. Each chromosome is paired.

The gametes, however, are **haploid** – the nucleus of these cells (sperm, egg cell, male gamete in pollen grain) contains only one set of chromosomes. This is the result of the way that they are produced during meiosis.

In humans, the nucleus of diploid cells contains 46 chromosomes, and the nucleus of haploid gamete cells contains 23 chromosomes.

END OF EXTENDED

MONOHYBRID INHERITANCE

Some characteristics, such as the colour of your eyes, are passed down (inherited) from your parents, but other characteristics may not be passed down. Sometimes characteristics appear to miss a generation: for instance, you and your grandmother might both have dry earwax but both of your parents may have wet earwax.

Leopards occasionally have a cub that has completely black fur instead of the usual spotted pattern. It is known as a black panther but is still the same species as the ordinary leopard. Just as in humans, leopard chromosomes occur in pairs. One pair carries a gene for fur colour.

There are two copies of the gene in a normal body cell (one on each chromosome). The version of the gene (allele) may be identical but sometimes they are different, one being for a spotted coat and the other for a black coat.

Leopard cubs receive half their genes from each parent. Eggs and sperm cells contain only half the number of chromosomes of normal body cells. This means that egg and sperm cells contain only one of each pair of alleles. When an egg and sperm join together at fertilisation, forming a zygote that will develop into the new individual, it now has two alleles of each gene.

Different combinations of alleles will produce different fur colour:

spotted coat allele + spotted coat allele = spotted coat

spotted coat allele + black coat allele = spotted coat

black coat allele + black coat allele = black coat

The black coat only appears when *both* of the alleles for the black coat are present. As long as there is at least one allele for a spotted coat, the coat will be spotted because the allele for a

△ Fig 17.6 Two spotted leopard parents may produce offspring with a spotted coat or a black coat.

spotted coat over-rides the allele for a black coat. It is the **dominant** allele. A dominant allele is the allele that is expressed in the phenotype. Alleles like the one for the black coat are described as **recessive**. The recessive allele is the allele that is not expressed in the phenotype unless there are two copies present.

An individual with two identical alleles for a gene is said to be **homozygous** (*homo* means 'the same') for that gene.

An individual with two different alleles for a gene is said to be **heterozygous** for that gene (*hetero* means 'different').

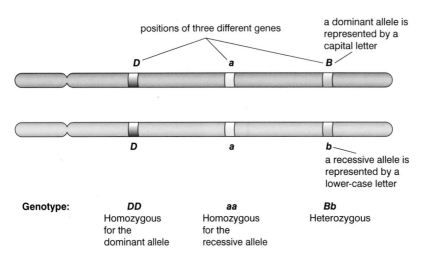

△ Fig 17.7 Definitions in genetics.

Identical homozygous individuals that breed together will be pure breeding; heterozygous individuals that breed together will not be pure breeding. A leopard with a spotted coat may be homozygous for the spotted allele, or heterozygous. A leopard with a black coat can only be homozygous for the black allele.

QUESTIONS

1. 1. Define the following terms in your own words:

    a) *dominant* **b)** *recessive* **c)** *homozygous* **d)** *heterozygous*.

2. How many alleles for a particular gene would be found in:

    a) a body cell **b)** a gamete **c)** a zygote?

3. EXTENDED A sperm cell of a leopard contains 19 chromosomes. How many chromosomes are there in the nucleus of a leopard's body cell? Explain your answer.

Monohybrid crosses

An individual's combination of genes is his or her **genotype**. An individual's combination of physical features is his or her **phenotype**. Your genotype influences your phenotype.

We can show the influence of the genotype in a **genetic diagram**. This uses a capital letter for the dominant allele and a lower case letter for the recessive allele.

Using the example of the leopards, **B** stands for the dominant allele for a spotted coat and letter **b** stands for the recessive allele for the black coat. Two spotted parents who have a black cub must each be carrying a **B** and a **b**. The genetic diagram below shows the possible genotypes and phenotypes of the offspring.

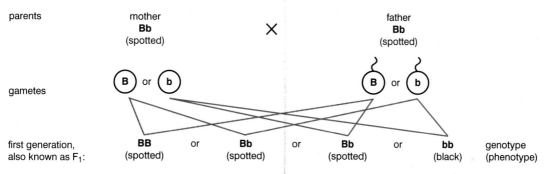

△ Fig 17.8 Three different genotypes are possible from the cross in this diagram. The probability of each genotype is 1BB : 2Bb : 1bb.

Because we are looking at a characteristic (fur colour) controlled by one gene, this is an example of a **monohybrid cross**. *Mono* means 'one', and a *hybrid* is produced when two different types breed or cross.

Another type of genetic diagram is known as a *Punnett square*. The example above can be shown in a Punnett square. The four boxes at the bottom right show the possible combinations in the offspring.

			male Bb spotted	
			gametes	
			B	b
female Bb spotted	gametes	B	BB spotted	Bb Spotted
		b	Bb spotted	bb black

Probabilities and predictions

If you cross two individuals that are homozygous for the same alleles, then you will always get offspring that are homozygous for those alleles. We say that these individuals are pure-breeding. If you cross heterozygous individuals, you will get variety in the offspring. So heterozygous individuals are not pure-breeding.

When two heterozygous parents are crossed, the phenotype of the offspring with the dominant allele and the offspring with the recessive allele appears in the ratio of 3 : 1. The 3 : 1 ratio refers to the probabilities of particular combinations of alleles, so the chance of having an offspring with the phenotype of the dominant allele is three times the chance of having an offspring with the phenotype of the recessive allele.

In the example of the leopards, there is a 1 in 4, or 25% chance of a leopard cub being black. This is because the offspring must inherit two recessive alleles (one from each parent) in order for the offspring to be homozygous and for the phenotype to be expressed (visible).

With a large number of offspring in an *actual* cross of two heterozygous leopard parents, you would expect something near the 3 : 1 ratio of spotted to black cubs. However, because it is a matter of chance which sperm cell fertilises which egg cell, you should not be too surprised if a small litter – for example, of four cubs – contained two black cubs, or none.

Using the example of leopard coat colour and a Punnett square, we can also look at what happens if we cross homozygous recessive and heterozygous individuals:

			male Bb spotted	
			gametes	
			B	b
female bb black	gametes	b	Bb spotted	bb black
		b	Bb spotted	bb black

The predicted outcome from this cross is a 1 : 1 ratio of spotted to black colouring. This gives a 1 in 2, or 50% chance of a cub from these parents being spotted or being black.

In order to gain higher marks, you will need to be able to predict probabilities of outcomes from any monohybrid cross. Practice drawing genetic diagrams to make sure you are confident with them.

Can you predict what will happen if a homozygous spotted coat leopard is crossed with a heterozygous spotted coat leopard?

			male Bb spotted	
			gametes	
			B	b
female BB spotted	gametes	B	BB spotted	Bb spotted
		B	BB spotted	Bb spotted

In this case, although some of the cubs born are likely to be homozygous and some heterozygous, they will all have spotted coats. They will have the same phenotype but not the same genotype.

QUESTIONS

1. Define *monohybrid inheritance* in your own words.

2. Rabbits have a gene for coat colour – the allele for brown coat is dominant over the allele for black coat colour. Using the letter B for the dominant allele, and b for the recessive allele, write down all the possible genotypes and phenotypes for this gene. Explain your answers.

3. Using your answers from Question 2:

   a) Construct a genetic diagram to show the possible offspring from a cross between a male rabbit that is homozygous for the dominant allele and a female rabbit that is homozygous for the recessive allele.

   b) What is the probability of producing a black baby rabbit from this cross?

Developing investigative skills

In an investigation into the inheritance of a characteristic, students used red beads to represent dominant alleles and blue beads to represent recessive alleles.

As a homozygous dominant individual produces gametes that only contain the dominant allele, all the red beads were placed into a beaker to represent the gametes for this individual. As a homozygous recessive individual produces gametes that only contain the recessive allele, all the blue beads were placed into another beaker to represent the gametes for this individual.

To model what would happen in a cross between these two individuals, they took one gamete (bead) from one pot and paired it with one gamete (bead) from the other pot and wrote down the genotype and phenotype for that 'offspring'. This showed that all the offspring from these parents would be heterozygous (one red, one blue bead).

Devise and plan investigations

❶ Describe and explain how you would adapt this method to represent a cross between two heterozygotes. (Hint: Make sure you use enough beads to get a reasonable approximation of the actual result to the expected result.)

Analyse and interpret data

Some students carried out an investigation like this that started with two 'parents' heterozygous for a characteristic.

❷ Each pot started with 40 beads. How many red beads and how many blue beads were in each of the two pots? Explain your answer.

Only 20 selections were made from the two beakers, to produce the 'offspring'. The results are shown in this table.

Number of red/red pairs in 'offspring'	5
Number of red/blue pairs in 'offspring'	12
Number of blue/blue pairs in 'offspring'	3

❸ Draw a genetic diagram for this cross, to show the predicted probabilities of genotypes and phenotypes. (Hint: remember to choose letters for the alleles and explain which allele is modelled by the red beads and which by the blue beads.)

❹ Describe how the actual results differ from the expected results.

Evaluate data and methods

❺ Comment on the difference between the expected and actual results.

❻ Explain how you would adjust the method to help improve the results.

MENDEL'S PEAS

Gregor Mendel (1822–1884) was the first person to study genetic inheritance in a thorough and scientific manner. He chose characteristics in peas to study because he could see clear differences in characteristics and patterns in their inheritance. He started by crossing plants with the same characteristics many times, until he was certain that they were pure-breeding.

He then made hundreds of crosses of the same kind. He started by removing the anthers of each flower. Then he brushed pollen from a plant he had chosen for one parent on to the stigma of the other 'parent' and covered the flower to prevent other pollen getting in.

From his results, Mendel was able to show that alleles generally do not mix effects in the phenotype, but that a dominant allele in a heterozygote prevents the recessive allele being expressed.

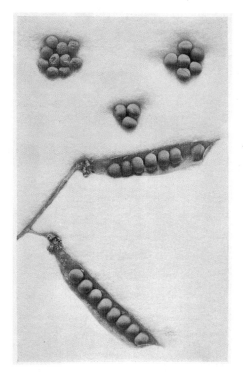

△ Fig 17.9 The results of one of Mendel's crosses for pea form and colour. (Note that each pea is the result of a separate cross between a pollen grain and an egg cell.)

1. Why was it important that the parent plants were pure-breeding?

2. Why did Mendel need to carry out hundreds of crosses before drawing a conclusion?

3. Pea flowers are pollinated by insects. How could Mendel be certain that no chance fertilisations took place?

4. At the time Mendel carried out his work, people couldn't understand how a characteristic could be present in one generation, 'disappear' in the next generation and then reappear in the next. Using genetic diagrams, and a characteristic of your choice, show how this happens when starting with pure-breeding parents for the dominant and recessive characteristics.

5. Explain the importance of a thorough and scientific method for drawing reliable conclusions.

Different types of cross

Test crosses

Breeders can use a cross with a homozygous recessive individual to test whether an individual with the dominant phenotype is homozygous or heterozygous for the dominant allele. For example, a plant breeder may have a tall pea plant. The allele for tallness (T) is dominant over the allele for dwarfness (t). How can the plant breeder find out if the plant is TT or Tt?

- A cross between a homozygous dominant (TT) and homozygous recessive (tt) will produce all heterozygous (Tt) offspring, and so all offspring will have the phenotype of the dominant allele.
- A cross between a heterozygous dominant (Tt) and a homozygous (tt) recessive will have a 50% chance of producing offspring that have the phenotype of the dominant allele (tall) and a 50% chance of producing offspring with the phenotype of the recessive allele (dwarf).

(Try drawing genetic diagrams to confirm this for yourself.)

This kind of cross is known as a **test cross**.

Co-dominance

In the leopard example above, one allele of the gene pair for coat colour was dominant and the other was recessive. When both alleles of a gene pair in a heterozygote are expressed in the phenotype, with neither being dominant or recessive to the other, this is called **co-dominance**.

Human blood types are determined by three different alleles of the same gene: I^A, I^B and I^o (note that I represents the gene and the superscript letter shows the allele). I^A results in the production of the A antigen in blood, I^B results in the production of B antigen, I^o produces no antigen. The I^o allele is recessive but the I^A and I^B alleles are co-dominant. These three possible alleles can give us the following allele pairs:

$I^A I^A$ $I^B I^B$ $I^o I^o$ $I^A I^B$ $I^A I^o$ $I^B I^o$

These six different genotypes give us four different phenotypes: the four different human blood groups A, B, AB and O.

- The phenotype of blood group A can have the genotype of $I^A I^A$ or $I^A I^o$ allele pairs because I^A is dominant over recessive I^o.
- The phenotype of blood group B can have the genotype of $I^B I^B$ or $I^B I^o$ allele pairs because I^B is dominant over recessive I^o.
- The phenotype of blood group AB has the genotype of the two co-dominant alleles, $I^A I^B$.

- The phenotype of blood group O can only have the genotype I^oI^o, the recessive allele pair.

We can use genetic diagrams to predict the outcomes of crosses that involve co-dominant alleles.

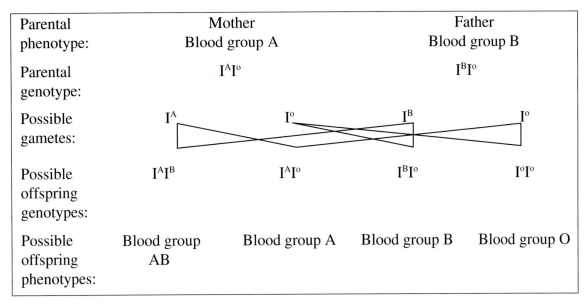

	Mother	Father
Parental phenotype:	Blood group A	Blood group B
Parental genotype:	I^AI^o	I^BI^o
Possible gametes:	I^A $\quad$ I^o	I^B $\quad$ I^o
Possible offspring genotypes:	I^AI^B $\quad$ I^AI^o	I^BI^o $\quad$ I^oI^o
Possible offspring phenotypes:	Blood group AB $\quad$ Blood group A	Blood group B $\quad$ Blood group O

Δ Fig 17.10 This genetic diagram predicts the outcome of crosses between one parent who is blood group A, and one who is blood group B.

A cross between a parent who is heterozygous for blood group A and a parent who is heterozygous for blood group B produces a predicted ratio of 1 : 1 : 1 : 1 for children with each of the four blood groups, giving a 25%, or 1 in 4 chance that a child will inherit any one of the four blood groups.

QUESTIONS

1. Explain why a test cross can identify the genotype of an individual with the dominant phenotype.

2. Define *co-dominance*.

3. Draw a genetic diagram to show the inheritance of blood group from a mother who is blood group O and a father who is AB.

END OF EXTENDED

Sex determination and inheritance

If you take all the chromosomes from a body cell, you can arrange them into pairs. This is because you inherit one chromosome of each pair from your father and one from your mother.

In the nucleus of a human body cell there are 46 chromosomes that form 23 pairs. In all but one of these pairs, the two chromosomes of the pair always look identical. We call these 22 pairs the autosomal chromosomes. The chromosomes of the other pair are identical in women, but differ in men. These are called the **sex chromosomes**. The sex chromosomes of women are called XX and in men are called XY.

When the gametes are produced, they each receive one of the sex chromosomes. So egg cells all contain an X chromosome, but sperm cells may contain an X chromosome or a Y chromosome. As a result of the way the sperm cells are produced about 50% are X and 50% are Y.

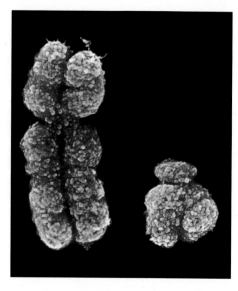

△ Fig 17.11 The human X and Y chromosomes are different shapes.

During fertilisation, one sperm cell fuses with one egg cell. We can use a Punnett square to show the possible combinations of sex chromosomes in the offspring.

		father's gametes	
		X	Y
mother's gametes	X	XX (female)	XY (male)
	X	XX (female)	XY (male)

This shows that there is a 50%, or 1 in 2 probability of any child being a boy or a girl. The ratio of boys to girls born in a family is often not 1 : 1, but over the whole human population about equal numbers of baby boys and baby girls are born.

QUESTIONS

1. Which sex chromosomes would be found in the cells of an adult woman?

2. Which sex chromosomes would be found in the cells of a baby boy?

3. A couple have three boys. What is the chance of their next child being a girl? Explain your answer.

Sex-linked characteristics

You can see from Fig 17.11 that the human Y chromosome is much shorter than the X chromosome. This because the Y chromosome is missing part of the DNA (i.e. some of the genes) that are found on the X chromosome. This affects the inheritance of characteristics produced by these genes. For women, the pattern of inheritance is as you have already seen for genes on other chromosomes. But for men, the pattern of inheritance is different. We call characteristics produced by these genes **sex-linked characteristics** because of the different pattern of inheritance in men and women. A greater proportion of men have the characteristic than women.

There are many examples of sex-linked characteristics, including **colour blindness**. This is not true blindness, but is the inability to distinguish some colours from others. It occurs because some of the cone cells in the eye (see Topic 14) fail to produce the protein that responds to light. The most common form of colour blindness makes it difficult to distinguish between red and green, but there are other forms.

◁ Fig. 17.12 People who suffer from colour blindness may not be able to see the umbrella in the centre of this colour blindness test.

The allele that causes red–green colour blindness is recessive. This means that a women with the colour blindness allele on one X chromosome and a normal colour allele on the other X chromosome will not be colour blind. The inheritance of these alleles by daughters is as above for the monohybrid inheritance of a recessive allele. So they will only be colour blind if they inherit a colour blindness allele from both parents.

If this woman has sons, however, there is an equal chance that they inherit either allele. If they inherit the normal allele, they will have normal colour vision. If they inherit the colour blindness allele, they will be colour blind. This is because the Y chromosome that they inherit from their father has no equivalent allele. Even if the father has a normal colour vision allele on his X chromosome, this will not affect any of his sons, as they only inherit the Y chromosome from him.

We can use a genetic diagram or Punnett square to show the inheritance of sex-linked characteristics. In this case, we need to show both the sex chromosome and the allele. So, for example, we could use X^R for the normal colour vision allele on the X chromosome, and X^r for the colour-blind allele. There is no allele for this on the Y chromosome, so we show this just as Y.

This Punnett square shows the inheritance of colour blindness from a mother who is a carrier for the colour-blindness allele, and so has normal colour vision, and a father who has normal colour vision. Note that we have to identify the sex and characteristic in the phenotype of the offspring.

		father's gametes	
		X^R	Y
mother's gametes	X^R	$X^R X^R$ (female, colour vision)	$X^R Y$ (male, colour vision)
	X^r	$X^R X^r$ (female, colour vision [carrier])	$X^r Y$ (male, colour blind)

From these parents, there is a 50 : 50 chance (50% probability, 1 : 1 ratio) that a son will be colour blind. However, no daughters will be colour blind.

QUESTIONS

1. Explain what is meant by a *sex-linked characteristic*.

2. A girl is born colour blind. Identify the possible genotype and phenotype of each of her parents, and explain your answer.

END OF EXTENDED

MITOSIS

Organisms grow by the division of cells, when the body cells split in two. Before the cell can split, its nucleus must first divide in two. This kind of division is used to produce new body cells in growth, the repair of damaged tissues and replacement of cells in the body. It is also the way that single-celled organisms reproduce and is the only type of cell division involved during asexual reproduction (reproduction that does not involve sex cells), as you saw in Topic 16. This type of cell division, in which the new cells are genetically identical to the original cell, is known as **mitosis**.

Before a cell divides in mitosis, its chromosomes are duplicated (copied). During mitosis, the copies of the chromosomes separate, so that one copy of each chromosome ends up in each of the new (daughter) cells. This is why the **daughter cells** are genetically identical to the original cell.

Stem cells

Once cells have differentiated in the body (such as into muscle or nerve cells), they lose the ability to divide and produce different kinds of cell. However, some cells in differentiated tissue remain unspecialised. These are called **adult stem cells**. Adult stem cells retain the ability to divide and produce some types of differentiated cell, usually those in the tissue where they are found. Their role is to replace damaged cells and to produce new cells for growth (such as when muscles increase in size after puberty in boys and through exercise).

Adult stem cells are found in any differentiated tissue, even in the fetus, but we call them adult stem cells to distinguish them from stem cells in the early embryo. **Embryonic stem cells** can divide to produce daughter cells that can become almost any kind of differentiated cell.

Stem cells are increasingly being studied for use in the treatment of disorders caused by faulty cells, such as Type 1 diabetes or after heart disease. Although embryonic stem cells can be used more easily than adult stem cells to produce any kind of body cell for these treatments, there are other problems with their use.

MEIOSIS

During sexual reproduction, a male gamete fuses with a female gamete. If each gamete had the same number of chromosomes as a normal body cell, the zygote would end up with twice as many chromosomes as normal. Instead, gametes are produced by a different form of cell division called **meiosis**. This is a **reduction division** because the cells produced by meiosis have a reduced number of chromosomes, just one chromosome of each pair – half the normal number of chromosomes. These cells are called haploid cells. When the gametes fuse during fertilisation, they restore the normal number of chromosomes, creating a diploid cell with pairs of chromosomes again.

Cells produced by meiosis are not identical. This means that, during fertilisation where there is a random chance that any one male gamete will fuse with the female gamete, the offspring produced will be different from each other. We say they show variation.

QUESTIONS

1. a) Which form of cell division produces new body cells?

b) Explain why this is important to the organism.

2. The diagram shows the life cycle of a human.

Copy the diagram and annotate it to show:

- when meiosis and mitosis occur

- which cells are diploid and which are haploid.

3. **EXTENDED** Name the form of cell division that is found in organisms that reproduce by: (a) sexual reproduction, (b) asexual reproduction.

4. **EXTENDED** Explain the importance of meiosis in producing variation in offspring.

End of topic checklist

Key words

adult stem cell, allele, base, chromosome, co-dominance, colour blindness, diploid, dominant, DNA, gene, genetic code, genetic diagram, genotype, haploid, heterozygous, homozygous, inheritance, meiosis, mitosis, monohybrid cross, mRNA, phenotype, recessive, ribosome, sex chromosome, sex-linked characteristic, test cross

During your study of this topic you should have learned:

◯ Inheritance is the transmission of genetic information from generation to generation.

◯ A chromosome is a long thread of DNA, made up small sections of DNA called genes.

◯ A gene codes for a specific protein or characteristic.

◯ Genes have alternative forms called alleles that produce variations in the protein or characteristic.

◯ EXTENDED The order of bases in a DNA gene determines the order of amino acids that make up the protein it codes for.

◯ EXTENDED DNA controls how the cell works by controlling the proteins produced in the cell, including enzymes.

◯ EXTENDED To make a protein, the DNA base code is copied as mRNA, which moves out of the nucleus into the cytoplasm and to a ribosome. On the ribosome, the mRNA code is used to build the amino acid chain of the protein.

◯ EXTENDED All body cells have the same genes, but they produce different proteins because not all the genes are expressed.

◯ EXTENDED A haploid cell has a nucleus that contains one set of chromosomes.

◯ EXTENDED A diploid cell has a nucleus that contains two sets of chromosomes, and human diploid cells have 23 pairs of chromosomes.

◯ Dominant alleles in the genotype are always expressed in the phenotype, but recessive alleles are only seen in the phenotype when there is no dominant allele (there are two copies of the recessive allele).

◯ A homozygous individual has two copies of the same allele; a heterozygous individual has different alleles for the gene.

○ Two identical homozygous individuals that breed together will be pure-breeding, but heterozygous individuals are not pure-breeding.

○ Monohybrid inheritance is the inheritance of a characteristic controlled by one gene. The predicted outcome of any cross can be shown in a genetic diagram, including a Punnett square.

○ EXTENDED Co-dominant alleles are expressed equally in the phenotype, as shown by the inheritance of blood group in humans.

○ The sex of offspring is determined by the sex chromosomes inherited at fertilisation. In humans, a child that inherits two X chromosomes (XX) is female and a child that inherits an X and a Y chromosome (XY) is male.

○ EXTENDED A sex-linked characteristic, such as colour blindness, is one that is controlled by a gene located on a sex chromosome, making it more common in one sex than in the other.

○ Mitosis is the division of the nucleus of a body cell to produce two genetically identical cells. Mitosis produces new cells during growth and repair of body cells and in asexual reproduction.

○ EXTENDED Before mitosis, the chromosomes are duplicated.

○ EXTENDED During mitosis, one copy of each chromosome moves into each daughter cell, which results in two diploid cells that are genetically identical to each other.

○ Meiosis is a nuclear division result in genetically different cells such as in the production of gametes.

○ EXTENDED Meiosis is a reduction division producing haploid cells from a diploid cell, and produces variation by forming new combinations of maternal and paternal chromosomes.

End of topic questions

Note: The marks awarded for these questions indicate the level of detail required for the answers. In the examination, the number of marks awarded to questions like these may be different.

1. Write two sentences that correctly link all the following words to explain how they are related: *characteristic, chromosome, DNA, gene, nucleus, protein.* **(2 marks)**

2. Explain why there are two sexes in humans, using the inheritance of sex to support your answer. **(4 marks)**

3. The form of earwax in humans is controlled by one gene. The dominant allele produces wet-type earwax, and the recessive allele produces dry earwax.

   a) Using appropriate symbols, draw a genetic diagram to show the inheritance of earwax between a man with dry earwax and woman who is heterozygous for the characteristic. **(3 marks)**

   b) Describe the predicted probability of genotypes and phenotypes in their children. **(2 marks)**

   c) Explain why it is possible that their three children all have dry earwax. **(2 marks)**

4. EXTENDED A plant breeder had two plants of the same species that she knew were homozygous. One had pure white flowers and one had pure red flowers. She transferred pollen from one plant to the stigmas of the other plant.

   All the seed produced grew into plants with flowers that were red with white splashes. Explain why the gene in this example shows co-dominance. **(3 marks)**

5. a) EXTENDED About 5% of men in the US have red–green colour blindness, but only about 0.5% of US women have the condition. Explain why. **(1 mark)**

   b) Explain why a girl can only inherit the condition if both her parents have the colour-blindness allele. **(1 mark)**

   c) Identify from which parent a boy inherits colour blindness, and explain your answer. **(1 mark)**

   d) Use a Punnett square or genetic diagram to predict the phenotypes of offspring from a colour-blind woman and a man with normal colour vision. **(2 marks)**

   e) Suggest where a scientist looking for the gene that controls colour blindness in human chromosomes should look and explain why. **(1 mark)**

6. EXTENDED Draw up a table to summarise the similarities and differences between mitosis and meiosis in terms of: number of cells produced, whether daughter cells are genetically identical or different, whether daughter cells are haploid or diploid, and what its purpose is. **(8 marks)**

7. EXTENDED Explain why a life cycle needs a stage in which meiosis occurs before fertilisation. **(2 marks)**

Even as children we recognise that some organisms are only usually found in particular places: fish in water, thick-furred mammals where it is cold, camels where it is dry. The adaptations of each organism help it to survive and produce young in that particular environment. Within each species, though, individuals are not identical. They show variation, that is little differences between them. Some are better suited to the environment than others. Natural selection by the environment will lead to the better-adapted individuals producing more young.

CONTENTS

18

Variation and selection

△ Red blood cells from a person who is heterozygous for the sickle cell allele.

Variation and selection

INTRODUCTION

There is a huge range in variation between all the people on Earth today. We differ in many characteristics, such as size, skin colour, strength and hair type. Some of these characteristics are caused by genes and may stay the same throughout life. Some are also affected by the environment and so may change as we grow. Even though there is so much variation between people, we all belong to one species, *Homo sapiens*.

△ Fig 18.1 How many variations can you spot between these individuals of the human species?

KNOWLEDGE CHECK

✓ Variation can be inherited or caused by the environment.
✓ Genes are small parts of the genetic information (DNA) found in the nucleus of a cell.

LEARNING OBJECTIVES

✓ Define *variation* as the differences between individuals of the same species.
✓ Distinguish between phenotypic and genetic variation.
✓ **EXTENDED** Describe how phenotypic variation is caused by both genes and the environment.
✓ Describe discontinuous variation as a limited number of distinct phenotypes.
✓ **EXTENDED** State that continuous variation is mostly caused by environmental factors.
✓ **EXTENDED** Describe how discontinuous variation is mostly caused only by genes.
✓ Investigate continuous and discontinuous variation.
✓ Define *mutation* as a change in a gene that produces new alleles.
✓ Describe how the rate of mutation can be increased by ionising radiation and by some chemical mutagens.
✓ **EXTENDED** Define *gene mutation* as a change in the base sequence of DNA.
✓ **EXTENDED** Describe the cause, signs and symptoms of sickle cell anaemia and how it can be inherited.
✓ **EXTENDED** Describe how the allele that causes sickle cell anaemia can help to protect against malaria.
✓ Define the term *adaptive feature*.
✓ **EXTENDED** Define what is meant by the *fitness* of an individual for survival in the environment.
✓ Interpret information about the adaptive features of a species.
✓ **EXTENDED** Explain how xerophytes and hydrophytes are adapted to their environments.
✓ Describe natural selection in terms of the best-adapted organisms having a better chance of passing on their genes to the next generation.
✓ **EXTENDED** Know that natural selection can lead to populations becoming better adapted to the environment.

✓ **EXTENDED** Describe how adaptation to the environment can lead to natural selection.

✓ **EXTENDED** evolution is the change in characteristics of a population over time as the result of natural selection.

✓ **EXTENDED** Resistance to antibiotics in bacterial populations is an example of natural selection.

✓ Describe the term *selective breeding.*

✓ **EXTENDED** Distinguish between natural and artificial selection.

✓ **EXTENDED** Describe how selective breeding can be used to improve domesticated animals and crop plants.

VARIATION

No two people are the same. Similarly, no two trees (of the same species) are exactly the same in every way. For example, they have different heights, different trunk widths and different numbers of leaves. Variation exists between members of the same species. We say that they show **phenotypic variation** because their features look different. Some of these differences are caused by differences in genes, which is **genetic variation**.

△ Fig 18.2 Tongue-rolling: some people can roll the edges of their tongues inwards, whereas others cannot.

Phenotypic variation can be divided into two different types depending on how you are able to group the measurements.

- **Discontinuous variation** (sometimes called discrete variation) is where a characteristic can have one of a limited number of specific phenotypes with no intermediates. For example, gender (you are either male or female), blood group (you are group A, B, AB or O), or tongue-rolling (you can either roll your tongue or not).

- **Continuous variation** is where a characteristic can have any value in a range: for example, body weight and length of hair. It results in a range of phenotypes between two extremes.

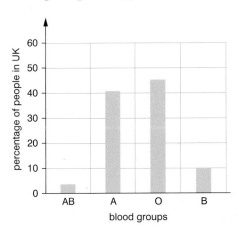

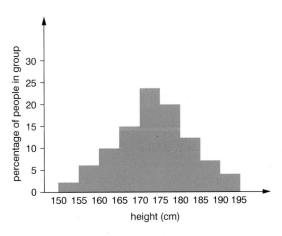

△ Fig 18.3 Charts showing discontinuous variation in human blood groups (left) and continuous variation in human height (right).

The variation in appearance of characteristics in an individual may have various causes:

- **environmental causes**, such as your diet, the climate you live in, accidents, your surroundings, the way you have been brought up and your lifestyle
- **genetic causes** in characteristics that are controlled by your genes, such as eye colour and gender.
- Many characteristics are influenced by both *environment* and *genes*. For example, people in your family might tend to be tall, but unless you are healthy when you are growing you will not become tall, even though genetically you have the tendency to be tall. Other examples are more controversial, such as human intelligence, where it is unclear how far environment or genes contribute to variation.

Discontinuous variation is caused by genetic variation alone. Continuous variation is usually the result of a combination of variation caused by genes and the environment.

QUESTIONS

1. Explain what is meant by *variation*.

2. Name two types of variation of characteristics in a species, and give an example of each.

3. EXTENDED Describe the source of the variation in each of these types of variation and explain your answer.

Mutation

A **mutation** is a change in the genetic code (DNA) of an individual. For example, it can produce a new allele of a gene (see Topic 17).

A **gene mutation** is a change in the base sequence of the gene. It can happen when the DNA of a cell is copied, such as in cell division. This is rather like mis-spelling a word when you are copying text, where you use one wrong letter and end up with a different word (e.g. bold instead of bond). The different word can completely change the meaning of the sentence. Similarly, the error in the DNA can produce a different allele of the gene and a different form of the protein it produces.

A gene mutation may produce a new version that is:

- beneficial for the organism, giving it an advantage over other individuals of the species; for example, fair skin is a mutation that has happened in human populations several times as they moved into areas of northern Europe and Asia because it allows the individual to make more vitamin D from sunlight than those with darker skin

- neutral, which means it has no obvious effect; many mutations fall into this category and can only be identified by looking in detail at the genetic code
- harmful to the organism, either causing the early death of the embryo, or making the individual less able to survive than other individuals; many inherited diseases are caused by mutations of genes that produce proteins that are important in key processes.

Sickle cell anaemia

A mutation in the gene that produces haemoglobin creates an allele that produces sickle-haemoglobin. This form of haemoglobin changes the shape of red blood cells when oxygen concentration is low. In people who are homozygous for the sickle cell allele, this can cause many health problems, such as pain in limbs and damage to organs when red blood cells get stuck in capillaries. It can also lead to a shortage of red blood cells in the blood (anaemia) as the liver removes the sickle-shaped cells, resulting in **sickle cell anaemia**. The full condition is referred to as *sickle cell disease*.

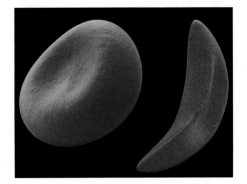

△ Fig 18.4 Red blood cells from a person who is heterozygous for the sickle cell allele. Most red blood cells are the normal disc shape, but some form the sickle shape when blood oxygen concentration is low. The red blood cells of a person who is homozygous for the sickle cell allele will all change shape at low blood oxygen concentration.

Sickle cell disease can only be inherited from parents who have at least one sickle allele for the gene. If the parents are heterozygous for sickle-haemoglobin, they may not be aware that they have the allele, and so producing a child that develops full sickle cell disease may be unexpected.

We can show the inheritance of sickle cell disease from two heterozygous parents using a Punnett square. Here H represents the allele that produces normal red blood cells, and h represents the sickle allele.

rbc = red blood cells

			Father Hh	
			Gametes	
			H	h
Mother Hh	Gametes	H	HH normal rbc	Hh mostly normal rbc
		h	Hh mostly normal rbc	hh sickle cell disease

The chance of these parents having a child with sickle cell disease is 1 in 4, 1 : 3 or 25%.

Sickle cell disease (from the homozygous condition) is harmful, and can shorten life. However, the heterozygous condition seems to be advantageous in warm humid areas where **malaria** occurs. Malaria is caused by a blood parasite, injected into the blood by the bite of an *Anopheles* mosquito. It causes around 1 million deaths each year, mainly in young children. People who have one sickle cell allele are more likely to survive infection with malaria than people who have no sickle cell alleles. So the occurrence of the sickle cell allele is more common in areas where malaria is found (see the section on natural selection below).

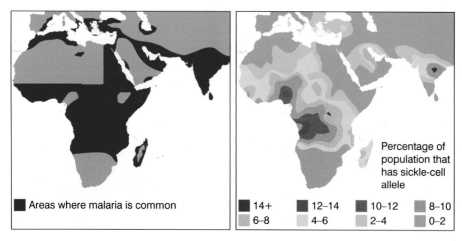

Areas where malaria is common

Percentage of population that has sickle-cell allele

14+   12–14   10–12   8–10
6–8   4–6   2–4   0–2

Δ Fig 18.5 These maps showing where malaria is common and the percentage of the population with at least one copy of the sickle cell allele suggest that there is a relationship between these factors.

END OF EXTENDED

Causes of mutation

The incidence of mutation can be increased beyond the natural rate as the result of:

- exposure to **ionising radiation**, such as gamma rays, X rays and ultraviolet radiation
- chemical **mutagens**, such as some of the chemicals in tobacco.

These factors may change the genetic code directly or cause it to be mis-copied more frequently during cell division.

One of the most obvious effects of radiation or chemical mutagens is to damage the control mechanisms that instruct a cell to stop dividing at the right time. The continuing division of cells produces a lump of unspecialised tissue called a **cancer**. Cancers that take over the space of other tissues can eventually cause death. In Europe and North America, the different forms of cancer are the greatest cause of death from disease.

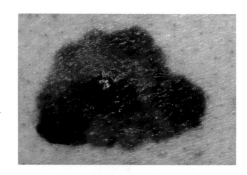

Δ Fig 18.6 This skin cancer was caused by too much ultraviolet radiation from sunlight.

1. Define the term *mutation* in your own words.

2. Name two different causes of gene mutation and give an example of each.

3. EXTENDED Describe the cause of sickle cell anaemia and explain how it is inherited.

4. EXTENDED Explain the relationship between the distribution of the sickle cell allele and areas where malaria is common.

ADAPTIVE FEATURES

An **adaptive feature** is a feature of an organism that helps it to survive well and reproduce in the environment in which it lives. These features are inherited and passed from generation to generation in the genes. For example, fish have fins and a streamlined body that are adaptive features to moving through water, and reptiles lay leathery shelled eggs, which is an adaptive feature for reproducing on land (so that the eggs don't dry out) (see Topic 1).

Different environments offer different challenges for survival and reproduction, including:

• effects of temperature – too hot or too cold are challenging environments for many organisms, but some species are adapted to living successfully in frozen regions such as at the poles or where it is very hot such as in deserts

• effects of water – not being able to get enough water is a problem for many species, but some have adaptations that enable them to survive and reproduce successfully even in desert conditions

• lack of light – plants need light for photosynthesis, but many animals also depend on the presence of light for vision – although you won't find plants in the depths of a dark cave, you will find animals that are adapted to living without light.

Δ Fig 18.7 In spring, the mountain hare replaces its thick white winter fur with a thinner brown fur. The white winter fur provides camouflage against snow and thick insulation against the cold. The brown summer fur provides camouflage against bushes and dead grass and is thinner to increase heat loss on a hot day. The large ears and all round vision help the hare to spot predators at a distance. Large feet give it good grip on snow and rough mountain ground.

Fitness

When we talk about *fitness* generally, we usually mean how good we are at exercise. However, fitness in terms of the environment has a very different meaning. It means the probability that an organism will survive and reproduce in its normal environment. An organism that is better able to survive and reproduce in that environment is said to have a higher **fitness**.

The adaptive features that an organism inherits will affect its fitness to the environment. Those organisms with features that are better adapted to the environment will have a higher fitness.

hump a store of fat that is used to release water and energy from respiration when drinking water is not available

large eyelashes, and nostrils that close to keep out sand during sandstorms

an ability to drink large volumes of water when drinking water is available (much larger in proportion to body weight than other organisms)

wide feet to stop feet sinking into soft sand

Δ Fig 18.8 Camels have many adaptations for surviving well in desert conditions of heat and drought.

Hydrophytes and xerophytes

Plants live in many different conditions, where the supply of water may vary greatly. To survive well, plants need to be well adapted to the conditions in which they live.

Hydrophytes are plants that live in water.

- Hydrophyte plants have no problem getting sufficient water for photosynthesis and transpiration. So their stomata may remain open all the time. Floating plants usually have their stomata on the upper surface, where they can exchange gases more easily with the air.
- These plants may have very small roots because they can also extract nutrients from the surrounding water through other tissues. The water will also support the plant, so roots may do little more than help to keep a plant in place.

Δ Fig 18.9 These floating pond plants have almost no roots because the water supports them.

- Many hydrophytes have large air spaces in their leaves, to help keep their leaves near the surface of the water where there is more light for photosynthesis.

Few plants live where there is very little water, such as in deserts. In these places the light may also be very intense during the day. The air temperature may range from beyond 40 °C during the day to below zero at night. It is not surprising, therefore, that many plants cannot survive in these conditions. Those plants that are well adapted to a lack of water are called *xerophytes*.

Xerophytes may have some or all of these adaptations:

- big root systems that penetrate a large volume of soil and may reach down a long way, to capture as much water from the soil as possible
- reduced or no leaves, to reduce the rate of transpiration (leaves may be reduced to spines to deter herbivores)
- green stems for photosynthesis to replace leaves
- stomata sunk deep into pits in the leaf or stem surface, to reduce the rate of transpiration
- thickened leaves or stems that contain cells that store water (**succulent**)
- hairy surfaces to reduce air flow across stomata, reducing transpiration during the day, and acting as insulation at night.

△ Fig 18.10 Cactuses show many features typical of xerophytes.

END OF EXTENDED

QUESTIONS

1. Explain what is meant by an *adaptive feature*.

2. Give one adaptive feature of (a) a mountain hare and (b) a camel, and explain how those adaptive features help the animal to survive in its normal environment.

3. EXTENDED Explain what is meant by the *fitness* of an organism in relation to its environment.

4. EXTENDED Sketch a diagram of a desert plant such as a cactus, and annotate it to show how it is adapted to survive in the desert.

SELECTION

In any environment the individuals that have the best adaptive features are most likely to survive and reproduce. This results in **natural selection** as follows:

- In any population of organisms there is variation between the individuals.
- When organisms reproduce, they produce more offspring than the environment is able to support. This will mean that there is competition between the offspring for food, or for mates or other resources that are limited. This competition results in a 'struggle for survival'.

- The offspring will have inherited their characteristics from their parents. However, they will have slightly different combinations of variations in characteristics than their parents as the result of sexual reproduction. Offspring with variations in adaptive features that help them compete better for resources, and get more of what they need, will have a better chance of surviving to adulthood and reproducing.
- Those individuals that have variations in features that are not as well adapted will be more likely to die and not reproduce.
- So the better-adapted individuals have a better chance of passing on their features to the next generation through reproduction. This means that in the next generation there will be more individuals with the better-adapted variations in features.

Example of natural selection

In any population of organisms, such as a species of flower in a field, there will be variation in characteristics as a result of the variation in their alleles. For our example, let's consider height in sunflowers.

△ Fig 18.11 Taller plants are better adapted to receiving more sunlight on their leaves.

- Some individual plants of this species will grow taller than others, as a result of variation in the alleles of their genes (see Fig. 18.11).
- Taller plants grow their leaves higher up the stalk, capturing more sunlight for photosynthesis and shading shorter plants so that those get less sunlight.
- So taller plants are able to make more food, and therefore make more seed than shorter plants.
- Embryos in the seeds from the tall plants will have inherited the 'tallness' alleles from the parent plants.
- There will be more seed with 'tallness' alleles, so when they germinate there are likely to be a greater proportion of tall plants in the next generation.

- Over more generations the height of this species of plant in this area will increase because taller plants are more likely to survive and reproduce than shorter plants.

It is a factor of the environment (light intensity) that has caused this change in the population. We call this *natural selection*, because a natural factor appears to select individuals with some characteristics more than others, making it possible for them to pass on their genes to the next generation more successfully.

EXTENDED

Evolution

If the environment does not change, selection does not change. This will favour individuals with the same characteristics as the parents. If the environment changes, or a mutation produces a new allele, selection might now favour individuals with different characteristics or with the new allele. So the individuals that survive and reproduce will have a different set of alleles that they pass on to their offspring. This will bring about a change in characteristics of the species – in other words, it will produce **evolution**.

REMEMBER

Natural selection gives some individuals a survival or reproductive advantage over others with different characteristics. When describing the stages in evolution of a species by natural selection, make sure you identify why each new development gives the organism an advantage over those individuals that have not changed.

Evolution means 'change over time' – in terms of organisms, it usually means how species change in their adaptive features over time as a result of natural selection. Usually this takes hundreds, thousands or even millions of years, making it difficult to see evolution in action.

Evidence from the fossil record is helpful in talking about evolution. For example, over 100 million years ago some species of dinosaur evolved feathers to provide insulation of the skin over the whole body. Some longer feathers also possibly evolved for display, to attract a mate. Over time, some species of feathered dinosaur evolved larger forelimbs, with longer feathers, possibly to help them glide to escape predators. From these, the first birds evolved strong wing muscles that allowed them to fly.

△ Fig 18.12 Reconstruction of a dinosaur with feathers, from fossil evidence.

Antibiotic resistance in bacteria

Natural selection results in a *process of adaptation*, which means that over generations those features that are better adapted to the environment become more common. That means populations of organisms become better suited to their environment. An example of this is the development of antibiotic resistance by bacteria.

Antibiotics are chemicals that are used to kill bacteria when they cause infection (see Topic 15). The first antibiotic that was developed was penicillin (see Topic 20). Antibiotics were first used widely to treat injured soldiers during the Second World War and since then have saved millions of lives. However, more recently, the evolution of bacteria that are resistant to antibiotics has become a major problem, causing many human deaths from infections each year.

The evolution of antibiotic resistance is a good example of evolution through natural selection. It happens like this:

- a patient suffering from a bacterial infection is treated with an antibiotic, for example penicillin
- the bacterial infection is caused by millions of bacteria of one species, and the individual bacteria within that population will show variation
- some bacteria, as a result of random mutation, may have an allele for a new characteristic that means the penicillin doesn't kill them as quickly as the other bacteria – we say these bacteria have developed **antibiotic resistance**
- unless the full course of antibiotics is taken the few that are more resistant will survive and reproduce
- the number of resistant bacteria in the patient may increase enough that the resistant bacteria escape from the body and are passed to another person
- the newly infected person, if they become ill as a result of the infection, cannot be treated with penicillin because it will not kill the resistant bacteria; so the doctor will have to use a different antibiotic to control the infection.

Over time, some bacteria have developed resistance to a larger range of antibiotics, and many species show multiple resistance – resistance to many kinds of antibiotics. Now there are very few new antibiotics to use on multiple-resistant types of bacteria, and doctors are concerned that there will be an uncontrollable increase in the numbers of deaths from bacterial infections that used to be treatable.

The rate of evolution of a new variation of a characteristic is related to how well it is favoured by natural selection. Antibiotics are an example of a *strong selecting factor* – only those bacteria that are most resistant to them will survive and the rest will die. So evolution of antibiotic resistance happens quickly.

END OF EXTENDED

QUESTIONS

1. Define *natural selection* in your own words.

2. Explain the importance of the following factors in natural selection:

   (**a**) variation in the population, (**b**) competition, (**c**) adaptive features.

3. EXTENDED Explain how natural selection results in populations becoming better suited to the environment.

4. EXTENDED Draw a diagram, such as a cartoon strip, to explain how antibiotic resistance develops in a bacterial species.

Selective breeding

Selective breeding (also known as *artificial selection*) is when a breeder chooses which parent organisms to breed from. The choice is usually for desirable features, such as those that have economic importance. Examples include increasing the size of farm animals kept for meat, and increasing egg size in chickens. It may be done for other reasons too, such as to develop breeds of dogs that make good pets, or to produce new colours of flowers in plants grown for horticulture.

As many characteristics are controlled by genes, by breeding together organisms that show the nearest form to a desired characteristic the breeder is more likely to get offspring that also have the desired characteristic (such as large size). If the breeder continues to select individuals with the largest size (say), over time the average size of the organisms will increase. Artificial selection may also be done to combine particular multiple characteristics.

EXTENDED

Example of selective breeding

One example of the improvement of a crop plant is the breeding of wheat plants to develop a variety that has a large seedhead (that gives lots of grain, which we use for food) but a short stalk (which means the plant wastes less energy in producing parts that we don't use, but also helps to support the large seedhead better in strong winds).

The plant breeders start by crossing a wheat plant with a long stalk and a large seedhead with a wheat plant that has a short stalk and small seedhead; there may be some offspring with the advantageous combination of short stalk and large seedhead. Selecting from the offspring that have the best combinations of these characteristics over many generations can produce a new variety with the perfect combination of these characteristics.

For the best marks, be prepared to explain the inheritance of characteristics through selective breeding in terms of the inheritance of genes and alleles that you have already learnt.

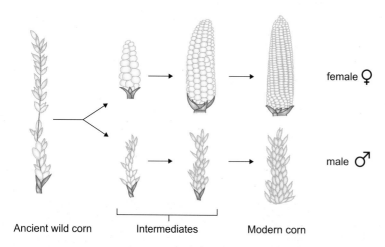

Ancient wild corn   Intermediates   Modern corn

Δ Fig 18.13 Over centuries of selective breeding, the ancient wild corn (maize) has developed into the modern breeds of corn that have the large seed cobs that we harvest.

The same process can be done with domesticated animals, by breeding together individuals that show the best features, to produce new breeds. It too can take many generations to improve the animal breed, and it can take longer than with plants, as animals generally take longer to become mature enough for reproduction.

Note that plants of the same species but with distinctively different characteristics are called **varieties**, whereas animals of the same species with distinct characteristics are called *breeds*. As they are still of the same species, different plant varieties can interbreed and different animal breeds can interbreed.

END OF EXTENDED

TULIP MANIA

Plants are also bred in horticulture, for gardens, for houseplants and cut flowers, to improve the colour, shape and form of the flowers and leaves. This is because people like new things.

For example, tulips were introduced to Europe in the 1500s from Turkey. They were so exotic that they became a luxury item that all wealthy people had to have. Plant breeders rapidly developed new varieties through selective breeding, such as flowers with different-coloured lines or specks on the petals.

At the peak of 'tulip mania' in the Netherlands in the 1630s, single tulip bulbs were being sold for more than 10 times the annual income of a skilled crafts-man. Prices suddenly collapsed in 1637, mainly because people got bored with tulips.

△ Fig 18.14 A completely black flower is almost impossible to breed, but that doesn't stop people wanting to try to produce it because many people would pay a lot of money for something so rare.

QUESTIONS

1. Who carries out selective breeding, and why?

2. Give two examples of selective breeding.

3. EXTENDED Describe the process of selective breeding.

4. EXTENDED Describe the difference between natural selection and selective breeding.

End of topic checklist

Key words

adaptive feature, antibiotic resistance, continuous variation, discontinuous variation, evolution, fitness, gene mutation, hydrophyte, ionising radiation, malaria, mutagen, mutation, natural selection, selective breeding, sickle cell anaemia, xerophyte

During your study of this topic you should have learned:

○ Variation is the differences between organisms of the same species.

○ EXTENDED Phenotypic variation in characteristics in a species may be caused by genes, environment or a combination of the two.

○ Continuous variation produces a range of phenotypes between two extremes.

○ Discontinuous variation produces a limited number of distinct phenotypes with no intermediates.

○ Mutation is a change in the genetic code in a gene that can produce a new allele.

○ EXTENDED A gene mutation is a change in the base sequence of DNA.

○ The rate of mutation can be increased by ionising radiation (such as gamma rays, X rays and ultraviolet radiation), and by chemical mutagens (such as the chemicals in tobacco smoke).

○ The sickle cell allele causes sickle cell anaemia in a homozygous individual, which affects the haemoglobin in red blood cells and may result in pain in limbs, damage to organs and anaemia.

○ EXTENDED The sickle cell allele gives people who are heterozygous for the condition some protection against infection by malaria.

○ An adaptive feature is an inherited feature that helps an organism to survive and reproduce in its normal environment.

○ EXTENDED Adaptive features improve the fitness of an organism to its environment, which means that the organism has a greater chance of surviving and reproducing.

○ EXTENDED Xerophytes are plants with adaptive features for living in drought conditions.

○ EXTENDED Hydrophytes are plants with adaptive features for living in water.

○ Natural selection is the struggle for survival between individuals in a population for limited resources, which results in the better-adapted organisms having a greater chance of surviving, reproducing and passing on their features to the next generation.

○ **EXTENDED** That natural selection can lead to populations becoming better adapted to the environment.

○ **EXTENDED** Evolution is the change in adaptive features of a population or species over time as the result of natural selection.

○ **EXTENDED** Antibiotic resistance in bacteria is an example of evolution by natural selection.

○ **EXTENDED** Artificial selection can change the characteristics of domesticated animals and crop plants to produce varieties with economic importance.

End of topic questions

Note: The marks awarded for these questions indicate the level of detail required in the answers. In the examination, the number of marks awarded to questions like these may be different.

1. In a student class, a survey was carried out of the variation shown in some features.

a) Of the 35 students, 28 were able to roll their tongue and 7 could not. There were no students who could partly roll their tongue. Which type of variation does tongue-rolling show? Explain your answer. **(2 marks)**

b) Describe another type of variation in humans, and give an example. **(2 marks)**

c) Explain how this type of variation differs from the type shown by tongue-rolling. **(1 mark)**

2. Skin cancer is the most common form of cancer in light-skinned people. The majority of skin cancers are not life threatening if treated early.

a) Cancer may be caused by a mutation to a gene in a cell. What does *mutation* mean? **(1 mark)**

b) Name two types of cause of mutation. **(2 marks)**

c) What is the most likely cause of skin cancer? Explain your answer. **(2 marks)**

d) The graph in Fig. 18.15 shows the number of new cases of skin cancer in Sweden between 1970 and 2005.

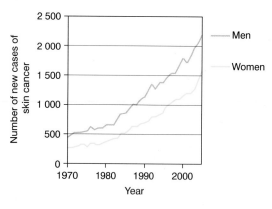

△ Fig 18.15 Cases of skin cancer in Sweden over the last 40 years.

(i) Describe the curves shown on the graph. **(2 marks)**

(ii) Suggest one possible reason for the trend shown in both curves. Explain your answer. **(2 marks)**

3. EXTENDED Look at the maps of distribution of malaria and sickle cell allele in Fig. 18.5.

a) Most people who have the sickle cell allele inherited it from a parent. Name one other source of the sickle cell allele. Explain your answer. **(2 marks)**

b) Explain why, in areas where malaria is not commonly found, such as northern Asia, the presence of the sickle cell allele is at a very low level. **(3 marks)**

c) Explain why, in areas where malaria is common, the percentage of people with the sickle cell allele is higher than in areas where malaria is not commonly found. **(3 marks)**

4. Polar bears are the largest predator in northern polar regions. They particularly hunt seals, which have good eyesight.

a) Describe one adaptive feature of the polar bear that helps to increase their chances of catching seals. Explain your answer. **(2 marks)**

b) Describe one adaptive feature that helps them to survive in the cold conditions of the polar region. Explain your answer. **(2 marks)**

△ Fig 18.16 This polar bear is on the hunt for seals.

5. EXTENDED Fig. 18.17 shows a section through a cactus stem. This cactus is normally found in rocky deserts.

a) Sketch the main features of the cactus stem and label it to show how they improve the fitness of the plant to its environment. **(6 marks)**

b) What is the name given to plants with features like the cactus? Explain your answer. **(2 marks)**

6. Using an example of your own choice, explain how natural selection can result in some individuals of a population passing on more genes to the next generation than others. **(3 marks)**

7. EXTENDED Describe in words or pictures the evolution of bacteria that are resistant to many types of antibiotics. **(4 marks)**

△ Fig 18.17 Section through a cactus stem.

Human activity can have a huge impact on food chains and food webs, and even lead to the extinction of whole species. The introduction of just 24 wild rabbits into Australia in 1859 resulted in a rapidly spreading population that has decimated huge areas of diverse environments, causing havoc to native animal and plant species. Various attempts to keep the rabbit population in Australia in check have been attempted, for example by introducing the rabbit disease myxomatosis. Even so, scientists estimate that rabbits still cost Australian farmers more than $200 million annually in lost production, in addition to the ongoing damage that they wreak on the natural environment.

CONTENTS

19

Organisms
and their
environment

△ Plants make their food by using light energy from the Sun.

△ Fig 19.1 Alligators can survive for months without food, although they are always on the lookout for a good meal.

Organisms and their environment

INTRODUCTION

All animals need to eat, to provide the fuel for respiration. Some animals such as the common shrew need to consume two or three times their body weight of insects, slugs and worms every day in order to survive. They live life quickly, being on the hunt for food for most of the time, especially at night. By contrast, alligators only need to feed about once a week, and can live for months without food. They live life much more slowly than shrews, waiting in ambush for prey to get close before attacking. Most animals eat on average somewhere between these extremes, although adult mayflies have no mouthparts and never eat. They live their brief lives of a few days using energy stored from earlier stages in their life cycle, as their only purpose is to reproduce, after which they die.

KNOWLEDGE CHECK

- ✓ Respiration is the release of energy from food molecules.
- ✓ During photosynthesis, light energy is transferred by plants to sugars as chemical energy.
- ✓ Energy released by respiration is used for a range of purposes, including making new body tissue.
- ✓ Organisms that feed on one another can be displayed in a food chain that shows who eats what.
- ✓ Food chains within a habitat can be combined to produce a food web.
- ✓ Water is essential for many life processes.
- ✓ Carbohydrates, proteins and lipids all contain carbon.
- ✓ Proteins also contain nitrogen.
- ✓ Plants lose water to the environment through their leaves, in transpiration.
- ✓ Decomposers digest dead organic material releasing some of the products of digestion into the environment.
- ✓ A healthy diet is needed for healthy growth and reproduction.
- ✓ Famine is caused by unequal distribution of food, droughts, flooding and war.
- ✓ Modern technology has resulted in increased food production.

LEARNING OBJECTIVES

✓ Identify the principal source of energy input to biological systems.

✓ Define the terms *food chain, food web, producer, consumer, herbivore* and *carnivore*.

✓ **EXTENDED** Explain that energy is transferred in a non-cyclical way between the environment and organisms, and back to the environment.

✓ Interpret food chains and food webs, and use them to describe the effect of humans on habitats.

✓ Draw, describe and interpret *pyramids of numbers*.

✓ **EXTENDED** Describe how energy is transferred between trophic levels.

✓ **EXTENDED** Define the terms *trophic level* and *decomposer*.

✓ **EXTENDED** Explain why there are limits to the number of trophic levels in a food chain.

✓ **EXTENDED** Explain why it is more efficient in terms of energy loss for humans to eat crop plants rather than to eat animals that are fed crop plants.

✓ **EXTENDED** Describe, draw and interpret pyramids of biomass and compare them with pyramids of numbers.

✓ Describe stages in the carbon cycle, including respiration, photosynthesis, decomposition and combustion.

✓ **EXTENDED** Discuss the effects of combustion and deforestation on carbon dioxide in the atmosphere.

✓ Describes stages in the water cycle, including evaporation, transpiration, condensation and precipitation.

✓ **EXTENDED** Describe stages in the nitrogen cycle, including the roles of bacteria and decomposers.

✓ Define the term *population*.

✓ Describe how food supply, predation and disease can limit the rate of population growth.

✓ **EXTENDED** Define the terms *community* and *ecosystem*.

✓ **EXTENDED** Name the phases of a sigmoid population growth curve.

✓ **EXTENDED** Explain the factors that affect the phases of a sigmoid population growth curve.

✓ Describe the increase in human population size and growth and its social implications.

✓ **EXTENDED** Discuss reasons for the increase in human population.

ENERGY FLOW

Plants make their food (sugars) from carbon dioxide and water using light energy from the Sun. In systems terminology, sunlight is the energy input for plants.

Most food chains on the surface of the Earth begin with photosynthesising plants. This means that the Sun is the main input of energy into biological systems, such as food chains and food webs.

SCIENCE IN CONTEXT

ENERGY INPUT FROM THE SUN

As a result of the curvature of the Earth, the amount of light energy from the Sun that falls on every square metre is greatest at the Equator, and decreases as you move towards the poles. The tilt of Earth's axis in relation to the Sun causes variation in the amount of sunlight energy received by high latitude regions at different times of the year, causing seasons.

These differences in energy received have major effects on the ecosystems in each region. Parts of the world near the Equator that receive sufficient rainfall, such as tropical rain forests, have a greater productivity of plants in a year than other regions. This greater productivity supplies more food for animals, leading to a greater productivity of animals – some of these areas are the most biodiverse on the planet.

The seasonal effects in high-latitude regions result in rapid plant growth in summer months and virtually no growth during the winter, although some of this effect is the result of lack of heat energy from the Sun as much as lack of light energy.

FOOD CHAINS AND FOOD WEBS

Food chains

You should be familiar with food chains from your earlier work. A **food chain** shows 'who eats what' in a habitat. For example, in Fig.19.2, owls eat shrews, shrews eat grasshoppers, grasshoppers eat grass. (Remember, the arrows in a food chain show the direction of energy flow.)

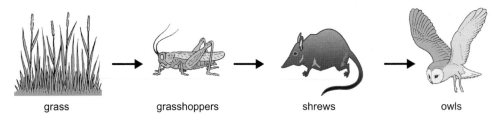

grass   grasshoppers   shrews   owls

△ Fig 19.2 An example of a food chain.

Each level in a food chain shows a separate level at which that species is feeding.

- Grass – this is the **producer** level, because grass is a plant and produces its own food (organic nutrients) using light energy during photosynthesis. All food chains start with a producer level.
- Grasshoppers – these are the primary consumers, '**consumer**' because they eat the grass and 'primary' because they are the first eaters of other organisms in the food chain. This level may also be called **herbivores**, because they eat plant material.

- Shrews – these are consumers too, but they are specifically secondary consumers because they eat the primary consumers. They are also called **carnivores**, because they eat meat.
- Owls – these are also consumers, but they are specifically tertiary consumers because they eat the secondary consumers. They are also carnivores.

If anything ate owls, they would be quaternary consumers, but food chains often don't reach that level. Animals at the highest trophic level in a food chain may also be called the top consumers, or top predators. All animals are consumers, because they eat other organisms to get their food, in contrast to plants, which are producers.

EXTENDED

Each feeding level of a food chain is called a **trophic level**. So producers are one trophic level, primary consumers (or herbivores) are the trophic level that feeds on producers, and so on. We also use the concept of trophic levels in food webs and pyramids of numbers or biomass, as you will see later in this Topic.

What isn't shown in a food chain is what happens to all the dead plant and animal material that isn't scavenged. This material decays as a result of the action of **decomposers**, such as fungi and bacteria. As you saw in Topic 1, fungi digest their food by secreting enzymes outside their hyphae; they then absorb the dissolved food materials. Many bacteria also do this. However, only some of the digested food materials are absorbed – the rest are released into the environment. Decomposers play an essential role in ecosystems, as you will see later in the nitrogen cycle.

◁ Fig 19.3 The hyphae of this fungus are growing through the dead tree and secreting enzymes that cause the wood to break down into simpler chemicals.

END OF EXTENDED

OTHER PRODUCERS

Not all producers are plants, and not all producers use light energy. There are species, mainly bacteria, which produce their own food without the presence of light energy from the Sun. Instead they get the energy they need for the formation of sugars from chemical reactions.

These bacteria are the source of food for food chains and webs that exist where there is no sunlight, such as deep in oceans and in underground caves. Be careful to avoid the statement that 'all life on Earth depends on the Sun', as this is an oversimplification and not totally accurate.

Energy in food chains

We can look at food chains in terms of energy. Plants use energy from light to build new substances. These substances act as stores of energy. A herbivore gains this store of energy, by ingestion, when it eats the plant. Some of that energy becomes stored in the substances in the animal's body, and so can be ingested by any animal that eats it. So we can define a food chain also as the transfer of energy between organisms by ingestion.

Food webs

If we look more closely at food chains, it is rare to find an organism that is eaten by just one other species, or a predator that feeds on just one type of prey. It may also be the case that a predator may feed on different kinds of organism – an **omnivore**, for example, is a primary consumer when feeding on plants, but a secondary or tertiary consumer when eating other animals. So food chains within a habitat are linked together to form a **food web**. A food web is a better description of the feeding relationships in a habitat and shows how living organisms are interconnected.

Food webs still usually group the organisms according to their feeding level. For example, in the simplified food web shown in Fig.19.4, the rabbit, squirrel, mouse, seed-eating bird and herbivorous insect are all primary consumers and are placed just above the producer level.

There are usually many more species in a habitat than shown in Fig.19.4, and linking them all in one food web can get confusing. So food web diagrams may focus on the relationships between key organisms rather than all of them. For example, they may only include

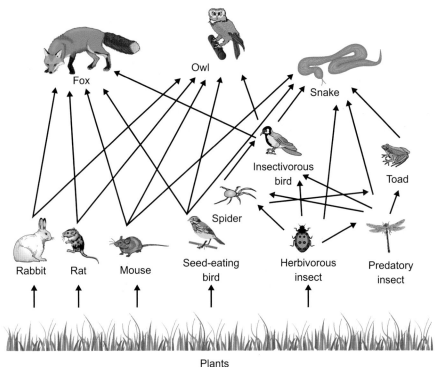

△ Fig 19.4 A simplified food web.

the most numerous species, or focus on the most vulnerable species. This can be helpful if you want to use the food web to predict what would happen to the ecosystem if the food web were changed in some way, such as by human activity.

You could use the food web shown to predict what would happen if the plants were sprayed with an insecticide. This would kill the herbivorous insects and so reduce the amount of food available to all the animals that feed on them.

Interpreting human impact on food chains and food webs

We can use food chains and food webs to help us understand the wider impact on habitats that we have when we affect particular organisms. For example, along the Atlantic coast of the USA there has been overfishing of large shark species. These species are predators of smaller fish, such as skate and rays. These smaller fish feed on shellfish, including scallops.

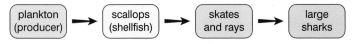

△ Fig 19.5 A marine food chain.

As the numbers of large sharks have decreased, there has been less predation of the smaller fish. So the numbers of skates and rays have greatly increased. This has had a major impact on the shellfish, with scallops becoming nearly extinct in several areas.

Many of the fish that we eat are predators higher up food chains, and so this effect of changing the population sizes of organisms lower in the food chain is being seen in many parts of the ocean.

We also affect food chains and webs when we introduce species from one area to another. This may happen intentionally, such as:

- to provide more food (for example, goats provide meat and milk)
- to control a pest species, such as introducing cane toads to Australia to control beetles that are pests of sugarcane plantations
- because the species is a pet (for example, cats and dogs).

Sometimes the introduction is accidental, such as the introduction of rats to some places because they were onboard the ships that transported humans to those places.

Goats have become a pest in many places, particularly on islands, because they eat much of the vegetation. This prevents new trees growing, and many of the local plants that are not adapted to being browsed like this also die out. Changing the plants that grow in the area will also change the animals that can live there.

Cats and rats have also become pests on islands because they eat many birds and their eggs. In New Zealand, many species of ground-nesting birds have become extinct because of these introductions.

Cane toads were introduced to Australia to control beetles that were attacking the sugarcane plantations in the northern regions. Unfortunately the toads didn't stay in the plantations, because they needed more shelter. So they moved out, and started eating small animals in other areas. This left less food for the predators of the local food web, including many species of small lizards. Population sizes of these lizards have decreased and some are at risk of extinction. The toad is now considered a pest in these areas.

◁ Fig 19.6 Cane toads have glands in their skin that produce chemicals that are toxic to many animals. So there are few predators in Australia that can eat them.

EXTINCTION IN HAWAII

A deep hole on one of the Hawaiian islands provides a 10 000 year record of the effects of humans on the plants and animals that lived there. Before humans arrived, the only organisms must have arrived by chance on the wind or water. Only a limited number of species could travel the thousands of miles from the mainland to the islands. Since the time that they arrived, they evolved into a range of new species that were found nowhere else. The birds, in particular, evolved into a wide range of forms, including some that were too large to fly and behaved more like pigs and goats, grazing the plants.

△ Fig 19.7 The Laysan albatross is now protected when it nests on Midway Island in Hawaii, although cats are still a threat to its eggs.

About 900 years ago the first bones of a rat appear in the deep hole. It arrived with people on a boat. More rat bones were found in the hole from since that time. Since 900 years ago, many island species have disappeared from the bone collection. Many species of birds, including the large species, became extinct. Only birds that nest on the islands and then leave for the rest of the year are still found in Hawaii. All the species of land snails, which were an important food for predators on the islands, became extinct, and this affected other species in the island food web.

The rats, and other species that humans brought to the island, including cats and goats, changed the island food web forever.

QUESTIONS

1. Use your own words to define the following terms: *producer, consumer, herbivore, carnivore.*

2. EXTENDED Use your own words to define the following terms: *decomposer, trophic level.*

3. Name the principal source of energy to an ecosystem. Explain your answer.

4. Distinguish between a food chain and food web.

5. Describe how food webs can be (a) useful and (b) difficult to draw.

EXTENDED

Energy transfers in biological systems

Plants transfer the energy from light into stored energy inside them. This energy is transferred to animals when they digest and assimilate plant food to make new substances in their body tissue.

The energy that a plant receives from light, or that an animal gets in its food, is always greater than the amount of energy it stores in the substances in its tissues. This is because some of the energy that it takes in is transferred to the environment in various forms. The energy losses from plants and animals differ in some ways.

Energy losses from plants

The amount of energy from sunlight that falls on the Earth's surface varies at different times of day and year, and varies in different parts of the world (with places near the Equator receiving more light energy than places nearer the poles). On average, tropical areas receive between 3 and 5 kWh/m^2 per day (which is about the same energy as a one-bar electric heater left on for 3–5 hours).

Plants use only a tiny proportion of this for many reasons, as shown in Fig.19.8. It has been estimated that most plants only transfer about 1% to 2% of the energy in the light that falls on them into chemical energy in their tissues (**biomass**). This is the energy available to a herbivore that eats the plant.

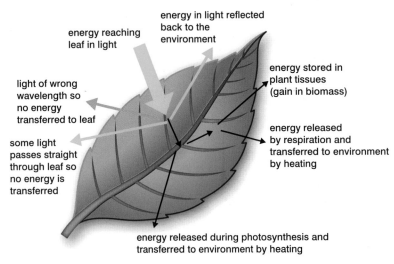

energy in light reflected back to the environment

energy reaching leaf in light

energy stored in plant tissues (gain in biomass)

light of wrong wavelength so no energy transferred to leaf

energy released by respiration and transferred to environment by heating

some light passes straight through leaf so no energy is transferred

energy released during photosynthesis and transferred to environment by heating

Δ Fig 19.8 Energy gains and losses of a plant.

Energy losses in animals

When an animal eats, the food is digested in the alimentary canal and the soluble food molecules are absorbed into the body. The undigested and unabsorbed food in the alimentary canal is egested as faeces (see Topic 7).

Absorbed food molecules may be used for different purposes in the body:

- to produce new animal tissue or gametes for reproduction
- as a source of energy for respiration
- converted to waste products in chemical reactions.

The energy stored in the food molecules may stay in the body stored in body tissue, or it may be transferred to the environment stored in waste chemicals such as urine. When food molecules are broken down during respiration and other reactions, some of the energy released from the molecules is transferred to the environment by heating, through the processes of conduction, convection and radiation. So only a small proportion of the energy stored in the animal's food is converted into energy stored in its body tissues as an increase in the animal's biomass.

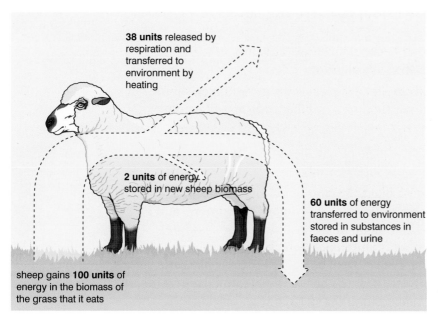

△ Fig 19.9 The energy flow through a sheep.

REMEMBER

Energy transfer efficiency is the amount of energy stored in the body tissue at a particular trophic level compared with the amount in the previous level. Calculating the energy transfer efficiency between trophic levels involves the estimation of many values. This means that the transfer efficiencies you may find in textbooks and on the internet are only best estimates and must not be taken as exact.

In addition, many sources quote a value of 10% as the efficiency of energy transfer between any trophic level and the one above. Calculations of efficiency vary from about 0.2% to around 20% for different organisms in different ecosystems. This gives an *average* of 10%, but over such a large range this is not very reliable. It is better to prepare to explain how energy is gained and lost between trophic levels, in order to explain the shape of pyramids of energy and lengths of food chains, than to quote specific values for energy transfer efficiency.

QUESTIONS

1. Draw a flowchart to show the energy gains by and losses from a plant leaf.

2. Draw a flowchart to show the energy gains by and losses from a herbivore.

3. Explain why the amount of energy stored in an organism's tissues is always less than the amount of energy that it gained.

END OF EXTENDED

Pyramids of numbers and biomass

The flow of energy through the feeding levels, from producers to top consumers, in a food chain or food web can be investigated using simple diagrams.

Pyramids of numbers

In many food chains, if you look at the number of organisms in each level you will find far more producers than primary consumers, and far more primary consumers than secondary consumers. For example, a few tigers eat a larger number of antelopes, which eat a far larger number of grass plants. We can use these data to create a **pyramid of numbers**, as shown in Fig.19.10. Each bar in the pyramid represents a different feeding level, arranged in order starting with producers at the bottom and ending with the top consumer at the top. The width of each bar is drawn to scale, representing the numbers of individuals in the level.

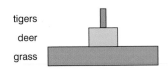

tigers
deer
grass

△ Fig 19.10 A typical pyramid of numbers.

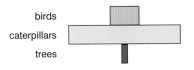

birds
caterpillars
trees

△ Fig 19.11 An inverted pyramid of numbers.

These diagrams are called 'pyramids' because their shape is often wider at the base and narrower towards the top. However, this isn't always the case. Imagine one large tree, on which hundreds of caterpillars feed, on which many birds feed. This pyramid of numbers produces a shape with a very narrow base, as shown in Fig.19.11. This is sometimes called an *inverted* pyramid of numbers.

Gathering data for a pyramid of numbers is relatively simple, because you just have to count the number of organisms in each trophic level within the area of observation.

Pyramids of biomass

It is not surprising that, in the example of tree/caterpillars/birds, you get an inverted pyramid of numbers, because one tree is huge in comparison with the tiny caterpillars that feed on it. If you measure **biomass** (the mass of living material) in the organisms instead of number, you can avoid this problem.

The biomass of each trophic level is usually calculated as the average dry mass of one individual multiplied by the total number of individuals. This is usually within a given area, so the values will be in mass per unit area. If you draw these values to scale, you can produce a **pyramid of biomass**.

Fig 19.12 shows what happens if you produce a pyramid of biomass for the tree/caterpillars/birds example from before. Using the biomass of the organisms produces the anticipated pyramid shape.

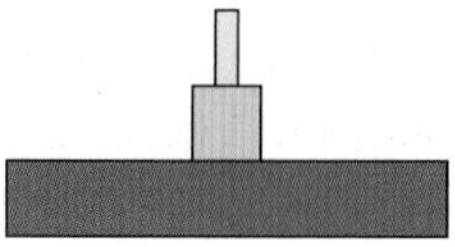

△ Fig 19.12 A pyramid of biomass.

Note that dry mass is used when constructing pyramids of biomass. This is the mass without any the water in the body, because water is relatively heavy and water content in a body can vary a lot depending on the state of hydration. Measuring dry mass may involve killing at least one organism of each type, so that the tissues can be dried fully in an oven and the masses averaged to give an average biomass per individual. Tables of average biomass can be used in order to avoid killing any organisms, but this adds another level of estimation to the process, and so may decrease the reliability of the data in the diagram even further.

Pyramids of biomass produce problems of their own. The mass of the tree is actually a measure of the biomass accumulated over many years. This is often called the standing crop. The insects living off it may have been produced and consumed in a matter of days and so do not accumulate biomass in the same way. This produces the correct shape for the pyramid but creates a different problem.

The growth of plankton in an area of sea was measured over a few days and a pyramid of biomass created (see Fig.19.13). Again the pyramid is inverted. This is due to 'undersampling' of the algae in the food web, which is caused by the relatively short life-span of the algae compared with the longer-lived herbivorous organisms. Unlike the tree, algae do not produce a significant standing crop so do not provide a significant base layer for the habitat.

To help you understand this, think of a shop that sells fruit. In the morning, the shopkeeper will fill the shelves with fruit, and during the day customers will take fruit from the shelves to buy. The 'standing crop' of fruit on the shelves will look smaller in the afternoon than in the morning. Only if the shopkeeper continually restocks the shelves will the standing crop be the same throughout the day.

△ Fig 19.13 An inverted pyramid of biomass.

Developing investigative skills

Some students were collecting data on the abundance of plants and snails on some school grounds so that they could construct ecological pyramids.

Devise and plan investigations

❶ Draw a food chain for these organisms, and identify each feeding level.

❷ Write a plan for this investigation, to explain how the students could gather reliable data for a pyramid of numbers.

Demonstrate and describe techniques

❸ Explain fully how they could convert the data for a pyramid of numbers into a pyramid of biomass.

Analyse and interpret data

The students collected the following data for their pyramid of numbers.

sample site	1	2	3	4	5
number of plants	46	75	39	28	22
number of snails	4	8	5	1	2

❹ Calculate a mean number for each feeding level.

❺ Use your mean values to draw a pyramid of numbers.

The students calculated the following mean values of dry mass for one organism in each level:
plant 38 g, snail 6 g.

❻ Use these values to construct a pyramid of biomass for these organisms.

❼ Describe and explain the shape of the pyramid of numbers.

❽ Describe and explain the shape of the pyramid of biomass.

The fact that there are energy losses to the environment at each trophic level explains the shape of the pyramids. It also explains the fact that food chains are rarely more than four or five organisms in length. Any organism expends energy when looking for food, and the more scattered the food, the more energy is lost in moving about to find it. Top consumers usually have to hunt over large distances to find enough food. If an organism fed exclusively on them, it would expend more energy hunting for its food than it would gain from eating it.

Human food chains

Humans are **omnivores**, meaning we get our energy from eating both plant and animal tissues. This gives us choice of what we eat, but these choices have an impact on what we grow and how we use ecosystems.

Consider two food chains that include humans:

- crop plant (e.g. wheat grain) → herbivore (e.g. cow) → human
- crop plant (e.g. wheat grain) → human

If we consider these food chains in terms of energy flow, we can see that if humans eat the grain, there is much more energy available to them than if they eat the cows that eat the grain. This is because energy will be lost from the cows in the system. So it is energetically more efficient within a crop food chain for humans to be herbivores than to be carnivores.

In reality, we often use animals to gather plants that either we cannot eat (e.g. grass), or that are too widely distributed for us to collect (e.g. tiny algae in oceans, which form the food of fish that we eat).

END OF EXTENDED

QUESTIONS

1. Define the term *pyramid of numbers*.

2. Explain, with an example, how you would produce a pyramid of numbers for a community with three feeding levels.

3. EXTENDED Define the term *pyramid of biomass*.

4. EXTENDED Explain why a pyramid of biomass is more likely to give a pyramid shape than a pyramid of numbers.

5. EXTENDED Sketch pyramids of biomass for the two food chains including humans given above, and use these to explain why it is energetically more efficient for humans to eat the crops than feed them to animals that we then eat.

NUTRIENT CYCLES

Unlike energy, which is transferred through organisms and eventually to the environment in a way that is not useful to the organisms, nutrients continually transfer between the environment and organisms and back again, in what is described as **nutrient cycles**. Examples are the carbon cycle, water cycle and nitrogen cycle.

The carbon cycle

Carbon is continually cycled through the living and non-living parts of ecosystems, in different forms at different stages of the **carbon cycle**. Carbon dioxide from the atmosphere is converted to complex carbon compounds in plants during photosynthesis. This is often called the 'fixing' of carbon by plants. Respiration in plants returns some of this fixed carbon back to the atmosphere as carbon dioxide. Carbon in the form of complex carbon compounds passes along the food chain. At each stage, some of this carbon is released as carbon dioxide to the atmosphere as the result of respiration.

When organisms die, their bodies decay as they are digested by decomposers. Some of the complex carbon compounds are taken into the bodies of the decomposers, where some may be converted to carbon dioxide during respiration. Carbon dioxide may also be released directly into the atmosphere during decay.

Combustion

If dead organic material is buried too quickly by sediment or water for decomposers to cause decay, and remains buried, then it may be converted to other complex carbon compounds. Peat is formed when mosses and other plants are buried in swampy ground for hundreds of years. Over many millions of years, where there were once huge forests growing in swampy regions, heat and pressure have turned the organic material into coal. Heat and pressure over many millions of years also produces oil from the decaying bodies of tiny marine organisms that were buried in sediment at the bottom of oceans. Peat, coal and oil are **fossil fuels**. We can release the carbon from the complex carbon compounds in fossil fuels into the air as carbon dioxide during combustion, when we burn them.

Fig 19.14 Water excludes air from the ground, which prevents decay organisms from respiring. So dead plant material in waterlogged ground builds up over time, forming peat. Peat can be burnt as a fuel, although this is being discouraged so that peat bog habitats can be protected.

REMEMBER

Make sure you are certain what form carbon is in (carbon dioxide or complex carbon compounds such as carbohydrates) at each stage of the carbon cycle.

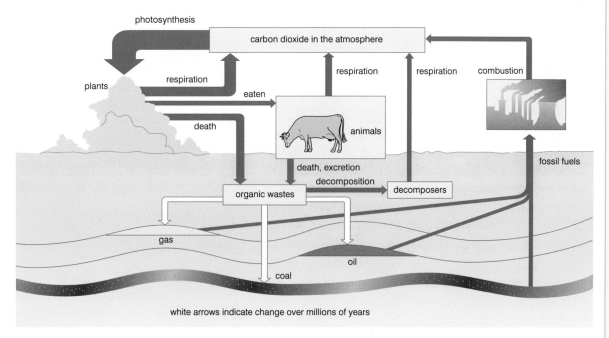

△ Fig 19.15 A summary of the carbon cycle.

The effects of large-scale deforestation and combustion

Deforestation is the permanent destruction of large areas of forests and woodlands. It usually happens in areas that provide quality wood for furniture and to create farming or grazing land.

Forests act as a major carbon store because carbon dioxide is taken up from the atmosphere during photosynthesis and used to produce the chemical compounds that make up the tree. When forests are cleared, and the trees are either burnt or left to rot, this carbon is released quickly into the air as carbon dioxide. This rapidly increases the proportion of carbon dioxide compared with oxygen in the air surrounding the forest. In addition, the amount of oxygen removed from the local atmosphere by plants for photosynthesis may also drop, changing the balance between carbon dioxide and oxygen in the atmosphere locally.

On the scale of deforestation in the Amazon Basin, the amount of carbon dioxide released is so great that it cannot be brought back into balance as a result of photosynthesis. This additional carbon dioxide remains in the atmosphere.

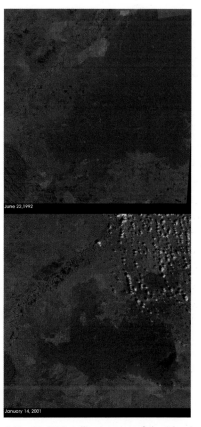

△ Fig 19.16 Satellite images of the island of Sumatra show the extent of deforestation between 1992 (top photo, land mostly green) and 2001.

Over the past 10 000 years or so, as a result of photosynthesis and respiration and other physical processes, the exchange of carbon between organisms and the atmosphere resulted in little change in the amount of carbon dioxide in the atmosphere. On average, over one year about 120 billion tonnes of carbon dioxide are removed from the atmosphere by photosynthesis, and a similar amount is returned by respiration.

During the past 250 years, however, combustion of forests and fossil fuels as a result of human activity has added increasing amounts of CO_2 to the atmosphere. Today about 5.5 billion tonnes of carbon dioxide are added to the atmosphere every year through human activity, particularly through combustion of fossil fuels.

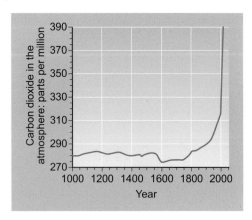

△ Fig 19.17 Atmospheric carbon dioxide concentration from 1000 CE to recent times.

Compared with 120 billion tonnes through natural processes, this may not seem a lot, but there is no process that balances this addition. So the concentration of carbon dioxide in the atmosphere is increasing. It is this additional carbon dioxide in the atmosphere that most people believe is causing global warming and climate change.

QUESTIONS

1. Describe the role of the following in the carbon cycle:

   (a) respiration, **(b)** photosynthesis, **(c)** decomposition.

2. In what form is carbon when it is in the following stages of the carbon cycle?

   (a) Earth's atmosphere, **(b)** plant tissue, **(c)** fossil fuels

3. **EXTENDED** Describe the effect of large-scale deforestation on the oxygen and carbon dioxide concentrations of the atmosphere.

The water cycle

Water (H_2O) is essential to life processes. Without water, most organisms usually die within a few days. Fortunately, the world's water does not get used up; it is constantly recycled.

Most of the world's water is in the oceans. Some evaporates into the atmosphere as water vapour. Water vapour is transported in the atmosphere by air movement until it condenses into liquid water droplets in clouds. It eventually falls as precipitation, such as rain or snow. Some returns straight to the ocean, but some falls on land. Much of this water drains into rivers and returns to the oceans.

Plants take up water through their roots and lose it through transpiration through their leaves. Within the plant, water is used for transport of dissolved substances in the phloem, for photosynthesis to make glucose and to keep cells turgid to support the plant. Animals get the water they need from their food, through respiration, and directly from the environment when they drink. They lose water to the environment through evaporation and through excretion of urine.

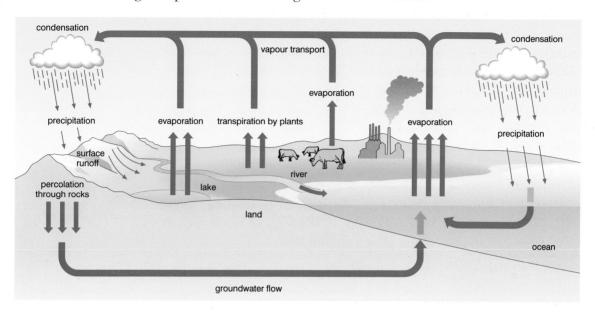

△ Fig 19.18 A summary of the water cycle.

QUESTIONS

1. Define the following terms, and give an example of each from the water cycle:

a) *evaporation*, **b)** *transpiration*, **c)** *condensation*, **d)** *precipitation*.

2. Starting with water in a pond, describe two different routes that water may take through the water cycle before returning to the pond, one through living organisms and the other not through organisms.

3. Explain the importance of the water cycle for life.

EXTENDED

The nitrogen cycle

Living things need nitrogen to make proteins, which are used, for example, to make new cells during growth. Air is 79% nitrogen gas (N_2), but nitrogen gas is very unreactive and cannot be used by plants or animals.

The **nitrogen cycle** describes the way in which nitrogen passes between the living and non-living parts of an ecosystem. Animals take in nitrogen in the form of proteins when they eat plant tissue or animal tissue. They break down the proteins to amino acids in digestion and convert them into new proteins in their own body tissue (see Topics 7 and 17). Any amino acids that the body does not need are broken down in the liver during deamination, and the nitrogen returned to the environment, as urea in urine (see Topic 13).

As plants don't eat, they can't take their nitrogen in as proteins. Instead they absorb nitrogen in the form of nitrate ions (NO_3^-) from the soil water around their roots (see Topic 6). They then convert these ions into the proteins they need.

Nitrate ions are present in the soil as a result of several processes, one non-living and the others as the result of living organisms. The non-living process is lightning, which generates large amounts of energy that cause atmospheric nitrogen to react with oxygen. This forms nitrate ions, which dissolve in rain and fall to the ground, where they remain in soil water.

The biological processes that produce nitrate ions are much more important. The first begins with organic material containing complex nitrogen compounds, such as proteins, in the form of faeces or urine from animals, and as dead plant and animal tissue.

- This material decays as a result of decomposers, releasing nitrogen in the form of ammonium ions into the soil.
- Some bacteria in the soil can take in ammonium ions and produce nitrite ions (NO_2^-). Other soil bacteria can take in nitrite ions and produce nitrate ions.
- Both kinds of bacteria are called **nitrifying bacteria** because their action adds soluble nitrogen to the soil water, and this process is known as **nitrification**.

The other biological process that makes nitrogen available to plants as nitrates also involves bacteria. These bacteria are unusual because they can convert nitrogen gas from the atmosphere directly into a form that plants can use. They are called **nitrogen-fixing bacteria** and the process is called *nitrogen fixation*. Some of these bacteria live free in the soil and some grow in root nodules (small lumps on the roots) of some kinds of plants, especially legumes (plants of the pea and bean family).

Nitrifying bacteria can only grow in aerobic conditions, when there is plenty of oxygen in the soil. In waterlogged conditions, air in the soil is pushed out, so these bacteria cannot grow. These conditions favour another type of bacteria, which can respire anaerobically. As they grow, they convert nitrates back to nitrogen gas, which escapes to the atmosphere. They are called **denitrifying bacteria**, because they remove nitrates from the soil and make it less fertile for growing plants. This process is called *denitrification*.

△ Fig 19.19 Some legume plants produce special nodu on their roots in which nitrogen-fixing bacteria live.

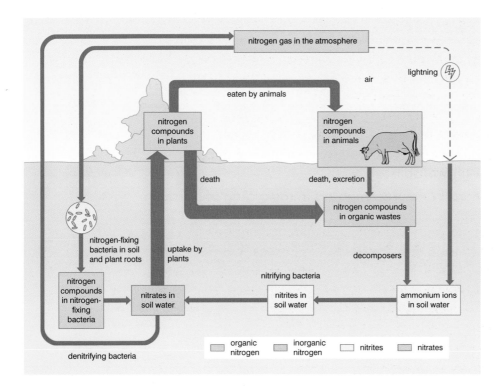

△ Fig 19.20 A summary of the nitrogen cycle.

SCIENCE IN CONTEXT

MAINTAINING SOIL FERTILITY

As plants grow, they remove nitrates from the soil. In natural communities, those nitrates are returned to the soil when the plants die and decay, or when the animals that ate them die and decay. However, when we grow crops, we usually remove the plants from the ground, taking the nitrates (in the form of nitrogen compounds in plant tissue) away. This reduces the amount of nitrates in the soil each year.

Farmers can return some nitrates to the soil by spreading animal manure (faeces and urine mixed with straw) or by growing legume crops in some years.

Millions of tonnes of nitrogen-containing fertiliser are made each year by chemical processes. These are used to fertilise fields to provide food for the growing human population.

△ Fig 19.21 Farmers sometimes plant legume crops in order to add nitrogen to the soil. The following year another crop, such as potatoes or cabbages, will grow better without additional fertiliser.

These processes often use energy from fossil fuels, which are non-renewable resources. There is concern that, if we do not find other ways of making these fertilisers, global food production may decrease as reserves of fossil fuels are used up.

1. Describe what is meant by:

   a) nitrifying bacteria

   b) nitrogen-fixing bacteria

   c) denitrifying bacteria.

2. Explain the importance of nitrifying bacteria in the nitrogen cycle for the fertility of soils.

3. Explain the importance of decomposers in the cycling of nitrogen.

Developing investigative skills

Students were given some young wheat plants and some young legume plants growing in separate pots. The plants had been grown from seed. The seed for the legume plant had been inoculated with nitrogen-fixing bacteria so that it developed root nodules containing the bacteria. The students were also given two nutrient solutions for watering the plants: one that contained all nutrients and one that contained all nutrients except nitrogen.

Devise and plan investigations

❶ Write a plan, using this equipment, to investigate the effect of nitrogen on the growth of legume and non-legume plants. Make clear how your investigation is designed to produce reliable results.

❷ Write a suitable prediction for your investigation.

Analyse and interpret data

The table shows the results of the investigation carried out by the students.

Plants	Wheat		Legume	
Nutrient solution used for watering	all nutrients	without nitrogen	all nutrients	without nitrogen
Height at start (cm)	5.2	4.8	3.6	4.1
Height at end (cm)	20.6	13.6	18.1	19.3

❸ For each plant calculate the percentage increase in height from the start to the end of the experiment.

❹ Describe the differences in growth between the plants.

❺ Explain the differences in growth of the wheat plants.

❻ Explain the difference in results for the legume plants.

❼ Draw a conclusion for this experiment.

Evaluate data and methods

❽ Identify any weaknesses in this method.

❾ Explain how the method should be improved so that a more reliable conclusion can be produced.

END OF EXTENDED

POPULATION SIZE

A **population** is a group of organisms of the same species that live in the same environment at the same time. So we might talk about a population of mahogany trees in a forest, or a population of pill millipedes living in a rotting log.

Other ecological terms

The term *population* is a key term in the study of organisms in their habitats: what we call **ecology**.

- A population is a group of organisms of the same species living in the same area at the same time.
- Within that area there will be populations of different species – all the species that form the food web. All these populations together are called a **community**.
- An **ecosystem** is the community of organisms and their environment in an area that interact together.

If we consider a lake as an example of an ecosystem, within that lake there are physical factors such as:

- the amount of light at different levels in the lake
- the temperature in different parts of the lake
- parts where the bottom of the lake is rocky and parts where there is sediment that animals can burrow into.

There is also a community of organisms including populations of different species of plants, microscopic animals and larger fish.

The physical factors affect where some organisms can live, but the organisms also change the physical factors, for example by creating shelter or shade. So within the ecosystem, the physical factors and biological factors (the community) continually interact.

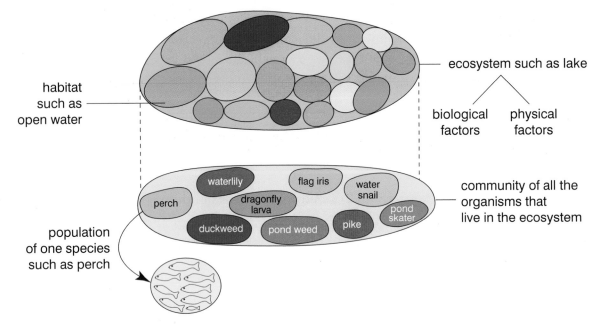

△ Fig 19.22 Definitions in ecology.

END OF EXTENDED

QUESTIONS

1. Define the term *population*.

2. EXTENDED In your own words, define the term *ecosystem*, and give two examples.

3. EXTENDED In your own words, define the term *community*.

4. EXTENDED Describe how an *ecosystem*, *community* and *population* are inter-related.

Human population change

When we talk about a human population we may mean a local population of people living in a town, or the global human population, which is all the people in the world. This is because humans are able to move around and mix in a much more general way than most species.

The size of a population depends on various factors:

- the number of new individuals as a result of reproduction, i.e. births
- the number of individuals lost from the population, i.e. deaths
- for some populations, there may be **emigration**, as individuals move out to other areas, or **immigration**, as individuals come in from other areas.

Births and immigration will increase the number of individuals, whereas deaths and emigration will decrease the number of individuals, in the population. So any change in population size will depend on the balance between these:

Change in population size = current population size + [births + immigration] − [deaths + emigration]

- If [births + immigration] is greater than [deaths + emigration], the population will increase in size.

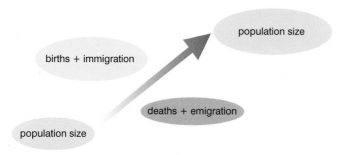

△ Fig 19.23 How a population increases.

- If [deaths + emigration] is greater than [births + immigration], the population will decrease in size.

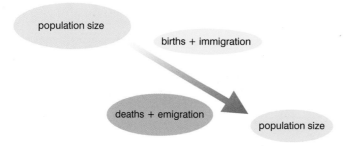

△ Fig 19.24 How a population decreases.

- The greater the difference between [births + immigration] and [deaths + emigration], the more rapid the change in population size – that is the rate of population growth. (A decrease in population size is often described as 'negative growth'.)

Any factor that affects the number of births or deaths, or the number immigrating or emigrating, will affect the rate of population growth.

Food supply

Food supply may affect several of the variables in the population size equation. When there is plenty of food, **birth rate** (the number of births in a particular time) may increase. Survival rate of the young may also increase, so **death rate** (the number of deaths in a particular time) may decrease. Emigration may also decrease because there is food for all, and immigration may increase as individuals arrive from areas where there is less food.

So, when food supply is good, the population will most probably grow. And when food supply is poor, the population growth will more likely be negative and the population size will decrease.

Predation

The food supply for a predator is its prey. So, when there is plenty of prey, the population size of the predator will probably increase. This can have a negative effect on the population size of the prey species, particularly when the predator only feeds on one or two prey species. The death rate, by predation, of the prey species will increase, which may cause a decrease in population size of the prey. That, in turn, means the food supply for the predator decreases, leading to starvation and/or reduced birth rate for the predator.

A well-known example of this cyclical effect of predator and prey population change is shown by the snowshoe hare and lynx, which live in northern Canada. The hare is a herbivore, and the lynx feeds mainly on hares. Studies using evidence of numbers of animals killed for their fur between 1845 and 1935 show regular cycles.

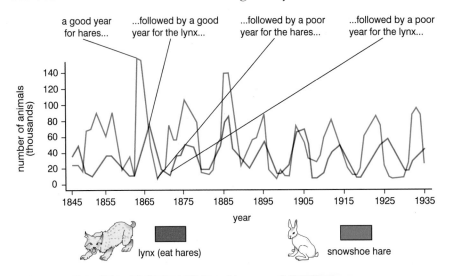

△ Fig 19.25 The relationship between lynx and hare population size.

These cycles were interpreted as the predator population size controlling the prey population size through predation, and in return prey population size controlling the predator population size as a result of food supply. Further research has suggested that the population size of the hares is controlled more by the availability of their food, than by the number of lynxes. However, the sudden immigration of a large number of predators could cause a rapid decrease in population size of a prey species.

EXTENDED

A predator–prey cycle like the one shown by hares and lynxes is virtually unknown in nature, because most predators feed on more than one or a few species of prey. If predator numbers are high, when one prey population decreases (and the prey became more difficult to find), the predator usually hunts a more common prey. So the change in prey population size is rarely as large as shown by the snowshoe hares.

Disease

Disease can increase the death rate. It can also reduce the birth rate by affecting the mothers. Disease is more likely to be common when food supply is limited, because organisms are not as able to fight off infection when they are not fully healthy. So the combination of limited food and disease can cause a decrease in population size and growth.

Infectious diseases need to be transmitted from one individual to another, so they will have a greater impact on death rate when the population is already large. They will have a more limited impact on a small population where the individuals are fairly widely spread in the area.

QUESTIONS

1. Name two variables that increase population size and two variables that decrease population size.

2. Give an example of an environmental factor that can result in an increase in population growth, and explain why it has this effect.

3. Give examples of two environmental factors that can decrease population growth and explain why they have this effect.

Sigmoid population growth curve

If you measure the growth of a population of microorganisms growing in a fermenter, you will get a curve similar to the one shown below. Note that the conditions within the fermenter are maintained to provide an ideal environment so that the microorganisms grow as rapidly as possible.

The shape of this curve gives it its name, a **sigmoid population growth curve**. This curve has four distinct phases, as shown in Fig.19.26.

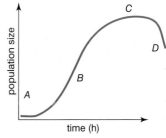

- The level phase at the start (A) is known as the **lag phase**.
- The stage when population size is rapidly increasing (B) is known as the **exponential phase** or **log phase**.
- This is followed by a stage at which population size does not change (C), which is called the **stationary phase**.
- The final stage is where the population size decreases (D), which is known as the **death phase**.

△ Fig 19.26 A sigmoid population growth curve has four distinct phases, as described in the text.

The change from one phase to the next in a sigmoid growth curve is a result of changing conditions within the environment in which the organisms are growing, caused by the organisms themselves.

- In the lag phase, the organisms are adapting to the environment, e.g. making new enzymes to suit the nutrients in the food supply, before they can grow sufficiently to reproduce. Also there are so few individuals at the start that it takes a while for numbers to increase in a way that is measurable.
- In the exponential or log phase, the growth rate is **exponential**, meaning that the increase at any point is dependent on the number just beforehand. This is when the food supply is abundant, so birth rate is rapid and death rate small. The main factor limiting population growth at this point is the number of new individuals that can be produced, i.e. the birth rate.
- In the stationary phase, population growth levels out. This occurs when some factor in the environment, such as a nutrient, becomes limited because it is not being replenished, increasing the death rate and decreasing the birth rate so that they become equal. Unless more nutrient is added at this point, the stationary phase will continue until the nutrient becomes severely limiting.
- In the death phase, the population decreases, either because food has become very scarce or something produced by the organisms (such as a metabolic waste) increases to a high enough concentration to become toxic. This causes the death rate to increase further and the birth rate to fall, so that death rate exceeds the birth rate.

Organisms in natural environments are unlikely to show a sigmoid population growth curve because they are affected by many other factors, such as changing physical conditions of temperature or light, predators and disease. They may also be able to migrate from the area when conditions get difficult.

QUESTIONS

1. Name the four phases of a sigmoid growth curve.

2. Give an example of where a population of organisms may have a sigmoid growth curve. Explain your answer.

3. EXTENDED Explain why a sigmoid growth curve shows the four phases that you named in your answer to Question 1.

END OF EXTENDED

Human population size

Today there are over 7 billion people living on Earth. One hundred years ago there were about 1.7 billion people. In one hundred years from now estimates suggest there could be anything from 5.5 billion to 14 billion people. This variation depends on predictions for birth rate and death rate in different parts of the world.

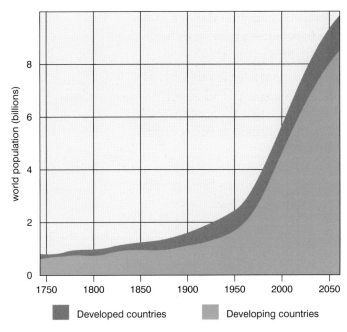

△ Fig 19.27 The change in human population size since 1750, and as predicted using average values for birth and death rate to 2050.

From the graph in Fig.19.27 we can see that:

• the total growth in global human population seems to follow the lag and log phases of a sigmoid growth curve
• the rate of growth in developed countries was greatest between about 1900 and 1950, and since then has become more constant
• the rate of growth in developing countries is still increasing rapidly
• the prediction from now to 2050 is an increase for all countries, but a slowly decreasing rate for developing countries.

If we think about the causes of the rapid increase in human population size, the key factors include:

• a more rapid increase in birth rate due to a greater abundance of food as a result of improved technology
• a decrease in death rate as a result of improved medicine, hygiene and health care.

Some predictions of future population size suggest that growth rate will slow down as birth rate falls in developing countries due to improved birth control.

REMEMBER

There are many ways of displaying human population growth, each with a different focus or message to tell. Look carefully at each chart or diagram and try to work out its 'message', and how that links to the social implications, both locally and globally, of the growth of the human population.

END OF EXTENDED

Another way of looking at population growth is to look at the age structure of a population.

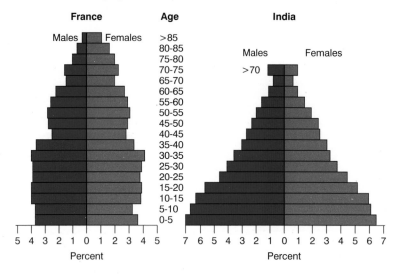

△ Fig 19.28 The age structures of the populations of France and India.

This can help us see in more detail what is happening in a particular population, and help to predict the impact of those changes.

The example compares the age structure of the population living in France (a developed country) and in India (a developing country), and the shapes of these charts are quite typical of the two groups of countries. From the graphs we can see that:

- in France more people live beyond the age of 70 than in India – this is the result of better food, hygiene and medical care generally in France than in India
- there are almost equal numbers of people in each five-year group up to the age of 40 in France, while there are many more younger people than older people in India – this is because improving food supply and medical care in India is increasing the number of children born, while in France the birth rate is much lower as couples choose to have fewer children and start their families at an older age.

SCIENCE IN CONTEXT **PLANNING FOR THE FUTURE**

Population size and growth are important factors that are considered by governments, scientists and others, when planning for the future. This includes planning for new roads, buildings, food supplies and developments in the health service, as well as predicting the impact of any changes on the environment and other species so as to mini-mise their effects and protect the world around us from our activities. (See also Topic 20.)

Social implications of human population growth

Human population growth has implications on a global, regional and local scale, for the environment and for the way we will be able to live with each other (the **social implications**) in the future.

On a global scale, the concerns are mainly around food supply, and being able to supply sufficient food for everyone, distributed so that nobody suffers from starvation or malnutrition.

On a countrywide or regional scale, where countries have a large proportion of younger people, one concern is providing sufficient jobs and homes for these people when they are old enough, as well as all the other things that people consider important in

△ Fig 19.29 A favela in the Morumbi district of Sao Paulo, Brazil. Although some people live in the expensive high-rise buildings, poor people live in the slum buildings, where living conditions are poor.

life, such as transport or internet access. In countries where the birth rate has already fallen, and people live until they are much older than the normal working age, there is a concern with there being enough money generated by the country to support older people who no longer work, including the additional health care that they need.

On a local scale, many people are moving from farmlands to cities, where there may be a better chance of work, food and health care. If the population of the city increases too quickly, this can lead to large areas of slum development, where there is poor hygiene, poor quality buildings and little space. This increases the risk of rapidly spreading infectious diseases, as well as general unrest in people that can lead to violence.

QUESTIONS

1. Describe the rate of growth of the global human population over the past 150 years.

2. Explain why there are different predictions of global human population growth over the next 100 years.

3. Give two reasons why human population growth rate differs in different countries.

4. Give two examples of social implications of the human population growth in cities (include one positive and one negative implication in your answer).

End of topic checklist

Key words

biomass, birth rate, carbon cycle, carnivore, combustion, community, consumer, death rate, decomposer, deforestation, denitrifying bacteria, ecosystem, food chain, food web, fossil fuel, herbivore, nitrifying bacteria, nitrogen cycle, nitrogen-fixing bacteria, nutrient cycle, omnivore, population, producer, pyramid of biomass, pyramid of numbers, sigmoid population growth curve, social implications, trophic level, water cycle

During your study of this topic you should have learned:

◯ Producers are organisms that make their own organic nutrients (food), such as plants that use sunlight to produce sugars through photosynthesis.

◯ Consumers are organisms that gain energy by feeding on other organisms. There are different levels of consumer, depending on their position in a food chain.

◯ A herbivore is an animal that eats plants, and a carnivore is an animal that eats other animals.

◯ A food chain shows the transfer of energy between organisms as a result of feeding, starting with a producer.

◯ A food web is an interconnection of food chains that share some organisms.

◯ How to define decomposer as an organism that gets its energy from dead or waste organic material.

◯ Food chains and food webs can be used to interpret the impact of human activity such as overharvesting of fish and introduction of foreign species to a habitat.

◯ **EXTENDED** A trophic level is a feeding level within a food chain, food web or pyramid of numbers or biomass.

◯ **EXTENDED** Energy is gained at each trophic level as it is transferred from light in plants or from food in animals to make new body tissue.

◯ **EXTENDED** Energy is transferred to the environment at each trophic level as heat energy from respiration, and also as chemical energy from animals in the form of faeces and urine.

◯ **EXTENDED** That a food chain is rarely more than five trophic levels in length because the top trophic level within the chain contains too little energy to support another trophic level.

◯ **EXTENDED** That it is more efficient in energy terms for people to eat crop plants than to feed the plants to animals that they then eat.

○ A pyramid of numbers is a diagram drawn to scale that shows the numbers of organisms at each level in a food chain.

○ EXTENDED A pyramid of biomass is a diagram drawn to scale that shows the biomass of organisms at each level in a food chain.

○ EXTENDED A pyramid of biomass is a better way to represent a food chain than a pyramid of numbers because the biomass is a better measure of the amount of energy in each trophic level.

○ The carbon cycle can be represented as a diagram that shows how photosynthesis, respiration, decomposition and combustion contribute to the transfer of carbon between organisms and the environment.

○ The water cycle can be represented as a diagram that shows how evaporation, transpiration, condensation and precipitation contribute to the transfer of water between the air, ground and organisms.

○ EXTENDED Combustion and deforestation can rapidly increase the carbon dioxide concentration in the atmosphere.

○ EXTENDED The nitrogen cycle can be represented as a diagram that shows how nitrogen is transferred between organisms and the environment, and highlights the importance of bacteria in the processes of nitrification, denitrification and nitrogen fixation within the cycle.

○ A *population* is a group of organisms of one species living in the same area at the same time.

○ Food supply, predation and disease can affect population growth.

○ EXTENDED A *community* is all the populations of different species that live in an ecosystem, and an ecosystem is a unit of a community and the environment with which they interact.

○ EXTENDED The phases of a sigmoid population growth curve are the lag phase, the exponential (log) phase, the stationary phase and the death phase. Each stage has different causes.

○ The human population has grown rapidly over the past 250 years, and this has social implications, including food supply and starvation.

○ EXTENDED An ecosystem is the community of organisms and the environment with which the organisms interact.

End of topic questions

Note: The marks awarded for these questions indicate the level of detail required in the answers. In the examination, the number of marks awarded to questions like these may be different.

1. The photograph in Fig.19.30 shows lions eating a dead zebra. Before the lions killed the zebra, the zebra had been feeding on grass.

△ Fig 19.30 Lions eating their kill.

a) Is the lion a carnivore or herbivore? Explain your answer. **(2 marks)**

b) At which level of a food chain does the zebra feed? **(1 mark)**

c) Draw a food chain for the organisms shown in the photograph. **(2 marks)**

d) Lions also feed on the herbivores gazelle and wildebeest. Use all these organisms to draw a food web for the African grassland. **(3 marks)**

2. **EXTENDED** In a tropical forest, the layer of dead leaves (called the leaf litter) on the forest floor is usually very thin at all times of the year. In temperate woodlands (where there are seasons of summer and winter), many trees drop their leaves in the autumn and grow new ones in the spring.

a) Tropical trees drop a few leaves at a time at any time of year. What happens to the leaves on the ground? Explain your answer as fully as possible. **(2 marks)**

b) The leaf litter in a temperate woodland is deep all through winter, when it may be cold enough for snow, until it gets warm again in spring. Then the leaf litter disappears. Explain these observations as fully as you can. **(3 marks)**

△ Fig 19.31 A temperate woodland in winter.

3. In a garden there are five lettuces. There are 40 caterpillars feeding on the lettuces until two thrushes (insectivorous birds) eat all the caterpillars.

   a) Draw a pyramid of numbers for this food chain. **(3 marks)**

   b) Describe the limitations of this pyramid. **(2 marks)**

   c) EXTENDED Describe the difficulty of preparing the data for a pyramid of biomass for these organisms. **(2 marks)**

4. Use the food web in Fig.19.4 to predict what would happen to the following species if all the herbivorous insects were killed by insecticide. Explain your answers.

   a) predatory insects **(2 marks)**

   b) insectivorous birds **(2 marks)**

   c) mice **(2 marks)**

   d) snakes **(2 marks)**

5. Fig.19.32 shows a pyramid of numbers for a food chain early in the year. Later in the year the caterpillars change into butterflies and fly away to feed on flowers.

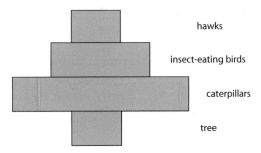

△ Fig 19.32 A pyramid of number at one time of year.

   a) Which organisms are the primary consumers in this food chain? Explain your answer. **(2 marks)**

   b) Explain why this pyramid is not the usual pyramid shape. **(1 mark)**

   c) Suggest what this pyramid would look like for the same food chain in late summer. Explain your answer. **(2 marks)**

   d) EXTENDED The data in this pyramid were converted to a pyramid of biomass. Suggest the shape of the pyramid of biomass. Explain your answer. **(2 marks)**

6. EXTENDED Explain as fully as you can why a food chain is unlikely to include more than five trophic levels. **(6 marks)**

7. EXTENDED Food chains in northern regions on Earth may be much shorter than food chains in tropical rain forests. Thinking only in terms of energy, try to explain this difference. **(4 marks)**

8. EXTENDED A farmer feeds wheat grain grown in his fields to his chickens, to fatten them up for meat. Explain the error of this in terms of trophic energy efficiency. **(2 marks)**

9. Imagine one water molecule in the ocean. Write bullet point notes as an outline for a children's story describing the journey of the water molecule through the water cycle. Include the processes of evaporation, condensation, transpiration and precipitation in your notes. **(7 marks)**

10. The graph in Fig.19.33 shows the change in carbon dioxide concentration above a forest over 2 days, and the light intensity just above the top of the trees.

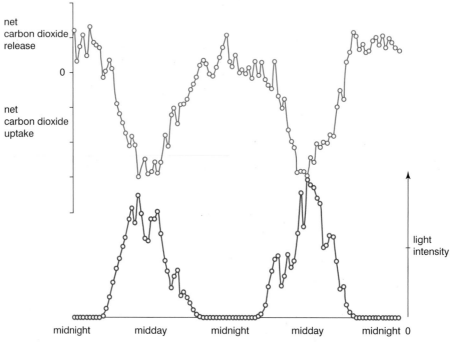

△ Fig 19.33 Changes in light intensity and carbon dioxide concentration above a forest.

a) Explain the changes in light intensity shown in the graph. **(2 marks)**

b) Explain the changes in carbon dioxide concentration shown in the graph. (Remember there are more organisms than just the trees in the forest.) **(4 marks)**

11. a) EXTENDED Explain why waterlogged soils, such as swamps and bogs, usually have very low concentrations of nitrates. **(3 marks)**

b) Sundew plants live in waterlogged soils of swamps and bogs. They have sticky hairs on some leaves that are special adaptations for catching insects. Once the insect is trapped, the leaf rolls up and enzymes are secreted to digest the animal. The digested

△ Fig 19.34 This sundew plant has trapped an insect, which it will digest.

liquid is absorbed by the plant. Suggest why these adaptations are important to the sundew. **(3 marks)**

12. EXTENDED 'Without bacteria in the soil, there would be no plants and no animals.' Explain this statement. **(5 marks)**

13. A population of mice live in field. Predict the change in population growth of the mice as a result of the following factors. Explain each of your answers.

a) The crop in the field ripens, producing a lot of grain (a favourite food of the mice). **(4 marks)**

b) The local fox families produce many offspring. (Foxes feed their young on mice.) **(2 marks)**

14. EXTENDED The graph in Fig.19.35 shows that the growth in human population has been exponential up to about the year 2000 CE.

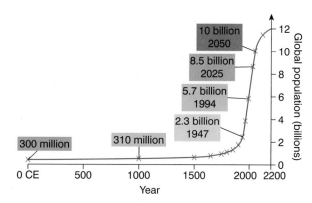

△ Fig 19.35 Change in global human population size since 0 CE, as predicted up to 2200 CE.

a) What is meant by *exponential* growth? **(1 mark)**

b) Suggest why the global human population has this shape up to about 2000 CE. **(1 mark)**

c) Describe the predicted shape of the graph up to the year 2200 CE. **(1 mark)**

d) Explain why the prediction gives this shape. **(2 marks)**

e) Suggest one global and one local social implication of this increase in human population to 2200 CE. **(2 marks)**

Microorganisms such as bacteria have long been engineered to produce useful proteins for commercial and industrial applications. Advances in biotechnology have over more recent decades led to a new era in medicine that is enabling the development of highly effective drugs that are not based on chemical compounds, but on proteins and other biological molecules. More recently, domesticated animals, such as cattle and rabbits, have been engineered to secrete therapeutic proteins into the milk, which can be purified out and used to treat some rare and devastating human diseases.

CONTENTS

20
Biotechnology and genetic engineering

△ Many crops are being genetically modified to improve their ability to grow well and provide the food we need for a growing human population.

Biotechnology and genetic engineering

△ Fig 20.1 This mouse has been modified with the genes of a jellyfish that make it glow in the dark.

INTRODUCTION

All living organisms are constructed from their genetic code. In organisms that have cells with nuclei, this genetic code is in the form of DNA. Even organisms such as bacteria that don't have nuclei still use DNA to carry their genetic code. As a result of evolution the genetic code in all organisms is decoded in exactly the same way. This means that a piece of DNA taken from one organism, such as the gene that causes a jellyfish to glow in ultraviolet light, and placed in the nucleus of a completely different organism, such as a mouse, will be decoded in the same way as it was originally: so that the mouse glows like a jellyfish in ultraviolet light.

This may seem not very useful, but it has important applications. Inserting the glow gene into cancer cells in humans would help researchers see how the cells move around inside the body, and this could possibly help with treatment.

KNOWLEDGE CHECK

✓ Bacteria are single-celled prokaryote organisms with a simple cell structure.
✓ Some bacterial cells contain plasmids of genetic material in addition to the bacterial chromosome.
✓ Anaerobic respiration is the release of energy from glucose molecules without the presence of oxygen.
✓ Digestive enzymes are catalysts that increase the rate of breakdown of substrate molecules into smaller molecules.
✓ Antibiotics are drugs that are taken to kill or slow the growth of bacterial infections in the body.
✓ Genes are small sections of DNA that code for a particular feature or protein.

LEARNING OBJECTIVES

✓ State that bacteria are useful in biotechnology and genetic engineering because they can produce complex molecules and reproduce rapidly.
✓ **EXTENDED** Explain that bacteria are useful in biotechnology and genetic engineering because there are no ethical concerns over their manipulation, they share the genetic code with other organisms, and they contain plasmids.

✓ Describe the role of anaerobic respiration in yeast during production of ethanol for biofuels, and during bread-making.

✓ Investigate the use of pectinase in producing fruit juice.

✓ Investigate the use of enzymes in biological washing powders.

✓ **EXTENDED** Investigate the use of lactase to produce lactose-free milk.

✓ **EXTENDED** Describe the use of *Penicillium* mould to produce penicillin.

✓ **EXTENDED** Explain how fermenters are used to produce penicillin.

✓ Define the term *genetic engineering*.

✓ Give examples of genetic engineering.

✓ **EXTENDED** Outline the process of genetic engineering using bacteria.

✓ **EXTENDED** Discuss the advantages and disadvantages of genetically modified crops.

BIOTECHNOLOGY AND GENETIC ENGINEERING

As you have seen in previous topics, humans use organisms in many ways as resources, such as for food or for building materials. We also use organisms to make other products, such as extracting chemicals from plants and animals to use as drugs (see Topic 15). This use of organisms to make other products is an example of **biotechnology**, and we have been doing this in different ways for thousands of years.

As our understanding of organisms and our ability to manipulate them have increased, we have developed new ways to use organisms for our needs, including genetic engineering (which is described in more detail below).

Bacteria are particularly useful organisms in biotechnology and genetic engineering because they produce complex molecules. For example, certain bacteria added to milk produce enzymes that break down chemicals in the milk and change it to yoghurt. Bacteria are also useful because they reproduce rapidly, so that the amount of chemicals they produce can also rapidly increase.

◁ Fig 20.2 The 'blue' bits in this blue cheese are due to the Penicillium added to the cultures.

The bacterial chromosome and plasmids are made of DNA – the same DNA that is found in the chromosomes of animals and plants. This means that all organisms share the same genetic code – a gene that codes for a particular protein in one organism will code for the same protein in another organism. The presence of plasmids in bacteria, separate from the main bacterial chromosome, is useful because they are small and easy to extract and handle.

When we try to manipulate animals and animal cells for these purposes, many people have ethical concerns about how the animals may be harmed as they are manipulated and grown. This means they believe that using animals in this way is wrong. People do not have the same concerns about using bacteria like this, often because they think that bacteria do not feel pain or distress as animals may do. This is another useful feature of bacteria, making them useful in biotechnology and genetic engineering. So it can be easier to use bacteria in biotechnology than to use other, more complex organisms.

END OF EXTENDED

QUESTIONS

1. Write a definition of the term *biotechnology* in your own words.

2. Explain why bacteria are useful in biotechnology.

3. EXTENDED Explain why people may have fewer ethical concerns over the manipulation of bacteria than they have about the manipulation of animals.

BIOTECHNOLOGY

Yeast and biofuels

In Topic 12 you learnt about the anaerobic respiration of yeast. This is where yeast cells break down glucose to release energy without the use of oxygen. The products of this reaction are ethanol (an alcohol) and carbon dioxide. Ethanol is increasingly being used as a **biofuel**, that is a fuel made from living organisms rather than a fossil fuel such as oil, coal or gas. In countries such as Brazil and the USA, biofuel is partly replacing petrol as the fuel for cars and other vehicles.

Plant materials are used as the substrate for producing ethanol. Sometimes the waste parts of crop plants, such as the stalks, are used, but sometimes crops are grown specially and the whole crop is harvested for making ethanol. In some places, people are concerned that this is reducing the land area available for the local people to grow the food they need.

△ Fig 20.3 This biofuel plant produces ethanol from the breakdown of waste crop material by yeast.

The plant materials are crushed or chopped into small pieces to help release the sugars and starch in the plant cells. Yeast is then added to break down the sugars and starch to produce ethanol. The liquid is separated from the remaining solid plant tissue and treated to remove much of the water. This leaves a concentrated solution of ethanol, which can be used as a fuel.

Yeast and bread-making

Yeast has been used for thousands of years to make bread. A bread dough made without yeast doesn't rise. Adding yeast makes a bread that is softer, more spongy and has a different flavour. This sponginess is caused by the carbon dioxide given off during the anaerobic respiration of yeast. (Note that yeast will respire anaerobically when there are plenty of sugars, even if there is oxygen available.)

△ Fig 20.4 Bread dough rising as a result of yeast. The dough in the top tin has risen after dough similar to that in the lower tin was left for an hour in a warm place.

Before the yeast is added to the flour for making bread, it is first mixed with a sugar solution and kept warm. This activates the yeast, which means that the yeast cells start to grow and divide as they begin to break down the sugars. The activated yeast solution is mixed with flour, and any flavourings for the bread, and the mixture is kneaded to make a dough in which the yeast and flour are thoroughly mixed. The dough may be shaped at this stage, into loaf or roll shapes. It is then left in a warm place for a while.

During this time the bread rises, which means it increases in volume. As the yeast breaks down the sugars and starch in the dough it releases carbon dioxide and ethanol. The carbon dioxide gas is trapped within the dough, forming bubbles. When the dough has risen, it is placed in a hot oven to bake. The baking kills the yeast and evaporates the ethanol, but the bubbles remain in the dough, making a spongy-textured bread.

Pectinase and fruit juice

Fruit juice is produced by squeezing the juice out of fruit. Chopping up the fruit before squeezing helps to release a lot more juice from the fruit cells. However, not every cell is broken open, and so a lot of juice remains trapped inside whole cells.

Pectinase is an enzyme that breaks down a chemical called pectin, which is one of the chemicals found in plant cell walls that helps to hold plant cells together. If pectinase is added to the chopped fruit before it is squeezed, it helps to break open more cell walls. This makes it possible to squeeze out even more juice from the same amount of fruit.

Developing investigative skills

Some students were asked to investigate the effect of pectinase on the amount of fruit juice produced from one variety of apples. They were given a solution of pectinase enzyme, some apples and access to a water bath set at 30 °C.

Devise and plan investigations

❶ Describe how you would set up this investigation, using the equipment offered to the students. Remember to explain how variables should be controlled.

❷ Write a prediction for your investigation and explain your prediction.

Analyse and interpret data

The students measured the following volumes of juice squeezed from the same mass of apple pulp in each case.

	Volume of juice (cm³)
without enzyme at room temperature (20 °C)	12.6
with enzyme at room temperature (20 °C)	13.4
with enzyme at 30 °C	15.1

❸ Describe the results.

❹ Explain the differences in the results using your scientific knowledge.

❺ Draw a conclusion from this investigation.

Evaluate data and methods

❻ Explain why the water bath was set at 30 °C and not at a higher temperature.

❼ Explain why the same mass of fruit pulp must be used in each test.

Biological washing powders

Many of the stains that need washing out of our clothes are organic molecules, such as oil from our skin, protein from blood, and fat and protein from our food. Detergents made from soap can remove some of these stains, particularly if used with hot water. However, it can take a lot of time and effort to get these stains out of the clothes and make them clean again.

Biological washing powders contain digestive enzymes similar to the ones that help to break down food in your alimentary canal. The enzymes have two advantages:

- they work quickly to break down large molecules into small ones that can easily be washed away in the washing water
- they are effective at much lower temperatures than washing powders that contain no enzymes, which means that the water does not need to be heated as much, and that saves time and energy.

△ Fig 20.5 A biological washing powder will get these stains out more quickly and easily than soap and hot water.

Enzymes have an optimum temperature at which they work fastest. So the best cleaning happens at the optimum temperature for the enzymes in the washing powder. This can be investigated by testing the cleaning power of biological and non-biological washing powders at different temperatures on the same range of 'stains' on materials.

Lactose-free milk

Lactose is the form of sugar that occurs in milk. Human babies are born with the ability to produce the enzyme **lactase** in their alimentary canal. Lactase digests lactose to simple sugars that can be absorbed into the body through the wall of the small intestine (see Topic 7). Most people lose the ability to make lactase in their body as they grow older, although some people, such as those who live in northern Europe, East Africa and Mongolia, keep the ability to make lactase all their life.

People who stop making lactase as they get older are not only unable to digest lactose, the milk they drink can upset their digestion and cause nausea, flatulence or diarrhoea. This is known as lactose intolerance. These people are unable to drink milk or eat milk products such as cheese and yoghurt.

△ Fig 20.6 Lactose-free milk can be drunk by people who are lactose-intolerant.

Milk can be made lactose-free by adding lactase and leaving the milk to stand for a while to allow the enzyme to break down the lactose. Although the enzyme works more slowly at lower temperature, it is important to keep the milk in a cool place to prevent bacteria in the milk breaking down some of the proteins in the milk and turning it sour.

QUESTIONS

1. Which product of anaerobic respiration of yeast is important in the following: **(a)** bread-making, **(b)** manufacture of biofuel?

2. Describe the effect of pectinase in the production of fruit juice.

3. Explain why biological washing powders clean more effectively than soap and hot water at cooler temperatures.

4. EXTENDED Explain the use of lactase to produce lactose-free milk.

EXTENDED

Producing penicillin

Penicillin was the first antibiotic that was discovered (see Topic 15). Penicillin is naturally produced by the fungus *Penicillium* in order to protect the fungus from infection by some kinds of bacteria. Since the discovery of penicillin, methods have been developed to grow the *Penicillium* fungus on a large scale. The fungus secretes penicillin into the fluid surrounding it. The penicillin can then be extracted from the fluid and used to make antibiotic medicine that can help us to fight off bacterial infections in our body.

Penicillin is made on an industrial scale by growing the *Penicillium* fungus in a large vessel called a **fermenter**. Conditions inside the fermenter need to be controlled to help the fungus grow as quickly as possible.

- Nutrients needed for growth are added to replace those that are used up. These include an energy source, such as glucose, for respiration. They also include other nutrients needed for the synthesis of new cell materials, such as a nitrogen source (ammonia, for example) for making proteins and nucleic acids.
- The reactions of respiration release heat energy. If the temperature of the mixture gets too high, this could affect the enzymes and slow down the rate of growth. A cooling jacket is used to remove excess heat, and the temperature inside the fermenter is monitored continually.
- The pH is continually monitored because if it varies too far from the optimum pH for the enzymes, the rate of growth will slow. If needed, the pH of the solution is adjusted using buffer chemicals.
- *Penicillium* is aerobic, so the fungus needs a continuous supply of oxygen in the form of air bubbled through the mixture in the fermenter.
- The mixture in the fermenter is continually agitated by stirring, to make sure the fungal cells don't all settle to the bottom and so that all the materials in the fermenter are well mixed.
- Before a new batch of culture is added to the fermenter, it is sterilised by passing steam through it. Also, all solutions added to the fermenter are sterilised. These aseptic precautions make sure that no other microorganisms are added to the fermenter, which could affect the growth of the fungus.

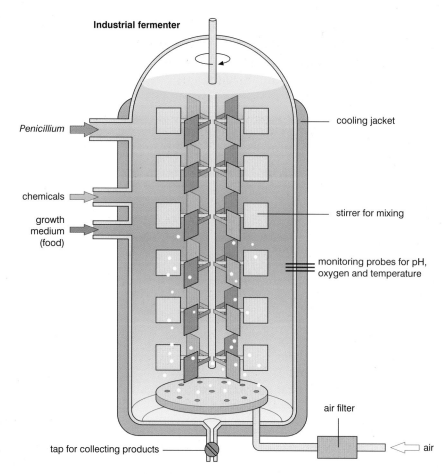

Industrial fermenter

Penicillium

chemicals

growth
medium
(food)

cooling jacket

stirrer for mixing

monitoring probes for pH,
oxygen and temperature

air filter

tap for collecting products

air

△ Fig 20.7 The structure of an industrial fermenter for the growth of *Penicillium* fungus.

Once the process has been going long enough for the mixture in the
fermenter to contain enough product, some of it is drained through a
tap at the bottom of the fermenter. The mixture is then processed to
extract the product. More culture and nutrients can be added to the
fermenter to replace what has been drained off, so that the process can
continue without stopping.

END OF EXTENDED

QUESTIONS

1. **EXTENDED** Explain what is meant by an *industrial fermenter*.

2. **EXTENDED a)** Name four conditions inside a fermenter that are
   controlled while the microorganisms are growing.

   b) For each condition named in **(a)**, explain why it might change
   and why it needs to be controlled.

3. **EXTENDED a)** What is meant by *aseptic precautions*?

   b) Why are these needed when preparing the fermenter before
   adding the fungus?

GENETIC ENGINEERING

Genetic engineering (also called *genetic modification*) is the cutting out of a gene from one organism and its insertion into the DNA of another organism so that the gene is expressed and produces its characteristic. The DNA that is formed when the gene is inserted is called the *recombinant DNA*, and the organism containing the recombinant DNA is called a *transgenic organism*, or sometimes a *genetically modified organism* (GMO).

An organism may also be genetically engineered by removing (sometimes called 'knocking out') or changing a particular gene.

There are many examples of genetically modified organisms that have been produced.

- The human gene that codes for insulin has been removed from a human chromosome and inserted into a bacterium. The bacterium produces human insulin that can be purified and used by people who need to inject insulin to control diabetes.
- Crop plants, such as wheat or maize, have been genetically modified to contain a gene from a bacterium that produces a poison that kills insects. When pests, such as caterpillars, eat the plants the broken cells produce the poison, which kills the pests.
- Crop plants have also been genetically modified to make them resistant to a herbicide (plant-killing chemical). This means that when the herbicide is sprayed over the growing crop it kills weeds without harming the crop plants.

◁ Fig 20.8 A field containing a GM crop and weeds after spraying with herbicide.

- Some crops have been genetically modified to contain additional vitamins. For example, 'golden rice' has been genetically modified to contain genes from another plant and from a bacterium. These genes help the rice to produce a chemical in the rice grain that is turned into vitamin A in the human body. The scientists who made 'golden rice' hoped that it could be grown in places where people suffer from diseases caused by a lack of vitamin A in their diet, and so help to prevent these diseases.

Genetically modified crops

In some countries, large areas of GM crops such as soya, maize and rice are grown, but in other parts of the world countries have decided against growing them. This is because, although many advantages are given for growing GM crops, there are also concerns about their impact on the environment.

The advantages given for growing GM crops include:

- less use of chemicals such as herbicides and pesticides, which should be better for other organisms in the environment and save time, effort and costs for the farmer
- increased yield of food from the crops because they are not competing with weeds for water and nutrients, or not suffering from as much pest damage.

The disadvantages include:

- reduced biodiversity, because there are fewer plant species where herbicide has been used, which will reduce the food available for insects and therefore for insect-eating birds
- increased cost of seed, because the company that produces it will charge more for GM seed to recover the costs of developing it – this can make the seed too expensive for poor farmers who cannot compete with the production of large, more wealthy farms
- increased dependency on use of particular chemicals, such as the herbicide that the plants are resistant to, which can increase costs for farmers
- a risk that the inserted genes may be transferred to similar wild plants in the environment through pollination – for example, this would make herbicide-resistance in a crop plant useless, as the weeds would also be unaffected by the herbicide.

It can be difficult to assess the claims made by opposing views on GM crops. For example, although the companies that produce GM seed suggest that its use will increase yield, scientific research suggests that in many cases this doesn't happen because inserting a gene can affect the ability of the plant to grow as well as non-GM plants. Many environmental groups also argue that GM crops are unsafe for eating. However, there is no scientific evidence to suggest that these foods have any effect on health.

An example of genetic engineering

One of the best examples of genetic engineering is the insertion of the gene that codes for human insulin into bacteria, causing the bacteria to produce human insulin. Insulin is a hormone needed by some people who are diabetic and unable to make their own insulin. They have to inject the hormone every day to control their blood glucose concentration (see Topic 14).

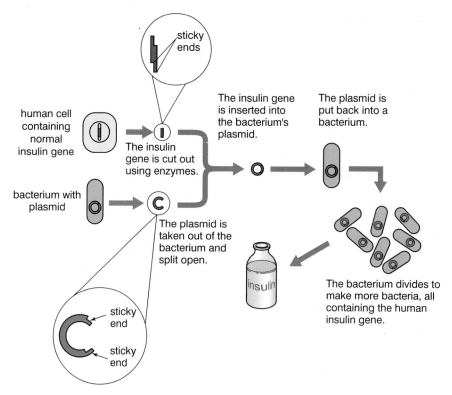

△ Fig 20.9 The process of genetic modification of bacteria to make insulin.

- The human insulin gene is identified in human DNA and cut out using a **restriction enzyme**. This leaves **'sticky ends'**, where there are a few bases on one strand of the DNA that are not paired with bases on the other strand.
- Many copies of the gene are made.
- Bacterial plasmids are extracted and cut open using the same restriction enzyme, to produce sticky ends that match those on the insulin gene.
- The plasmids and genes are mixed together, and a ligase enzyme added to join the sticky ends.
- The plasmids are put back into bacterial cells, which are then tested to check if they contain the inserted insulin gene. Any plasmids that do not contain the gene are discarded.
- The recombinant plasmids act as vectors when they are inserted into bacteria. These bacteria now produce human insulin.
- The bacteria are cultured on a large scale in a fermenter.

△ Fig 20.10 Human insulin being produced in a plant in Russia.

This produces large quantities of human insulin quickly and relatively cheaply. Before this method was developed, insulin was extracted from animals, such as pigs, that were grown specially for this purpose, then killed and the insulin extracted from their pancreas. The advantages of using genetically modified bacteria not only include the larger quantities that are produced more rapidly and at a cheaper price, but also the insulin produced from bacteria is like natural human insulin and so less likely to cause a reaction in the human body than using insulin from another animal.

If new genes are introduced into the cells of an animal or plant embryo in an early stage of development then, as the cells divide, the new cells will also contain copies of the new gene.

Only if the gamete cells contain the new gene, can it be passed on to offspring.

SCIENCE IN CONTEXT

THE ADVANTAGES OF GM INSULIN

Insulin is a hormone that is essential for the control of blood glucose concentration (see Topic 14). Some people are unable to produce insulin – they have Type 1 diabetes. They need to inject insulin regularly to keep their blood glucose concentration under control.

Before the development of transgenic bacteria containing the human insulin gene, insulin was extracted from the pancreas of domesticated animals. It was not only a slow and expensive process; the insulin produced by other species is slightly different from human insulin, so it could cause other problems in people.

As the gene expressed in transgenic bacteria is the human gene, these bacteria produce insulin that is identical to human insulin. Also, growing the bacteria in a fermenter produces much larger amounts of insulin, more rapidly and more cheaply than the old process.

QUESTIONS

1. Explain what we mean by *genetic engineering*.

2. Give two examples of organisms that have been genetically engineered.

3. EXTENDED Give one advantage and one disadvantage of GM crops.

4. EXTENDED Use the example of bacteria modified to produce human insulin to explain how genetic engineering is carried out.

End of topic checklist

Key words

biofuel, biological washing powder, biotechnology, fermenter, genetic engineering, lactase, pectinase

During your study of this topic you should have learned:

○ Bacteria are useful in biotechnology and genetic engineering because they can make complex molecules, and they reproduce rapidly.

○ EXTENDED Bacteria are also useful in biotechnology and genetic engineering because they share the genetic code with other organisms, they contain plasmids, and people are not concerned about their manipulation and growth.

○ Ethanol produced during anaerobic respiration in yeast is useful as a biofuel.

○ Carbon dioxide produced during anaerobic respiration in yeast is useful in making bread rise.

○ Pectinase is an enzyme that is used to break down plant cell walls, which increases the production of fruit juice.

○ Enzymes in biological washing powders help to break down organic chemicals in stains at a lower temperature and more easily than non-biological detergents.

○ EXTENDED The enzyme lactase can be used to break down lactose in milk so that people who are lactose-intolerant can drink it without reaction.

○ EXTENDED *Penicillium* is the fungus that produces the antibiotic penicillin.

○ EXTENDED Fermenters can be used to produce penicillin on a large scale.

○ Genetic engineering is the taking of a gene from an individual of one species and placing it in another species so that it produces the characteristic.

○ How to give examples of genetic engineering, including the insertion of the human insulin gene into bacteria, the insertion of genes into crop plants that makes them resistant to a herbicide or to attack by insect pests, and the insertion of genes into crop plants so that they produce additional vitamins.

○ EXTENDED Advantages of growing GM crops include reducing the amount of chemicals needed to help the crop grow well, and possible increased yield of food from the crop.

○ EXTENDED Possible disadvantages of growing GM crops include decreased biodiversity, increased risk of transfer of inserted genes to wild plants and increased cost to the farmer of seed.

○ EXTENDED Human insulin is produced from bacteria by inserting the human gene into bacterial plasmids, inserting the plasmids into bacteria and growing the bacteria on a large scale in a fermenter.

End of topic questions

Note: The marks awarded for these questions indicate the level of detail required for the answers. In the examination, the number of marks awarded to questions like these may be different.

1. This car is being filled with biofuel.

△ Fig 20.11 Some cars run on biofuel.

a) Explain what we mean by *biofuel*. **(1 mark)**

b) Biofuel is produced during the anaerobic respiration of yeast. Write a word equation for this reaction and identify the product that is the biofuel. **(2 marks)**

c) Name one substrate (starting material) that can be used to produce biofuel using yeast. **(1 mark)**

d) Describe two advantage of using biofuels to replace fossil fuels. **(2 marks)**

2. A manufacturer advertises 'Snow White' as a biological washing powder guaranteed to get clothes clean.

a) Explain what is meant by a *biological washing powder*. **(1 mark)**

b) The chemicals that make the washing powder 'biological' are produced by bacteria. Describe one advantage of using bacteria in biotechnology. **(1 mark)**

c) Explain why the biological washing powder can get clothes cleaner faster and at a lower temperature than soap and water. **(2 marks)**

d) Explain why there is no advantage to using biological washing powders at higher temperatures than described on the packaging. **(2 marks)**

3. EXTENDED Penicillin is produced in fermenters.

a) What is penicillin? **(1 mark)**

b) Which organism is used to produce penicillin? **(1 mark)**

c) Give one reason why penicillin is produced in a fermenter. **(1 mark)**

d) Explain why the fermenter needs to be cooled during the process. **(2 marks)**

4. This crop of maize (sweet corn) has been genetically engineered.

△ Fig 20.12 This maize crop has been labelled to show that it has grown from genetically engineered (modified) seed.

a) Explain what we mean by *genetic engineering*. **(1 mark)**

b) Give one example of a feature that has been given to a crop plant by genetic engineering. **(1 mark)**

c) Give one example of genetic engineering of a different organism, other than a plant. **(1 mark)**

5. EXTENDED 'Golden rice' is an example of a genetically modified rice. This variety produces a chemical in the rice grains that is changed into vitamin A in the human body.

a) Explain why golden rice was developed. **(2 marks)**

b) Outline the process that was used to produce golden rice. **(2 marks)**

c) Describe one disadvantage of golden rice. Explain your answer. **(2 marks)**

d) Explain why some people are against growing GM crops on health grounds. **(1 mark)**

6. EXTENDED **a)** Explain why bacteria need to be genetically engineered so that they produce human insulin. **(2 marks)**

b) Explain why bacteria can produce human insulin. **(2 marks)**

c) Describe the role of the following in producing genetically engineered bacteria: (i) restriction enzymes, (ii) DNA ligase, (iii) 'sticky ends', (iv) plasmids. **(4 marks)**

There is probably no place on Earth that is not affected by human activity. An estimated 40% of the land surface is cultivated to produce food, either from crops or animals. Changing land use, so that it produces food or provides places for us to live and work, destroys habitats for other organisms. The the waste we produce causes pollution of land, water and air unless it is properly controlled. As the human population grows, we must find ways of reducing our impact on ecosystems, so that we conserve resources and the many organisms with which we share the Earth.

CONTENTS

21

Human influences on ecosystems

△ Deforestation in the mountains of British Columbia Canada, destroys the habitats of many species of plants and animals that depend on the trees.

△ Fig 21.1 Before humans arrived on St Helena this landscape would have been covered with dense tropical rainforest.

Human influences on ecosystems

INTRODUCTION

St Helena is an isolated island in the Atlantic Ocean. The first people to reach the island arrived in 1502. The human population of the island slowly increased to over 1000 people in the 1700s, and around 4500 people live here now.

The first people to arrive on St Helena found many plants and animals that were unique to the island. As people cleared the dense tropical forest, to make space for building and for growing crops and keeping herd animals, many of these unique species became extinct.

The introduction of animals that didn't naturally live there, such as cats, goats and rats, also had a devastating effect on wildlife. Cats catch and kill small animals and birds, and rats steal and eat eggs from bird nests. Many of the lower areas near the sea are now completely bare of vegetation as a result of grazing by goats.

KNOWLEDGE CHECK

✓ Earth's atmosphere is affected by human activity (such as deforestation and combustion of fuels) and by natural processes (such as volcanoes).
✓ Development of the environment can be sustainable or non-sustainable.
✓ Organisms that cannot adapt to changing conditions fast enough may go extinct.

LEARNING OBJECTIVES

✓ Discuss ways in which food production has increased due to technology.
✓ **EXTENDED** Discuss problems of world food supplies and those that contribute to famine.
✓ Describe the negative impacts of large-scale monocultures of crops and of intensive livestock production.
✓ Describe reasons for habitat destruction.
✓ Describe the effects of deforestation on organisms, soil, water and air.
✓ **EXTENDED** Explain the effects of deforestation on organisms.
✓ Describe the sources and effects of pollution due to chemicals used in farming or nuclear fall-out.

✓ Describe how eutrophication can result from fertiliser leaching into water, and how this can harm fish.

✓ EXTENDED Explain how eutrophication is caused, and how it can lead to the death of organisms.

✓ Describe how sewage and chemical waste can pollute water.

✓ EXTENDED Discuss the effects of non-biodegradable plastics on the environment.

✓ EXTENDED Discuss the causes and effects of acid rain and how these can be reduced.

✓ Name two greenhouse gases and explain how human activities are contributing to their release.

✓ Describe the polluting effects of greenhouse gases.

✓ EXTENDED Explain how greenhouse gases may cause climate change.

✓ EXTENDED Describe the impact of female contraceptive hormones in water.

✓ Describe what is meant by a *sustainable resource*.

✓ EXTENDED Explain how forests and fish stocks can be conserved.

✓ EXTENDED Explain how sustainable management may be carried out.

✓ Describe the need for conservation of fossil fuels.

✓ Give examples of resources that can be recycled or reused.

✓ Explain why species may become endangered or extinct.

✓ Describe how sewage is treated to make it safe.

✓ Describe how endangered species may be conserved.

✓ EXTENDED Explain some reasons for conservation programmes.

FOOD SUPPLY

Our food comes mainly from crop plants and animals such as cows, fish and chickens. In order to increase food production, we have developed many technologies. Modern technologies that help to maximise food production include:

- use of agricultural machinery, which includes machines that are designed for specific tasks, such as sowing seed, spreading fertiliser or harvesting the crop – this makes it possible to carry out these tasks much more quickly and over larger areas

- use of fertilisers to give plants the nutrients that they need for rapid and healthy growth, and so produce a greater harvest (yield) – we now make over 500 million tonnes of fertilisers by chemical processes each year to spread on crop fields

- killing the pests using chemicals called *pesticides* increases the amount of food produced from a crop – pests are animals that damage crop plants by eating them, which reduces their growth and yield

- use of herbicides – plant growth is also reduced if the plant is competing with many neighbouring plants (weeds) for water and nutrients from the soil – using herbicides (plant-killing chemicals) that specifically kill the weeds will allow the crop plants to grow better and produce a bigger yield

- **selective breeding** (Topic 18) can be used to produce crop plants and animals with characteristics that result in more food for us.

Using all these technologies has helped world food production to grow continually, as shown in Fig. 21.2.

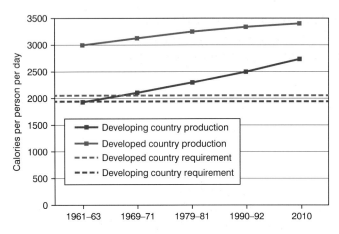

△ Fig 21.2 World food production from 1961 to 2010.

Problems with world food supplies

Although world food production is increasing, especially as new technologies become more available to farmers in developing countries, not everyone in the world has enough food to eat. According to the Food and Agriculture Organisation (FAO) of the United Nations, about 14% of people in the world do not get enough food, and starvation kills around 6 million children every year. Most of the people who do not have enough food live in very poor countries, where there is not enough money to buy in the new technologies.

World food production does produce more than enough food for everyone to have enough to eat. One problem is that the food is not distributed to everyone equally. People in developed countries have access to far more food, and eat more every day, than people in poor areas of the world.

Famine (widespread hunger) occurs in areas where crops fail year after year due to drought, as in parts of eastern Africa. It may also occur after

◁ Fig 21.3 People in refugee camps are most likely to suffer from famine unless there are sufficient food supplies brought in from other places.

major floods, such as those that happened in low-lying areas of Pakistan. The biggest cause of famine is warfare, which not only destroys crops and animals, but also displaces large numbers of people to refugee camps when they try to escape from the fighting.

END OF EXTENDED

Problems caused by food production

Growing large amounts of food for the global human population requires a lot of land. This can lead to large-scale deforestation and habitat destruction, as described later in this Topic. It can also have other negative impacts.

Many crop plants, such as rice, potatoes and wheat, are grown as large-scale **monocultures**. *Mono* means 'one', and a monoculture is one type of crop grown in a large area.

◁ 21.4 This crop of soybean is being grown as a monoculture.

Growing monocultures over a large area can be useful, because the farmer only needs a limited range of machinery to look after and harvest the crop. However, it can also cause problems.

- There is plenty of food for pests that feed on the crop. Pest populations can rapidly increase in size to a point where they damage the crop and reduce the amount of food that can be harvested from the plants. Farmers have to spray with chemical pesticides to keep the pest numbers under control.
- Only a very few species of animal can feed on the crop, so this means there are few food chains in the area. This reduces the range of species, or **biodiversity**, in the region. Use of pesticides can make this worse, if the chemicals kill species other than the pest species. This reduction in biodiversity is thought to be one of the factors responsible for the decrease in bee numbers (see Topic 16), which is of major concern for crops that need bees as pollinators.

◁ Fig 21.5 Clearance of forest for grazing large herds of cattle is still a major cause of deforestation and habitat destruction in the Amazon region.

Livestock production is the growing of animals for use as food for people. Growing a large number of livestock needs large areas of grassland for grazing.

Large areas of grassland are almost monocultures, so they also greatly reduce biodiversity in the area. If the numbers of grazing livestock are not properly controlled, there may be overgrazing, where too much grass is eaten. This not only reduces the amount of food for the livestock, it can also permanently damage the area by removing plants that hold the soil together. Wind and rain can then remove the soil, causing soil erosion (see below). After this, fewer plants will be able to grow in that ground.

Large numbers of the same kind of animal in the same area can attract a large number of pests, so the livestock need to be monitored and treated if they become ill.

QUESTIONS

1. Describe four ways in which modern technology has increased food supply.

2. a) Describe one negative impact of the large-scale monoculture of crop plants.

   b) Describe one negative impact of large-scale intensive livestock production.

3. EXTENDED Give reasons why people in some areas of the world suffer from famine.

HABITAT DESTRUCTION

We change and destroy habitats not only when we grow large areas of crops, or grassland for grazing livestock. We also use large areas of ground for building houses, factories and offices, and the road networks that link them.

Habitat destruction also occurs when we clear land to extract natural resources such as limestone rocks, coal and minerals (e.g. iron and copper). Pollution from the mining activities can damage the environment even further by adding poisonous chemicals to the water, or by creating large areas of waste.

Habitat destruction can also happen in the oceans as a result of human activity, such as:

△ Fig 21.6 This open cast mine for copper-containing rocks has cleared an area the size of a mountain.

- oil spills from container ships or from oil rigs can poison marine animals and clog up the feathers of sea birds
- fertilisers in river water can cause eutrophication (see section on Water Pollution) when the water reaches the oceans, producing a rapid increase in algal growth, which can poison other organisms
- warming of the oceans as a result of climate change caused by the enhanced greenhouse effect (see below) can make it unsuitable for the growth of corals, which is resulting in large-scale damage of many coral reefs around the world.

△ Fig 21.7 This river kingfisher has been badly affected by an oil spill.

Deforestation

Deforestation is the permanent destruction of large areas of forests and woodlands. It usually happens in areas that provide quality wood for furniture, such as the tropical hardwood forests of Malaysia, or to create farming or grazing land (all over the world).

Deforestation can result in many kinds of damage to the environment and the organisms that live there, including:

- extinction of organisms when there is nowhere left that is suitable for them to live
- loss of soil
- flooding
- carbon dioxide build-up in the atmosphere because there are not enough trees to store the carbon after photosynthesis.

EXTENDED

Forests act as a major carbon store because carbon dioxide is taken up from the atmosphere during photosynthesis and used to produce the chemical compounds that make up trees. When forests are cleared, and the trees are either burnt or left to rot, this carbon is released quickly as carbon dioxide. This rapidly increases the proportion of carbon dioxide compared with oxygen in the air surrounding the forest. On the scale of deforestation in the Amazon Basin, the amount of carbon dioxide released is so great that it cannot be brought back into balance as a result of photosynthesis.

Deforestation also has an effect on the water cycle. Trees draw ground water up through their roots and release it into the atmosphere by transpiration. As forest trees are removed the amount of water that can be held in an area decreases, which in turn can cause either increasing or decreasing rainfall in the area.

Removing the protective cover of vegetation from the soil can also result in **soil erosion**. This is where the soil is washed away by rain. The top layers of soil are the ones that contain the most nutrients, from the decay of dead vegetation, so soil erosion removes essential nutrients from the land. Soil nutrients are also lost by **leaching**, which is the soaking away of soluble nutrients in soil water because there are few plant roots in the soil to absorb the nutrients and lock them away in plant tissue. This loss of nutrients from the soil is permanent, and makes it very difficult for forest trees to regrow in the area, even if the land is not cultivated.

◁ Fig 21.8 This satellite image of a river estuary in Madagascar shows large amounts of soil in the water (orange). This is a result of deforestation near the river.

Loss of plant species due to deforestation will result in a loss of animal species in the same community, because of their feeding relationships in the food web. Many tropical rainforests are areas of high biodiversity, where many organisms live. They also contain many species found nowhere else because they have evolved together in an energy-rich and relatively unchanging environment. Destruction of tropical rainforests, such as in the Amazon Basin, is causing a high rate of extinction of species.

END OF EXTENDED

QUESTIONS

1. a) Give two causes of habitat destruction on land as a result of human activity.

b) Give two causes of habitat destruction in the oceans as a result of human activity.

2. EXTENDED Explain these terms:

a) deforestation

b) soil erosion

c) leaching.

3. EXTENDED Explain how deforestation may affect:

a) the water cycle

b) soil fertility

c) atmospheric carbon dioxide.

REMEMBER

In your exams, you may be given examples of ecosystems that have been damaged, polluted or conserved other than the ones discussed in this Topic. You will be expected to apply the principles you have learnt here to the examples you are given.

POLLUTION

Pollution is the adding of substances to the environment that cause harm. Many human activities can lead to pollution of water, land and air.

Pollution due to pesticides

A **pesticide** is a chemical used to kill pests. Pesticides include:

- **insecticides**, used to kill insect pests that damage a crop
- **herbicides**, used to kill plants that compete with a crop (i.e. a weed).

Plants do not provide food just for humans. A wide range of other animals and insects will eat crop plants if they are not protected. These animals damage the plants by eating parts of their leaves, or sucking out sap (e.g. aphids). Damaging the plants reduces their ability to make food and produce new tissue, so they don't grow as well and don't produce as great a crop yield. We call these animals **pests**, because they are a problem to us.

△ Fig 21.9 Locusts are pests of many plant species. A swarm of locusts may destroy crops over large areas.

Traditionally insect pests were controlled by hand, picking the pests off the plants, or by using domesticated animals, such as chickens, to eat them. Today, in the huge crop fields that we commonly use, the main control is by using chemical poisons that kill insects. These insecticides are sprayed on to the plants and eaten by the insects when they feed on the plants. The chemicals kill or harm the insects, which reduces the damage they cause, and so increases crop growth and yield.

Although insecticides are useful, there are problems with using them. Some insecticides kill not only the pest species but also other insect species in the community. This can have two drawbacks.

- Killing lots of different types of insect in an area will reduce the amount of food available for any animals that specialise in eating insects, such as insectivorous birds. This will affect other organisms in the food web, because of the way that they depend on each other.
- If the other species killed are predators of the pest then, once the insecticide has been washed away by rain, it is possible for the pest species to return and increase in number even more rapidly, causing even more damage to the crop.

THE PROBLEM WITH DDT

Some insecticides can cause other problems higher up the food chain, through bioaccumulation when the toxin is stored in tissue. A good example of this is DDT, an insecticide used widely in the 1950s and 1960s. DDT is stored in fatty tissues in animals. A small amount in the body may have no noticeable effect on the animal, so predators that eat insects treated with DDT may not be obviously harmed. However, the more insects they eat, the more DDT is stored in their tissues – the DDT accumulates. Predators that feed on these animals will absorb much higher doses of DDT than are in the environment, and store the DDT in their tissues. At high doses DDT is toxic to larger organisms too. In birds it can also cause eggs to be laid with thinner shells than normal, which break more easily, killing the developing chick inside. In the 1960s it became clear in the USA and Europe that numbers of birds of prey, which are top consumers in food webs, were decreasing rapidly as a result of poisoning by DDT and eggshell thinning. DDT was then banned for use in agriculture in the USA and Europe.

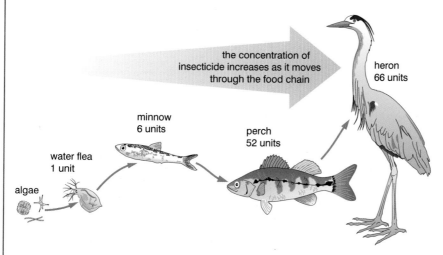

the concentration of insecticide increases as it moves through the food chain

heron
66 units

minnow
6 units

perch
52 units

water flea
1 unit

algae

Δ Fig 21.10 DDT affected many food chains. In this food chain, the figures give the relative concentration of DDT in each type of organism.

A growing problem with insecticides is that pest species are evolving resistance to the chemicals. This is because any individuals that survive the use of an insecticide are more resistant than those that are killed, so the individuals that reproduce have offspring that carry the genes for resistance. Farmers have responded by using greater amounts of insecticide, which only increases the damaging effects of the insecticide on the environment.

Herbicides can be used to kill the plants in the field that are not the crop. They are usually sprayed on to a field where they selectively kill weeds, leaving the crop plants unaffected. This clears any plants that might compete with the crop plants for nutrients, water and light. So the crop plants can grow more rapidly and produce a greater yield.

The use of herbicides may help increase yield, but they can cause damage to the environment.

- Many weeds are important food plants for a wide range of insect species. So removing all the weeds reduces the food and shelter available for them. Some of the insects will be pests of the crop, so removing the weeds might be helpful. However, some of the insect species may be predators of insect pest species, so clearing the weeds will make it easier for insect pest species to increase in number more quickly. Some farmers now leave a strip of weed plants around their crops to encourage the increase in predator insect species.
- Some herbicides quickly break down in the soil to simple substances that are no danger to the environment. However, some include highly dangerous substances that can poison soil organisms and anything that eats them. These herbicides are now banned in most countries, but as they don't break down easily, some areas still contain toxic concentrations in the soil.

QUESTIONS

1. Define the term *pesticide* in your own words.
2. Describe, with examples, the advantages of using pesticides on crops.
3. Give one example of a problem caused by using the following on a crop:
   a) an insecticide
   b) a herbicide.

Pollution due to nuclear fall-out

Nuclear fall-out contains radioactive particles that get into the environment from accidental leakage of radioactive materials, such as from a nuclear power station or processing plant, or as a result of an explosion involving nuclear material.

If particles are thrown high into the atmosphere by an explosion, they may be transported by winds over long distances before they fall to the ground. Larger particles will fall out more quickly, and so nearer to the site of the explosion, than smaller particles, which may travel hundreds of miles.

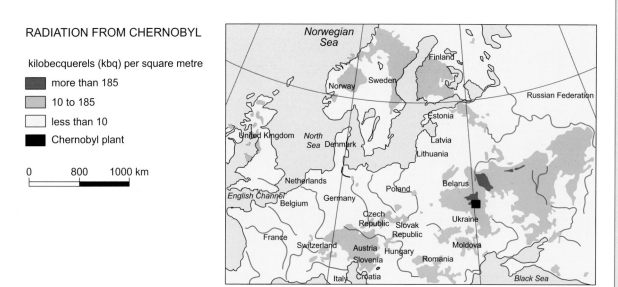

RADIATION FROM CHERNOBYL

kilobecquerels (kbq) per square metre

- more than 185
- 10 to 185
- less than 10
- Chernobyl plant

0   800   1000 km

△ Fig 21.11 Nuclear fall-out from the explosion at the Chernobyl nuclear reactor in 1986.

Many kinds of radioactive particles may be released in an explosion like the one at the Chernobyl reactor in 1986. Some decay to non-radioactive particles quite quickly, and so are unlikely to cause harm. Others keep their radioactivity for longer and may cause damage if they touch living material, such as by burning tissue or causing cancers. Radioactive particles of elements that are normally stored in tissue, such as iodine, can cause greater problems because they can be passed along the food chain in animal tissue. This can result in increasing amounts of radioactivity in each trophic level of the food chain, leading to a greater risk of damage in animals higher up the food chain. The most notable effect on human health as a result of the Chernobyl explosion was an increase in the proportion of children and young people with thyroid cancers since 1986.

QUESTIONS

1. Explain what is meant by *nuclear fall-out*.

2. Give two examples of causes of nuclear fall-out.

3. Explain the spread of nuclear fall-out from the Chernobyl explosion shown in the map above.

4. Describe one danger from nuclear fall-out.

Pollution due to discarded plastics

Plastics are used to make a huge number of products. Many of these plastics are **non-biodegradable**, which means that they cannot be decayed by the action of decomposers such as fungi and bacteria. If left in the environment, they may remain there unchanged for tens, or even hundreds, of years.

One way of dealing with plastic refuse has been to place it in landfill tips. The problem is that, once covered over, that land can be only be used for a few purposes. It cannot be used for growing crops or grass for herd animals, due to the risk of leakage of poisonous chemicals. It can only be used for building on several decades after burial, when the ground has settled and no decay gases are being produced.

Plastic that gets into water systems may end up out at sea, where it collects in huge areas, commonly called 'garbage patches', where the oceans circulate.

◁ Fig 21.12 Much of the pollution in oceans and on sea shores is caused by discarded plastic.

The plastic is a form of pollution because:

- plastic bags may be swallowed by animals such as turtles that mistake them for their prey, jelly fish
- plastic nets and ropes may entangle organisms so that they die of starvation
- the plastic may be broken down to release toxins that affect organisms in the area
- the plastic may break down into small particles, called nurdles, that are swallowed by animals that mistake them for food.

Research has shown that at least 267 species worldwide have been affected by plastic marine debris.

1. Describe two problems with the decay of non-biodegradable plastics.

2. **EXTENDED** Explain why dumping non-biodegradable plastics in landfill sites is being restricted.

3. **EXTENDED** Explain why non-biodegradable plastics are causing pollution in oceans.

Water pollution

Pollution of rivers, lakes and seas may also be caused by the addition of chemicals, from farming, human waste or from chemical production.

Sewage is human waste, faeces and urine, which we all produce and need to dispose of. Faeces and urine contain high concentrations of many nitrogen-containing substances, and so are good sources of nutrients for plants and microorganisms. In fact, farmers often use animal waste as manure to spread on their fields to increase crop production.

In areas where many people live, sewage disposal is a big problem. Many cities have sewage management systems, to carry the sewage in pipes to treatment centres where it can be broken down, or far from the city.

△ Fig 21.13 In some fast-growing cities there are no proper systems for removing and treating sewage.

When untreated sewage is added to water, the nutrients in it dissolve into the water. This leads to eutrophication (see below) and, like the addition of artificial fertilisers to water, can increase plant and algal growth, resulting in an increase in bacterial growth, a fall in oxygen concentration in the water, and death of aquatic organisms. In addition, human waste contains many bacteria, some of which can cause infection, leading to vomiting, diarrhoea, fever and even death.

Even when sewage is treated properly to reduce the amount of nutrients it contains, and to remove pathogens, it may still contain concentrations of some substances that can cause harm to organisms. Female sex hormones are used in the contraceptive pill (see Topic 16). Women taking these pills excrete the hormones in their urine. Sewage treatment breaks down some of the hormones, but tiny amounts may be left in the water that is returned to the natural water systems, such as rivers.

These tiny amounts can affect other animals. For example, some male fish in these rivers have a reduced sperm count and may even produce eggs instead of sperm. This is known as **feminisation** of males, as the males show female features. There is also a concern that drinking water taken from these rivers may contain sufficient concentrations of the hormones to affect men and reduce their sperm count.

Water pollution can be caused by other substances. Many industries produce liquid waste that is easiest to dispose of into water systems. In most places there are strict laws about what can and cannot be released into rivers, streams and lakes. Some substances, like sewage, lead to eutrophication. Others are toxic, such as the metals copper, mercury and lead and some organic chemicals. These must be cleaned completely from any waste water that drains into water systems. This is to prevent the toxins being absorbed by plants and animals and passing into food chains where they can cause damage.

SCIENCE IN CONTEXT   THE MINAMATA POLLUTION DISASTER

One of the worst water pollution incidents occurred in Japan between about 1932 and 1968. A chemical factory released a mercury-containing chemical into Minamata Bay in waste water from the industrial processes. In the bay, shellfish and fish absorbed the mercury. When people ate the shellfish and fish, the mercury was absorbed and stored in their bodies. Over 10 000 people eventually absorbed so much mercury that it caused many different kinds of damage to them, including to muscles, nerves, vision and speech. Over 2000 people died as a direct result of the mercury.

Δ Fig 21.14 Taisuke Mitarai, 69 years old, suffers the effects of mercury poisoning as a result of the Minamata disaster.

Fertilisers and eutrophication

Fertilisers are chemicals that farmers use on fields to add nutrients, such as nitrates, that help the crops to grow better and so produce greater yields. However, if a farmer adds more fertiliser to a field than the crop plants can absorb, the remaining nutrients will soak away in ground water into nearby streams and rivers. Also, if there is heavy rainfall soon after the fertiliser has been spread on a field, the nutrients will dissolve in the rainwater and run off the surface of the field into streams and rivers.

The adding of nutrients to water is called **eutrophication**. The nutrients in the water will have the same effect on plants and algae in the water as they have on plants that grow on land, and will encourage them to grow faster. As they grow faster, they respire more rapidly, taking oxygen from the water. This leaves less oxygen in the water for other organisms, such as fish, and those organisms may die.

EXTENDED

The effects of eutrophication on an aquatic ecosystem can be explained in the following way.

- Eutrophication increases the rate of growth of photosynthesising organisms (producers) in the water, in particular algae and plants that grow at the surface of the water.
- If the plants and algae at the surface grow so much that they block light to plants that grow deeper in the water, the deep-water plants will die because they cannot photosynthesise.
- This will provide more food for decomposers, such as bacteria, which will increase in numbers rapidly.
- The bacteria respire more rapidly in order to make new materials for growth and reproduction. Respiration takes dissolved oxygen from the water, reducing the oxygen concentration of the water.
- Other aquatic (water-living) organisms find it increasingly difficult to get the oxygen they need from the water for respiration.
- If the amount of oxygen dissolved in the water falls too low, many organisms, particularly active animals such as fish, will die.
- The decay of dead organisms in the water provides more nutrients, so more bacteria grow, respire and take more oxygen from the water.
- Eventually, most of the large aquatic plants and animals in the water may die.

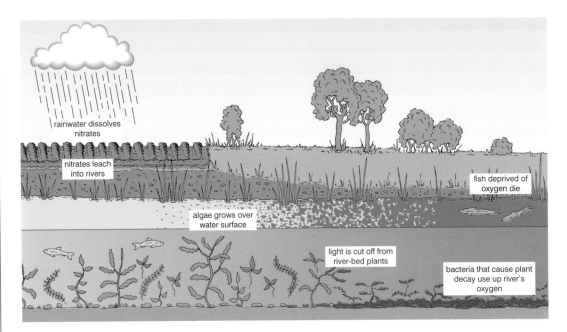

△ Fig 21.15 Eutrophication can lead to the death of water organisms.

Labels in figure:
- rainwater dissolves nitrates
- nitrates leach into rivers
- fish deprived of oxygen die
- algae grows over water surface
- light is cut off from river-bed plants
- bacteria that cause plant decay use up river's oxygen

REMEMBER

Eutrophication is often wrongly defined as the pollution of water and death of aquatic organisms. This is incorrect – eutrophication is simply the adding of nutrients. It comes from the Greek word *eutrophia,* meaning 'healthy or adequate nutrition'. Adding nutrients that the ecosystem can use normally may be an advantage, but adding them in excess may lead to the death of aquatic organisms as a result of the depletion of dissolved oxygen in the water. So excess nutrients can cause pollution.

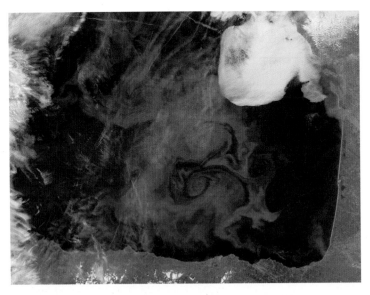

△ Fig 21.16 Large-scale algal growth can be seen in satellite photos. This algal bloom occurred in the Baltic Sea in 2010 as a result of fertilisers being washed off the surrounding land.

END OF EXTENDED

QUESTIONS

1. Describe *three* sources of water pollution.

2. Describe one other danger from sewage in water systems, apart from eutrophication.

3. Explain what we mean by *eutrophication*.

4. Give two reasons why the use of artificial fertiliser on a field could cause eutrophication of a nearby stream.

5. Describe how eutrophication can lead to the death of fish in a stream.

6. EXTENDED Draw a flow diagram to explain how sewage can cause eutrophication and water pollution.

AIR POLLUTION

Sulfur dioxide

Since the Industrial Revolution began in northern Europe in the 1700s, humans have burnt increasing quantities of fossil fuels (such as coal, oil and natural gas) to provide energy for industrial processes. Burning fossil fuels gives off many gases, including sulfur dioxide (SO_2).

Sulfur dioxide is an acidic gas that is highly soluble in water, forming sulfuric acid when it dissolves. Acid damages cells and delicate tissues directly. If breathed in, the sulfur dioxide can dissolve in the moisture lining the lungs and damage the delicate tissues of the alveoli. This can lead to breathing problems for life.

Acid rain

Sulfur dioxide in the air can combine with water droplets in clouds to form sulfuric acid. When the water droplets fall as rain, it is more acidic than usual, so we call it **acid rain**.

Acid rain can cause damage directly to living organisms. Plants may have their leaves damaged, so they can no longer photosynthesise and grow well. Animals with soft skin, such as fish and amphibians (frogs and toads), may have their skin damaged by the acid rain falling in the ponds, lakes and rivers where they live. Single-celled organisms, such as protoctists, are even more likely to be damaged.

Acid rain can also cause damage indirectly. In soil, it can cause some mineral ions to dissolve into the soil water (leaching). Some of these ions, such as aluminium ions, are poisonous to some organisms. Other ions may be more easily washed out of the soil, away from plants that need them, so that plant growth is reduced.

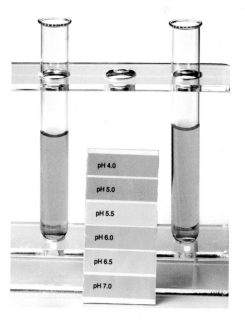

△ Fig 21.17 The pH of normal rainwater (left) is about 5.6, but acid rain (right) can have a pH of less than 3.0.

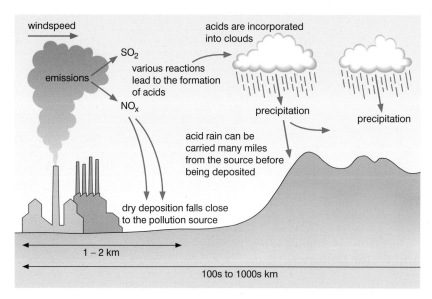

△ Fig 21.18 Acid rain can be transported many kilometres from where the acidic gases were released into the air.

Damaging some organisms in a food web will have an impact on other organisms because of the way that organisms in an ecosystem depend on each other. Species that feed on those damaged by acid rain will either do more badly or move away from the area. However, some species can tolerate acidity better than others, so they will benefit by having more space to live in.

◁ Fig 21.19 This species of lichen can only grow where there is no pollution in the air.

Developing investigative skills

You can investigate the effect of acid on the germination of seeds by adding acid to the water used to water growing seedlings.

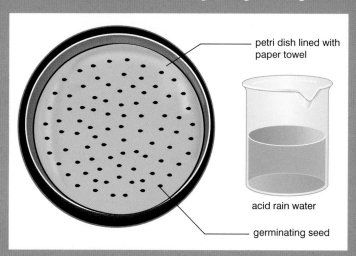

petri dish lined with paper towel

acid rain water

germinating seed

△ Fig 21.20 Apparatus for the investigation into the effect of acid rain on germinating seeds.

Devise and plan investigations

❶ Write a plan for an investigation on the effect of different acidic pHs on the germination of seeds, using the apparatus shown in Fig. 21.20.

Demonstrate and describe techniques

❷ Describe any hazards with your plan and how you should protect against them.

Analyse and interpret data

The graph shows the results from an investigation into the effect of different pHs on the germination of wheat seeds.

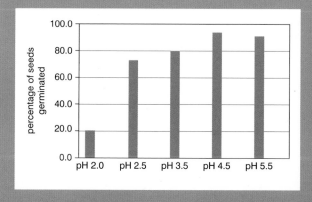

△ Fig 21.21 Results from the investigation.

❸ Use the graph to draw a conclusion about the effect of acid rain on wheat.

Reducing sulfur dioxide emissions

Most of the fossil fuels that we burn are either used in industry, particularly for the generation of electricity, or in vehicle engines. Over the past few decades, particularly in Europe and the USA, efforts have been made to reduce emissions of sulfur dioxide.

- Sulfur dioxide is removed ('scrubbed') from the gases given off from combustion as they pass up the chimneys of factories and power stations, so that it is not released into the atmosphere.
- Sulfur compounds are removed from petrol and diesel fuels before they are burnt in vehicle engines.

These efforts have resulted in a decrease in sulfur dioxide in the air, but more needs to be done to solve this problem completely.

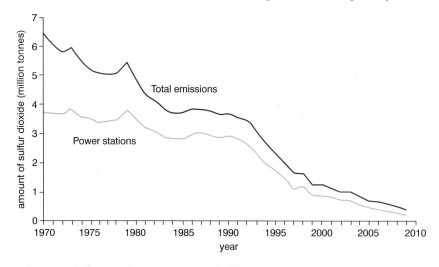

△ Fig 21.22 Sulfur dioxide emissions from the UK.

END OF EXTENDED

QUESTIONS

1. Explain why sulfur dioxide in the air is a form of pollution.

2. EXTENDED Use Fig. 21.18, showing how acid rain is formed, to:

    a) explain how human activity contributes to acid rain

    b) explain why acid rain is not just a problem for places where there is a lot of industry.

3. EXTENDED Describe the different ways in which acid rain can damage organisms and ecosystems.

Pollution by greenhouse gases

There are many gases in the Earth's atmosphere, but one group plays an important role in keeping the Earth's surface warm. These gases are called the **greenhouse gases** and they include:

- carbon dioxide – produced naturally from respiration of living organisms (see Topic 19)

- methane – produced during the decay of organic material, such as in swamps, and in the digestion of food in the alimentary canal.

Human activities are increasing the proportion of some greenhouse gases in the atmosphere.

- Carbon dioxide is increasing as a result of combustion of fossil fuels.

- Methane is increasing as a result of the increasing numbers of people and livestock, and from the release of the gas from artificial wetlands such as rice paddy fields.

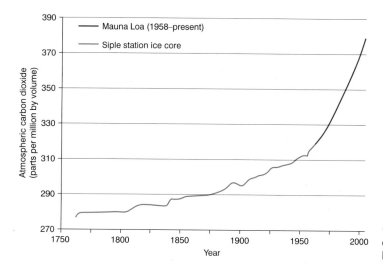

◁ Fig 21.23 Change in the concentration of carbon dioxide in the Earth's atmosphere between 1750 and 2004.

Average global surface temperature has also been rising over the past few centuries. Global temperatures can vary over a wide range due to many natural factors, such as the amount of radiation received from the Sun, which varies due to a predictable but complex cycle. However, many scientists are certain that the recent increases in temperature are the result of increased emissions of greenhouse gases from human activity, resulting in an **enhanced greenhouse effect**, or what is commonly called **global warming**.

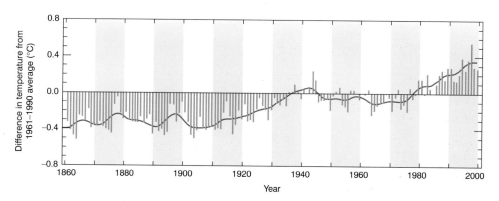

△ Fig 21.24 Variation of the Earth's surface temperature, calculated as the difference in average temperature between 1961 and 1990.

Many features of our climate are the result of differences in local surface temperatures in different places, such as the speed of winds or amount of precipitation. Predictions from computer modelling of the effects of global warming suggest that different parts of the world, at different times, may experience **climate change,** such as an increase in:

- the number and strength of storms
- drought
- flooding as a result of increased rainfall and rising sea levels
- hotter summers and warmer winters
- cooler, wetter summers and colder winters.

These changes will not only affect humans, but whole ecosystems, potentially increasing the rate at which species become extinct. This will have greater impacts as a result of the interdependency of organisms through food webs in communities.

The greenhouse effect

Short-wave radiation from the Sun warms the ground and the warm Earth gives off heat as longer-wave radiation. Much of this radiation is stopped from escaping from the Earth by the greenhouse gases and returns to warm the Earth's surface. This is known as the **greenhouse effect**.

The greenhouse effect is responsible for keeping the Earth warmer than it otherwise would be. The greenhouse effect is normal, and important for life on Earth. Without it, it is estimated that the surface of the Earth would be about 33 °C cooler than it is now. All water on the surface of the Earth would be frozen, and very little life could exist in these conditions.

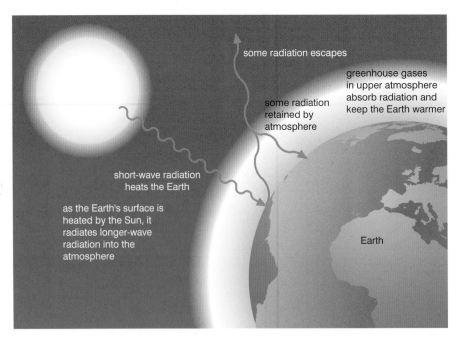

some radiation escapes

greenhouse gases in upper atmosphere absorb radiation and keep the Earth warmer

some radiation retained by atmosphere

short-wave radiation heats the Earth

as the Earth's surface is heated by the Sun, it radiates longer-wave radiation into the atmosphere

Earth

△ Fig 21.25 The greenhouse effect on Earth.

Additions of greenhouse gases to the atmosphere as a result of human activity are thought to increase the greenhouse effect, producing what some call an **enhanced greenhouse effect**. This is pollution because, in causing global warming, it could damage many species and the environment.

SCIENCE IN CONTEXT — LIFE ON MARS OR VENUS?

The importance of the greenhouse effect can be seen by comparing the conditions on the surfaces of Earth, Venus and Mars. Mars has a relatively thin atmosphere, and although it is composed mainly of carbon dioxide, the effect of this as a greenhouse gas is limited. The average surface temperature on Mars is about −55 °C, varying from about 27 °C during the day at the equator to −143 °C at the poles at night. By contrast, Venus has a much denser atmosphere than Earth, and it consists mainly of carbon dioxide with clouds of sulfur dioxide. These gases create a very strong greenhouse effect, heating the surface of Venus to an average of around 460 °C. It is not surprising, therefore, that Earth is the only planet in our Solar System where we know that life has evolved.

REMEMBER

Be very careful not to confuse the natural greenhouse effect, which is essential for life on Earth, with the enhanced greenhouse effect and global warming as a result of the release of additional greenhouse gases from human activity.

END OF EXTENDED

QUESTIONS

1. Give examples of natural causes and human causes of emissions of the following gases:

   a) carbon dioxide

   b) nitrous oxide

   c) methane.

2. Give three examples of the consequences of global warming.

3. EXTENDED Distinguish between the greenhouse effect and the enhanced greenhouse effect.

CONSERVATION

Conservation means 'protection', to prevent long-term damage. We can conserve resources so that they don't run out, or conserve habitats so that we protect the species that live in them.

We use many resources from the Earth. Some, such as food and water, are renewable or **sustainable resources** because they will not run out. Sustainable resources that may seem unlimited, such as fresh water and wood, are limited by the rate at which they can be produced. So this means that they also need conserving and managing carefully.

Other resources, such as the fossil fuels of coal, oil and gas, are **non-renewable resources**, because what we use cannot be replaced. These are the resources that cause most concern because, once we have used them all, we will not be able to produce any more. These resources need to be conserved by reducing the amount we use and finding other, sustainable resources to replace them.

△ Fig 21.26 Reusing and recycling can reduce our need for using more non-renewable resources.

Sustainable development

Sustainable development is the development of technology and the environment to support the needs of an increasing human population without harming the environment. The rest of this Topic covers the conservation of resources and habitats, and looks at ways that different areas of development can be made more sustainable.

Often when we are developing the ways in which we use resources, we have to balance conflicting demands. Conflict may come from the needs of different groups of people, such as the need of logging companies to earn money compared with the need of local people to gather food and firewood from the area in which they live. Conflict may occur between the needs of people and the needs of other organisms in the area, such as between elephants that need food and damage the crops of local farmers who grow the crops to feed their families.

Conflict may also occur between the needs of people now and needs in the future, such as harvesting all the fish we need to feed people now, which may cause overfishing that damages fisheries for the future.

For development to be sustainable, people need to cooperate at local, national and international levels in their planning and management of resources.

When you are studying examples of conservation, you should consider the conflicts involved in each case, and how they can be resolved in a way that is sustainable. You should also consider at which levels (local, national and international) that cooperation is needed to bring about sustainable development.

END OF EXTENDED

Fossil fuels

The fossil fuels coal, oil and gas, supply most of our energy needs. They are burnt in power stations to generate electricity, and are used to power vehicles for transport. In addition they are an important source of chemicals for the plastics and other manufacturing industries.

Fossil fuels are non-renewable resources, in the sense that we use them at a far greater rate than it takes to make them. It is difficult to predict how much longer the resources we know about will last, as it depends on how quickly we use them.

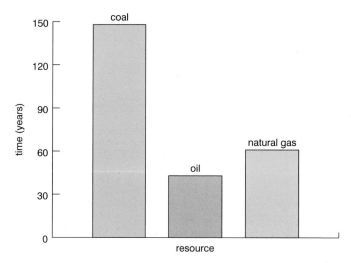

Δ Fig 21.27 At the current global rates of use fossil fuels might only last this long. However, there may be other sources of the fuels that have yet to be discovered.

We use these resources not only as fuels, but as the raw materials for other processes. For example, almost all the plastics that are made start with oil as a raw material. Even if we reduce our rate of use, fossil fuels will eventually run out, so we need other sources of energy and raw materials to replace them.

Wood

We use wood for many purposes, such as for building, for making furniture, as firewood and for making paper. Wood is a sustainable resource because when the trees are cut down they can be planted again. However, it is not as simple as this because trees can take many years to grow. So forests need careful managing to make sure that the use is sustainable. This means making sure there as many trees in the future as there are being cut down and used now.

EXTENDED

Forests used to produce wood for making paper are now grown mostly as cash crops. This means that areas of mature trees that are cut down for making paper are quickly replanted with similar trees so that there will be wood for paper in future years. It may take 30–50 years before the trees mature, so large areas of land may be covered in these plantations.

Some tropical woods, such as teak and mahogany, have been particularly chosen for making furniture because they are very attractive. This has caused great problems in areas where they grow, such as Malaysia and Indonesia, because these trees have been taken from ancient forests and not replanted. The damage done to the forests when the trees are removed harms not only the environment but also the lives of the local people, who do not benefit from the sale of the wood.

There are now several schemes that aim to make this use of wood more sustainable, by monitoring the timber companies and making sure that they manage the forests properly. Timber from these companies is labelled and tracked to the products that it is used to make. This means the person buying the products can be sure that they are buying sustainably. Education, to teach companies how to manage forests sustainably and to teach customers how to buy sustainably, will help to conserve the world's forests.

△ Fig 21.28 As soon as an area of timber plantation is cut down, more trees are planted to replace them.

△ Fig 21.29 The Forest Stewardship Council (FSC) is one scheme that certifies wood from forests that are managed sustainably. People who buy these wood products know that they are not causing damage to the world's forests.

END OF EXTENDED

Fisheries

In 2009 around 120 million tonnes of fish were eaten by people across the world, and this number continues to increase each year. The number of fish in an area is called the *fish stock*. Stocks of many kinds of fish that we eat have greatly decreased as a result of overfishing. Around one-third of all fishing areas around the world have been damaged by overfishing.

Fish stocks can be managed in ways that help to conserve the fish and allow us to harvest them sustainably so that there will be plenty of fish in the future.

△ Fig 21.30 Tuna fish are in such great demand for food there is a danger that soon there will be no tuna left in the oceans.

EXTENDED

Managing fish stocks sustainably includes controlling the number of fish caught each year, and the size of fish caught. Many species of fish only breed when they are over a certain age and a certain size. As we usually take the largest fish from an area, it is important not to take all the fish which are able to breed. Scientists study the populations of fish, to estimate the stock size and ages of the fish. Then governments can set legal **fishing quotas** that limit the amount of fish that can be caught in a year in each fishing area. This should allow enough large fish in each area to breed and produce more fish for future years. Anyone who has not been given a quota, or who takes more fish than is allowed in a quota, is fishing illegally and may be fined or sent to prison.

Where fish stocks are in danger in rivers and lakes, there may be efforts to re-stock the area. A few adult male and female fish are caught during the breeding season. They are 'milked' for their eggs and sperm and returned to their habitat. The eggs and sperm are mixed to fertilise the eggs, then the fertilised eggs are kept in water tanks in ideal conditions for hatching. The young fish are fed and looked after until they are large enough to return to the natural habitat. This avoids predation of the young fish in the natural habitat and improves growth because they do not have to look for and compete for food. So more fish survive to adulthood than if they hatched in the natural habitat.

END OF EXTENDED

1. Explain what is meant by the following terms:
a) *conservation* **b)** *sustainable resource*.

2. EXTENDED Explain what is meant by *sustainable development*.

3. Explain why fossil fuels need to be conserved.

4. EXTENDED Explain how the following can be managed sustainably: **a)** forests **b)** fish stocks.

Reusing and recycling

Some resources can be conserved by reusing or recycling. For example, reusing a plastic bag again and again, instead of throwing it away when it has been used once, reduces the amount of oil needed to make the plastic. This also reduces the amount of plastic waste that needs to be disposed of. Oil is a non-renewable resource, so reducing the amount we use helps to ensure that there is more oil for the future.

△ Fig 21.31 Many fleece jackets are made from recycled plastic.

Once the plastic bag is no longer usable, it may be **recycled**. This means melting the plastic bag and using it to make another plastic product.

Glass is produced from sand, with added chemicals, heated to a very high temperature to melt it. Glass is also easy to recycle. Waste glass is sorted into the different types and colours of glass, then crushed ready for melting and turning into new glass products such as jars and bottles. Using recycled glass to make new products instead of glass produced from sand requires much less energy. So even though there is little risk of us running out of sand in the future, recycling glass helps to conserve fossil fuels used for heating.

Paper recycling

Paper is made by pulping the wood from whole trees. This requires energy for preparing the wood, by stripping off the bark, and then crushing it. The crushed wood is then soaked with chemicals to help separate the wood fibres, and to bleach the wood so that white paper can be made. The wood pulp that is produced is used to make paper.

Used paper can also be recycled to produce more paper. Printed paper needs to have the ink removed first. Then the paper is mashed up in water to make pulp again. This pulp is used to make more paper. Recycled paper is not as strong or as bright a white as new paper, but it is useful for many purposes.

Although wood is a renewable resource, there is a limit to how quickly it can grow. And wood is used for many purposes other than paper, such as for building. So recycling paper means that more new wood is available for those other purposes, or that the land used for growing trees could be used for growing something else, such as crops, or left as forest to protect habitats for other organisms.

Recycling paper also:

- saves energy, because less energy is needed to produce the pulp from old paper than from trees
- reduces the amount of chemicals used, particularly the bleaching chemicals that can cause water pollution
- reduces the amount of paper dumped in landfill sites.

Recycling water

Around two-thirds of the Earth is covered in water, but most of this is salt (sea) water. If we drink this, or use it on our crops or give it to our animals, it will cause problems because the concentration of solutes in the salt water is greater than in living cells. Drinking salt water can cause living cells to lose water by osmosis, and so causes dehydration.

Living organisms need fresh water. Fresh water is not equally distributed across the Earth's surface. Some parts of the world may receive metres of rain each year; other parts may only receive a few millimetres of precipitation in a decade. People need water not only to drink, to water crops and for their animals, but also for cooking and washing. It is not surprising that many people live close to a source of fresh water, such as a river or lake.

△ Fig 21.32 An area of drought in Somaliland, Africa, where very little can grow.

As the human population grows, the need for fresh water increases. This is partly because there are more people using the same freshwater sources, but also because people spread out into surrounding areas where fresh water may not be as plentiful.

We are also capable of polluting water, with sewage, chemicals and fertilisers. So this can reduce the amount of fresh water available to us, as well as to other organisms.

DWINDLING FRESHWATER RESOURCES

Early this century it was calculated that humans use about 60% of the available fresh water on the Earth every year. That was when the global human population was around 6 billion. The projected human population for 2050 was 10 billion at that time, which raises concerns about the availability of fresh water not only for all the humans and their needs, but also for all the wild organisms that share the water with us.

In many places, sewage (human waste) is disposed of by washing it away into pipes using water. The pipes carry the liquid to sewage treatment plants, where the organic waste can be removed. The water is cleaned so that it can be returned to the water system without causing eutrophication.

The treatment includes several stages.

- First stage: the waste water (including sewage) is screened to remove inorganic material such as sand, gravel and grit.
- Second stage: the waste water is passed through treatment beds, where microorganisms feed on the organic material and break it down to smaller molecules, such as carbon dioxide, water and mineral ions.
- Third stage: the water is treated with chemicals to remove dissolved minerals that are toxic. Chlorine is added to kill microorganisms.
- The water may receive extra processing to make it pure enough for use as drinking water, but at this point is safe to return to water systems.

△ Fig 21.33 During the second stage of water treatment, air is bubbled through the waste water to encourage rapid growth of aerobic microorganisms that break down organic material in the water.

The solid organic material that is collected from the water may be used as a fertiliser on fields, or in a biodigester, where it is broken down by microorganisms to release methane. The methane gas can be used as a fuel.

QUESTIONS

1. Explain why fresh water resources need to be conserved.

2. Explain why fossil fuels need to be conserved.

3. **EXTENDED** Describe how water is recycled.

4. **EXTENDED** Explain why recycling paper makes economic sense.

Conservation of organisms and habitats

Conservation can also refer to the protection of species and their habitats, so that the species can continue to survive and reproduce successfully. If the number of organisms in a population falls too low, the organisms may have difficulty in finding mates for reproduction and the population will die out. If this happens to all the populations of these organisms, the species will become **extinct**.

EXTENDED

Even if the population survives extinction, if numbers are very low there will be little genetic variation between individuals. This will mean that the population will be at greater risk of extinction as a result of random changes in the environment (see Topic 18).

END OF EXTENDED

The International Union for the Conservation of Nature (IUCN) Red List shows which species are **endangered** (at risk of extinction) and is used to help conservationists prioritise which species to protect.

Organisms can become endangered as a result of several human activities.

- Climate change may occur as a result of changes in the atmosphere from combustion of fossil fuels and from methane. If conditions change too much, the organisms may not be adapted to the new conditions and so will die, or move to areas to which they are better suited. For example, plants and animals adapted to living in cold places may need to move nearer to the polar regions or higher up mountains, if the climate gets warmer.

- The destruction of habitats, such as by deforestation or pollution, destroys the places where organisms live. If the destruction is on a large scale, there may be nowhere else left for the organism to live.

- Some species have been hunted to extinction, or to near extinction. Hunting may be: for food, as in the case of the dodo, which became extinct in 1681; for useful

△ Fig 21.34 All species of tiger are hunted for their fur or other body parts, for fun or to protect local people. This skin of a Siberian tiger was taken from poachers by an anti-poaching force. Tiger numbers in the wild are now so small that all species may become extinct in the next decade or so.

parts of the organism, such as fur skins of tigers or the ivory tusks of elephants; or just for fun.

- Pollution can poison organisms or change the conditions in the habitat so that they can no longer live there.
- Introducing species to an area can cause extinction by affecting the food web. For example, the introduced species may become a predator of the local species – as happened with the cane toad in Australia or rats in Hawaii (see Topic 19). The introduced species will also affect local species if it becomes a competitor for food or space.

Species may be conserved by breeding them in safe places. For example, animals may be kept in zoos, wildlife parks or nature reserves and bred in **captive breeding programmes** to increase their numbers. Botanic gardens are places where plants that are at risk of extinction in the wild are kept and conserved. Endangered plant species may be conserved by growing them or by keeping their seeds in **seed banks**. However, if the habitats they lived in are not conserved as well, then there is little point in trying to return the species to the wild.

THE HAWAIIAN GOOSE

A successful example of conservation is the survival of the Hawaiian goose. When James Cook visited the island of Hawaii in 1778 there was an estimated population of around 25 000. As a result of hunting the geese for food, and the introduction by people of predators such as pigs and cats, there were only about 30 birds by 1952.

A few breeding pairs were brought back to Slimbridge in the UK in the 1950s, where they bred successfully. Since then more birds have been bred in zoos and wildfowl sanctuaries around the world. Some have also been successfully re-introduced to national parks on an island near Hawaii where they are protected.

Δ Fig 21.35 A Hawaiian goose.

Education to change people's attitudes plays an important part in conserving endangered species. For example, people used to travel to Africa to hunt and kill large animals such as elephants and lions, but now they visit as tourists to photograph them instead. Elephants are still at risk of being shot, either for their ivory tusks or because they damage crops of local people. Changing attitudes of people who might buy ivory products will reduce the market for ivory, and placing bee hives near crops (elephants can hear the bees and tend to avoid going close to them) could help to protect crops without harming the elephants.

Conservation programmes

Conservation programmes may be carried out at local, national or international level to protect species and habitats.

△ Fig 21.36 There are only a few thousand snow leopards left in the wild, but they are still hunted for their fur. Captive breeding programmes in zoos across the world aim to prevent extinction of this species and could provide animals to return to the wild when hunting has stopped.

- Captive breeding programmes may be coordinated between zoos and wildlife parks in different parts of the world, to prevent extinction even if the species becomes extinct in its natural environment.
- Seed banks collect seed from all over the world to guard against extinction of plants due to climate change.
- Nature reserves on land and in the water prevent human activities that might damage areas containing species that are endangered, or vulnerable habitats that are rare.
- Wild varieties of crop plants are conserved either as seed or as growing plants to make sure we have sources of genes in the future for plant breeding. They can be used to produce new varieties of crops that are better able to fight off pests and diseases and to cope with climate change such as drought.
- Plants may also be collected from the wild and conserved as a source of chemicals that could, in the future, be developed to produce new drugs for use against diseases.

QUESTIONS

1. Explain the meaning of these terms:

   a) *endangered*

   b) *captive breeding programme*

   c) *seed bank*.

2. Identify *three* ways in which human activities may cause a species to become endangered.

3. Explain how conservation programmes can protect organisms and their habitats.

END OF EXTENDED

End of topic checklist

Key words

acid rain, biodiversity, captive breeding programme, climate change, conservation, deforestation, endangered, eutrophication, extinct, famine, feminisation, global warming, greenhouse effect, greenhouse gases, herbicide, insecticide, leaching, monoculture, non-biodegradable, nuclear fall-out, pesticide, pollution, recycled, seed bank, sewage, soil erosion, sustainable development

During your study of this topic you should have learned:

○ Modern technology has increased food production through the use of machinery, fertilisers, insecticides, herbicides and selective breeding.

○ Large-scale monocultures of crop plants can increase the need for chemicals to control pests and fertilise the soil, and reduce biodiversity.

○ Intensive livestock production can damage habitats through overgrazing and increase the need for pesticide use.

○ EXTENDED As the human population grows, the need for food rises, which may increase the use of resources on land and in water and have an increasing impact on other organisms.

○ EXTENDED Famine may be caused by an unequal distribution of food, as well as by environmental problems such as drought and flooding.

○ Habitat destruction may occur to provide more space for growing crops and livestock and for building. It may also happen when minerals and fossil fuels are extracted from the ground and as a result of pollution in the oceans.

○ We can damage a habitat by introducing new species to food webs and food chains, which affects the local species that live in the habitat.

○ Deforestation can damage the environment by causing species to become extinct, increasing loss of soil and the risk of flooding, and by resulting in more carbon dioxide in the atmosphere.

○ Why deforestation has undesirable effects on the environment.

○ Pollution of water and land may be caused by chemicals used in farming, such as insecticides, herbicides or by nuclear fall-out.

○ Pollution of water may also be caused by discarded rubbish, chemical waste, untreated sewage and fertilisers.

○ Eutrophication caused by the addition of nutrients to water sources, is the increase in nutrients in water from fertilisers or untreated sewage, which may lead to the death of organisms such as fish due to lack of oxygen in the water.

○ EXTENDED Eutrophication caused by the addition of nutrients to water sources, increases the rate of growth of surface plants and algae that block light to plants lower in the water. Lower plants die and are decayed by bacteria that remove oxygen from the water for respiration. This leaves little oxygen in the water for other organisms such as fish.

○ EXTENDED Plastics that are non-biodegradable may damage aquatic and land ecosystems because they do not decay.

○ EXTENDED Increased levels of female contraceptive hormones in water may be causing feminisation of male aquatic organisms and a reduced sperm count in men.

○ Air may be polluted by gases from human activities, including methane and carbon dioxide. Increased release of carbon dioxide and methane into the air may be causing an enhanced greenhouse effect, which could lead to climate change.

○ EXTENDED Sulfur dioxide pollution of the air can cause acid rain, which damages the environment.

○ A sustainable resource is one that can be removed from the environment without causing long-term damage, and without it running out.

○ Non-renewable resources, such as fossil fuels, need conserving so that they will last for longer.

○ Resources such as forests and fish stocks can be maintained in a way that reduces long-term damage through education, legal quotas and re-stocking.

○ EXTENDED Making forests and fish stocks sustainable involves education, legal quotas and re-stocking.

○ Paper, glass and plastics can be reused or recycled to help conserve resources.

○ Waste water containing sewage can be treated to make the water in it safe to be returned to the environment or for human use.

○ EXTENDED Sustainable development aims to provide for the increasing needs of humans without harming the environment.

○ EXTENDED Sustainable development needs to manage conflicting demands and may need planning and cooperation at local, national and international levels.

○ Species may become endangered or extinct as a result of climate change, habitat destruction, hunting, pollution or the introduction of new species.

End of topic checklist continued

○ Endangered species can be conserved through monitoring and protection of species and habitats, captive breeding programmes, seed banks and education.

○ **EXTENDED** If the size of a population decreases, it will decrease genetic variability, which makes the population more at risk of extinction if conditions change.

○ **EXTENDED** Conservation programmes aim to reduce extinction, protect vulnerable habitats, and maintain nutrient cycling and provision of resources.

End of topic questions

Note: The marks awarded for these questions indicate the level of detail required in the answers. In the examination, the number of marks awarded to questions like these may be different.

1. Using the graph of world food production in Fig. 21.2, describe and suggest explanations for the changes in food production in developing countries since 1961. **(2 marks)**

2. EXTENDED Explain as fully as you can why, although there is enough food for every human on Earth, some people are still starving. **(4 marks)**

3. In the Amazon Basin large areas of rainforest have been cut down to make space for growing livestock such as cattle.

    a) Give one reason why some people have decided to keep livestock instead of leaving the rainforest to grow. **(1 mark)**

    b) Suggest *one* advantage of this change, and explain your answer. **(2 marks)**

    c) Give *two* disadvantages of this change. **(2 marks)**

4. EXTENDED If rainforest is cleared on a large scale and then left to recover, it is rare that the same species of plants and animals return to the area, even after many years. Explain why this happens, referring to soil fertility, climate and biodiversity in your answer. **(4 marks)**

5. Rivers and lake that are used for water supplies may be monitored to make sure that the water in them is safe for use. One way of monitoring is to measure the amount of oxygen that is used by the water (the oxygen demand) over a period of 5 days.

    a) Why might concentration of oxygen decrease in the water? Explain your answer. **(2 marks)**

    b) In this test would polluted water use more oxygen than unpolluted water? Explain your answer. **(2 marks)**

Another way of monitoring the water is to sample the small organisms that live in it. Some species, such as worms, are better adapted for living in water that has a low oxygen concentration. Other species, such as mayfly larvae, need a high concentration of oxygen in the water.

    c) Which of the two species above would be more common in polluted water? Explain your answer. **(2 marks)**

    d) What does *adapted* mean? **(1 mark)**

    e) Why might sampling the organisms be a better measure of the long-term health of the water than measuring the oxygen demand of the water? **(2 marks)**

6. In parts of Europe, farmers now use satellite technology to help them see which parts of a field need additional fertiliser, and how much fertiliser they need.

a) Why do farmers add fertiliser to their fields? **(1 mark)**

b) What might happen if a farmer adds too much fertiliser to a field? **(1 mark)**

c) Explain as fully as you can how this could result in water pollution. **(4 marks)**

d) Is this referring to the use of satellite imaging technology, or the use of fertilisers as a technology to improve crop growth/yield ? **(2 marks)**

7. a) Explain the meaning of the term *pollution*. **(1 mark)**

b) Name two human activities that are major sources of sulfur dioxide in the atmosphere. **(2 marks)**

c) Explain how sulfur dioxide in the air can lead to acid rain. **(2 marks)**

d) Sketch a diagram to show how sources of sulfur dioxide in one region could result in acid rain in another region. **(3 marks)**

e) Explain why sulfur dioxide causes pollution. **(2 marks)**

8. EXTENDED The graph in Fig. 21.37 shows the results of surveys of populations of birds on farmland in the UK between 1966 and 2009, compared with the 1966 level (set at 100 for easier comparison). The farmland birds were split into two groups: generalist species that are found on a range of other habitats as well as farmland, and specialists that live and breed almost exclusively on farmland habitats.

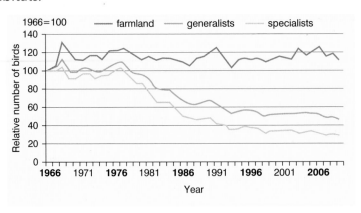

△ Fig 21.37 Numbers of farmland birds between 1966 and 2009.

Of the five species of specialist seed eaters, all decreased in number up to 1986, after which one (goldfinches) increased while the rest continued to decrease. Of the three species of insect eaters, all species decreased in number to about 1996, after which numbers seem to have stabilised.

a) Describe what the graph shows. (2 marks)

b) Suggest reasons for the difference between changes in population size for generalist and specialist species. (2 marks)

c) Goldfinches are farmland birds that have increased in number since about 1986, possibly because people are feeding more birds in their gardens over winter. Suggest one possible cause for the continuing decrease in other species. (1 mark)

d) In 1988 farmers in the European Union were encouraged to set aside some of their land for wildlife each year. Explain the role of local, national and international agreements in conservation. (2 marks)

Doing well in examinations

INTRODUCTION

Examinations will test how good your understanding of scientific ideas is, how well you can apply your understanding to new situations and how well you can analyse and interpret information you have been given. The assessments are opportunities to show how well you can do these.

To be successful in exams you need to:

✓ have a good knowledge and understanding of science
✓ be able to apply this knowledge and understanding to familiar and new situations
✓ be able to interpret and evaluate evidence that you have just been given.

You need to be able to do these things under exam conditions.

OVERVIEW

Ensure you are familiar with the structure of the examinations you are taking. Consult the relevant syllabus for the year you are entering your examinations for details of the different papers and the weighting of each, including the papers to test practical skills. Your teacher will advise you of which papers you will be taking.

You will be required to perform calculations, draw graphs and describe, explain and interpret biological ideas and information. In some of the questions the content may be unfamiliar to you; these questions are designed to assess data-handling skills and the ability to apply biological principles and ideas in unfamiliar situations.

ASSESSMENT OBJECTIVES AND WEIGHTINGS

For the Cambridge IGCSE examination, the assessment objectives and weightings are as follows:

✓ A: Knowledge with understanding (50%)
✓ B: Handling information and problem solving (30%)
✓ C: Experimental skills and investigations (20%).

The types of questions in your assessment fit the three assessment objectives shown in the table.

Assessment objective	Your answer should show that you can...
A Knowledge with understanding	Recall, select and communicate your knowledge and understanding of science.
B Handling information and problem solving	Apply skills, including evaluation and analysis, knowledge and understanding of scientific contexts.
C Experimental skills and investigations	Use the skills of planning, observation, analysis and evaluation in practical situations.

EXAMINATION TECHNIQUES

To help you to work to your best abilities in exams, there are a few simple steps to follow.

Check your understanding of the question.

✓ **Read the introduction to each question carefully before moving on to the questions themselves**.

✓ Look in detail at any **diagrams, graphs** or **tables**.

✓ Underline or circle the **key words** in the question.

✓ **Make sure you answer the question that is being asked** rather than the one you wish had been asked!

✓ Make sure you understand the meaning of the '**command words**' in the questions.

REMEMBER

Remember that any information you are given is there to help you to answer the question.

EXAMPLE

✓ **'Give', 'state', 'name'** are used when recall of knowledge is required, for example you could be asked to give a definition or provide the best answers from a list of options.

✓ **'Describe'** is used when you have to give the main feature(s) of, for example, a biological process or structure.

✓ **'Explain'** is used when you have to give reasons, e.g. for some experimental results or a biological fact or observation. You will often be asked to 'explain your answer', i.e. give reasons for it.

✓ **'Suggest'** is used when you have to come up with an idea to explain the information you're given – there may be more than one possible answer, no definitive answer from the information given, or it may be that you will not have learned the answer but have to use the knowledge you do have to come up with a sensible one.

✓ **'Calculate'** means that you have to work out an answer in figures.

✓ **'Plot'** and **'Draw a graph'** are used when you have to use the data provided to produce graphs and charts.

Check the number of marks for each question

✓ Look at the **number of marks** allocated to each question.

✓ Look at the **space provided** to guide you as to the length of your answer.

✓ Make sure you include at least as many points in your answer as there are marks.

✓ Write neatly and keep within the space provided.

REMEMBER

Beware of continually writing too much because it probably means you are not really answering the questions. Do not repeat the question in your answer.

Use your time effectively

✓ Don't spend so long on some questions that you don't have time to finish the paper.

✓ Check how much time you have left regularly.

✓ If you are really stuck on a question, leave it, finish the rest of the paper and come back to it at the end.

✓ Even if you eventually have to guess at an answer, you stand a better chance of gaining some marks than if you leave it blank.

ANSWERING QUESTIONS

Multiple choice questions

✓ Select your answer by placing a cross (not a tick) in the box.

Short-and long-answer questions

✓ In short-answer questions, **don't write more than you are asked for**.

✓ You may not gain any marks, even if the first part of your answer is correct, if you've written down something incorrect later on or which contradicts what you've said earlier. This may give the impression that you haven't really understood the question or are guessing.

✓ In some questions, particularly short-answer questions, answers of only one or two words may be sufficient, but in longer questions you should aim to use **clear scientific language**.

✓ Present the information in a logical sequence.

✓ Don't be afraid to also use **labelled diagrams** or **flow charts** if it helps you to show your answer more clearly.

Questions with calculations

✓ **In calculations always show your working**.

✓ Even if your final answer is incorrect you may still gain some marks if part of your attempt is correct.

✓ If you just write down the final answer and it is incorrect, you will get no marks at all.

✓ Write down your answers to as many **significant figures** as are used in the numbers in the question (and no more). If the question doesn't state how many significant figures then a good rule to follow is to quote three significant figures.

✓ Don't round off too early in calculations with many steps – it's always better to give too many significant figures than too few.

✓ You may also lose marks if you don't use the correct **units.** In some questions the units will be mentioned, e.g. calculate the mass in grams; or the units may also be given on the answer line. If numbers you are working with are very large, you may need to make a conversion, e.g. convert joules into kilojoules or millimetres into metres.

Finishing your exam

✓ When you've finished your exam, **check through** your paper to make sure you've answered all the questions.

✓ Check that you haven't missed any questions at the end of the paper or turned over two pages at once and missed questions.

✓ Cover over your answers and read through the questions again and check that your answers are as good as you can make them.

REMEMBER

You will be asked questions on investigative work. It is important that you understand the methods used by scientists when carrying out investigative work.

More information on carrying out practical work and developing your investigative skills are given in the next section.

TEACHER'S COMMENTS

a) i) It is important to know the features of different groups of organisms and be able to label these.

   A Correct – nucleus.

   B Correct – vacuole.

   C Incorrect – the outer layer of the hypha is the wall.

   D Incorrect – the membrane is the next layer within the wall, pushed up against the wall.

   E Correct – cytoplasm.

ii) Correct – the hyphae of moulds such as Mucor have a large central vacuole.

The answer is correct in that the hyphae have a wall, but this cannot be described as a 'cell wall' as the hyphae are not divided into cells. To be completely correct, the student simply had to repeat this information from part a) i).

Exam-style questions

Note: The questions, sample answers and marks in this section have been written by the authors as a guide only. The marks awarded for these questions indicate the level of detail required in the answers. In the examination, the number of marks awarded to questions like these may be different.

Sample student answer

Question 1

The diagram shows the structure of a part of an organism called Mucor.

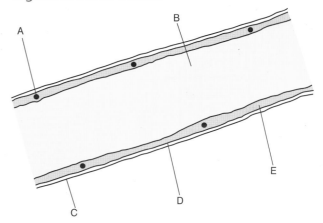

a) i) The diagram shows the structure of the organism Mucor. Name each of the parts A–E. Use the words in the box below. (5)

cytoplasm	membrane	nucleus
starch grain	vacuole	wall

A	*nucleus*	✓ ①
B	*vacuole*	✓ ①
C	*membrane*	✗
D	*wall*	✗
E	*cytoplasm*	✓ ①

Exam-style questions continued

ii) State **two** features the organism has in common with plants. **(2)**

Mucor has a large central vacuole. ✓ ①

Mucor has a cell wall. ✓ ①

iii) EXTENDED Give one feature that tells you that Mucor is a fungus. **(1)**

It has many nuclei lying in the cytoplasm. ✓ ①

b) EXTENDED Describe how moulds such as Mucor feed. **(4)**

Mucor lives on its food, e.g. bread, and secretes enzymes into it. ✓ ①

The food is absorbed over the surface of the fungus. ✓ ①

c) EXTENDED Yeast is another type of fungus. State one major difference between Mucor and yeast. **(1)**

Yeast is single-celled. ✓ ①

(Total 14 marks)

iii) Correct. The student could have chosen from a selection of features but was only asked to give one for the mark.

b) The answer is correct, but the student could have added that food is digested outside the mould, and that this process is called saprotrophic nutrition.

c) Correct – the mycelium of Mucor has many nuclei distributed through the cytoplasm, with no cell boundaries; yeast is made up of single cells.

Question 2

This question is about the variety of living organisms.

a) Four types of living organism are listed as A to D below:

A: bird	B: bony fish	C: mollusc	D: nematode

  i) Which **two** organisms have backbones? **(2)**

 ii) Which organism has a shell? **(1)**

iii) Which organism has jointed legs? **(1)**

iv) Which organism has an exoskeleton? **(1)**

  v) Which organism is shaped like a tube? **(1)**

b) The illustration below shows an animal called the duck-billed platypus.

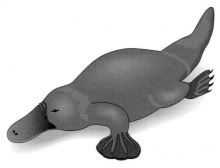

   i) State **one** characteristic, visible in the diagram, that is typical of all mammals. **(1)**

   ii) State **one** characteristic of the duck-billed platypus, **not** visible in the diagram, that is typical of all mammals. **(1)**

   iii) State **one** characteristic of the duck-billed platypus that is not typical of other mammals. **(1)**

(Total 9 marks)

Question 3

This question is about the characteristics of living things.

a) Copy and complete the sentences by writing the most appropriate word in each space.

Use only words from the box.

detect	development	energy	gravity
growth	light	location	nutrition
position	respiration	respond	sensitivity

.... is the taking in of substances needed for energy and for .... and ....

.... is a series of reactions that take place in living cells to release .... from nutrient molecules so that cells can use this to keep them alive.

.... is the ability to .... and .... to changes in external and internal conditions.

Movement causes a change in .... of the organism. In animals, this involves their entire bodies. Plants often move parts of their body in response to external stimuli, such as .... and .... **(12)**

b) Define the term excretion. (3)

c) Which of the characteristics shown by living things are shown by a motor car? (4)

(**Total 19 marks**)

Question 4

All organisms are classified.

a) Describe how scientists classify organisms into groups. (1)

b) Describe why the binomial system is used to name living organisms. (2)

c) The following is a list of four animal species.

PANTHERA LEO	Homo Sapiens	Lumbricus terrestris	pieris brassicae

  i) Which animal species above is written correctly using the binomial system? (1)

  ii) Define the term species. (2)

  iii) In the correctly-named organism in the box above, which part of the name defines the species? (1)

(**Total 7 marks**)

EXTENDED Question 5

Not everyone agrees that viruses should be called living things. Use your knowledge of viruses and the characteristics of living things to discuss whether or not viruses should be classed as living. (4)

(**Total 4 marks**)

Question 6

When scientists discover a new species, they classify it.

a) Explain why it is important to classify all organisms. (2)

b) The diagrams show the structure of the fore limbs of some animals.

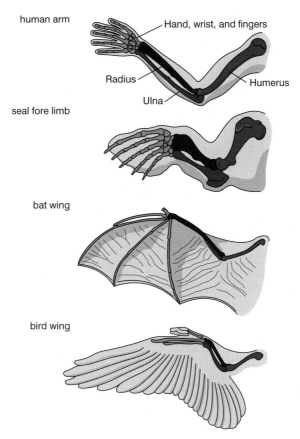

All of these organisms are vertebrates.

  i) State the major characteristic of vertebrates. (1)

  ii) Using information from the diagram, explain how scientists know that these organisms can be placed into the same group. (1)

  iii) Describe the major differences between the wing of the bat and the bird. (3)

c) What feature do scientists currently use when investigating the relationships of organisms? (1)

(**Total 8 marks**)

EXTENDED Question 7

The diagrams below show five different types of arthropod.

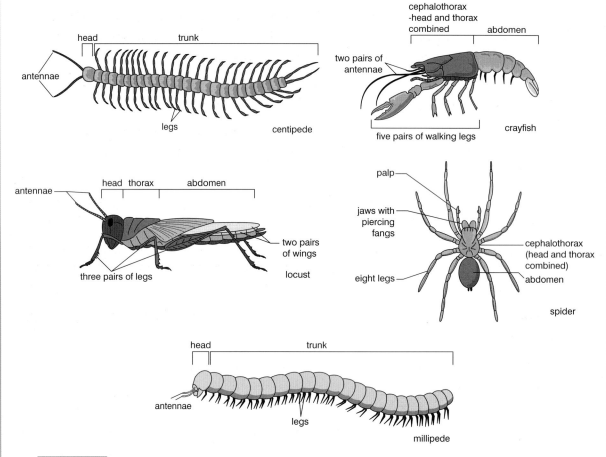

a) EXTENDED State **two** major features of arthropods.   (2)

b) Construct a dichotomous key to identify the five organisms.   (5)

(Total 7 marks)

Question 8

Most living organisms are made up of cells.

a) Copy and complete the sentences by writing the most appropriate word in each space.

The .... holds the cell together and controls substances entering and leaving the cell. The .... is the jelly-like substance contained within the cell. It is where many different chemical processes occur.

The .... is the control centre of the cell and contains genetic material as .... These control how a cell grows and works.

Plant cells also have features that are not found in animal cells. These include the ...., made of ...., which gives the cell extra support and defines its shape.

Many plant cells have a large central, permanent .... that contains cell sap. It is used for storage of some chemicals, and to support the shape of the cell.

Plant cells exposed to the light contain .... These contain the green pigment ...., which absorbs the light energy that plants use for the process of .... **(10)**

b) The levels of organisation in multicellular organisms include cells, tissues, organs and systems.

State whether each of the following structures is a cell, tissue or organ.

Structure	Cell	Tissue	Organ
Blood			
Brain			
Liver			
Muscle			
Neurone			
Ovum			
Skin			
Sperm			

(8)

(Total 18 marks)

Exam-style questions continued

Question 9

The light micrograph shows a cell from the liver of a human.

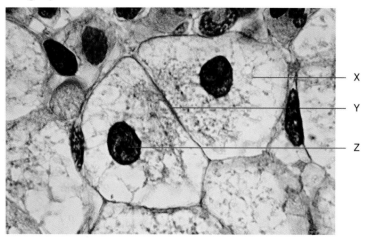

a) State the functions of the three structures highlighted above. **(6)**

b) EXTENDED Calculate the width, in micrometres, of the longer dimension of cell A, as shown by the line. Show your working. **(2)**

c) How many liver cells, laid side-to side, would there be in a piece of liver tissue 1 cm across? Show your working. **(2)**

(Total 10 marks)

EXTENDED Question 10

A Biology student set up an investigation in which three cubes of different sizes were cut from an agar jelly block. The agar jelly contained a red indicator that turns blue in the presence of alkali.

The cubes were placed in an alkali. The student measured the time taken for the cubes to turn completely blue.

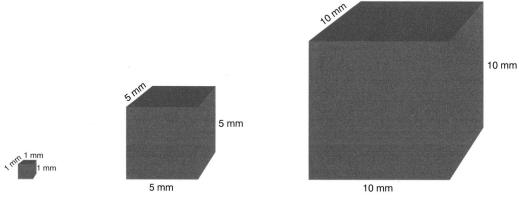

a) What is the name of the process that causes the alkali to penetrate the agar jelly? **(1)**

b) EXTENDED The student used cubes of three dimensions:

Dimensions of cube, mm
1 × 1 × 1
5 × 5 × 5
10 × 10 × 10

For each cube, calculate its:

  i) surface area

 ii) volume

iii) surface area : volume ratio. (9)

Dimensions of cube/mm	i) Surface area of cube/mm²	ii) Volume of cube/mm³	iii) Surface area : volume ratio
1 × 1 × 1			
5 × 5 × 5			
10 × 10 × 10			

c) EXTENDED Explain the relationship between surface area and volume as the cube increases in size. (1)

d) EXTENDED During the biology lesson, the alkali penetrated the two smaller cubes, but by the end of the lesson, the 10 mm × 10 mm × 10 mm cube had still not turned completely blue.

  i) Explain these results. (3)

 ii) Explain what implications this has for organisms of increasing size. (3)

(Total 17 marks)

Question 11

A student cut a number of cylinders from a potato and weighed them. These were placed in sucrose solutions of different concentrations.

After one hour, the cylinders were removed, blotted dry and reweighed. The student calculated the percentage change in mass for each cylinder. The results are shown in the table.

Concentration of sucrose/g per cm³	Percentage change in mass of potato cylinders				Average percentage change in mass
	Experiment 1	Experiment 2	Experiment 3	Experiment 4	
0.0	+31.4	+33.7	+31.2	+32.5	
0.2	+20.9	+22.2	+22.8	+21.3	
0.4	−2.7	−1.8	−1.9	−2.4	
0.6	−13.9	−12.8	−13.7	−13.6	
0.8	−20.2	−19.7	−19.3	−20.4	
1.0	−19.9	−20.3	−21.1	−20.3	

a) Calculate the average percentage changes in mass for each of the sucrose concentrations. (6)

b) i) Draw a graph of these results. Join the points with a line of best fit. (4)

   ii) At what concentration of sucrose was there no net movement of water? (2)

   iii) Describe the changes in mass over the range of sucrose concentrations. (3)

   iv) State the process involved in these changes in the potato cylinders. (1)

(Total 16 marks)

Question 12

The table below lists some molecules that are important biologically.

a) Give the units that each one of the following biological molecules is made up of.

Biological molecule	Units that make up the molecule	
Glycogen		(1)
Fats		(2)
Proteins		(1)
Starch		(1)

b) Describe a test that can be carried out in the laboratory for the following carbohydrates:

   i) glucose (5)

   ii) starch. (4)

(Total 14 marks)

EXTENDED Question 13

A company that produces enzymes publishes information sheets of their performance. The graphs below show the performance of an enzyme, pectinase, at different pHs and temperatures.

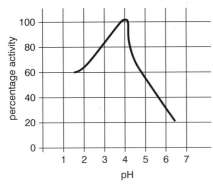
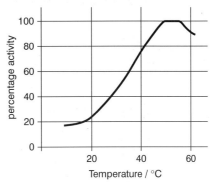

a) Describe and explain the effect of:

  i) pH   **(6)**

  ii) temperature, on the activity of the enzyme pectinase.   **(5)**

b) A student finds an information sheet on the effect of pH on the activity of a protease called papain, from the papaya plant.

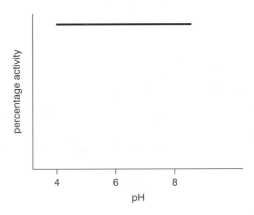

  i) EXTENDED State two proteases produced by the human gut.   **(2)**

  ii) A student says that the graph shows that papain is unaffected by pH. Is the student correct? Explain your answer.   **(2)**

(Total 15 marks)

EXTENDED **Question 14**

a) In humans, proteases are produced by the stomach, pancreas and small intestine. Copy the diagram and show the location of these organs. (3)

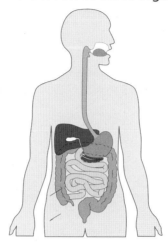

b) The graphs show the effect of pH on the activity of two proteases that break down proteins.

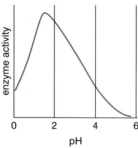

stomach protease

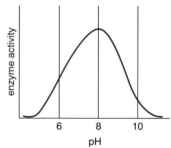

small intestine protease

i) EXTENDED What are the optimum pHs of stomach and small intestine proteases? (2)

ii) Describe an experiment to investigate the effect of temperature on the breakdown of a named food molecule. (5)

(Total 10 marks)

TEACHER'S COMMENTS

a) i) Correct. As light intensity increases, the rate of photosynthesis increases, because light energy supplies energy for the process of photosynthesis. At a certain point, the graph levels off, so any further increase in light intensity after that point will result in no further increase in photosynthesis. At this point, some other factor must be limiting, for example carbon dioxide, and preventing any further increase.

ii) One mark has been awarded for the correct graph. The student has not responded to the second part of the question- explain the shape of the graph you have drawn. To gain a second mark, the student needed to explain that as carbon dioxide was a factor that was limiting the rate of photosynthesis where the graph levels off, in a higher concentration of carbon dioxide, the graph will continue to a higher point (i.e. a higher rate of photosynthesis) until it

Plants respond to the light available.

a) The graph below shows the effect of light intensity on photosynthesis in a single-celled plant.

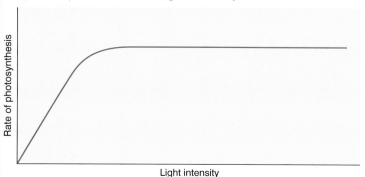

Rate of photosynthesis

Light intensity

i) Describe and explain the effect of light intensity on the plant. (4)

Increasing light intensity increases the rate of photosynthesis up to a certain point. ✓ ①

This is because light energy is needed for photosynthesis. ✓ ①

The graph stops getting steeper because increasing the light intensity can't increase the rate of photosynthesis any more. ✓ ①

This is because another factor is limiting the rate of photosynthesis. ✓ ①

The investigation was also carried out in a high concentration of carbon dioxide.

ii) Sketch a graph of what you would expect so you can compare it with the graph above. Explain the shape of the graph you have drawn. (3)

Exam-style questions continued

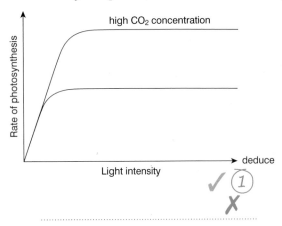

high CO_2 concentration

Rate of photosynthesis

Light intensity

deduce

✓ ① ✗

again levels off. The third mark would have been awarded for stating that at this point, with light and carbon dioxide being available, another factor (e.g. temperature) must be preventing any further increase in the rate of photosynthesis.

b) A scientist investigating the response of plants to light placed:

- one group in the light, given even illumination
- one group of plants in the dark, and
- one group exposed to light from one side.

The plants were in an atmosphere of radioactive carbon dioxide, and after five hours, the amount of radioactive auxin in the area below the shoot tip was measured. The scientist's results are shown below.

b) The student has correctly identified that there is no significant difference between the amount of auxin in the plants in the light, the dark or those illuminated on one side. A further mark is gained by correctly stating that this shows that light has no effect on the production of auxin.

To gain further marks, the student needed to provide a more in-depth explanation using the results, such as 'This shows that light has no effect on the production of auxin. In the plant illuminated from one side, about 71% of the auxin in the plant is on the dark side, so as the total auxin was unaffected by light, the auxin must have been redistributed from the light to dark side.'

	Plants in the light	Plants in the dark	Plants exposed to light from one side	
			Dark side	Lighted side
Total radioactive auxin/ counts per minute	2985	3004	2173	878

Explain fully what these results show about the effect of light on auxin in the plants. **(4)**

There is not much difference between the amount of auxin in the plants in the dark, the plants in the light or the plant that was half in the light and half in the dark. ✓ ①

This shows that altering the levels of light does not make any difference to the production of auxin. ✓ ①

(Total 11 marks)

Question 16

The leaf is the main organ of photosynthesis.

a) Write a word and symbol equation for photosynthesis. (5)

b) EXTENDED Explain how the leaf is adapted to exchanging gases required for photosynthesis. (5)

c) Chemical substances in a plant are transported in the xylem and phloem.

Copy and complete the table below.

	Phloem	Xylem
Substances transported	(2)	(2)
Substances are transported:		
from	(1)	(1)
to	(1)	(1)

(8)

(Total 18 marks)

Question 17

The diagram shows a section through a leaf.

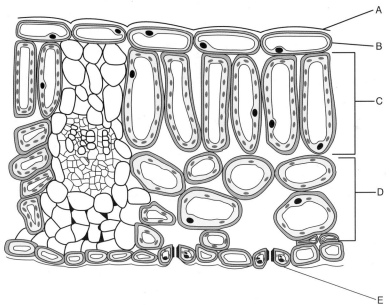

a) Name parts A–E shown in the diagram. (5)

b) The leaf is the main organ of photosynthesis. Write a word equation for photosynthesis. (3)

c) Define the term *transpiration*. (3)

d) Describe a technique used to investigate the effect of temperature on transpiration rate. (7)

(Total 18 marks)

EXTENDED Question 18

a) The diagram below shows a section of a plant root surrounded by soil particles.

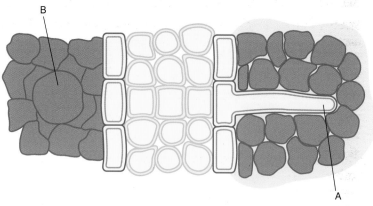

i) Identify the parts of the plant root, A and B. (2)

ii) **EXTENDED** Explain the importance of water potential in the uptake and transport of water by plant roots. (7)

b) The effect of osmosis on animal cells is different from its effect on plant cells.

i) **EXTENDED** Explain how osmosis is involved in the body's response to a cholera infection. (5)

(Total 15 marks)

Question 19

The circulatory system has several functions, including the transport of substances, temperature regulation and defence.

The diagram shows the structure of the heart.

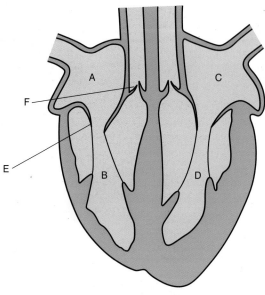

a) Name the chambers of the heart, A, B, C and D. (4)

b) Copy and complete the table for each of the different components of the blood.

Component of blood	Function
Red blood cells	
White blood cells	
Platelets	
Plasma	

(8)

(Total 12 marks)

Question 20

a) Describe how the back flow of blood in the heart is prevented. (4)

b) EXTENDED Explain why the wall of the left ventricle is four times as thick as the wall of the right ventricle. (4)

c) EXTENDED The blood system is involved in the body's immunity.

   i) Describe how the body can develop passive immunity. (1)

   ii) Explain how a vaccination can make a person immune to a particular disease. (5)

d) Describe the function of vaccination. (1)

e) Explain how vaccination works. (3)

(Total 18 marks)

Question 21

a) Yeast, a fungus, is used in the production of biofuel.

   i) Give the word equation for the production of ethanol by yeast. (2)

   ii) Describe how yeast cells are involved in the process. (1)

b) Compare the energy produced by yeast undergoing anaerobic respiration with yeast undergoing aerobic respiration. (1)

(Total 4 marks)

Question 22

The diagram shows the urinary system of humans.

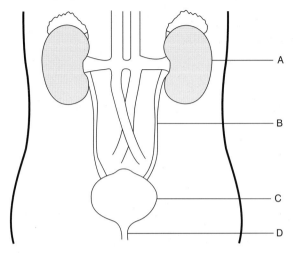

a) Identify the parts of the urinary system, A, B, C and D. (4)

b) Name another excretory organ of humans and one chemical that it excretes. (2)

c) The table below shows the composition of urine.

Substance	Concentration in urine
Water	96.0 cm^3 per 100 cm^3
Glucose	0.0 g per 100 cm^3
Salts	1.8 g per 100 cm^3
Urea	2.0 g per 100 cm^3

Under normal conditions, on average, a person excretes 1500 cm^3 of urine every day.

   i) Why and where is urea produced in the body? (2)

   ii) State **one** factor that affects the volume and concentration of urine produced, and explain how these are affected. (3)

(**Total 11 marks**)

Question 23

This question is about plants' responses towards stimuli.

Copy and complete the sentences by writing the most appropriate word in each space.

Growth in response to the direction of light is called ....
If the growth is towards light, it is called .... ,
as shown by plant ....

Growth in response to gravity is called .... Plant roots are
.... This response helps the plant
.... to grow .... , so the plant can
obtain the .... it needs.   **(Total 8 marks)**

Question 24

The nervous system is involved in the body's response to stimuli.

a) When a person puts her hand on a hot object, she removes it quickly using a reflex
   action.

   i) Draw a diagram to show the reflex arc involved.   (6)

   ii) Shortly after she removes her hand, she realises that she has touched a hot
      object. Explain how this occurs.   (3)

b) EXTENDED What is the name of the other system involved in the body's coordination?
   How does the response of this system differ from the nervous system?   (4)

                                                                          (Total 13 marks)

EXTENDED **Question 25**

The diagram shows the structure of an industrial fermenter used to culture a microorganism that produces a medicinal drug.

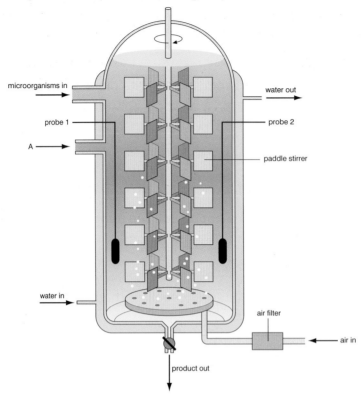

a) State why many drugs are produced with microorganisms rather than manufactured from chemical raw materials. **(2)**

b) i) Suggest what may be pumped into the fermenter at point A. **(1)**

ii) Suggest two factors that probes 1 and 2 may be designed to measure. **(2)**

c) In the fermenter, explain fully the use of:

i) the paddle stirrer **(2)**

ii) water circulating around the fermenter. **(3)**

d) Give one way in which the manufacturer ensures that this microorganism grows rather than others. **(1)**

e) What type of respiration is the microorganism carrying out in the fermenter? Explain your answer. **(2)**

(Total 13 marks)

Question 26

a) The passage below describes the process of sexual reproduction.

Use suitable words to complete the sentences in the passage.

Sexual reproduction is the most common method of reproduction for the majority of larger organisms, including almost all animals and plants. To produce a new organism, two .... fuse. This process is known as .... **(2)**

Usually, sexual reproduction involves .... parent organisms of the same species. The .... formed is genetically different from each of the parents. **(2)**

b) **EXTENDED** Give one advantage and one disadvantage of:

   i) asexual reproduction. **(2)**

   ii) sexual reproduction. **(2)**

c) **i)** Label the diagram of the human female reproductive system. **(6)**

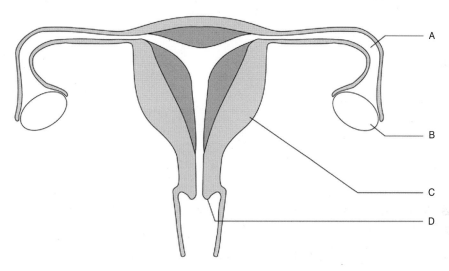

   ii) Draw a flow chart to illustrate the processes involved in labour and birth. **(6)**

d) State **one** method of each type of birth control:

   i) chemical **(1)**

   ii) barrier **(1)**

   iii) surgical. **(1)**

(Total 23 marks)

Question 27

Flowers are adapted to be pollinated by insects or by the wind.

a) Name the structures of an insect-pollinated flower shown in the diagram below. **(10)**

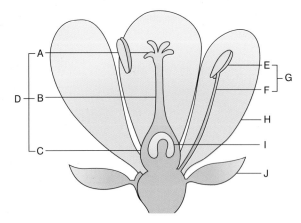

b) Explain how each of the structures is adapted for pollination in wind-pollinated flowers:

   i) petals   **(2)**

  ii) stigma   **(2)**

 iii) stamens   **(2)**

 iv) pollen grains.   **(2)**

(Total 18 marks)

EXTENDED Question 28

This question is about reproduction.

a) The diagram shows a human sperm.

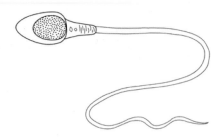

Explain how the sperm is adapted to fertilising a human egg.   **(4)**

b) Explain the roles of hormones in controlling the menstrual cycle and preparing the uterus for a fertilised egg.   **(3)**

c) Discuss the advantages of breast-feeding compared with bottle-feeding.   **(3)**

(Total 10 marks)

Question 29

People are either able to roll their tongue into a U-shape, or unable to roll their tongue. Tongue rolling is controlled by a single pair of genes which has two alleles.

a) The diagram shows a pair of chromosomes:

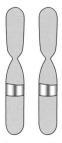

Genotype TT:
can roll tongue

a) i) Correct – dominant.

The rest of the answer is too vague. It should be more specific, such as 'The two letters making up the genotype are written in upper case.'

i) Is the allele for tongue rolling dominant or recessive? Explain your answer. **(2)**

Dominant ✔ ①

The letters are capitals. ✗

ii) Write down the other possible genotypes related to tongue rolling, along with their phenotypes. **(2)**

Tt - The phenotype is a tongue roller. ✔ ①

tt - The phenotype is non tongue roller (cannot roll tongue). ✔ ①

b) A couple who can both roll their tongues have children.

i) Give the possible genotypes of the man and the woman. **(2)**

The couple could be TT ✔ ①

or Tt. ✔ ①

ii) Both statements are correct, but only two marking points have been addressed. The student is correct, that unless both parents were Tt, all children would be tongue rollers, but the answer would benefit from two statements of explanation:

First of all, it should be made clear that as both the man and woman can roll their tongue, the must have at least one T allele.

There should then be a sentence of explanation to link the statements, such as:

'Without the presence of a t allele in both parents, all the children would be tongue rollers.'

ii) Their first child cannot roll his tongue; the second one can.

What does this tell you about the genotypes of the couple? Explain your answer fully. **(4)**

The genotype of both the man and women must be Tt. ✓ ①

Because otherwise all the children would be tongue rollers. ✓ ①

iii) Show the genetic cross involved. **(4)**

Tt   x   Tt ✓ ①

↓

TT   Tt   tT   tt ✓ ①

(Total 14 marks)

⁹⁄₁₄

iii) The diagram illustrates the cross correctly, but lacks detail.

The best way of illustrating the cross is to use a Punnett square, showing each stage of the cross:

the genotypes of the parents

the different alleles that could be passed on to the offspring from the mother and father (the alleles in the egg cells and sperm cells)

the possible combinations of alleles in the offspring (genotypes)

the possible phenotypes produced.

		Mother possible alleles in eggs	
		T	t
Father possible alleles in sperm	T	TT Tongue roller	Tt Tongue roller
	t	Tt Tongue roller	tt Non tongue roller

A further point is the way in which the student has written the third possible genotype in their answer (tT). Although not incorrect, the convention is to write the dominant allele first, so it should be written Tt.

Question 30

The diagram shows a cell and some of the structures in it.

Identify the structures 1, 2, 3, 4 and 5.

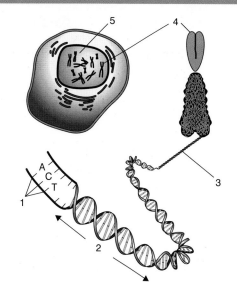

(Total 5 marks)

Question 31

A disease called cystic fibrosis is caused by a faulty allele of a recessive gene.

The family tree below shows the occurrence of cystic fibrosis in a family.

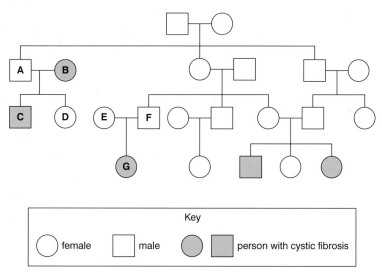

Key

○ female   ☐ male   ● ■ person with cystic fibrosis

a) Give the genotypes of the following members of the family, explaining how you come to your decision:

   i) father A   **(2)**

   ii) daughter D   **(2)**

   iii) parents E and F.   **(3)**

b) In the part of the family tree with the people A–G, identify the carriers of cystic fibrosis.   **(4)**

(Total 11 marks)

EXTENDED **Question 32**

Codominance is seen in the genetic traits of a number of organisms, including humans. It is a condition where both alleles of a gene pair are both expressed as neither is dominant over the other.

a) The coat colour of some cattle shows incomplete dominance.

Some cattle have alleles that produce red hairs; others have alleles that produce white hairs. Cattle that have a combination of both alleles have red and white hairs. Their coat colour is described as *roan*.

i) Draw genetic diagrams to show the following crosses and predict the ratios of offspring produced.

Use C^R to represent the allele for red hair and C^W to represent the allele for white hair.

A red bull and a white cow. (6)

A roan bull and a white cow. (8)

b) In the inheritance of human blood groups, the alleles for blood group A and blood group B are dominant to the allele for blood group O. The alleles for blood group A and B are codominant.

Use I^A to represent the allele for blood group A, I^B to represent the allele for blood group B, and I^O to represent the allele for blood group O.

What is the probability of a father with blood group A and a mother with blood group B having:

i) a child with blood group A (4)

ii) a child with blood group O? (4)

(Total 22 marks)

Question 33

Haemophilia is a sex-linked condition in which blood fails to clot.

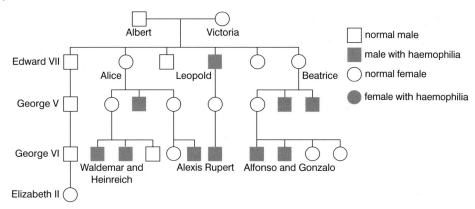

The simplified pedigree shows the inheritance of haemophilia through the royal families of Europe in the descendants of Great Britain's Queen Victoria and Prince Albert.

a) Using the letters H for normal, and h for haemophiliac, state the genotypes for Queen Victoria and Prince Albert. Explain your answer. **(7)**

b) Explain why it is mostly males who are affected by the condition. **(4)**

c) Explain why haemophilia has not occurred in the current British royal family Edward VII through to Elizabeth II. **(2)**

(Total 13 marks)

Question 34

A horse has a chromosome number of 64.

a) State whether each statement refers to mitosis, meiosis, both or neither. **(6)**

i) The chromosome number in each daughter cell is 64.

ii) The daughter cells are haploid.

iii) Two identical cells are produced.

iv) The nuclear membrane breaks, disappears at the beginning, and is reformed at the end of the process.

v) Some variability occurs in the alleles of parent and daughter chromosomes.

vi) Occurs when new red blood cells are produced in the blood of the horse.

b) Explain why a horse's gametes are produced by meiosis. **(5)**

(Total 11 marks)

Question 35

The food web below shows the relationship of some of the organisms on a rocky shore.

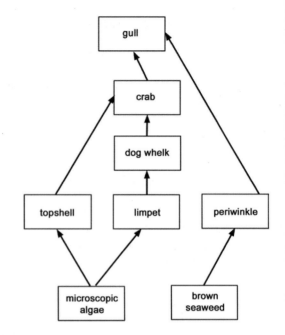

a) **EXTENDED** In the food web, state which organisms are:

  i) producers   (2)

  ii) primary consumers   (3)

  iii) secondary consumers.   (3)

b) In an ecosystem, the numbers of crabs is severely reduced.

  i) State **one** reason for the reduction of an organism in an ecosystem.   (3)

  ii) Describe the impact on dog whelks, limpets and gulls in the food web.   (5)

c) A student investigated the distribution of a species of brown seaweed and periwinkles down a rocky shore. Her results are shown here.

Distance below high water on seashore/ metres	Distribution of organisms	
	Observed distribution of brown seaweed	**Density of periwinkles/ mean number of periwinkles per m²**
0	Absent	0
10	Rare	16
20	Occasional	52
30	Abundant	156
40	Abundant	128
50	Occasional	44
60	Rare	12

Suggest two reasons for the distribution of the periwinkles.   (2)

(Total 18 marks)

Question 36

Nutrients are cycled in nature.

a) The passage below describes the stages in the carbon cycle.

Use suitable words to complete the sentences in the passage. **(9)**

.... from the atmosphere is converted to complex carbon compounds in .... by the process of .... This is often called carbon ....

Plants are then often eaten by ...., which build up their own complex carbon compounds.

The process of .... in both plants and animals, returns some of this carbon back to the atmosphere as ....

When organisms die, their bodies decay as they are worked on by .... Some of the complex carbon compounds are taken into the bodies of these organisms, where some may be converted to carbon dioxide during their ....

b) EXTENDED By what other process does carbon dioxide enter the air? **(1)**

(Total 10 marks)

Question 37

The graph shows the actual and projected changes in human populations in developed and developing countries from 1750.

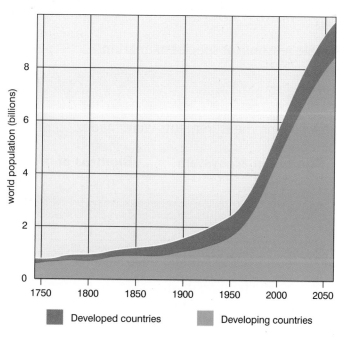

a) Describe the change in population growth from 1750 to 2050. (8)

b) Explain reasons for:

   i) time periods where the population growth is slow (2)

   ii) rapid increases in human population size. (2)

c) The graph shows human population size and estimated extinctions of organisms.

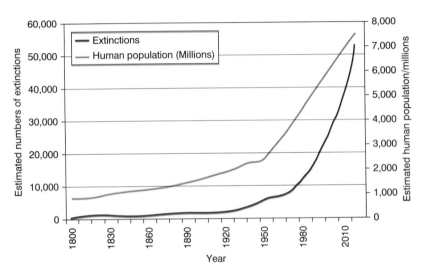

   i) Describe the patterns in human population growth and species extinctions. (2)

   ii) Explain why the numbers of species extinctions are estimated and not actual numbers. (2)

   iii) State **five** possible reasons for species extinction. (5)

(Total 21 marks)

EXTENDED **Question 38**

In an ecosystem, the following measurements were made.

Organism	Number in ecosystem	Biomass of organisms/g
Oak trees	1	500 000
Aphids	100 000	100
Ladybirds	200	10

a) Draw a food chain to illustrate the feeding relationships of the three organisms. (3)

b) Using a sketch, compare the feeding relationships in the food chain using a pyramid of numbers and a pyramid of biomass. (2)

c) EXTENDED Explain one advantage and one disadvantage of using a pyramid of biomass to illustrate feeding relationships. (2)

d) EXTENDED In observations of the ecosystem, ladybirds were seen to be fed on by spiders, and spiders fed on by blackbirds.

    i) Draw a food chain to illustrate these feeding relationships. (1)

    ii) Explain fully why food chains longer than this are rare. (5)

(Total 13 marks)

EXTENDED Question 39

The diagram shows the nitrogen cycle. Name the organisms missing from the diagram.

(4)

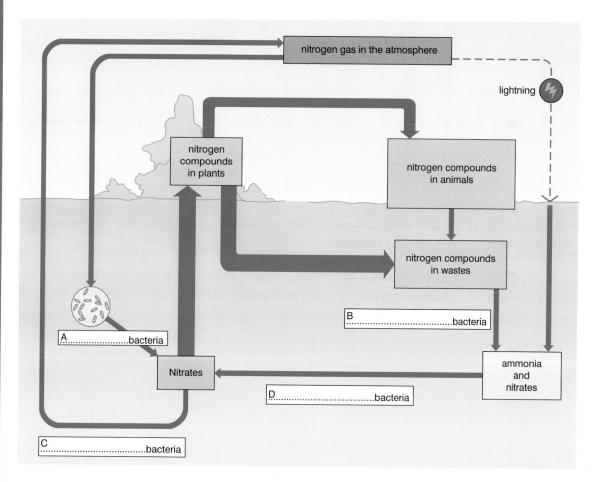

(Total 4 marks)

Question 40

The diagram shows part of a kidney.

a) EXTENDED Name parts A–H shown in the diagram. (8)

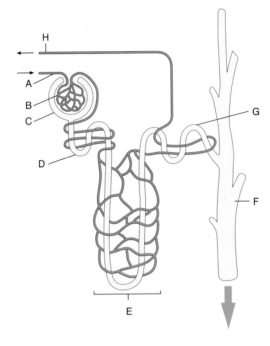

b) The table shows the concentration of certain substances in the plasma, glomerular filtrate and urine of a healthy person.

Substance	Concentration in plasma/g per 100 cm³	Concentration in glomerular filtrate/g per 100 cm³	Concentration in urine/g per 100 cm³
Amino acids	0.05	0.05	None
Glucose	0.10	0.10	None
Salts	0.90	0.90	<0.90 – 3.60
Protein	8.00	None	None
Urea	0.02	0.02	2.0

Referring to the structures in **a)**, explain the changes in concentrations of each of the four types of substance. (4)

c) EXTENDED The diagram shows what happens when someone is using a dialysis machine.

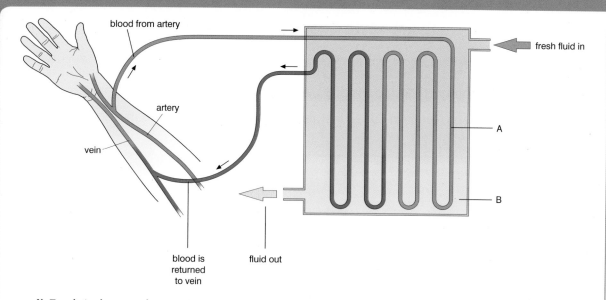

i) Explain how, when a patient is receiving dialysis, blood cells and blood proteins are prevented from leaving the blood. (1)

ii) Suggest how the treatment is able to remove urea from the blood, but keep the concentration of glucose in the blood at a normal level. (3)

d) **EXTENDED** Discuss two advantages and two disadvantages of the use of kidney transplants compared with dialysis. (4)

(Total 20 marks)

Question 41

Fruit juices are often produced using the enzyme pectinase.

Describe an experiment to show that fruit juice can be extracted from fruit more effectively by the addition of pectinase. (8)

(Total 8 marks)

Question 42

a) Define fully the term *genetic engineering*. (4)

b) **EXTENDED** State one reason why improving the characteristics of an organism by genetic engineering might be preferable to improving characteristics by selective breeding. (1)

c) State one medical application of genetic engineering. (1)

(Total 6 marks)

EXTENDED **Question 43**

a) Outline the technique used to modify bacteria so that they produce insulin. **(6)**

b) Explain why it is better to produce insulin using bacteria, rather than obtain it from livestock such as cattle. **(4)**

(Total 10 marks)

Question 44

The table gives information on how the land area covered by forest has changed from 1990 to 2005.

Country	Area covered by forest/millions of hectares		Area of forest lost from 1990 to 2005/%
	1990	**2005**	
Bolivia	109.9	58.7	46.6
Brazil	851.5	477.7	
Colombia	113.9	60.7	
French Guiana	9.0	8.1	
Peru	125.5	68.7	
Suriname	16.3	14.8	
Venezuela	91.2	47.7	

Data from http://rainforests.mongabay.com/deforestation_alpha.html

a) EXTENDED Calculate the area of forest lost for each country, as a percentage of the area in 1990. The first one has been done for you. **(6)**

b) During the time period 1990 to 2005, in which country is there:

  i) the greatest deforestation? **(1)**

  ii) the least deforestation? **(1)**

c) Suggest two reasons for deforestation. **(2)**

d) List the effects of deforestation. **(5)**

(Total 15 marks)

TEACHER'S COMMENTS

a) **i)** Correct.

ii) The answers given for carbon dioxide and nitrous oxide are detailed and correct.

For methane, the student has not appreciated that the graph has been drawn to the scale on the right hand axis, which ranges from 0–2000 ppb. This has meant that although the trends have been described, the values of methane concentration are incorrect.

It is important to check scales carefully when reading data from graphs. The answer should therefore be:

'The concentration of methane has shown a very slow, slight upward trend from 0 to around 1750, ranging from 650 ppb to around 750 ppb.'

'Then after a slight dip, a steep increase to around 1925 ppb in 2005.'

Question 45

This question is about the enhanced greenhouse effect and global warming.

a) The graph shows the concentration of greenhouse gases in the air from the Year 0 to 2000.

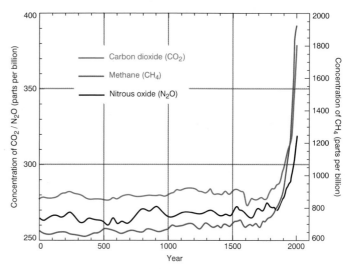

i) Which greenhouse gas was present in the highest concentration in the air in 2000? **(1)**

Methane ✓ ①

ii) Describe the trends in the changes of the concentration of each greenhouse gas from 0 to 2005. **(6)**

The concentration of carbon dioxide has been fairly stable at around 280 parts per billion from 0 to 1600. ✓ ①

Then, after a dip, it shows a steep increase to 380 ppb in 2005. ✓ ①

Exam-style questions continued

The concentration of nitrous oxide has shown a little fluctuation from 0 to around 1800, ranging from 265-275 ppb. ✓ ①

But there has been a steep increase to around 320 ppb in 2005. ✓ ①

The concentration of methane has shown a very slow, slight upward trend from 0 to around 1750, ranging from 255 ppb to around 260 ppb. ✗

But then a steep increase to around 390 ppb in 2005. ✗

iii) How has human activity contributed to the change in the concentration of carbon dioxide in the air? **(2)**

Carbon dioxide production has increased from the burning of fossil fuels in transport, heating and cooling, and in manufacture. ✓ ①

iii) The student has written a good answer for the contribution of the burning of fossil fuels to the increase in carbon dioxide. These all refer to the burning of fossil fuels, however, and the student could have picked up the second mark by referring to deforestation.

b) i) The student has picked up two marks, but for the third mark, has not mentioned the fact that sulfur hexafluoride has the longest lifetime – a greenhouse gas that's around for a shorter time will make less of a contribution to the greenhouse effect.

b) The table gives information on several greenhouse gases.

Gas	Chemical formula	Lifetime (years)	Global Warming Potential*
Carbon dioxide	CO_2	Variable	1
Methane	CH_4	12	21
Nitrous oxide	N_2O	114	310
CFC-11	CCl_3F	45	3 800
CFC-12	CCl_2F_2	100	8 100
Sulfur hexafluoride	SF_6	3 200	23 900

*The **Global Warming Potential (GWP)** is a measure of how much heat a greenhouse gas traps in the atmosphere relative to that trapped by the same mass of carbon dioxide. A GWP is calculated over a time interval. The values in the table are for a 100-year time scale.

From: IPCC/TEAP (2005) *Special Report on Safeguarding the Ozone Layer and the Global Climate System: Issues Related to Hydrofluorocarbons and Perfluorocarbons* [Metz, B., et al. (eds.)]. Cambridge University Press.

i) Which greenhouse gas contributes most to global warming?
Explain your answer. (3)

Sulfur hexafluoride ✓ ①

It has the highest GWP. ✓ ①

ii) Explain how greenhouse gases result in the greenhouse effect and global warming. (6)

Shortwave radiation from the Sun passes through the Earth's atmosphere and warms the ground. ✓ ①

The warmed Earth gives off longer wave radiation that is prevented from leaving the earth by greenhouse gases in the atmosphere. ✓ ①

ii) This is a good answer, but the student has not mentioned the 'enhanced greenhouse effect'. The final marking point could have been extended:

'But increases in greenhouse gases as a result in human activity is leading to the enhanced greenhouse effect.'

'This is leading to a significant warming of the Earth called global warming.'

The trapping of the radiation leads to the Earth warming up, which is called the greenhouse effect. ✓ ①

The greenhouse effect is important, because without it, the temperature on the Earth would be 33°C lower – the Earth would be uninhabitable. ✓ ①

But increases in greenhouse gases as a result in human activity is leading to a significant warming of the Earth called global warming. ✓ ①

(Total 18 marks)

13/18

Question 46

Modern technology is used to increase the yields of crop plants.

a) One method used to increase crop yields is to apply fertilisers. List the effects, in sequence, when nitrates are washed from the fields and pollute water. **(4)**

b) Pesticides are often applied to crops.

i) Explain why pesticides are applied to crops. **(5)**

ii) Describe two negative impacts of pollution by one type of pesticide. **(2)**

(Total 11 marks)

EXTENDED **Question 47**

The effect of sewage into a river was monitored over a number of years. The results are shown in the graphs.

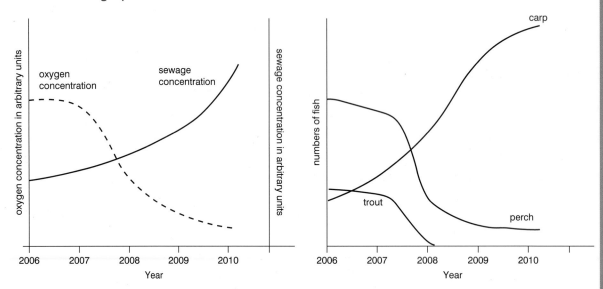

a) **i)** Describe the trends in sewage and oxygen concentration between 2006 and 2010. **(2)**

ii) Explain why sewage had this effect on the oxygen concentration in the water. **(3)**

b) Describe and explain the effects of the changing oxygen concentration on fish populations. **(6)**

(Total 11 marks)

Developing experimental skills

INTRODUCTION

As part of your Biology course, you will develop practical skills and have to carry out investigative work in science.

This section provides guidance on carrying out an investigation.

The experimental and investigative skills are divided as follows:

1. Using and organising techniques, apparatus and materials

2. Observing, measuring and recording

3. Handling experimental observations and data

4. Planning and evaluating investigations.

1. USING AND ORGANISING TECHNIQUES, APPARATUS AND MATERIALS

Learning objective: to demonstrate and describe appropriate experimental and investigative methods, including safe and skilful practical techniques.

Questions to ask:

How shall I use the equipment and chemicals safely to minimise the risks – what are my safety precautions?

✓ When writing a Risk Assessment, investigators need to be careful to check that they've matched the hazard with the concentration of a chemical used. Many acids, for instance, are corrosive in higher concentrations, but are likely to be irritants or of low hazard in the concentration used when working in biology experiments.

✓ Don't forget to consider the hazards associated with all the chemicals and biological materials, even if these are very low.

✓ You may be asked to justify the precautions taken when carrying out an investigation.

How much detail should I give in my description?

✓ You need to give enough detail so that someone else who has not done the experiment would be able to carry it out to reproduce your results.

How should I use the equipment to give me the precision I need?

✓ You should know how to read the scales on the measuring equipment you are using.

✓ You need to show that you are aware of the precision needed.

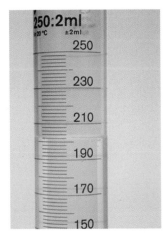

△ Fig. 6.1 The volume of liquid in a burette must be read to the bottom of the meniscus. The volume in this measuring cylinder is 202 cm³ (ml), not 204 cm³.

EXAMPLE 1

This is an extract from a student's notebook. It describes how she carried out an experiment to investigate the production of carbon dioxide by yeast at different temperatures.

What are my safety precautions?

a) Chemicals.

I have looked up the hazards associated with the chemical I am using:

Glucose (solutions from 0.05 to 0.25 M): LOW HAZARD

Although it is only a low hazard, it is still best to wear eye protection when using the solutions, especially as some of the liquids will be hot. It is also important to handle all chemicals carefully, and wipe up any spills of liquid.

COMMENT

The student has used a data source to look up the chemical hazards.

b) Organisms.

I found my information on yeast from the Fisher Scientific website:

Dried yeast may cause eye, skin, and respiratory tract
irritation. It is expected to be a low hazard for usual
handling. If the dust is inhaled, you should 'remove from
exposure and move to fresh air immediately'.

I will handle the powdered yeast carefully when making
up my suspension, trying to avoid making any dust.

COMMENT

The student has used a data source to look up the biological hazards.

c) Equipment

I must be careful when using the water bath not to get
water near the electrical sockets.

I need to handle the glassware (conical flask, gas syringe
and glass tubing) carefully. In particular, I need to
protect my hands with a towel (or glove) when linking
together the glass delivery tubes from the rubber bung in
the conical flask to the gas syringe with rubber tubing. The
tubing needs to be lubricated with water and I need to
hold my hands close together to limit the movement of
glass if a break occurs.

COMMENT

The student has suggested some sensible precautions.

How much detail should I give in my description?

The student's method is given below:

1 *A solution of 0.25 M glucose was made up by dissolving*
   45.00 g of glucose in water to make a litre of solution.

2 *100 cm³ of the glucose solution was transferred to each of*
   six conical flasks.

3 *The conical flask was transferred to a water bath at 20 °C.*
   It was left for a few minutes to reach the temperature.

4 *1.00 g of yeast was then added, and the mixture swirled to*
   mix in the yeast. The stop clock was started.

5 *The bung, on which I had placed tubing connecting it to*
   the gas syringe, was placed in the conical flask.

6 Every minute, the volume of carbon dioxide in the gas syringe was recorded.

7 The average volume of carbon dioxide produced per minute was calculated.

8 The experiment was repeated three times and the average rate of carbon dioxide production calculated.

9 The investigation was then carried out at 10 °C, 30 °C, 40 °C, 50 °C and 60 °C.

10 A graph was drawn of the average rate of carbon dioxide production over temperature.

COMMENT

The method is detailed and well written. The student has appreciated that it is important for the sugar solution to reach the temperature being investigated before the yeast is added.

2. OBSERVING, MEASURING AND RECORDING

Learning objective: to make observations and measurements with appropriate precision, record these methodically, and present them in a suitable form.

Questions to ask:

How many different measurements or observations do I need to take?

✓ Sufficient readings have been taken to ensure that the data are consistent.

✓ It is usual to repeat an experiment to get more than one measurement. If an investigator takes just one measurement, this may not be typical of what would normally happen when the experiment was carried out.

✓ When repeat readings are consistent they are said to be **repeatable**.

Do I need to repeat any measurements or observations that are anomalous?

✓ An **anomalous result** or **outlier** is a result that is not consistent with other results.

✓ You want to be sure a single result is accurate. So you will need to repeat the experiment until you get close agreement in the results you obtain.

- ✓ If an investigator has made repeat measurements, they would normally use these to calculate the arithmetical mean (or just mean or average) of these data to give a more accurate result. You calculate the mean by adding together all the measurements, and dividing by the number of measurements. Be careful though; anomalous results should not be included when taking averages.

- ✓ Anomalous results might be the consequence of an error made in measurement. But sometimes outliers are genuine results. If you think an outlier has been introduced by careless practical work, you should omit it when calculating the mean. But you should examine possible reasons carefully before just leaving it out.

- ✓ You are taking a number of readings in order to see a changing pattern. For example, measuring the volume of gas produced in a reaction every 10 seconds for 2 minutes (so 12 different readings). It is likely that you will plot your results onto a graph and then draw a **line of best fit**.

- ✓ You can often pick an anomalous reading out from a results table (or a graph if all the data points have been plotted, as well as the mean, to show the range of data). It may be a good idea to repeat this part of the practical again, but it's not necessary if the results show good consistency.

- ✓ If you are confident that you can draw a line of best fit through most of the points, it is not necessary to repeat any measurements that are obviously inaccurate. If, however, the pattern is not clear enough to draw a graph then readings will need to be repeated.

How should I record my measurements or observations – is a table the best way? What headings and units should I use?

- ✓ A table is often the best way to record results.

- ✓ Headings should be clear.

- ✓ If a table contains numerical data, do not forget to include units; data are meaningless without them.

- ✓ The units should be the same as those that are on the measuring equipment you are using.

- ✓ Sometimes you are recording observations that are not quantities. Putting observations in a table with headings is a good way of presenting this information.

EXAMPLE 2

How many different measurements or observations do I need to take?

A student cut a number of cylinders of tissue from a potato and weighed them, and recorded the mass of each cylinder. Six dishes were set up with each dish containing a different concentration of sucrose. Four potato cylinders were placed into each dish. After one hour, the cylinders were removed, blotted dry and reweighed. The student then calculated the percentage change in mass for each cylinder. The results are shown below.

Concentration of sucrose/M	Percentage change in mass of potato cylinders/g				Average percentage change in mass	Texture of potato cylinders (qualitative)
	Experiment 1	Experiment 2	Experiment 3	Experiment 4		
0.0	+31.4	+33.7	+31.2	+32.5	+42.9	Firm
0.2	+20.9	+33.4	+22.8	+21.3	+21.7	Firm
0.4	−2.7	−1.8	−1.9	−2.4	−2.2	Slightly soft
0.6	−13.9	−12.8	−13.7	−13.6	−13.5	Soft
0.8	−20.2	−19.7	−19.3	−20.4	−19.9	Floppy
1.0	−19.9	−20.3	−21.1	−20.3	−20.4	Very floppy

△ Table 6.1 Results for Example 2.

In this table of results:

✓ the description of each measurement is clear.

✓ the units are given.

✓ the data are recorded to the same number of decimal places, and decimal points are aligned.

✓ calculations of means are recorded to the appropriate number of significant figures.

The student has recorded four measurements for each concentration investigated.

With the exception of the cylinder in Experiment 2 in a concentration of 0.2 M sucrose (highlighted in the table), the repeats show good consistency.

Do I need to repeat any measurements or observations that are anomalous?

The result from the cylinder in Experiment 2 in a concentration of 0.2 M sucrose is not consistent with the other results for this concentration. It an anomalous result and is highlighted in the table. The student has not included this result in the calculation of the mean for this concentration.

EXAMPLE 3

How should I record my measurements or observations?

Here are some results of food tests carried out by an investigator:

Food substance tested	Colour change on heating with Benedict's solution
10% glucose solution	blue → green → yellow → orange → red
Biscuit	blue → greenish blue
Grape	blue → green → yellow → orange → red
Honey	blue → green → yellow → orange → red-brown
Potato	remained blue

△ Table 6.2 Results of some food tests.

Note the clear table headings. The right hand column doesn't simply say 'colour' but refers to colour *changes*.

COMMENT

Don't forget that some investigations might benefit from including both numerical data and observations, e.g. in the osmosis experiment in Example 2, the student also found it useful to include information on the firmness of the potato cylinders at the end of the experiment.

3. HANDLING EXPERIMENTAL OBSERVATIONS AND DATA

Learning objectives: to analyse and interpret data to draw conclusions from experimental activities which are consistent with the evidence, using biological knowledge and understanding, and to communicate these findings using appropriate specialist vocabulary, relevant calculations and graphs.

Questions to ask:

What is the best way to show the pattern in my results? Should I use a bar chart, line graph or scatter graph?

✓ Graphs are usually the best way of demonstrating trends in data.

✓ A bar chart or bar graph is used when one of the variables is a **categoric variable**, for example when one of the variables is the type of leaf, or species of organism.

✓ A line graph is used when both variables are continuous, e.g. time and temperature, time and volume.

✓ Scattergraphs can be shown to show the intensity of a relationship, or degree of *correlation*, between two variables.

✓ Sometimes a line of best fit is added to a scatter graph, but usually the points are left without a line.

When drawing bar charts or line graphs:

✓ Choose scales that take up most of the graph paper.

✓ Make sure the axes are linear and allow points to be plotted accurately. Each square on an axis should represent the same quantity. For example, one big square = 5 or 10 units; not 3 units.

✓ Label the axes with the variables (ideally with the independent variable on the x-axis).

✓ Make sure the axes have units.

✓ If more than one set of data is plotted use a key to distinguish the different data sets.

If I use a line graph, should I join the points with a line or a smooth curve?

✓ When you draw a line, do not just join the dots!

✓ Remember there may be some points that don't fall on the curve – these may be incorrect or anomalous results.

✓ A graph will often make it obvious which results are anomalous and so it would not be necessary to repeat the experiment

✓ If following the biological rhythms of an organism over a period of time, you should join the data points, point-to-point.

Do I have to calculate anything from my results?

✓ It will be usual to calculate means from the data.

✓ Sometimes it is helpful make other calculations, before plotting a graph (see Example 2). Other types of calculation include:

✓ the energy content of food *per gram* when burning a sample of food

✓ the volume of water taken up by a plant from the distance moved by a bubble in a potometer (volume = $\pi r^2 \times$ distance)

✓ the density of plants, e.g. as plants per m^2, or frequency of plants or animals, from sampling using a square frame called a quadrat

✓ Investigators also look for numerical trends in data, for example, the doubling of a reaction rate every 10 °C; the doubling of numbers of microorganisms every 20 minutes.

✓ Sometimes you will have to make some calculations before you can draw any conclusions.

Can I draw a conclusion from my analysis of the results, and what biological knowledge and understanding can be used to explain the conclusion?

✓ You need to use your biological knowledge and understanding to explain your conclusion.

✓ It is important to be able to add some explanation which refers to relevant scientific ideas in order to justify your conclusion.

EXAMPLE 4

What is the best way to show the pattern in my results?

A student did an experiment to compare the loss of water from leaves of three different species of tree – hazel, lime and oak.

He measured the mass of 10 leaves of similar size and hung the leaves on a line. After three hours, he removed the leaves and measured the masses of the leaves again and calculated the average loss of water in grams per hour.

Species	Average loss of water/g per hour
Apple	0.30
Hazel	0.05
Oak	0.01

△ Table 6.3 Results of Example 4.

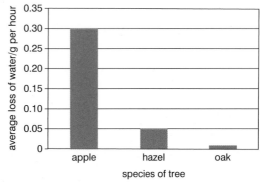

△ Fig. 6.2 Bar chart showing water loss from different leaves.

A bar chart or bar graph is used to display the data in this instance, as the type of leaf is a categoric variable.

EXAMPLE 5

What is the best way to show the pattern in my results?

A student investigated the effect of different light intensities on photosynthesis in pondweed.

He measured the oxygen collected over a number of days.

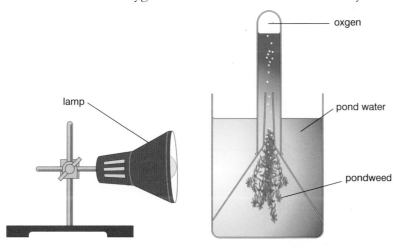

△ Fig. 6.3 Apparatus for Example 5.

A line graph is needed as both the volume of gas and time are continuous variables.

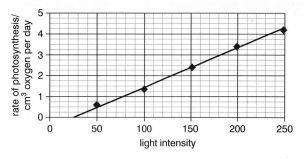

△ Fig. 6.4 Experimental results of Example 5.

If I use a line graph, should I join the points with a line or a smooth curve?

In this case the data fit a straight line most closely. You need to look at the shape that the points make to help you decide how to join them.

EXAMPLE 6

What is the best way to show the pattern in my results?

A student investigated the effect of applying different amounts of fertiliser to plants in the school grounds. He used a scatter graph to display the results he collected.

A scatter graph is most appropriate for displaying these data because each point represents one plant and is unrelated to another point. The results show a trend that should be described in the conclusion.

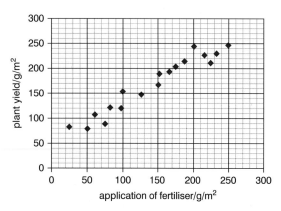

△ Fig. 6.5 Experimental results for Example 6.

EXAMPLE 7

If I use a line graph, should I join the points with a line or a smooth curve?

In an investigation on the activity of an enzyme at different temperatures, an investigator obtained a set of results that shows different phases.

Photographic film is made from a sheet of plastic coated with light-sensitive silver particles bonded by the protein gelatine. When the gelatine is broken down by a protease enzyme, the silver particles fall off, and the film becomes clear.

Photographic film was cut into five strips of equal size, and each strip was placed into a test tube. An identical volume of protease was added to the tubes, and each tube was kept at a different temperature.

The amount of time taken for each strip of film to become clear was measured and recorded.

Temperature/°C	Average time taken for breakdown of gelatine/s
4	3450
13	667
25	175
30	130
40	133
50	7140

△ Table 6.4 Table of results for Example 7.

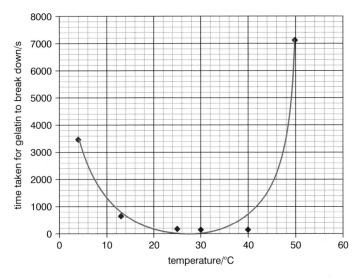

△ Fig. 6.6 Results for Example 7 with line of best fit plotted.

Do I have to calculate anything from my results?

The trend of how enzyme activity is affected by temperature is not well illustrated by the graph. It is shown better if the *rate of reaction* is calculated and plotted against temperature. The rate is the inverse of the time taken to break down the gelatine, i.e. 1 ÷ the time taken.

Temperature/°C	Average time taken for breakdown of gelatine/s	Rate of breakdown of gelatine (= 1/time)/s^{-1}
4	3450	0.00029
13	667	0.00150
25	175	0.00571
30	130	0.00769
40	133	0.00752
50	7140	0.00014

Δ Table 6.5 Table of results with rate column added.

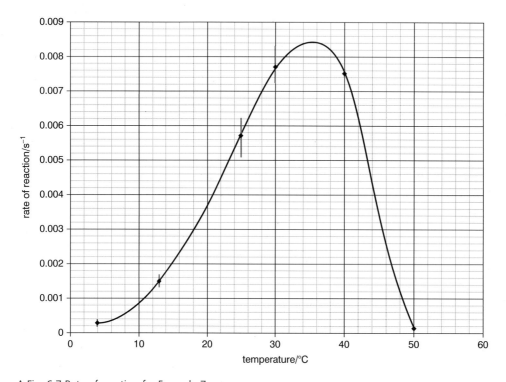

Δ Fig. 6.7 Rate of reaction for Example 7.

Note that on this graph, the student has also drawn range bars to show how the data points are arranged around the mean.

Rates can also be calculated by looking at the change in steepness/gradient of a line graph, or part of a graph.

Can I draw a conclusion from my analysis of the results?

The student wrote:

> Enzymes work best at a particular temperature. My graph suggests that the optimum temperature for protease is around 35 °C. At lower temperatures, enzymes work slowly because the molecules have less energy and move around more slowly, so there are fewer successful collisions between enzyme and substrate (gelatine) molecules.

Enzymes work by a lock and key mechanism, with the substrate fitting into the enzyme. At temperatures that are too high, the structure of an enzyme will be changed so that it will not work. This change is permanent and the enzyme is said to be denatured.

COMMENT

This is a good, concise conclusion and links the data to the mechanism of enzyme action.

4. PLANNING AND EVALUATING INVESTIGATIONS

4a Planning

Learning objective: to devise and plan investigations, drawing on biological knowledge and understanding in selecting appropriate techniques.

Questions to ask

What do I already know about the area of biology I am investigating, and how can I use this knowledge and understanding to help me with my plan?

✓ Think about what you have already learned and any investigations you have already done that are relevant to this investigation.

✓ List the factors might affect the process you are investigating.

What is the best method or technique to use?

✓ Think about whether you can use or adapt a method that you have already used.

✓ A method, and the measuring instruments, must be able to produce **valid** measurements. A measurement is valid if it measures what it is supposed to be measuring.

You will make a decision as to which technique to use based on:

✓ The accuracy and precision of the results required.

Investigators might require results that are as accurate and precise as possible but if you are doing a quick comparison, or a preliminary test to check a range over which results should be collected, a high level of accuracy and precision may not be required.

✓ The simplicity or difficulty of the techniques available, or the equipment required; is this expensive, for instance?

✓ The scale, for example using standard laboratory equipment or on a micro-scale, which may give results in a shorter time period.

✓ The time available to do the investigation.

✓ Health and safety considerations.

What am I going to measure?

✓ You need to decide what you are going to measure.

✓ You need to choose a range of measurements that will be enough to allow you to plot a graph of your results and so find out the pattern in your results.

✓ You might be asked to explain why you have chosen your range rather than a lower or higher range.

✓ The factor you are investigating is called the **independent variable**. A **dependent variable** depends on the value of the independent variable that you select.

How am I going to control the other variables?

✓ These are **control variables**. Some of these may be difficult to control. This may be especially difficult if you are carrying out an ecology investigation in the field, where varying factors such as light and temperature are impossible to control.

✓ You must decide how you are going to control any other variables in the investigation and so ensure that you are using a fair test and that any conclusions you draw are valid.

What equipment is suitable and will give me the accuracy and precision I need?

✓ The *accuracy* of a measurement is how close it is to its true value.

✓ Precision is related to the smallest scale division on the measuring instrument that you are using, e.g. when measuring the distance moved by the bubble in Method 3, a rule marked in millimetres will give greater precision that one divided into centimetres only.

✓ A set of precise measurements also refers to measurements that have very little spread about the mean value.

✓ You need to be sensible about selecting your devices and make a judgement about the degree of precision. Think about what is the least precise variable you are measuring and choose suitable measuring devices. There is no point having instruments that are much more precise than the precision you can measure the least precise variable to.

What are the potential hazards of the equipment, chemicals, organism and technique I will be using and how can I reduce the risks associated with these hazards?

✓ Investigators find out about the hazard associated with chemicals using CLEAPSS Student Safety Sheets or a similar resource. Information on biological hazards can be found in the CLEAPSS Laboratory Handbook.

✓ Be prepared to suggest safety precautions when presented with details of a biology investigation.

EXAMPLE 8

You have been asked about the design and planning of an investigation on carbon dioxide production by yeast under different conditions.

What do I already know?

You may have already learned about the role of yeast in the production of alcohol/beer. In the equation for anaerobic respiration of yeast, you can see that in the absence of oxygen, yeast uses sugars for (anaerobic) respiration, producing carbon dioxide and alcohol (ethanol).

As sugar is a reactant in the process, conditions that might affect the production of carbon dioxide on the process include the *concentration of sugar*, and the *type of sugar* may also be a factor.

The chemical reactions involved in this process are controlled by the yeast's enzymes, so you would expect this process to be affected by *temperature*.

Conditions that might be expected to affect the process are therefore:

✓ concentration of sugar

✓ type of sugar

✓ temperature.

You might be questioned on how to measure the effect these factors, or one of these factors, has on carbon dioxide production.

All of these factors are independent variables. The amount of carbon dioxide produced is the dependent variable because it is affected by the independent variables – concentration of sugar, type of sugar and temperature.

What is the best method or technique to use?

An investigator needs to set up an experiment so that they can measure the carbon dioxide produced by the respiring yeast.

Several methods are available to produce valid measurements.

Method 1

A simple way is to add some yeast to a sugar solution in a conical flask, as shown in the diagram below and count the bubbles produced in given time periods, e.g. every minute, or over a period of time, e.g. one hour.

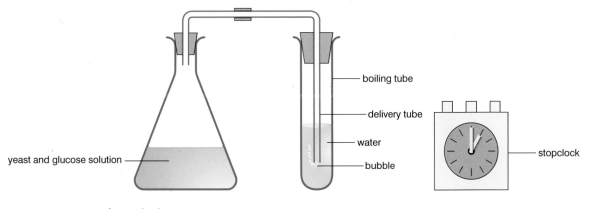

△ Fig. 6.8 Apparatus for method 1.

Method 2

An alternative method is to set up the yeast and sugar solution as before, but this time connect the glass tube to a gas syringe. This time, you can measure the volume of carbon dioxide produced in given time periods, e.g. every minute, or over a period of time, e.g. one hour.

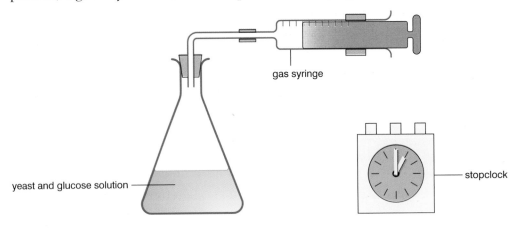

gas syringe

stopclock

yeast and glucose solution

△ Fig. 6.9 Apparatus for method 2.

Method 3

Another method is based on a smaller scale. The yeast and sugar solution is placed in a syringe, which is connected to a pipette that contains a bubble of water. The movement of the bubble is measured in given time periods, e.g. every minute, or over a period of time, e.g. one hour. It is less suitable for the temperature investigation, however, as it would be inadvisable to immerse the syringes in water baths.

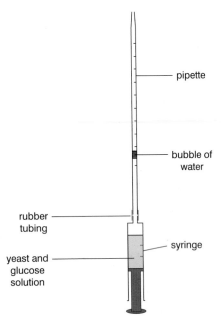

pipette

bubble of water

rubber tubing

syringe

yeast and glucose solution

△ Fig. 6.10 Apparatus for method 3.

Choosing the method:

✓ Accuracy and precision: methods 2 and 3 would be preferred when accurate and precise results are needed. Method 1 cannot be used to actually measure volume of carbon dioxide, but would be best for a preliminary test or a quick comparison.

✓ Micro-scale: method 3 might be most suitable here.

✓ Time available: method 3 might be most suitable, as smaller volumes are involved and the investigation could be carried out more quickly.

✓ Health and safety considerations are less relevant here.

What am I going to measure?

You need to make a measure of the amount of carbon dioxide produced using different concentrations of sugar, different types of sugar, or at different temperatures.

The **independent variables** are the factors under investigation: the concentration of sugar, the type of sugar and the temperature.

The **dependent variables** are the measurements made: the number of bubbles per minute, the volume of carbon dioxide per minute, or the volume moved by the bubble.

Different concentrations of sugar

A sensible range of sugar concentrations to use might be based on concentrations that yeast might encounter in nature, or might be used to produce different beers in a brewery. The investigator here chose to use concentrations ranging from 0 M to 0.25 M (at intervals of 0 M, 0.05 M, 0.10 M, 0.15 M, 0.20 M and 0.25 M), as a preliminary test showed that these concentrations would give suitable results in the time period allocated. Concentrations chosen were no higher as the investigator realised that these might have an osmotic effect; water could be drawn from the yeast cells by osmosis, and not function.

The investigator plotted a graph using the results from the six different concentrations to look for a pattern in those results.

Different types of sugar

Here, the investigator decided to use sugars commonly found in nature, or in malted barley in brewing, that yeast might use for respiration. These included fructose, glucose, lactose, maltose and sucrose.

Different temperatures

It would be sensible to choose a range of temperatures that yeast would encounter in nature or in a brewery. Respiration in yeast is a series of enzyme-controlled reactions. In most cases, enzymes work best around 40 °C, and cease to function above around 60 °C. It was decided, therefore, to measure carbon dioxide production at five different temperatures (10 °C, 20 °C, 30 °C, 40 °C, 50 °C and 60 °C). Again, this would be sufficient to allow the investigator to plot a graph of results and so find any pattern in the results.

How am I going to control the other variables?

The investigator must ensure that any differences in carbon dioxide production must be the result of, in the different investigations, sugar concentration, type of sugar and temperature, and not the result of some other factor. In other words, it must be a fair test and produce valid measurements.

So, the investigator must decide what other factors could affect the experiment and try to keep these constant. These are the control variables.

Factor under investigation/ independent variable	Factors to be kept constant				
	Yeast concentration	Sugar concentration	Type of sugar	Temperature	Length of investigation
Sugar concentration	Yes	No – vary	Yes	Yes	Yes
Type of sugar	Yes	Yes	No – vary	Yes	Yes
Temperature	Yes	Yes	Yes	No – vary	Yes

△ Table 6.6 Variables in Example 8.

EXAMPLE 9

In this experiment, the production of heat from germinating seeds is being investigated. Some seeds have been placed in an insulated flask (Thermos flask) and their temperature measured over a period of time.

But a rise in temperature alone would not be sufficient to demonstrate that it is the respiring seeds that are causing this rise. Some other factor could be involved. So an identical experiment is set up, but this time with seeds that have been killed. So any change in the temperature must be the result of the living seeds' respiration. Both sets of seeds are also sterilised with disinfectant so that any temperature rise can't be down to the growth of microorganisms on the seeds.

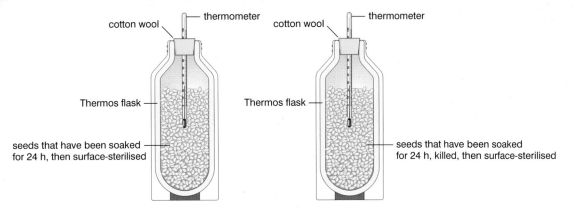

△ Fig. 6.11 Apparatus for Example 9.

What equipment is suitable and will give me the accuracy and precision I need?

You now know what you will need to measure and so can decide on your measuring devices.

Referring back to Example 8:

Measurement	Quantity required	Equipment
Mass of yeast	1.00 g	Balance measuring up to two decimal places
Volume of sugar solution	100 cm³	100 cm³ volumetric flask
Temperature	10–60 °C	Thermometer, with 1 °C precision
Time	One minute intervals	Stop watch (1 s precision)

△ Table 6.7 Suitable equipment for experiment.

You will need to be sensible about selecting your equipment and make a judgement about the degree of accuracy. The accuracies of equipment need to be comparable. It would be not appropriate to measure the yeast that was put in every conical flask accurately without measuring the volume of sugar solution poured onto each flask to a similar level of accuracy.

What are the potential hazards of the equipment and how can I reduce the risks?

In Example 8, the chemical hazards are as follows:

Fructose solution	LOW HAZARD
Glucose solution	LOW HAZARD
Lactose solution	LOW HAZARD
Maltose solution	LOW HAZARD
Sucrose solution	LOW HAZARD
Yeast, dried	LOW HAZARD

These indicate that there are no specific hazards the investigator needs to be aware of. However, when handling *any* chemicals, it would be sensible to wear eye protection.

In terms of the equipment and technique, the major hazards are:

✓ handling hot liquids (at 50 °C and 60 °C).

✓ when connecting tubing together.

✓ possible contact between water and electrical sockets.

4b Evaluating

Learning objective: to evaluate data and methods.

Questions to ask:

Do any of my results stand out as being inaccurate?

✓ You need to look for any anomalous results or outliers that do not fit the pattern.

✓ You can often pick this out from a results table (or a graph if all the data points have been plotted, as well as the mean, to show the range of data). The investigator has not included this result in the calculation of the mean for this concentration. It may be a good idea to repeat this part of the practical again, but it is not necessary if the results show good consistency.

What reasons can I give for any inaccurate results?

✓ When answering questions like this it is important to be specific. Answers such as 'experimental error' will not score any marks.

✓ It is often possible to look at the practical technique and suggest explanations for anomalous results.

✓ When you carry out the experiment you will have a better idea of which possible sources of error are more likely.

✓ Try to give a specific source of error and avoid statements such as 'the measurements must have been wrong'.

Your conclusion will be based on your findings, but must take into consideration any uncertainty in these introduced by any possible sources of error. You should discuss where these have come from in your evaluation.

Error is a difference between a measurement you make, and its true value.

The two types of errors are:

✓ random error

✓ systematic error.

With **random error**, measurements vary in an unpredictable way. This can occur when the instrument you are using to measure lacks sufficient precision to indicate differences in readings. It can also occur when it is difficult to make a measurement. If two investigators measure the height of a plant, for instance, they might choose different points on the compost, and the tip of the growing point to make their measurements.

With **systematic error**, readings vary in a controlled way. They're either consistently too high or too low. One reason could be down to the way you are making a reading, for example taking a burette reading at the wrong point on the meniscus, or not being directly in front of an instrument when reading from it.

What an investigator *should not* discuss in an evaluation are problems introduced by using faulty equipment, or by using the equipment inappropriately. These errors can, or could have been, eliminated, by:

✓ checking equipment

✓ practising techniques before the investigation, and taking care and patience when carrying out the practical.

Overall, was the method or technique I used accurate enough?

✓ If your results were good enough to provide a confident answer to the problem you were investigating the method probably was good enough.

✓ If you realise your results are not precise when you compare your conclusion with the actual answer it may be you have a **systematic error** (an error that has been made in obtaining all the results). A systematic error would indicate an overall problem with the experimental method.

✓ If your results do not show a convincing pattern then it is fair to assume that your method or technique was not precise enough and there may have been a **random error** (i.e. measurements vary in an unpredictable way).

If I were to do the investigation again, what would I change or improve upon?

✓ Having identified possible errors it is important to say how these could be overcome. Again you should try and be absolutely precise.

✓ When suggesting improvements, do not just say 'do it more accurately next time' or 'measure the volumes more accurately next time'.

✓ For example, if you were measuring small volumes, you could improve the method by using a burette to measure the volumes rather than a measuring cylinder.

✓ Other errors arise from accuracy of measurement. And investigations can also often be improved by extending the range (e.g. temperature, time, pH, etc.) over which it is carried out.

Do any of my results stand out as being inaccurate?

In Example 2, the results from the cylinder in Experiment 2 in a concentration of 0.2 M sucrose are not consistent with the other results for this concentration. The **anomalous result** or **outlier** is highlighted in the table.

EXAMPLE 10

What reasons can I give for any inaccurate results?

In this example, the pH of yoghurt was monitored during its production using a data logger. The data logger gave very precise, consistent readings. First, it had to be set, or *calibrated*, using solutions of known pH (called buffers).

In Example 2, it's possible that the potato cylinder had not been blotted dry properly before its mass was measured.

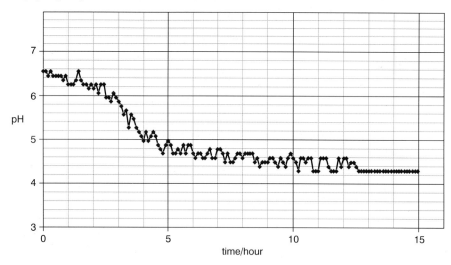

△ Fig. 6.12 Experimental results for Example 10.

EXAMPLE 11

In an investigation on the energy content of food, an investigator used the apparatus below to find the energy content of a piece of pasta.

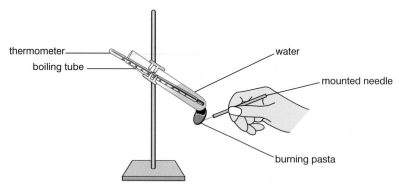

△ Fig. 6.13 Apparatus for Example 11.

Was the method or technique I used accurate enough?

The value obtained by the investigator was 1272 joules of energy per gram of pasta. This value was much lower than the value of 13 440 joules per gram of pasta printed on the packet.

The main problem with this method is that it relies on the transfer of all the chemical energy in the food to heat energy, which is used to warm the water. But using this equipment, the transfer is nowhere near 100 percent. Reasons for this are:

✓ conversion of the chemical energy to other forms of energy

✓ incomplete combustion of the food

✓ poor transfer of heat from the burning pasta to the water.

Measurements of the temperature rise may also be inaccurate because the heat energy is not evenly distributed through the water.

If I were to do the investigation again, what would I change or improve upon?

It is possible to improve the accuracy of energy values of food in the school laboratory by modifying the method above or using different equipment. The transfer of heat to the container holding the water (in this case, a boiling tube) can be improved, and the container could also be insulated. Many investigators use a device called a bomb calorimeter to overcome these problems. The food is burned inside the bomb calorimeter.

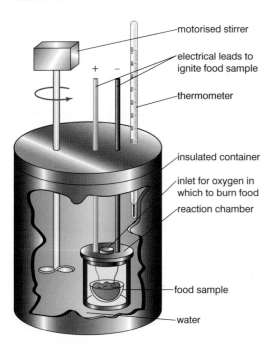

motorised stirrer

electrical leads to ignite food sample

thermometer

insulated container

inlet for oxygen in which to burn food

reaction chamber

food sample

water

△ Fig. 6.14 Improved apparatus for Example 11.

Glossary

absorption The movement of digested food molecules from the alimentary canal into the blood.

abstinence Not doing, such as avoiding sexual intercourse.

accommodation How the lens of the eye changes so that objects at different distances are focused on the retina.

acid rain Rain that contains higher than normal concentrations of dissolved acidic gases, such as sulfur dioxide and nitrogen oxides, which causes the rain to have a lower pH than normal.

acrosome A bag of enzymes at the front of a sperm cell that makes it possible for the sperm nucleus to enter the egg cell.

active immunity The production of immunity in the body by an infection or immunisation.

active site The space in an enzyme into which the substrate molecule fits.

active transport The movement of molecules across a cell membrane using energy from respiration; movement is often against a concentration gradient.

adaptive feature A feature that helps an organism to survive well in its environment.

addiction When the body cannot function properly without a drug.

adrenaline The hormone produced by the adrenal glands that prepares the body for action.

adult stem cell A cell in differentiated tissue that can still divide to form a range of cell types.

aerobic respiration Respiration (the breakdown of glucose to release energy) using oxygen.

AIDS Acquired immunodeficiency syndrome, caused by the human immunodeficiency virus.

alimentary canal The tubular part of the digestive system, from mouth to anus.

allele One version of a gene, producing one form of the characteristic that the gene codes for.

alveoli The tiny bulges of the air sacs in lungs where gases diffuse between the air in the lungs and the blood (singular: alveolus).

amino acid The basic unit of a protein.

amniotic fluid Fluid surrounding the developing fetus in the uterus.

amniotic sac The tough membrane surrounding the developing fetus and amniotic fluid in the mother's uterus.

amylase An enzyme that digests starch.

anabolic steroids Substances with a particular structure that cause the body to develop more muscle and bone, and which may be misused by sports people.

anaerobic respiration Respiration (the breakdown of glucose to release energy) without oxygen (also called *fermentation*); in animal cells produces lactic acid; in plant cells and yeast produces ethanol and carbon dioxide.

anatomy The study of the body structure of organisms.

ancestor A related organism that lived in the past.

ante-natal care Care of a pregnant woman before the birth of her baby.

anther The male part of flower that produces pollen.

antibiotic resistance Resistance in bacteria to the effect of an antibiotic that normally kills them.

antibiotics Drugs used to treat infections caused by bacteria, fungi or protoctists (mainly bacteria) but not those caused by viruses.

antibodies Chemicals produced by some white blood cells, which attack pathogens.

antigens Chemicals on the surface of cells, including pathogens, that are specific to the cell.

aorta The largest artery, which receives blood from the left ventricle of the heart.

arteriole Small blood vessel that connects an artery to a capillary.

artery Blood vessel that carries blood away from the heart.

artificial insemination Placing sperm artificially in the uterus of a woman, often part of fertility treatment.

asexual reproduction Production of young without fertilisation.

assimilation When absorbed food molecules are taken into cells and used to make new substances.

atrium (plural *atria*) One of two chambers of the heart that receive blood from veins and pumps it into the ventricles.

auxin A plant hormone that controls growth of roots and shoots.

balanced diet The intake of food that supplies all the protein, fat, carbohydrate, vitamins and minerals that the body needs in the right amounts.

base A subunit of DNA, of which there are four: A, C, G, T. The order of bases forms the genetic code.

Benedict's reagent Solution that changes colour in the presence of reducing sugars, used to test for their presence in a food sample.

biconcave A shape in which the middle is pressed inwards, making a red blood cell thinner in the middle than at the edges.

bile The liquid produced by the liver and stored in the gall bladder, which is highly alkaline and emulsifies lipids.

binomial system A system of naming organisms using a genus and species name to identify a particular species.

biodiversity The range of variation in species in an area.

biofuel A fuel made from plants or animals.

biological catalyst A catalyst of reactions inside living organisms.

biological washing powder A powder containing enzymes, used for cleaning clothes.

biomass The mass of a living organism.

biotechnology The use of organisms to make products.

birth rate The number of births within a particular time.

biuret test The test used to indicate the presence of protein in a food sample.

bladder The organ of the excretory system that stores urine from the kidneys until it is released to the environment.

bronchioles The tiny tubes in the lungs that carry air to the alveoli.

bronchitis A disease of the lungs that produces a hacking cough as a result of damage to the cilia by smoking or infection.

bronchus The division of the trachea as it joins to the lungs.

cancer A disease caused by uncontrolled division of cells.

canine A tooth with a pointed shape, behind the incisors in the mouth, which holds food while other teeth bite and chew.

capillary Smallest blood vessel, found within every tissue, which exchanges substances with the cells.

captive breeding programme Where animals are bred in zoos and wildlife parks to help protect them from extinction.

carbohydrate A large molecule, such as starch or glycogen, made of many simple sugars.

carbon cycle How the element carbon cycles in different forms between living organisms and the environment.

carcinogenic Causes cells to produce cancers, such as some of the chemicals in tobacco smoke.

carnivore An animal that eats animals.

carpel The female structure in flowers that contains one or more ovaries and their stigmas and styles.

carrier protein A protein that lies across the cell membrane and transports ions or molecules through the membrane.

catalyst A substance that increases the rate of a chemical reaction, such as an enzyme.

cell membrane The structure surrounding cells that controls what enters and leaves the cell.

cell wall A layer of cellulose that surrounds plant cells, giving them support and shape. Bacterial cells also have a cell wall outside the cell membrane.

cellular respiration See respiration.

cement A material that holds the tooth tight in the jaw and gum.

central nervous system The brain and spinal cord.

chemical digestion The breakdown of large molecules into smaller ones using enzymes.

chlorophyll The green chemical in chloroplasts that captures light energy for photosynthesis.

chloroplast An organelle found in plant cells and some protoctist cells that can capture energy from light for use in photosynthesis.

cholera Disease caused by the cholera bacterium, which releases a toxin in the small intestine. The toxin causes secretion of salts into the alimentary canal, which draws water out of the body by osmosis, resulting in severe diarrhoea.

chromosome A long DNA molecule that is found in a cell nucleus.

cilia Tiny hairs that project from a cell surface and that move things across the cell surface.

ciliated cell A cell that has cilia on its surface.

circulatory system The organ system that transports substances around the body.

cirrhosis A form of liver damage, often caused by excessive long-term alcohol use.

class A group of orders that share key features.

classification The grouping of things by how similar their features are.

climate change Change to wind, rainfall and temperature as a result of the greenhouse effect.

clone An individual that is genetically identical to other individuals.

co-dominance When both alleles for a gene are expressed in the phenotype.

cohesion Where molecules stick together, such as water molecules in the xylem of a plant.

colon The medical name for the large intestine.

colour blindness An example of a sex-linked characteristic that is found more commonly in men than in women.

combustion Burning, such as that of fossil fuels.

community All the organisms that live in the same habitat.

complementary Being similar but opposite, like the shape of the space in an enzyme and the shape of its substrate.

concentration gradient The difference in the amount of a substance between two areas; diffusion is usually down the concentration gradient: molecules move from the area of high concentration to the area of low concentration.

condom A rubber sheath placed over the erect penis to act as a mechanical barrier against sperm.

cone Type of light-sensitive cell in the eye that responds to colour.

conservation The protection of species or habitats, to prevent their destruction.

constipation The slow movement of digested food through the intestines and rectum as a result of there being too little fibre in the food for peristalsis to be effective.

consumer An organism that gets its food by eating other organisms; an animal.

continuous variation Variation in a feature that can have any value (e.g. height).

contraception Birth control methods that prevent the fertilisation of an egg as a result of sexual intercourse.

contraceptive pill A pill containing sex hormones that prevent ovulation.

COPD (Chronic Obstructive Pulmonary Diseases) Diseases of the lung that include bronchitis and emphysema.

core temperature The temperature around the major organs of the heart and liver.

cornea The front part of the eye, where most light focusing occurs.

coronary heart disease Diseases such as angina, high blood pressure or heart attack, caused by the partial or complete blockage of a coronary artery, such as by cholesterol.

correlation When two factors vary in a similar way, suggesting that they are linked.

cortex The outer area of the kidney.

cuticle A waxy layer that covers leaves, particularly the upper surface, to reduce water loss from the leaf.

cytoplasm The jelly-like liquid inside the cell that contains the organelles and where many chemical reactions take place.

daughter cell A cell produced by division of a parent cell.

deamination Removal of the nitrogen-containing part of a protein molecule as it is broken down in the liver.

death phase The final phase of a sigmoid growth curve, where some factor in the environment prevents reproduction (e.g. lack of nutrients) or increases death rate (e.g. build-up of toxins) so that death rate greatly exceeds birth rate.

death rate The number of deaths in a particular time.

decomposer An organism that feeds on dead plants or animals, or animal waste.

deforestation The destruction of large areas of forest or woodland.

dehydration Loss of too much water.

denature When an enzyme stops working, which may be the result of high temperature or pH change.

denitrifying bacteria Soil bacteria that convert nitrates in the soil to nitrogen gas, which is released to the atmosphere.

dentine The main layer of tooth below the enamel and softer than enamel.

deoxygenated Lacking in oxygen.

deoxyribonucleic acid See *DNA*.

depressant A drug that slows down the rate of response of the body.

dialysis Artificial cleansing of the blood by passing it through dialysis fluid where diffusion of urea, excess proteins and water can occur.

diaphragm (birth control) A rubber cap placed over the cervix before sexual intercourse to prevent sperm entering the uterus.

diaphragm (respiratory system) A sheet of tissue situated below the lungs that controls breathing.

diarrhoea The production of large amounts of watery faeces.

dichotomous key A series of pairs of questions based on easily identifiable features that can be used to identify organisms.

dicotyledon A flowering plant that has two cotyledons in its seeds.

diffusion The net movement of molecules along a concentration gradient from a region of higher concentration to a region of lower concentration; it is a passive process (it does not require energy).

digestion The breakdown of large food molecules into smaller molecules.

digestive enzyme An enzyme found in the digestive system.

diploid A cell that contains two sets of chromosomes.

discontinuous variation Variation in a feature that can have only a particular number of possibilities (e.g. eye colour, fur colour, sex).

DNA (deoxyribonucleic acid) The chemical that forms chromosomes and carries the genetic code.

DNA analysis The study of the sequence of bases in DNA, used to identify evolutionary relationships between organisms.

dominant An allele that only needs to be present on one chromosome of a pair to produce its version of the characteristic.

double circulation A circulatory system as in humans where the blood passes through the heart to be pumped first to the lungs, then returned to the heart to be pumped to the rest of the body.

double helix The twisted ladder shape formed by a molecule of DNA.

drug A substance that, when taken into the body, changes or modifies the way one or more types of cell function.

ecology The study of organisms and their environment.

ecosystem The community of organisms and their environment in an area that interact together.

effector An organ that responds to the nervous system, such as a muscle or a gland.

egestion The removal of undigested material from the body (faeces) (compare with *excretion*).

egg cell The female sex cell.

electrocardiogram (ECG) A recording of the activity of the heart.

embryo Developing young, in which cell division and differentiation are taking place rapidly. The stage before a fetus.

embryonic stem cell A cell in the early embryo that is able to divide and produce most kinds of differentiated cell.

emigration The movement of individuals away from a population.

emphysema A disease of the lungs caused by damage to alveoli, which reduces the area for gas exchange in the lungs.

emulsify To break up large droplets of a lipid in an aqueous solution into smaller droplets.

enamel The hard outer covering of a tooth that protects the softer layers inside the tooth.

endangered When a species is at high risk of becoming extinct.

endocrine gland An organ that produces a hormone.

endoplasmic reticulum A system of membranes inside cells to which many ribosomes are attached.

enhanced greenhouse effect An increase in the greenhouse effect, most likely caused by the release of additional greenhouse gases from human activity.

enzyme A protein that acts as a biological catalyst, changing the rate of reactions in the body.

epidermis The layer of cells on the outer surface of a body or organ, such as a leaf.

eutrophication The addition of nutrients to water, which may lead to water pollution.

evaporation When particles in a liquid (e.g. water) gain enough energy to move fast enough and become a gas (as in water vapour).

evolution Change over time in the adaptive features of a population or species through the process of natural selection in response to changes in their environment.

excess More than is needed.

excretion Removal of waste (often toxic) substances such as carbon dioxide and urea in animals that have been produced from chemical reactions inside the body.

exoskeleton A hardened outer layer that provides support for the body, as in the arthropods.

expiration Breathing out.

exponential Where the next value depends on the previous value; for example, exponential growth, where the number of births depends on the number of mature females that can reproduce.

extinct When all individuals of a species have died.

faeces The undigested material that remains after digestion of food in humans.

family A group of genera that have similar features.

famine Starvation of many people in an area as a result of extreme shortage of food.

fat A solid lipid.

fatty acid One of the basic units of a lipid, along with glycerol.

female sterilisation Cutting the oviducts of a woman to prevent eggs reaching the uterus, and sperm from reaching eggs.

femidom The female equivalent of a condom, which prevents sperm entering the woman's body.

feminisation When male organisms show female features, for example after exposure to female sex hormones.

fermenter A large vessel in which microorganisms such as fungi and bacteria can be grown in controlled conditions that maximise the rate of growth.

fertile An organism that can breed and produce offspring.

fertilisation Joining of male and female sex cells.

fertility drug A drug used to stimulate a woman's ovaries to release eggs.

fetus The name given to the developing baby in the uterus.

fibre Plant material that is difficult to digest and keeps the food in the alimentary canal soft and bulky, aiding peristalsis. Also called *roughage*.

fibrin The fibrous protein produced to help blood clot.

fibrinogen A protein produced by the liver that is broken down to fibrin by an enzyme released by platelets at a site of damage to a blood vessel.

filtrate The liquid in a kidney tubule produced by filtration of the blood in the renal capsule.

filtration The separation of molecules as a result of size.

fishing quota A legal limit to the amount, size and species of fish that can be caught in a year.

fitness (environmental) How well adapted an organism is to its environment.

flaccid Wilting caused by loss of water by osmosis. The vacuole shrinks and does not push against the cell wall to give the plant support.

flagellum Large cell structure that moves back and forth to move the cell, such as the 'tail' of a sperm cell.

fluoride A soluble chemical that hardens tooth enamel; may be added to public water supplies to reduce risk of tooth decay.

food chain diagram A diagram that shows the transfer of energy from organism by ingestion.

food web diagram A diagram showing the feeding relationships between organisms in the same community.

fossil fuel Fuel formed from organic material, such as peat, coal and oil.

FSH (follicle-stimulating hormone) A pituitary hormone that controls the development of an egg in the ovary during the menstrual cycle.

gamete A sex cell.

gas exchange The exchange of gases between the air and the body across a gas exchange surface such as the lungs or a leaf.

gene A small section of DNA that codes for a protein.

gene mutation A change in base sequence of a gene.

genetic code The code formed by the order of the bases in DNA that instructs cells how characteristics should be produced.

genetic code The sequence of bases along one strand of DNA.

genetic diagram A diagram that displays how a characteristic may be inherited by offspring from the parents alleles.

genetic engineering The transfer of a gene from one organism into an organism of a different species so that the gene is expressed.

genotype The genetic code of an organism.

genus A group of species that share many features.

germination The start of plant growth from a seed, which only occurs when there is the right amount of oxygen and water and an appropriate temperature.

global warming A warming of the Earth's atmosphere, possibly as a result of an enhanced greenhouse effect.

glomerulus A small knot of capillaries in the renal capsule.

glycerol One of the basic units of a lipid, along with fatty acids.

glycogen Large carbohydrate that is stored in liver cells for use as an energy source.

graticule The scale viewed through a microscope, used to calculate the observed size of a structure.

gravitropism A plant's growth in response to gravity.

greenhouse effect The warming effect caused by greenhouse gases in the atmosphere that prevent some of the heat energy radiated by the Earth's surface from escaping into space.

greenhouse gases Atmospheric gases, such as carbon dioxide and methane, that trap some of the heat radiated from the Earth's surface and prevent it from escaping into space.

growth The permanent increase in body size and dry mass of an organism, usually from an increase in cell number or cell size (or both).

haemoglobin The red chemical in red blood cells that combines reversibly with oxygen.

haploid A cell that contains only one set of chromosomes, such as gametes.

heart The organ of the circulatory system that pumps blood.

heart attack When the heart stops working, due to a blockage of a coronary artery.

heart rate The number of heart beats in a given time, e.g. beats per minute.

heart transplant An operation in which a damaged heart is replaced with a healthy one.

herbicide A chemical that kills plants, often containing plant hormones for killing weeds.

herbivore An animal that eats plants.

heroin A dangerously addictive drug with powerful depressant effects.

heterozygous Where the two alleles for a gene are different in the genotype.

HIV Human immunodeficiency virus, transmitted during sexual intercourse, by blood, through the placenta or in breast milk, which causes AIDS.

homeostasis Keeping the internal environment of the body within safe limits.

homozygous Where the two alleles for a gene are the same in the genotype.

hormonal system The chemical response system of the body to changes in the environment.

hormone A chemical substance produced by a gland resulting in a change in another part of the body.

host An organism that is attacked by a pathogen.

humidity A measure of the concentration of water molecules in the air.

hydrophyte A plant adapted to live in water.

hygiene Keeping things clean, which helps to reduce the risk of transmission of a pathogen.

hypha A single thread of fungal mycelium (plural *hyphae*).

illegal Against the law, punishable as a crime.

immigration The movement of individuals into a population.

immune Cannot catch a transmissible disease.

immune system The system of the body that protects the body against infection; includes white blood cells.

implantation When the embryo settles into the thickened uterus lining.

incisor A flat-bladed tooth type at the front of the mouth for biting off pieces of food.

ingestion The taking of food into the alimentary canal.

inheritance the passing of inherited characteristics from one generation to the next.

insecticide A chemical used to kill insect pests.

insoluble A substance that does not dissolve.

inspiration Breathing in.

insulin The hormone produced by the pancreas that controls blood sugar concentration.

intercostal muscles Muscles between the ribs that help with breathing.

invertebrate An animal without a backbone.

in vitro fertilisation (IVF) When eggs are taken from a woman, and fertilised outside the body by sperm taken from a man.

involuntary Done without thought or control from the central nervous system, such as a reflex response.

ionising radiation Radiation, such as gamma rays, X rays and ultraviolet radiation, that can damage cells and produce mutations in genes.

IUD (intrauterine device) A mechanical barrier placed in the uterus to prevent the passage of sperm and the implantation of a fertilised egg in the uterus.

IUS (intrauterine system) An object placed inside the uterus that prevents pregnancy by the release of hormones.

kidney Organ that removes unwanted substances from the blood to produce urine.

kidney tubule Where urine is formed in the kidney by exchange of substances with the blood liquid filtered from the blood.

kinetic energy The energy carried by moving molecules.

kingdom A group of phyla that share key features.

kwashiorkor Protein energy malnutrition, usually seen in young children who have a diet that contains little protein.

labour The stage at the end of pregnancy when the muscles of the uterus wall start to contract strongly to push the baby out of the mother's body.

lactase The enzyme that breaks down lactose, the sugar found in milk, which can cause digestive problems in some people.

lacteal Tubes of the lymphatic system that carry fat droplets from the digestive system around the body.

lag phase The first phase of a sigmoid growth curve, where there is little change in number as organisms prepare for growth and reproduction.

larynx The 'voice box' at the top of the trachea, which produces sounds when air moves through it, e.g. when speaking.

leaching The loss of dissolved mineral nutrients in soil water as it soaks deep into the ground beyond the reach of plant roots.

lens The structure in the eye that produces fine focusing of an image on the retina.

LH (Luteinising Hormone) A pituitary hormone that controls when ovulation occurs in the menstrual cycle.

limiting factor A factor (e.g. light, temperature) that affects the rate of photosynthesis; it is the condition that is least favourable.

lipase An enzyme that digests lipids (fats and oils).

lipid Molecule made from fatty acids and glycerol.

livestock production The growing of animals as a source of food.

log phase The second phase of a sigmoid growth curve, where growth is rapid because birth rate greatly exceeds death rate, when conditions are ideal for growth.

lungs Organs in the human body where gas exchange takes place.

lymph Fluid in the lymphatic system.

lymphatic system A system of tubes that collects tissue fluid from the tissues and returns it to the blood system near to the heart.

lymphocyte A type of white blood cell that makes antibodies to attack a pathogen.

magnification The amount by which a microscope increases the observed size of a structure compared with its actual size: calculated by multiplying the eyepiece magnification with the objective magnification.

malaria A disease caused by the protoctist *Plasmodium*, transmitted by mosquito vectors.

malnutrition Not getting the right amounts and balance of nutrients and other essential substances in the diet, including a diet that has too much or too little of any of these.

mechanical digestion The breaking up of food into smaller pieces through biting and chewing by teeth.

medicinal drug A chemical substance used to treat a medical condition.

medulla Inner part of the kidney.

meiosis The form of cell division that produces four haploid, and genetically different, cells from a diploid parent cell; produces gametes.

memory cell A cell produced by lymphocyte blood cells that responds to a second infection by the same pathogen by releasing many more antibodies.

menstrual cycle The continuous sequence of events in a woman's reproductive organs; each cycle of ovulation (ripening and release of an egg) and menstruation (shedding of the unwanted uterus lining) takes about 28 days and is controlled by the hormones oestrogen and progesterone.

metabolism All the reactions that occur inside the body that keep an organism alive.

microvilli Tiny finger-like extensions of the cell membrane of the surface cells of villi.

mineral (mineral ion) Nutrients that plants and animals need in small amounts, such as nitrates that are needed for making amino acids.

mitochondria Cell structures in which respiration takes place.

mitosis The form of cell division that produces two identical diploid daughter cells from a diploid body cell, used for growth and repair in the body and in asexual reproduction.

molar A tooth type found at the back of the mouth that has a large grinding surface for chewing.

monocotyledon A flowering plant that has only one cotyledon in its seeds.

monoculture A large area of one crop species.

monohybrid cross The inheritance of a characteristic produced by one gene.

morphology The study of what organisms look like.

motor neurone (also called *effector neurone*) A nerve cell that carries electrical impulses from the central nervous system to an effector.

movement The ability to change the position of all or some of the body.

mRNA (messenger RNA) A copy of one strand of DNA that carries the genetic code out to a ribosome in the cytoplasm for building an amino acid chain.

mucus Slimy liquid that is produced by cells lining the trachea, bronchi and bronchioles.

multicellular An organism that has a body which contains many cells.

mutagen A chemical that produces mutations in genes.

mutation A change in the genetic code of an organism.

mycelium A mass of hyphae that forms the body of a fungus.

natural selection The influence of the environment on survival and/or reproduction, such that some characteristics are more successful at producing offspring than others.

negative feedback Where a change in a stimulus causes the body to respond by reversing that change, e.g. in controlling body temperature.

nerve A bundle of nerve cells.

net movement The sum of all the movements in different directions, e.g. the movement of all the particles being considered in diffusion or osmosis.

neurone A nerve cell.

neurotransmitter A chemical that can cross the gap in a synapse between two neurones.

nicotine The addictive chemical in tobacco smoke.

nitrifying bacteria Soil bacteria that convert ammonium ions to nitrite ions, and nitrite ions to nitrate ions; important in the nitrogen cycle.

nitrogen cycle How the element nitrogen cycles in different forms between living organisms and the environment.

nitrogen-fixing bacteria Bacteria found in the soil and in root nodules of some plants that can convert atmospheric nitrogen to nitrate ions.

non-biodegradable Something that does not break down quickly in the environment.

non-renewable resources Resources such as fossil fuels, which are limited and so cannot be replaced.

nuclear fall-out Radioactive dust that enters the environment after a nuclear leakage or explosion.

nucleus The organelle in plant and animal cells that contains the genetic material.

nutrient cycle How a nutrient cycles between living organisms and the environment.

nutrition The taking in of nutrients to the body from the environment.

obesity A condition of the body that has large amounts of fat.

oestrogen A hormone produced by the ovaries that helps to control the menstrual cycle and produces secondary sexual characteristics in girls.

oil A liquid lipid.

omnivore An animal that eats both plants and animals.

optimum pH The pH at which an enzyme works best.

optimum temperature The temperature at which an enzyme works best.

oral rehydration salt A dry mixture of substances that contain the right balance of substances for restoring the balance of the body upset by diarrhoea.

order A group of families that share key features.

organ A collection of tissues that together have a particular function (e.g. the kidney).

organ system A group of organs that work together to carry out a particular function (e.g. the digestive system).

osmosis The net movement of water molecules through a partially permeable membrane, from a solution that has a higher concentration of water molecules (a dilute solution) to one that has a lower concentration of water molecules (a more concentrated solution).

ovary (in plants and humans) A structure that contains egg cells.

oviduct A tube that carries the egg released from the ovary to the uterus; where fertilisation occurs.

ovulation When an egg is released by an ovary.

ovule Female structure in a flower that contains one egg cell.

oxygen debt The need for oxygen after anaerobic respiration to break down lactic acid.

oxygenated Containing a lot of oxygen.

palisade cell Cells in the upper part of a leaf that contain the most chloroplasts and carry out most of the photosynthesis in a leaf.

pancreas The organ that produces the hormone insulin.

partially permeable The condition of a membrane that lets some substances pass through but not others.

passive immunity Introducing antibodies against a pathogen, either by injection, or mother-to-baby contact through the placenta or breast milk, which gives only short-term protection against the pathogen.

passive The opposite of *active*, happening without the need for additional energy.

pathogen A disease-causing organism.

pectinase The enzyme that breaks down pectin in plant cell walls, and so helps to release more juice from plant cells in the production of fruit juice.

penicillin The antibiotic produced by the fungus *Penicillium*.

peripheral nervous system All the nerves that are not part of the central nervous system.

peristalsis The rhythmic muscular contractions of the alimentary canal that moves food from mouth to anus.

pest An organism that is causing a problem.

pesticide A chemical used to kill pests.

phagocyte A type of white blood cell that engulfs and destroys pathogens.

phagocytosis To flow and engulf, as when phagocytes engulf pathogens.

phenotype The visible characteristics of an organism as a result of its genes.

phloem The plant tissue that carries sucrose through the veins of a plant.

photosynthesis The process carried out in plant cells that makes sugars by combining carbon dioxide and water molecules using energy from light.

phototropism Growth of a plant in response to light.

phylum A group of classes that share key features.

physical digestion The breaking up of food particles, such as fats and oils, into smaller pieces (droplets) by substances in the alimentary canal, such as bile.

placenta A structure formed by the developing fetus that attaches to the wall of the mother's uterus and across which substances are exchanged between the mother and fetus.

plasma The liquid, watery part of blood that carries dissolved food molecules, urea, hormones, carbon dioxide and other substances around the body and also helps to distribute heat.

plasma protein A protein found in blood plasma.

plasmid A small circle of genetic material found in some bacteria in addition to the circular chromosome.

plasmolysed A plant cell in which the cell membrane is pulling way from the cell wall due to lack of water.

platelet Fragment of a much larger cell that causes blood clots to form at sites of damage in blood vessels.

pollen tube The tube that grows out of a pollen grain, down through the style, carrying the male gamete to the female gamete.

pollination The process in which pollen from one flower is transferred to another flower, before fertilisation can take place.

pollution The introduction of potentially harmful or toxic substances that cause damage to the environment, people and other organisms, often as a result of adding chemicals to the air, water or land.

population A group of organisms of the same species living in a particular habitat.

premolar A tooth type, found behind the canines, that helps with cutting off food and has a small grinding surface for chewing.

producer An organism that produces its own food; for example, plants using energy transferred from light in photosynthesis to produce glucose.

product A molecule that is formed during a reaction.

progesterone The hormone produced in the ovaries that helps to control the menstrual cycle.

prokaryote An organism that has a cell in which the genetic material lies free in the cytoplasm and has no nucleus, e.g. a bacterium.

protease An enzyme that digests proteins.

protein A large molecule that is made of many amino acids joined together.

protein energy malnutrition A condition caused by a diet that contains little protein, often causing kwashiorkor.

protein synthesis The process in which proteins are made inside a cell.

pulp cavity The soft layer in the middle of the tooth containing the blood vessels and nerves.

pupil Opening in the eye that lets light reach the retina.

pyramid of biomass A diagram that shows the biomass in different trophic levels of a food chain; often a pyramid shape.

pyramid of numbers A diagram that shows the number of individual organisms in different trophic levels of a food chain; often a pyramid shape.

reabsorption The taking of substances from the filtrate in a kidney tubule back into the blood in a capillary close by.

receptor organ An organ that receives information about the environment (such as eye or ear) and responds by stimulating a neurone.

recessive An allele that must be present on both chromosomes of a pair to produce its version of the characteristic.

recreational drug A drug that is not prescribed by a doctor, and is used for its effects.

recycle To make new materials using old ones rather than starting with raw materials.

red blood cell Blood cell that contains the red protein haemoglobin, which carries oxygen.

reduction division Cell division that reduces the number of chromosomes, such as meiosis.

reflex An automatic response to a stimulus.

reflex arc The pathway of neurones that an electrical impulse follows during a reflex response.

relay neurone A nerve cell in the central nervous system (also called *intermediate* or *connector neurone*) that forms a connection between other neurones.

renal capsule Cup-shaped structure at the start of a kidney tubule where ultrafiltration occurs.

reproduction The process of creating new members of a species.

respiration The chemical process in which glucose is broken down inside the mitochondria in cells, releasing energy and producing carbon dioxide and water.

restriction enzyme An enzyme that cuts DNA.

retina The layer of light-sensitive cells at the back of the eye.

rhythm method A natural method of birth control in which a couple avoid intercourse, or the penis is removed from the vagina before ejaculation, at the time in the menstrual cycle when the woman is most fertile.

ribosome Very small cell structure that carries out protein synthesis.

rod Type of light-sensitive cell in the eye that responds to brightness of light.

root hair cell A cell in the epidermis of roots that has a long extension of cytoplasm, where uptake of substances from soil water occurs.

saprotrophic nutrition The digestion of dead food material outside the body, as in fungi.

secondary sexual characteristic A feature that develops at puberty as a result of sex hormones.

secretion The release of chemicals that have been made inside the cell into the fluid outside the cell.

seed bank A large collection of many different species of seed stored for use in the future.

seed The structure formed from an ovule that contains the plant embryo and food stores.

selective breeding The breeding together of organisms that have desirable features.

sense organ An organ that responds to a stimulus by causing an electrical impulse in a neurone.

sensitivity The detection of changes (stimuli) in the surroundings by a living organism, and its responses to those changes.

sensory neurone A nerve cell that carries electrical impulses from a receptor to the central nervous system.

sewage Human waste, faeces and urine.

sex chromosome A chromosome that affects the sex of the individual, e.g. for humans XX in women and XY in men.

sex-linked characteristic A characteristic caused by a gene on a sex chromosome, expressed more frequently in one sex than the other.

sexual reproduction Production of new individuals by the fusion of a male and a female gamete.

sexually transmitted infection (STI) Infection transmitted by sexual intercourse, such as HIV.

shunt vessel Blood vessel that connects an arteriole directly to a veniole, so blood can bypass capillaries.

sickle cell anaemia A condition caused by the inheritance of two sickle cell alleles.

sigmoid population growth curve A growth curve with a typical shape in four phases, shown by populations living in ideal conditions in a limited area.

simple sugar A basic sugar unit (e.g. glucose) that can join together with other sugar units to make large carbohydrates such as starch and glycogen.

sink Part of a plant where a substance is converted into other substances for growth or storage, or is used – for example, sucrose is broken down to glucose and used in respiring cells.

social implications Effects on the way people live and work together.

soil erosion The washing away of soil as a result of wind and rainfall when there is little vegetation to hold on to the soil.

soluble Dissolves easily in a solvent, such as water.

source Where something is produced or enters the body, such as photosynthesising cells for glucose.

specialisation When a cell develops special features that help it work in a particular way.

species A group of organisms that share many features and can interbreed to produce fertile offspring.

specific Limited, usually to one or a few. For example, enzymes are specific because they only work with one or a few similar substrates.

sperm cell Male gamete in animals.

spermicide A chemical that kills sperm.

spongy mesophyll The layer of cells in the lower part of the leaf in which there are many air spaces, so increasing the internal surface area to volume ratio.

stamen The male structure in flowers that contains the anther.

starch A complex carbohydrate made from many glucose units.

starvation Eating too little food to supply the body with its need for energy and nutrients.

stationary phase The third phase of a sigmoid growth curve, where some factor becomes limiting, such as a nutrient, and birth rate and death rate are equal.

stent A short, wire mesh tube, inserted into a blood vessel to keep it open.

'sticky ends' Short stretches of unpaired bases at the ends of DNA cut by some kinds of restriction enzymes.

stigma The female structure in flowers to which pollen grains attach in pollination.

stimulus A change in the internal or external environment that produces a response by an organism.

stomata Tiny holes in the surface of a leaf (mostly the lower epidermis), which allow gases to diffuse into and out of the leaf.

style The structure that supports the stigma in a flower.

substrate A molecule that fits into an enzyme molecule at the start of a reaction.

succulent A plant with thick, fleshy water-filled tissue, adapted to living in dry conditions such as the desert.

sucrose Common sugar that is formed of pairs of glucose units.

sustainable development The development of technology and the environment to support increasing human needs for resources without harming the environment.

sustainable resources Resources that can be produced without harming the environment.

synapse Where two neurones connect.

synthesis The building of larger molecules from smaller ones, such as the formation of proteins from amino acids.

systemic pesticide A pesticide that is absorbed by a plant and carried through the phloem to all parts, so that pests eating any part of the plant are affected by the pesticide.

target organ An organ that is affected by a hormone.

tension A 'pull', such as the pull created by the cohesion of water molecules in xylem.

test cross A cross made between an individual with the dominant phenotype and a homozygous recessive to test if the dominant phenotype is heterozygous or homozygous.

testis The site of production of sperm in men.

testosterone The male sex hormone that is produced in the testes.

tissue A group of similar specialised cells that work together to carry out a particular function.

tissue fluid Fluid that surrounds cells.

tissue rejection When the immune system attacks and destroys 'foreign' tissue in the body, such as after an organ transplant.

toxic Poisonous.

trachea The tube leading from the mouth to the bronchi, sometimes called the windpipe.

translocation The movement of dissolved substances, such as sucrose and amino acids, through the phloem tissue of a plant.

transmissible disease A disease that can be passed from one host to another.

transpiration Evaporation of water vapour from the surface of a plant.

transplant An operation that places a healthy organ, such as heart or kidney, into a patient whose organ is not functioning well enough for healthy living.

trophic level A feeding level in a food chain or food web, e.g. producer, primary consumer.

tropism A growth response of a plant as a result of the environment.

turgid Plant cells that have a full vacuole and the cytoplasm pushes against the cell wall, giving the plant structure and support.

turgor pressure The pressure of the cytoplasm inside a cell against the cell wall.

Type 1 diabetes A disease caused by the immune system destroying cells in the pancreas that produce insulin.

urea The substance produced in the liver from the breakdown of amino acids that are not needed in the body.

ureter The tube connecting the kidney to the bladder.

urethra The tube that connects the bladder to the outside of the body.

urine Liquid produced by kidneys, containing water, urea and salts.

uterus Where a baby develops inside a mother.

vaccination Introducing a harmless version of a pathogen into the body to stimulate the immune system to respond and produce active immunity.

vaccine A harmless version of a pathogen used in immunisation.

vacuole A large sac found in the middle of many plant cells, containing cell sap.

valve Flaps in the heart, and in veins, that prevent the flow of blood in the wrong direction.

vascular bundle Tissue that forms the veins in plant roots, stems and leaves, containing xylem vessels and phloem cells.

vasectomy Cutting the sperm ducts of a man to prevent sperm leaving the body.

vasoconstriction The narrowing (constriction) of blood vessels.

vasodilation The widening of blood vessels.

vector An animal that carries a pathogen from one host to another.

vein (*animal*) A blood vessel that carries blood towards the heart. (*plant*) See *vascular bundle*.

vena cava The largest human vein that delivers blood from the body to the right aorta.

veniole (or venule) Small blood vessel that connects a capillary to a vein.

ventilation Moving air into and out of the lungs.

ventricle One of two chambers of the heart that receive blood from the atria and pump it out through arteries.

vertebrate An animal that has a backbone.

vesicle A small membrane-bound structure in a cell that contains substances such as enzymes or hormones.

villus Finger-like projection of the small intestine wall where absorption of digested food molecules occurs.

vitamin A nutrient needed by the body in tiny amounts to remain healthy, such as vitamins A, C and D.

voluntary Done consciously, after thought.

waste product A product of a chemical reaction that is not needed, such as oxygen in photosynthesis.

water cycle How water cycles in different states between living organisms and the environment.

water potential The potential for a solution to take up more water molecules; it is 0 for pure water and has a negative value for solutions.

water potential gradient The difference in water potential between two regions, e.g. in a plant.

withdrawal symptoms Effects caused by not getting sufficient amounts of a drug that the body has become addicted to.

xerophyte A plant that is adapted to live in very dry conditions.

xylem vessel A tube formed from dead cells in the vascular bundles of a plant, which carries water and dissolved substances from the roots to the leaves and other parts of the plant.

zygote A fertilised egg, formed from the fusion of a male gamete and female gamete.

Answers

The answers given in this section have beenwritten by the author and are not taken from examination mark schemes.

SECTION 1 CHARACTERISTICS AND CLASSIFICATION OF LIVING ORGANISMS

Characteristics of living organisms

Page 14

1. **a)** Any suitable answers for human, such as: movement – walking; respiration – combination of oxygen with glucose to release energy, carbon dioxide and water; sensitivity – vision; growth – increase in height; reproduction – having a baby; excretion – producing urine; nutrition – eating food.

    b) Any suitable answers for a specific animal, such as:
    movement – crawling; respiration – combination of oxygen with glucose to release energy, carbon dioxide and water; sensitivity – smell; growth – increase in length; reproduction – producing young; excretion – losing carbon dioxide through respiratory surface; nutrition – eating food.

    c) Any suitable answers for a plant, such as: movement – growing towards light; respiration – combination of oxygen with glucose to release energy, carbon dioxide and water; sensitivity – detecting direction of light; growth – increase in height; reproduction – producing seeds; excretion – diffusion of waste products out of leaf for photosynthesis (oxygen) and respiration(carbon dioxide); nutrition – taking in nutrients from soil and making glucose by photosynthesis.

2. Movement – to reach best place to get food or other conditions favourable for growth
    respiration – to release energy from food that can be used for all life processes
    sensitivity – to detect changes in the environment
    growth – to increase in size until large/mature enough for reproduction
    reproduction – to pass genes on to next generation
    excretion – to remove harmful substances from body
    nutrition – to take in substances needed by the body for growth and reproduction.

Concept and use of a classification system

Page 17

1. a group of organisms that share many features and that can interbreed and produce fertile offspring

2. Organisms are grouped according to how similar they are. The more similar their features, the more closely they are grouped, e.g. into species or genus rather than order or class.

3. Any suitable example, such as *Homo sapiens*, showing the two parts of the name, described as the genus name (the first part) and species name (the second part). Each species has a different binomial name.

4. EXTENDED It can be used to identify evolutionary relationships and it can help identify which species need conservation.

Methods of Classification

Page 18

1. EXTENDED Morphology is the study of what organisms look like. Anatomy is the study of the body structure of organisms.

2. EXTENDED Organisms that have a similar features and body structure may be more closely related than those that are more different. The disadvantage is that sometimes body structure and features are strongly affected by the environment, so distantly related organisms may look more similar than closely related organisms.

3. EXTENDED The sequence of bases in DNA is more similar in organisms that are closely related than in organisms that are more distantly related. So organisms with a similar DNA sequence have evolved from a more recent ancestor than those with DNA that is more different.

Features of organisms

Page 20

1. Cell surrounded by cell membrane (1) containing cytoplasm (1) and DNA. (1)

2. EXTENDED They are where proteins are made in protein synthesis.

3. EXTENDED respiration

4. EXTENDED Similar: contain genetic material; different: only have a protein coat, not a cell membrane or other features of cells of living organisms.

Page 21

1. Plant cells may contain chloroplasts, but animals cells do not.

2. Plants are usually not able to move around freely, but many animals can.

3. It is a plant because only plant cells contain chloroplasts.

Page 25

1. **EXTENDED** animals, plants, fungi, protoctists and prokaryotes; each kingdom with a suitable example

2. **EXTENDED** Bacterial cells have no nucleus / DNA lies free in cytoplasm, but animal cells have DNA in a nucleus.

3. **EXTENDED** a) cell walls, cannot move around
   b) no chloroplasts

4. **EXTENDED** Some protoctists contain a chloroplast and can photosynthesise as some plant cells do; others do not have chloroplasts and feed on other organisms, so are more like single animal cells.

Page 30

1. Table like the following.

Group	Key body features	Fertilisation	Production of young
bony fish	scaly skin, streamlined shape, fins and tail, gills	external	from eggs
birds	feathers and wings, constant body temperature	internal	from eggs
mammals	hair, mammary glands, constant body temperature	internal	live birth
amphibians	moist skin, metamorphosis between very different young and adult forms	external	from eggs
reptiles	tough scaly skin, varying body temperature	internal	from eggs

2. It is a vertebrate (backbone), and a bird, because only birds have feathers.

3. They all have a tough exoskeleton.

4. Myriapods have many segments and many legs. Insects have a three-part body with six legs and often two pairs of wings. Arachnids have a two-part body with eight legs. Crustaceans usually have a three-part body with two pairs of antennae on their head, and may have swimming legs on the abdomen as well as real leags on the thorax.

Page 32

1. **EXTENDED** Similarities: both have chloroplasts and are plants, both have roots and leaves. Differences: ferns reproduce using spores, flowering plants reproduce using flowers and seeds.

2. **EXTENDED** Dicotyledon plants have two cotyledons in the seed; monocotyledon plants only have one. Monocotyledons have long strap-like leaves with parallel veins; dicotyledons have broad leaves of many shapes with branching veins.

Dichotomous keys

Page 33

1. The key identifies organisms by using questions, where each question has only two possible answers. So with each question a group of different organisms is divided into two groups.

2. Any two suitable answers, such as: the key may not include sufficient differences between groups to place an organism at species level accurately; individuals vary within a species, so it may be difficult to decide if an individual does or does not have a particular feature; it might be the wrong time of year to identify particular features, e.g. plants don't have flowers at some times of the year.

Page 34

1. So that the user of the key can follow through the questions easily.

2. Any suitable solution that splits the three animals into a group of two and a single animal using one yes/no question, followed by another yes/no question that splits the group of two into two separate species. For example:
   Does it have black and white
   stripes all over the body?   yes – zebra
                   no – go to next
                   question
   Does it have black stripes?   yes – wildebeest
                   no – kudu

SECTION 2 ORGANISATION AND MAINTENANCE OF THE ORGANISM

Cell structure and organisation

Page 46

1. a) Drawing should be drawn with thin, clear pencil lines, no crossing out, to show the outline of the cell in the photograph and the central shape.

   b) Diagram should be labelled to show nucleus, cytoplasm and cell membrane.

2. cell wall, large vacuole, chloroplast

3. a) chloroplast
   b) large vacuole
   c) cell wall.

Page 47

1. **EXTENDED** Vesicles package substances in the cell, such as substances for release outside the cell or substances that are being stored in the cell. Mitochondria release energy during aerobic respiration. Ribosomes are where new proteins are formed.

2. EXTENDED Because they are too small to be seen properly with a light microscope.

3. EXTENDED The heart muscle cell because it needs a constant supply of energy for contraction, whereas the epithelial cell needs relatively little energy for its role as a lining of the heart walls.

Levels of organisation

Page 49

1. a) Any suitable two, such as: muscle tissue, nervous tissue, bone tissue.

   b) Any suitable two, such as: heart, liver, brain.

   c) Any suitable two, such as: nervous system, digestive system, circulatory system.

2. a) Any suitable two, such as: palisade cells, root hair cells.

   b) Any suitable two, such as: leaf, root.

Page 52

1. a) Lining some tubes in animal organs, such as the respiratory tract of humans; the cilia on the outside of the cells help move substances along inside the tubes.

   b) Throughout the body, conduct electrical impulses around the body.

   c) In blood; carry oxygen around attached to haemoglobin inside the cell.

   d) Near the tips of plant roots; have long cell extensions to increase surface area for absorption of materials into the root.

   e) In vascular bundles (veins) of plants; carry water and dissolved substances through the plant and help to support the plant.

2. Sperm cells are small, and have a tail for movement. Mitochondria provide energy for movement of the tail, and the acrosome contains enzymes that digest the egg cell membrane so the sperm nucleus can enter the egg cell for fertilisation. Egg cells are large and contain a lot of cytoplasm to provide nutrients for the fertilised cell during the early stages of division.

Size of specimens

Page 54

1. 2 mm

2. If you are not using a suitable magnification for the specimen you are looking at you may not be able to see what you want to. (It is most useful to start by focusing at a lower magnification and then moving up to the magnification you want to use.)

3. actual size $= \dfrac{2.5\,\text{mm}}{100}$

4. EXTENDED 0.025 mm = 25 µm

SECTION 3 MOVEMENT IN AND OUT OF CELLS

Diffusion

Page 64

1. Any answer that means the same as the following:

   net movement – the sum of movement in all the different directions possible

   diffusion – the sum of the movement of particles from an area of high concentration to an area of lower concentration in a solution or across a partially permeable membrane.

2. Passive, because no energy is provided by the cell for it to happen.

3. Only particles that are small enough to pass through the membrane can diffuse. Larger molecules cannot diffuse through the membrane.

Osmosis

Page 68

1. Any answer that means the same as the following: the net movement of water molecules from a region of their high concentration to a region of their lower concentration.

2. a) It is a passive movement of molecules as the result of a concentration gradient.

   b) Osmosis only considers the movement of water molecules; diffusion considers the solute molecules.

3. The strong cell wall prevents more water entering a plant cell than there is space for in the cell (i.e. when the cell is full of water). The cell wall gives cells that are full of water a specific shape, and this helps to support the plant, keeping it upright.

Water potential

Page 71

1. EXTENDED **a)** Not full of water.

   b) Full of water.

   c) The removal of water from a cell so that it shrinks in size (or the cell membrane surrounding the cytoplasm of a plant cell pulls away from the cell wall).

   d) The pressure caused by the water in the cytoplasm on the cell wall that prevents more water entering the cell.

2. EXTENDED The water potential of the cells inside the plant root is lower than the water potential of the soil water surrounding the root, so water moves down the water potential gradient into the root.

3. EXTENDED Diagram should show water molecules leaving the red blood cell as a result of osmosis and entering the solution. Labels should indicate a water potential gradient from the cell to the solution and indicate that the loss of water results in plasmolysis.

Active transport

Page 73

1. The absorption of a substance by a cell against its concentration gradient, using energy.

2. **EXTENDED** Uptake of nitrate ions by root cells in plants because plants need nitrate ions for making amino acids but they are in higher concentration inside plant cells than in soil water; uptake of glucose from digested food in the small intestine by epithelial cells of the villi in humans, because glucose is essential for use in respiration.

3. **EXTENDED** Energy comes from respiration. Makes it possible for carrier proteins to transport particles from one side of a membrane to the other against the concentration gradient.

SECTION 4 BIOLOGICAL MOLECULES

Carbohydrates, proteins and lipids

Page 79

1. **a)** fatty acids and glycerol **b)** simple sugars **c)** amino acids

2. Protein is formed from amino acids, carbohydrates from simple sugars; carbohydrates are often made from one kind of simple sugar, proteins from many different kinds of amino acids.

Page 80

1. **EXTENDED** The sequence of amino acids in the amino acid chain of a protein is what determines the way the chain will fold up to make the three-dimensional structure of the protein.

2. **EXTENDED** Enzymes have an active site that exactly matches the shape of the molecule that it joins with during a reaction. Antibodies have shapes that exactly match the shape of an antigen on a pathogen, which helps the immune system destroy the pathogen.

Water

Page 81

1. It is important because many substances dissolve in it.

2. **EXTENDED** In plants, substances are transported in xylem and phloem dissolved in water. In humans, substances dissolve in blood so they can be transported around the body.

The structure of DNA

Page 82

1. **EXTENDED** It is formed from two strands twisted together into a helical shape.

2. **EXTENDED** Base A always pairs with base T, and base C always pairs with base G.

Tests for food molecules

Page 85

1. **a) i)** A red-brick precipitate would form, because glucose is a reducing sugar. **ii)** The solution wouldn't change colour as there is no starch present.

   b) i) There would be no change in colour because sucrose and the starch in wheat flour are not glucose (reducing sugar). **ii)** The solution would turn blue-black because of the starch in flour.

2. Crush the walnut using a mortar and pestle, then:

   a) mix part with ethanol, decant the liquid and add water, if the mixture turns cloudy, then fat is present

   b) mix part with water to form a solution, add a few drops of biuret solution – if protein present, a blue ring forms at the surface, which disappears to form a purple solution

   c) mix part with water to form a solution, add a few drops of this solution to DCPIP, if the blue colour of the dye disappears then vitamin C is present.

SECTION 5 ENZYMES

Enzymes as catalysts

Page 91

1. a substance that speeds up the rate of reaction but remains unchanged at the end of the reaction

2. a chemical that is found in living organisms that acts as a catalyst

3. Without enzymes, the metabolic reactions of a cell would happen too slowly for life processes to continue.

4. A substrate is a molecule that an enzyme joins with at the start of a reaction. Substrate molecules are changed to product molecules during a reaction.

Enzyme action

Page 92

1. The sequence of amino acids in the amino acid chain determines the way the chain will fold up to make the three-dimensional structure of the protein.

2. **EXTENDED** the shape in an enzyme into which a substrate fits closely during a reaction

3. **EXTENDED** Only a substrate with a shape that is complementary to the shape of the active site can fit it into it. So an enzyme can only work with a particular shape of substrate.

Enzymes and temperature

Page 96

1. As temperature increases, the rate of the reaction will increase, up to a maximum point (the optimum) after which it decreases rapidly as the enzyme is denatured.

2. The optimum pH for pepsin is around pH 2, which is very acidic like the contents of the stomach. The optimum for trypsin is around pH 8, which is more alkaline like the contents of the small intestine. Each enzyme has an optimum pH that matches the environment in which they work, so that they act most efficiently there.

Enzymes and pH

Page 97

1. a) **EXTENDED** The cooler molecules are, the slower they move. So the longer it takes for the enzymes and substrate molecules to bump into each other and the substrate to fit into the active site. Therefore the cooler the temperature, the slower the rate of reaction.

b) As temperature increases, the atoms in the enzyme vibrate more. This changes the shape of the active site, making it more difficult for the substrate to fit into the active site and so slowing down the rate of reaction. Eventually, the atoms vibrate so much that the shape of the active site is destroyed and the enzyme is denatured.

2. **EXTENDED** At a pH above and below the optimum of pH 2, the shape of the active site is changed as the interactions between the amino acids in the enzyme are affected by the pH. This makes it more difficult for the substrate to fit into the active site, so the rate of reaction slows down.

SECTION 6 PLANT NUTRITION

Photosynthesis

Page 104

1.

$$\text{Carbon dioxide + water} \xrightarrow[\text{light energy}]{\text{chlorophyll}} \text{glucose + oxygen}$$

2. Without light, photosynthesis cannot take place in plant cells.

3. a)

EXTENDED $6CO_2 + 6H_2O \xrightarrow[\text{light energy}]{\text{chlorophyll}} C_6H_{12}O_6 + 6O_2$

b) Labels should show: CO_2 from air, H_2O from soil water, $C_6H_{12}O_6$ used in cells for respiration or converted to other chemicals for use in cells, O_2 released into air if not needed in respiration.

4. **EXTENDED** Most organisms other than plants get their energy in chemical form from the food that they eat. That energy was originally converted from light energy to chemical energy during photosynthesis in a plant cell and then transferred as chemical energy along the food chain.

Page 106

1. Test the leaf of a variegated plant for starch. Starch is only produced in the green parts of the leaf, where there is chlorophyll, so only the green parts of the leaf photosynthesise.

2. Heat in a water bath, keeping the ethanol away from open flames such as from a Bunsen burner, because ethanol gives off flammable fumes.

3. Place one de-starched plant in an atmosphere with no (or limited) carbon dioxide (due to potassium hydroxide) and one in an atmosphere high in carbon dioxide (due to carbon dioxide given off in a reaction between marble chips and dilute acid). Shine light on the plants. Test one leaf from each plant after several hours. Only the leaf in high carbon dioxide will have produced significant amounts of starch as a result of photosynthesis.

Page 110

1. **EXTENDED** A limiting factor is the factor that is limiting the rate of a reaction because it is the one in shortest supply at that particular time.

2. a) **EXTENDED** As light increases, so rate of photosynthesis increases.

b) As carbon dioxide increases, so rate of photosynthesis increases.

c) As temperature increases, the rate of photosynthesis increases up to a maximum, after which it decreases rapidly.

3. a) **EXTENDED** As light increases, more energy is supplied to drive the process of photosynthesis.

b) As carbon dioxide increases, so there is more reactant for the process.

c) As temperature increases, up to the maximum the particles in the reaction including enzymes are moving faster and bump into each other more. Above the maximum the rate of photosynthesis decreases because the enzymes that control the process start to become denatured.

Page 112

1. Carbon dioxide is soluble and acidic, so when more gas is being produced, such as during respiration, the solution becomes more acidic. When carbon dioxide is removed from the solution, such as during photosynthesis, the solution becomes less acidic.

Leaf structure

Page 114

1. Any four from: cuticle, epidermis, spongy mesophyll, palisade mesophyll, xylem.

2. **EXTENDED** Thin broad leaves, chlorophyll in cells, veins containing xylem tissue that transports water and mineral ions to the leaves and phloem tissue that takes products of photosynthesis to other parts of the plant, transparent epidermal cells, palisade cells tightly packed in a single layer near top of leaf, stomata to allow gases into and out of leaf, spongy mesophyll layer with large internal surface.

3. **EXTENDED** A large surface area helps to maximise the rate of diffusion, in this case diffusion of carbon dioxide into cells for photosynthesis and oxygen out of cells so that it can be released into the air.

4. **EXTENDED** It allows as much light as possible to pass through the epidermal cells to reach the palisade cells below, where there are chloroplasts.

Mineral requirements of plants

Page 115

1. Plants make their own foods and need to convert the carbohydrates made by photosynthesis into other substances, such as proteins, which contain additional elements.

2. **a)** Nitrogen is an essential element for making substances other than carbohydrates, such as proteins.

   b) Magnesium is needed to make chlorophyll, which is the green substance in plants.

3. **a)** **EXTENDED** Stunted growth: because without proteins, the plant cannot make new cells and will not grow well.

   b) Without enough magnesium the plant will not be able to make enough chlorophyll, so it will lose the green colour and become yellow. Any magnesium in the plant is transported to the new leaves, so that photosynthesis can continue there for making food for growth.

SECTION 7 HUMAN NUTRITION

Diet

Page 125

1. carbohydrates, proteins and fats

2. carbohydrates from pasta, rice, potato, bread, wheat flour; proteins from meat, pulses, milk products, nuts; fats from vegetable oils, butter, full-fat milk products, red meat

3. vitamins, minerals, water and fibre.

4. Vitamins and minerals are needed for maintaining the health of skin, blood, bones, etc. Water is needed to maintain the water potential of cells. Fibre is needed to help digested food to move easily through the alimentary canal.

5. **EXTENDED** Kwashiorkor is caused in young children by a diet low in protein. It results in swelling of the feet and abdomen, loss of muscle tissue, hair and teeth.

Page 128

1. Any answer along the lines of: different people need different amounts of energy every day; for example, active people need more than people who are seated for much of the day; men have a larger average body mass than women so will need more energy to support that extra tissue; some groups of people need more of a particular group of nutrients than others, e.g. pregnant women need additional iron.

2. Food that contains more energy than the body uses is converted into body fat, leading to obesity, which is associated with many health problems. A diet that is too low in energy leads to health problems as a result of low body weight.

3. **a)** Obesity is caused by a diet that contains too much energy, and is associated with many diseases.

   b) Starvation is a diet too low in energy and/or nutrients, leading to health problems from deficiency diseases or breakdown of muscle tissue for energy.

   c) Constipation is caused by too little fibre in the diet and may lead to diseases such as bowel cancer and diverticulitis.

The human alimentary canal

Page 131

1. Sketch should show the following labels correctly attached to organs shown on the diagram:

   - mouth, where food is broken down by physical digestion (chewing) and amylase enzyme starts digestion of starch in food

   - oesophagus moves food from mouth to stomach by peristalsis

   - stomach, where churning mixes food with protease enzymes and acid to start digestion of protein molecules

   - small intestine, where alkaline bile neutralises the acid chyme and enzymes from pancreas complete digestion of proteins, lipids and carbohydrates, and where digested food molecules are absorbed into the body

   - large intestine, where water is absorbed from undigested food

- rectum, where faeces are held until they are egested through the anus
- liver, where bile is made and where some food molecules are assimilated
- gall bladder, where bile is stored until needed
- pancreas, where proteases, lipases and amylase which pass to the small intestine.

2. Egestion is the removal of undigested food from the alimentary canal – food that has never crossed the intestine wall into the body. Excretion is the removal of waste substances that have been produced inside the body.

3. Peristalsis caused by contraction of the circular muscles of the alimentary canal, followed by relaxation as the longitudinal muscles contract.

Page 132

1. The production of large quantities of watery faeces.

2. Oral rehydration using a solution of clean water and rehydration salts or a mixture of sugar and salt.

3. **EXTENDED** Toxins produced by the cholera bacterium in the small intestine cause sodium ions to be secreted into the gut, which draws more water out of the body by osmosis.

Mechanical and physical digestion

Page 135

1. Chemical digestion uses chemicals (enzymes) to help break down large food molecules into smaller ones. Mechanical/physical digestion is the chewing by the teeth to break large pieces of food into smaller ones before swallowing, or the breaking up of large fat droplets into smaller ones by bile.

2. Incisors have a flat blade shape for biting off food. Canines have a sharp point for holding food while other teeth chew off pieces. Premolars and molars have grinding surfaces for chewing.

3. Brushing removes particles of food caught in the teeth. Bacteria growing on these particles can release acids that destroy the tooth enamel leading to tooth decay. So brushing prevents bacterial growth and tooth decay.

4. **EXTENDED** Bile helps to emulsify fats in food, breaking them up into much smaller droplets and creating a much larger surface area for lipase enzymes to act on.

Chemical digestion

Page 137

1. The digestive enzymes break down food molecules that are too large to cross the wall of the small intestine into smaller ones that can be absorbed across cell membranes and so enter the body. If we did not have enzymes, we would not be able to absorb many nutrients from our food.

2. a) amylase
   b) glucose

3. a) **EXTENDED** The acid increases stomach acidity, providing the right conditions for enzymes that digest food in the stomach.
   b) Bile neutralises the acidity of food from the stomach, providing the right conditions for enzymes that digest food in the small intestine. It also emulsifies fats, providing a larger surface area for lipase enzymes to work on.

Absorption of food

Page 139

1. The movement of digested food molecules across the alimentary canal (small intestine) wall into the body.

2. Small intestine (ileum) and large intestine (colon).

3. **EXTENDED** The larger the surface area, the more rapidly small molecules can be absorbed across the intestine wall into the body.

4. **EXTENDED** There are millions of villi on the surface of the intestine wall projecting into the alimentary canal. This greatly increases the surface area of the wall.

5. **EXTENDED** The capillaries provide a large blood supply to remove absorbed. Food molecules quickly so maintaining a high concentration gradient for diffusion; lacteals in the villi carry absorbed lipid molecules away to the rest of the body.

SECTION 8 TRANSPORT IN PLANTS

Transport in plants

Page 148

1. In vascular bundles that form veins throughout the roots, stems and leaves.

2. Xylem vessels are long continuous tubes formed from dead cells, which allow water and dissolved substances to pass easily through the plant.

3. Phloem cells link together to form continuous phloem tissue in the vascular bundles. They carry dissolved food materials, such as sucrose and amino acids, from the leaves where they are formed to other parts of the plants that use them for life processes or where they will be stored.

Water uptake

Page 150

1. It enters through the root hair cells, moves through the root cortical cells to the xylem in the centre of

the root. It moves through the xylem up the stem and into the leaves. In the leaves, it moves out of the xylem into the spongy mesophyll cells.

2. Place a stem of a plant in water containing food colouring. The colour will travel through the xylem with the water, and show where the xylem is in the stem, leaves and flowers.

3. **a)** osmosis, **b)** active transport

4. Diagram should include annotations like the following, at the appropriate point: soil water has higher concentration of water molecules than cytoplasm of cells in the root; water molecules enter root hair cells by osmosis; water molecules pass from cell to neighbouring cell by osmosis until they reach the xylem.

Transpiration

Page 154

1. evaporation from the surfaces of a plant, particularly from the stomata of a leaf into the air

2. Diagram should include annotations like the following, at the appropriate point: water molecules evaporate from surfaces of spongy mesophyll cells into air spaces; water molecules from air spaces move into and out through stomata into the air – diffusion (net movement) usually from inside leaf to outside; osmosis causes water molecules to move from xylem into neighbouring leaf cells, and then from cell to cell until they reach a photosynthesising cell or a spongy mesophyll cell; transpiration is the evaporation of water from a leaf.

3. Closing stomata reduces diffusion of water molecules out of the leaf. At night, oxygen is not needed for photosynthesis, so keeping stomata open would lose water unnecessarily.

4. **a)** When temperature is higher, particles move faster, so water molecules will diffuse out of the leaf more quickly.

   b) When air humidity is high, there is a high concentration of water molecules in the air. So more water particles will move from the air through the stomata into the leaf while water particles are moving out of the leaf into the air. This means the rate of diffusion will be lower.

5. **EXTENDED** Cohesion of water molecules means they stick to each other. So as water moves out of the xylem in the leaves, down its potential gradient into the spongy mesophyll cells, more water molecules are drawn up the xylem tube through the plant through cohesion of water. This causes a water potential gradient between the root cortical

cells and the xylem in the root, drawing more water into the xylem.

Translocation

Page 155

1. **EXTENDED** phloem

2. **EXTENDED** sucrose and amino acids

3. **EXTENDED** A source is a part of a plant where a substance is formed or enters the plant, e.g. (a) water from soil, carbon dioxide in air, and (b) glucose in photosynthesising cells. A sink is a part of a plant where the substance leaves or is converted into something else, e.g. (a) photosynthesising cells are a sink for water and carbon dioxide, (b) respiring cells and storage cells are sinks for glucose.

SECTION 9 TRANSPORT IN ANIMALS

Transport in animals

Page 162

1. to pump blood around the body

2. valves in the heart and veins

3. **EXTENDED** Blood passes twice through the heart for every once round the body – there are effectively two separate circulations of blood from the heart.

4. **EXTENDED** The pressure in the two circulations can be different, so the high blood pressure needed to get blood through all of the body doesn't damage the delicate capillaries in lung tissue.

Heart

Page 164

1. left atrium, right atrium, left ventricle, right ventricle

2. Arteries carry blood away from the heart; veins carry blood towards the heart. **EXTENDED** Mention arteriole and veniole in the correct order and give capillaries and shunt vessels as alternative routes.

3. **EXTENDED** vena cava, right atrium, right ventricle, pulmonary artery, pulmonary vein, left atrium, left ventricle, aorta

Page 166

1. taking a pulse count, listening to the heart, taking an ECG

2. Resting heart rate varies widely due to many factors, including age, health and fitness, so a single value for the average is too limited.

3. As level of activity increases, so heart rate increases.

4. EXTENDED Heart rate increases with exercise so the blood can circulate faster round the body, delivering oxygen and glucose to muscle cells for the increased rate of respiration to generate the energy needed for contraction. It also removes waste carbon dioxide from muscle tissue more rapidly to prevent it building up and affecting cells.

Page 169

1. to supply the oxygen and glucose needed for the heart muscle cells to respire and to remove waste carbon dioxide

2. smoking, diet containing a lot of saturated fat, stress, genetic factors

3. EXTENDED Eat a diet that is relatively low in saturated fat, don't smoke and try to control stress and the effects that it has on behaviour.

4. EXTENDED Any two from: surgery such as insertion of a stent to widen the artery; surgery such as heart transplant if heart too badly damaged; drugs to thin blood and reduce risk of blood clot.

Blood vessels and lymphatic vessels

Page 172

1. a) renal arteries, b) aorta, c) pulmonary veins

2. Arteries are large vessels with thick, elastic muscular walls; capillaries are tiny blood vessels with very thin walls that are often only one cell thick; veins are large vessels with a large lumen and valves to prevent backflow of blood.

3. EXTENDED The walls stretch as blood enters then, and slowly relax as the blood flows through, balancing out the pressure so that the change in pressure is reduced.

Page 173

1. EXTENDED In the capillaries, substances that are small enough to pass through the capillary wall diffuse out into the tissue fluid surrounding cells. Substances that are not absorbed by cells are taken into the lymphatic system, through the body and delivered back to the blood system.

2. EXTENDED The lymphatic system returns fluid to the blood that left the capillaries in tissue and did not return directly to the capillaries. It also produces lymphocytes.

Blood

Page 177

1.

Blood component	Function
plasma	carries dissolved substances, such as carbon dioxide, glucose, urea and hormones; also transfers heat energy from warmer to cooler parts of the body
red blood cell	carries oxygen
white blood cell	protects against infection
platelet	causes blood clots to form when a blood vessel is damaged

2. The biconcave disc shape increases surface area to volume ratio, so rate of diffusion of oxygen into and out of cell is maximised. Haemoglobin inside the cell binds with oxygen when oxygen concentration is high and releases oxygen when oxygen concentration is low. The cell has no nucleus, so there is as much room as possible for haemoglobin. The cell has a flexible shape so can squeeze through the smallest capillaries and reach all tissues.

3. Phagocytes engulf pathogens inside the body and destroy them. Lymphocytes produce antibodies that attack pathogens.

4. Damage to a blood vessel can create an easy route of infection into the body. So forming a blood clot where there is damage, as quickly as possible, helps to reduce the risk of infection.

SECTION 10 DISEASE AND IMMUNITY

Transmissable diseases

Page 185

1. a disease caused by a pathogenic organism that can be passed from one host to another

2. The host is a human, the pathogen is the virus.

3. Any three from: bacteria, viruses, fungi, protoctists.

Page 188

1. Direct: any one from blood (HIV, hepatitis B, hepatitis C) or semen (HIV, syphilis, gonorrhoea, other STI). Other examples may be correct.

   Indirect: water droplets in air (colds, flu); drinking water (cholera, typhoid, dysentery); contaminated surfaces (athlete's foot, food poisoning pathogens); insect bite (malaria, dengue fever).

2. an animal that carries a pathogen from one host to another

3. Any transmissible disease with a suitable description and explanation of how to control its spread.

Methods of defence

Page 189

1. a barrier that physically prevents entry into the body, e.g. nose hairs that filter air and thick skin

2. a chemical that destroys the pathogen, e.g. lysozymes in mucus and acid in stomach

3. White blood cells attack pathogens, either by engulfing and destroying them, or by producing antibodies that destroy pathogens.

Passive immunity

Page 193

1. a) EXTENDED chemical/protein on the surface of a pathogen cell to which antibodies attach

   b) protection from infection as a result of antibodies in the body

2. EXTENDED Part of the response of lymphocytes to an infection is to release memory cells into the blood. On a second infection, the memory cells respond by causing large quantities of antibodies to be released quickly. This destroys the pathogens before they cause disease.

3. EXTENDED Active immunity is caused by making the immune response produce antibodies and memory cells – it lasts a long time. Passive immunity is caused by giving a person antibodies – no memory cells are produced, so protection is only short-term.

Diseases caused by the immune system

Page 194

1. EXTENDED Type 1 diabetes (other auto-immune disorder answers are possible)

2. EXTENDED Instead of attacking pathogens, the immune system attacks and destroys cells in its own body. As the cells cannot function properly, this causes disease.

SECTION 11 GAS EXCHANGE IN HUMANS

The human respiratory system

Page 204

1. Exchange of gases between the body and the environment is by diffusion. Organisms need plenty of oxygen for respiration to provide energy for all life processes, and need to get rid of the waste carbon dioxide. So a rapid rate of diffusion supports a higher rate of respiration and all the other processes in the body.

2. The trachea carries air from the mouth down to the lungs; the bronchi (the two large divisions of the trachea as it reaches the lungs) are supported with rings of cartilage to prevent collapse during breathing; the bronchioles (the fine tubes in the lungs) carry the air to the alveoli; the alveoli (the bulges of the air sac) have a large surface area and are very thin for efficient diffusion of gases.

3. Sketch similar to Fig. 11.4, with annotations showing: thin lining of alveolar wall and wall of capillary allows rapid diffusion; high concentration gradients for gases between blood and air in alveolus due to continuous blood flow through capillary and ventilation of alveolus (lungs); large area of contact between capillary and alveolus, maximising area over which diffusion can occur.

4. EXTENDED The mucus traps particles and microorganisms that are in the air breathed in, and the cilia move the mucus and anything trapped in it up out of the lungs to the throat, where it can be swallowed. This protects the lungs from damage and infection.

Breathing in and out

Page 206

1. a) EXTENDED The muscle surrounding the diaphragm contracts so that the diaphragm flattens, pulling downwards on the thorax; the intercostal muscles contract, lifting the ribs out and up.

   b) These movements of the diaphragm and intercostal muscles increase the volume of the thorax, causing the volume of the lungs to increase and so drawing air into the lungs.

2. a) EXTENDED The diaphragm muscle relaxes, and is pushed upwards by the organs below it; the intercostal muscles relax, so the ribs fall back and down.

   b) These movements of the diaphragm and intercostal muscles reduce the volume of the thorax, so reducing the volume of the lungs, which pushes air out of the lungs.

Investigating the effect of exercise on breathing

Page 209

1. The percentage of oxygen is less in exhaled air than inhaled air. The percentage of carbon dioxide is greater in exhaled air than inhaled air. The percentage of water vapour is higher in exhaled air than inhaled air.

2. As level of exercise increases, rate and depth of breathing increase.

3. __EXTENDED__ There is less oxygen in expired air than inspired air because oxygen in the body is used for respiration. There is more carbon dioxide in exhaled air than inhaled air because the body produces carbon dioxide in respiration. There is more water vapour in exhaled air than inhaled air because water molecules evaporate from the surface of the alveoli due to warmth of the body.

4. __EXTENDED__ More exercise means more carbon dioxide is produced from an increased rate of respiration. Carbon dioxide is a soluble acidic gas so causes the body tissues and blood to become more acidic. A change in pH can affect many enzymes and so affect the rate at which life processes are carried out in the body. Slowing down the rate of life processes may harm the body.

SECTION 12 RESPIRATION

Aerobic respiration

Page 218

1. **a)**, **b)** and **c)**:

   glucose (*from digested food from alimentary canal*) + oxygen (*from air via lungs*) ⟶ carbon dioxide (*excreted through lungs*) + water (*used in cells or excreted through kidneys*) (+ energy (*transferred to other chemicals in cell processes*))

   b) glucose replaced by fats from hump, and very little water excreted through kidneys

2. inside cells

3. Any three from: muscles cells for contraction, synthesis of new molecules, such as proteins, for growth, active transport across cell membranes, passage of nerve impulses, maintenance of core body temperature.

4. __EXTENDED__ $C_6H_{12}O_6 + 6O_2 \longrightarrow 6CO_2 + 6H_2O$

Anaerobic respiration

Page 221

1. During vigorous exercise, they may not be able to get enough oxygen from the blood for all the energy they need for contracting. So the additional energy comes from anaerobic respiration.

2. Similarities: use glucose as substrate, produce energy, don't need oxygen. Differences: animals produce lactic acid, plants produce ethanol and carbon dioxide.

3. The amount of energy released from a mole of glucose molecules is much greater during aerobic respiration (c. 2900 kJ) than in anaerobic respiration (c. 150 kJ) in muscle cells.

4. Carbon dioxide is released by anaerobic respiration of glucose by yeast. Bubbles of the gas trapped in the dough makes it rise.

SECTION 13 EXCRETION IN HUMANS

Excretion

Page 228

1. The removal from the body of waste substances from metabolic reactions in cells.

2. They excrete carbon dioxide, which is the waste product of respiration.

3. They excrete urea, and excess water and mineral salts.

4. __EXTENDED__ They are toxic in large amounts in the body and so will cause harm.

Page 229

1.

Structure	Function
kidneys	produce urine by filtering waste substances from the blood
ureters	carry urine from kidneys to bladder
bladder	stores urine until it is released to the environment
urethra	links bladder to environment

2. water, urea, mineral salts

Changes in urine

Page 231

1. Amount of water taken into the body recently, environmental temperature, amount of exercise done recently.

2. **a)** Large quantity of pale yellow urine because it contains a lot of water.

   b) Small quantity of dark urine because it contains only a little water / water has been lost from the body by sweating during the exercise and leaves only a little for excretion by the kidneys.

3. __EXTENDED__ filtration and reabsorption

4. __EXTENDED__ Reabsorbed – any one from: water, glucose, mineral salts. Not reabsorbed: urea.

Kidney failure

Page 233

1. __EXTENDED__ Kidney dialysis, which cleans the blood artificially every few days, and kidney transplant, which places a healthy kidney into the patient's body and attaches it to the blood system to carry out natural blood cleaning.

2. **EXTENDED** You only need one kidney to keep blood cleaned sufficiently to remain healthy.

3. **EXTENDED** Normal kidney function: blood filtered in renal capsule – large amounts of water and soluble substances pass into the tubule; reabsorption of water, glucose and some ions, restores the correct balance of substances in the blood. Dialysis: substances exchanged only by diffusion between the blood and dialysis fluid.

4. **EXTENDED** Getting a kidney transplant depends on making a good tissue match between the patient and new kidney. The patient must wait until a suitable kidney becomes available, which may be a matter of luck (unless they have a relative willing to donate one of their kidneys).

5. **EXTENDED** Any two from: risk of tissue rejection, meaning another transplant would be needed, need to take drugs to suppress immune response for life, which increases risk of other infections (risk of having an operation).

SECTION 14 COORDINATION AND RESPONSE

Nervous control in humans

Page 241

1. The ability to detect and respond to changes in the external environment and internal conditions of the body.

2. A receptor detects a change in the environment, which is the stimulus. This causes a response from an effector in the body.

3. muscles and glands

4. Sensory neurones have long dendrons and axons that link the sense organ with the central nervous system.

   Relay neurones are short neurones with many dendrites, found in the central nervous system, that link sensory neurones to motor neurones or other relay neurones.

   Motor neurones have many dendrites to link with relay neurones and end on the effector, such as a muscle.

Synapses

Page 242

1. A chemical that is released at a synapse that crosses the gap and triggers an electrical impulse in the post-synaptic neurone.

2. They have a similar shape to a neurotransmitter and so can bind with the receptors in the post-synaptic neurone and trigger the same response as the neurotransmitter.

Page 244

1. A simple response of receptor > nerve > spinal cord > nerve > effector, which does not usually include the brain.

2. Reflex responses are very fast, which makes it possible to respond to a stimulus very quickly. Reflex responses are usually important in survival, e.g. to protect you from touching something dangerous, or blinking to protect the eye if something comes toward it.

3. **EXTENDED** A voluntary action is one that is consciously chosen (i.e. thought about), such as choosing what to eat. An involuntary reaction is one that is done unconsciously, such as blinking when something comes toward the eye.

Sense organs

Page 247

1. **EXTENDED** a) The cornea is transparent, so light passes through it easily into the eye.

   b) The pupil is a hole surrounded by the iris that lets light pass through to the back of the eye.

   c) The retina contains the light-sensitive cells that respond to light. The retina is also very dark, to absorb as much light as possible.

2. **EXTENDED** As light intensity increases, the pupil gets smaller, reducing the amount of light that can enter the eye. As light intensity decreases, the pupil gets larger, increasing the amount of light that can enter the eye.

   Pupil constriction in bright light happens because the radial muscle in the iris relaxes and the circular muscle contracts. Pupil dilation in dim light happens because the radial muscle in the iris contracts and the circular muscle relaxes.

3. **EXTENDED** Rod cells are found more around the periphery of the retina, and respond to light intensity, so we use them most when light levels are low. Cone cells are found more in the centre of the retina and respond to different colours of light, so we use them to distinguish colour when light levels are high.

Page 248

1. **EXTENDED** Light entering the eye from a near object needs to be refracted more than light from a distant object in order to focus it on the retina. The ciliary muscles contract, which reduces the tension on the ligaments that are attached to the lens. This allows the lens to become thicker and more rounded, which increases its focusing power.

2. <u>EXTENDED</u> For light from a distant object to be focused on the retina, the lens needs to be thin. So the ciliary muscles relax and the suspensory ligaments pull harder on the lens, causing it to flatten.

Hormones in humans

Page 250

1. a) A chemical messenger in the body that produces a change in the way some cells work.

   b) A gland that secretes hormones.

   c) An organ that contains cells that are affected by hormones.

2. When faced with attack, or when suddenly frightened.

3. It prepares the body for action by increasing the amount of oxygen and glucose delivered to muscle cells for rapid respiration, and improving vision.

4. <u>EXTENDED</u> The nervous system produces fast, short-term responses as a result of electrical impulses that pass along neurones between the receptor, central nervous system and effector. The hormonal system produces longer-term responses that are slower, by the secretion of chemical hormones from endocrine glands into the blood to travel to effector organs, where they cause a change in activity.

Homeostasis

Page 254

1. The maintenance of conditions inside the body within limits that allow cells to work efficiently.

2. Control of core body temperature (other answers possible).

3. Skin blood vessels dilate when the core body temperature is too high. This allows heat energy carried by the blood to reach the skin surface more easily and so be transferred to the environment more rapidly. Skin blood vessels constrict when the core body temperature falls too low. This reduces blood flow to near the skin's surface, so heat energy cannot be transferred as easily to the skin surface and so cannot be transferred to the environment as quickly. This keeps more heat energy within the body.

4. <u>EXTENDED</u> When a change in a stimulus causes a control centre to trigger the opposite change in response, so keeping a condition within limits.

5. <u>EXTENDED</u>

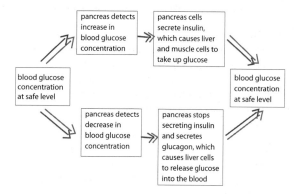

6. <u>EXTENDED</u> Symptoms: extreme thirst, weakness or tiredness, loss of weight, blurred vision. Treatment: regular injections of insulin into the fat beneath the skin.

Tropic responses

Page 258

1. A growth response of a plant to a stimulus.

2. a) Shoots grow towards light.

   b) Roots grow in the direction of the force of gravity.

3. <u>EXTENDED</u> Auxin is produced in the tip of the growing shoot and diffuses down the shoot. Auxin on the bright/light side of the shoot moves across the shoot to the darker side as it diffuses down the shoot. Cells on the dark side of the shoot elongate more than the cells on the light side of the shoot, so the shoot starts to bend as it grows so that the tip is pointing towards the light.

4. <u>EXTENDED</u> Auxins are absorbed into the leaves of broad-leaved weed plants more than into the leaves of grass-type crop plants. They cause the weed plants to grow so rapidly that they cannot sustain growth and die, leaving more space for the crop plants.

SECTION 15 DRUGS

Medicinal drugs

Page 269

1. a) A chemical that, when taken into the body, affects the way that the body works.

   b) A chemical that kills bacteria or prevents them from growing.

   c) When one type of bacteria is no longer killed or affected by an antibiotic.

2. Tetanus and bacterial meningitis will be affected, because they are caused by bacteria, but flu and viral meningitis won't, because they are caused by viruses.

3. **EXTENDED** Using antibiotics only when essential so that bacteria are not exposed to bacteria more often than necessary, as that is what causes the development of resistance; completing a course of antibiotics to reduce the risk that the more-resistant bacteria are passed on to somebody else.

Misused drugs

Page 270

1. It is against the law for the drug to be owned or used without permission, such as prescribed by a doctor.

2. Any two from: it is very addictive so difficult to give up, needs increasing amounts to produce the same effect as the body gets used to it, generally leads to crime to pay for the drug, may lead to infection by blood-borne diseases such as HIV as a result of sharing needles for injection.

3. **EXTENDED** It binds to receptors in the post-synaptic membrane of certain types of neurones in the brain that affect the way we feel and experience things.

Page 271

1. Because many people likes its effect of relaxation

2. Any three from: causes reaction time to lengthen, which is dangerous when fast responses are needed (e.g. when driving); in large amounts can lead to loss of self-control, which can result in violence, vomiting, unconsciousness.

3. Liver damage / cirrhosis because alcohol is taken to the liver for detoxification.

Page 273

1. Bronchitis – hacking cough caused by build-up of mucus in tubes of lungs as a result of damage to cilia; emphysema – shortage of breath due to breakdown of walls of alveoli so there is a smaller surface area for gas exchange in the lungs.

2. Nicotine is addictive, which makes smoking difficult to give up; carbon monoxide replaces oxygen on haemoglobin, reducing the amount of oxygen that blood can carry.

3. **EXTENDED** Both curves show a gradual increase over time up to a maximum. For smoking this is in the 1960s; for cancer deaths this is in the 1990s. The shape of the two curves is similar, which suggests that smoking increases the risk of cancer about 30 years later.

Page 274

1. **EXTENDED** A chemical with a particular structure that in the body stimulates the growth of tissues such as bone and muscle.

2. **EXTENDED** Increased size and strength of muscle are an advantage in sport, and give you a better chance of winning.

3. **EXTENDED** They harm the body, for example by increasing the risk of heart disease and liver damage; they have a harmful effect on the menstrual cycle in women; they limit bone growth in young people.

SECTION 16 REPRODUCTION

Asexual reproduction

Page 283

1. reproduction without the fusion of gametes, using a cell from only one parent

2. Binary fission is where the genetic material is copied and the cell splits in half. Only one cell is involved and there is no fusion of parent cells before division.

3. **EXTENDED** Advantages: no need for fertilisation, so reproduction faster and easier; if conditions remain stable, all new individuals will grow as well as the parent plant. Disadvantages: no genetic variation between plants, so if conditions change/the parent plant is susceptible to a particular disease, then all plants will do badly; this increases the risk that the plants in that area will all die.

Sexual reproduction

Page 285

1. a) The fusion of a male gamete and a female gamete to produce a zygote.

   b) The production of offspring from two parents as a result of fertilisation.

2. a) **EXTENDED** a sex cell or gamete such as a sperm, male gamete in a pollen grain, or an egg cell

   b) a zygote, or fertilised egg cell

3. **EXTENDED** Advantage: produces individuals with new variations of genetic material that increases the chance of survival when conditions change. Disadvantage: variation in offspring may also result in many offspring being less well adapted to environmental conditions than parent plants and so producing less harvest.

Sexual reproduction in plants

Page 287

1. Stigma, where pollen grains attach; style, which supports the stigma; ovary, which surrounds and protects the ovule, inside which is the female gamete.

2. Stamen, which includes an anther that contains pollen grains, inside which are the male gametes; filament, which holds the anther above the flower to help with shedding of pollen.

Page 292

1. Pollination is the transfer of pollen from a stamen to a stigma. Fertilisation is the fusion of the male gamete with the female gamete to form a zygote.

2. Any three from: wind-pollinated flowers usually small, no colour (white), make masses of lightweight pollen. Insect-pollinated plants usually large, may be brightly coloured, produce nectar and sometimes scent, make small amounts of larger pollen grains.

3. a) **EXTENDED** Can make less pollen; less waste of pollen as insects more likely to deliver pollen to flower than random distribution in wind.

   b) If the insect species die out, the plant will not get pollinated.

Page 296

1. When the embryo in a seed starts to grow, splitting the seed coat and increasing in size and complexity.

2. a) Seeds need a supply of oxygen for growth, although they may be able to start germination using anaerobic respiration.

   b) Seeds need water for germination and will not germinate in dry soil.

   c) Seeds need warmth for germination, although the amount of warmth they need may depend on where they naturally grow. Seeds from plants that live in colder areas may need a period of deep cold before they will germinate. Seeds from plants that live in areas prone to fire may not germinate until after a fire.

Sexual reproduction in humans

Page 298

1. Sketch should be similar to Fig. 16.20. Labels and annotations as follows:

   * testes, where sperm (male gametes) are produced

   * sperm duct, which carries sperm to urethra

   * prostate gland and seminal vesicles, which produce liquid in which sperm swim

   * penis, which when erect delivers sperm into vagina of female

   * urethra, the tube that carries sperm from sperm ducts to outside the body.

2. Sketch should be similar to Fig. 16.21. Labels and annotations as follows:

   * ovaries, where egg cells form

   * oviducts, which carry the eggs to the uterus and where fertilisation by sperm takes place

   * uterus, where embryo implants into lining and fetus develops

   * cervix, base of uterus where sperm are deposited during sexual intercourse

   * vagina, where penis is inserted during sexual intercourse.

3. **EXTENDED**

	Egg cell	Sperm cell
size	very large, 0.2 mm diameter	very small, 45 μm long
numbers	thousands in ovary but usually only one released each month	>100 million produced each day
mobility	unable to move on its own	self-propelling with tail

Page 300

1. a) The cell produced by fusion of a male gamete and female gamete.

   b) Formed from the division of cells in the zygote – until distinctive structures are obvious, such as limbs, when it becomes a fetus.

   c) Developing baby in the uterus (womb), from about 3 months after fertilisation.

2. In an oviduct.

3. In early stages, rapid cell division, and differentiation of cells to produce the main structures; later, development of nervous system and movement; increase in size and weight.

4. Provides nutrients from mother's blood and carries waste to mother's blood to be excreted.

Page 303

1. Care of the mother during her pregnancy to make sure she and the fetus are healthy.

2. Eating a healthy diet provides all the nutrients needed to keep the woman healthy and for the healthy development of the fetus. Alcohol intake should be limited, to minimise the effect of alcohol on the fetus. Additional nutrients such as folic acid are needed to prevent problems in the fetus, such as spina bifida.

3. Any two from: strong contractions of the uterus; blood-tinged mucus from plug lost from cervix; breaking of waters.

4. a) EXTENDED It usually provides the best balance of nutrients for the baby's growth, including antibodies that protect it from disease.

   b) If the mother was sick, or unable to produce sufficient milk for the baby.

Sex hormones in humans

Page 305

1. testosterone

2. oestrogen and progesterone

3. to make sexual reproduction possible, and to show that the individual is sexually mature

4. a) The release of an egg from an ovary.

   b) The changes that happen in the female reproductive system over about 28 days, including the development and breakdown of the uterus lining and ovulation.

5. EXTENDED Oestrogen: causes uterus wall to thicken and stimulates pituitary to secrete more LH

   progesterone: causes uterus wall to thicken even more, inhibits secretion of LH and FSH from pituitary.

   LH: causes ovulation/release of an egg from an ovary

   FSH: stimulates development of egg in ovary

Methods of birth control in humans

Page 309

1. To control when they have children and the number of children they have.

2. Abstinence, chemical methods (pill and IUD), surgical methods.

3. Because it depends on getting the timing right, and sperm survive for more than a day, so it is easy to misjudge the time when the woman is fertile.

4. They provide protection against transmission of sexually transmitted infections.

5. They prevent the sex cells getting to a place where they can meet.

6. EXTENDED Can help when a man is producing few sperm, by collecting and concentrating them before placing them in the woman's uterus, or using a sperm donor, when the man has no useful sperm.

7. EXTENDED Advantage: couple more likely to have children; disadvantage: risk of multiple births, which is more dangerous for the mother and for the babies.

Sexually transmitted infections (STIs)

Page 310

1. A disease that is transmitted in body fluids during sexual intercourse.

2. Through sexual body fluids during sexual intercourse; via blood through cuts or sharing of needles for injecting drugs; across the placenta from mother to fetus; through milk from mother to baby when breast-feeding.

3. EXTENDED The virus attacks the immune system, reducing the ability of the body to fight off other infections. This leads to AIDS.

4. EXTENDED Only have intercourse with a partner who is not infected with HIV; use barrier methods such as condoms or femidoms during intercourse.

SECTION 17 INHERITANCE

Chromosomes, genes and proteins

Page 321

1. gene, chromosome, nucleus, cell

2. A gene codes for a protein or characteristic; an allele is one form of the gene coding for a variation in the protein or characteristic. Any suitable example, e.g. gene for eye colour, allele for blue eye colour or brown eye colour.

3. the passing on of inherited characteristics from one generation to the next due to the passing on of genes that code for those characteristics.

4. EXTENDED TAACGATCCGA; A always pairs with T and G always pairs with C.

Page 322

1. a) EXTENDED The order of bases on the DNA strand is copied to form the strand of mRNA.

   b) The mRNA strand takes the genetic code from the DNA in the nucleus to the ribosome in the cytoplasm.

   c) The ribosome uses the order of bases on the mRNA strand to produce the amino acid chain of the protein.

2. EXTENDED Many of the genes are 'switched off' so they are not expressed.

Monohybrid inheritance

Page 324

1. a) The characteristic expressed in the phenotype when the organism has only one allele of that form.

b) The characteristic expressed in the phenotype when both genes in the genotype are the alleles for this form.

c) Having two identical copies of that allele for a particular gene.

d) Having different alleles for a particular gene.

2. a) 2 **b)** 1 **c)** 2

3. **EXTENDED** 38: because the body cell contains two copies of each chromosome

Page 327

1. the inheritance of a characteristic produced by one gene

2. genotype (the alleles in the chromosomes) BB, phenotype (what the organism looks like) brown; genotype Bb, phenotype brown (because the brown allele is dominant); genotype bb, phenotype black (because the organism doesn't have the brown allele)

3. a) The answer may be presented as a full layout diagram or a Punnett square, showing the adult genotypes and phenotypes (male BB brown and female bb black), the possible gametes produced (male B and B, female b and b), genotypes and phenotypes of possible offspring (BB brown, Bb brown, Bb brown, bb black).

b) This cross produces a theoretical probability of one black rabbit for every three brown rabbits, a ratio of 1 : 3, probability of 1 in 4 or 25%.

Page 329

1. So that, when the plants were bred together, the results in the offspring were not confused by a mix of alleles in one or both of the parents

2. Random variation is possible in the results. So the larger the sample, the more likely that any random variation will be averaged out.

3. He removed the stamens from every flower, so that pollen could not be transferred by insect. He also covered each flower after he had hand-pollinated it, so that other pollen could not get to the stigma.

4. Any characteristic may be used, with alleles appropriately designated with capital letter for dominant and lower-case letter for recessive allele. Parents used should show one with phenotype of dominant allele, homozygous, e.g. BB, and one parent with phenotype of recessive allele, i.e. bb. First cross will produce all individuals with phenotype of dominant allele but heterozygous in genotype, i.e. Bb. Crossing of these individuals will produce characteristic 1 BB : 2 Bb : 1 bb in genotype and 3 dominant characteristic to 1 recessive characteristic in next generation.

5. If Mendel had not been as thorough about his method, then his results would not have been as clear and predictable. So he would not have been able to have drawn clear and repeatable conclusions about the way characteristics are inherited in pea plants.

Page 331

1. **EXTENDED** The test cross is with the homozygous recessive, so if the individual with the dominant phenotype is heterozygous then some of the offspring produced will show the recessive phenotype, which is masked in a heterozygous individual.

2. **EXTENDED** When both alleles are expressed in the phenotype, and there is no dominance of one allele over the other.

3. **EXTENDED** Genetic layout diagram or Punnett square with following outcomes:

		father's gametes	
		I_A	I_B
mother's gametes	I_0	$I_A I_0$ blood group A	$I_B I_0$ blood group B
	I_0	$I_A I_0$ blood group A	$I_B I_0$ blood group B

Page 333

1. XX

2. XY

3. At each fertilisation there is a 50% chance that the X egg will be fertilised by an X sperm or a Y sperm. So the chance of the child being born male is 50%.

Page 334

1. **EXTENDED** a characteristic that is controlled by a gene on the sex chromosome, so that it is expressed more commonly in one sex than in the other

2. **EXTENDED** If a girl is colour blind, then she must have inherited one recessive allele for the condition from her father and one from her mother. So her father must have had an X chromosome with the recessive allele, and would have been colour blind, as there is no allele for this characteristic on the Y chromosome. Her mother could either have been homozygous for the recessive allele, and so colour blind, or heterozygous, with normal colour vision.

Meiosis

Page 336

1. a) mitosis

b) It produces cells that are identical.

2.

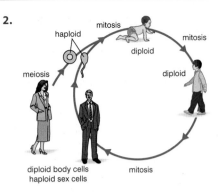

mitosis

haploid

mitosis

diploid

meiosis

diploid

diploid

mitosis

diploid body cells
haploid sex cells

3. EXTENDED **a)** meioisis **b)** mitosis

4. EXTENDED Meiosis produces non-identical cells, so there is variety in the gamete cells. When the gamete cells fuse, this will mean that the offspring will vary from each other.

SECTION 18 VARIATION AND SELECTION

Variation

Page 344

1. All the differences between individuals of the same species.

2. Discontinuous, e.g. gender or tongue-rolling; continuous, e.g. height or weight.

3. EXTENDED Discontinuous caused by alleles in genes, because there are a limited number of alleles for a gene that produce each different variation of the characteristic. Continuous caused by genes and environment because environmental factors affect the variation produced by genes, producing a range of variation.

Page 347

1. A change in the genetic code that produces a new allele that results in a different form of a characteristic.

2. Ionising radiation, such as ultraviolet radiation, X rays or gamma rays; chemical mutagens such as the chemicals in tobacco smoke.

3. EXTENDED A mutation in the haemoglobin allele results in a different form of the protein that changes shape at low blood oxygen concentrations.

4. EXTENDED The allele is present in greatest proportions where there is malaria because it helps the heterozygote to survive and reproduce and so pass on the allele to their offspring.

Adaptive features

Page 349

1. A feature that helps the organism to survive and reproduce in the environment in which it normally lives.

2. a) Any one from: white hair in winter (camouflage protects against being seen by predators); brown hair in summer (also camouflage protects against being seen by predators); thick fur in winter for insulation against cold; large feet for better grip on snow and loose rock for running away from predators.

b) Any one from: fat in hump provides energy and water from respiration when water and food are lacking; large feet make it easier to walk/run on loose sand; large eyelashes and nostrils that close prevent damage during sandstorms.

3. EXTENDED Fitness is how well adapted to the environment the organism is. The better-adapted organisms have a higher fitness.

4. EXTENDED Sketch of cactus with labels to show the following:

- extensive root systems to capture as much water as possible
- reduced or no leaves to reduce water loss by transpiration
- green stems for photosynthesis
- stomata sunk deep in pits in the stem to reduce rate of transpiration
- succulent stem (or leaves) to store water
- hairy surface to reduce rate of transpiration from stomata.

Selection

Page 353

1. Answer along the lines of: the influence of the environment on a characteristic, such that some variations of the characteristic are more successful at producing offspring than others and pas on their genes to the next generation.

2. a) If the individuals in a population are not all the same (there is variation), natural selection will favour some over others.

b) If there is competition between the variations, only those that are better adapted will be fit and healthy enough to produce offspring and pass on their genes.

c) Individuals with a particular variation of an adaptive feature may be more likely to survive and reproduce than individuals with other variations. So they are more likely to produce offspring that carry their alleles, and so those alleles will become more common in the next generation.

3. **EXTENDED** As the better-adapted individuals contribute more offspring to the next generation than those that are less well adapted, more individuals will have the alleles for the better adaptations. This means that the individuals in the next generation will be better suited to their environment than their parents.

4. **EXTENDED** Diagram should show the following: person infected with bacteria > bacteria grow in number inside patient > treatment of patient with antibiotics kills off least resistant bacteria but most-resistant bacteria survive > some of these bacteria escape into the environment from the patient and infect another person > the same antibiotic cannot be used on that patient as the bacteria are resistant.

Page 355

1. People who want to develop new varieties of plants and animals that have economic importance (will earn more money for the breeder).

2. Any two suitable examples, e.g. increased meat production of beef cattle, large eggs produced by chickens, unusual flower colours, crops that produce large amounts of grain.

3. **EXTENDED** Parent organisms with desirable characteristics are selected and bred together. Offspring with the best combination of characteristics are selected and then bred together. The process is repeated over many generations to produce a number of individuals that all exhibit the desired characteristics.

4. **EXTENDED** Natural selection is the selection by the environment for features that are best adapted to the conditions in that environment. Selective breeding is the selection of features by people of plants and animals that the people think are most useful or most attractive.

SECTION 19 ORGANISMS AND THEIR ENVIRONMENT

Food chains and food webs

Page 369

1. Producer: an organism that produces its own food from simpler materials, e.g. plants making carbohydrates in photosynthesis.

   Consumer: an organism that gets its food from eating other organisms, e.g. animal.

   Herbivore: an animal that eats plants.

   Carnivore: an animal that eats other animals.

2. **EXTENDED** Decomposer: an organism that gets its food from dead plants and animals or waste material, such as some fungi and bacteria.

Trophic level: the feeding level of an organism within a food chain or food web.

3. The Sun provides light energy, transferred as chemical energy to build plant tissue, which is then transferred as chemical energy through all other organisms in the ecosystem.

4. A food chain shows the relationship between one producer, one herbivore, the carnivore that eats the herbivore, etc.

   A food web shows the feeding relationships between all the organisms living in an area.

5. a) Food webs help us to understand the relationship between organisms in an area, and can help us predict what might happen to the organisms as a result of a change to the ecosystem.

   b) It can be difficult to organise the information in a food web because some organisms feed at many trophic levels, and it may not be possible to include all organisms (e.g. decomposers) on a food web because of space for the drawing.

Page 372

1. **EXTENDED** Energy in light from Sun (gain) > some reflected, some passes straight through, some wrong wavelength (losses) > energy in light transferred to chemical substances during photosynthesis > energy transferred to environment from photosynthetic reactions and from respiration by heating (losses) > energy stored in plant biomass.

2. **EXTENDED** Energy stored in food (gain) > energy in undigested food lost transferred to environment in faeces (loss) > energy stored in absorbed food molecules transferred to energy in waste products such as urea in urine and transferred to the environment (loss) > energy released in respiration transferred by heating to environment (loss) > energy stored in animal biomass.

3. **EXTENDED** Not all the energy gained is stored in new tissue in the organism. When the next trophic level feeds on the previous level, only the energy stored in the body tissue is available to it.

Page 375

1. A diagram showing the numbers of organisms at each trophic level in a food chain or food web in an area.

2. Any suitable example that includes producers, primary consumers and secondary consumers from a reasonable food chain. Count the number of individuals feeding at each level within the area. Draw a pyramid of three layers, starting with producers at the bottom and ending with secondary consumers at the top, with the bar for each level drawn to scale.

3. EXTENDED A diagram showing the biomass of organisms at each trophic level in a food chain or food web in an area.

4. A pyramid of biomass only shows the mass at a particular time in an area. If some trophic levels have a shorter life-span than others, they will be under-represented in the pyramid, which may cause an inverted shape.

5. EXTENDED The pyramid for plant/animal/human should show three layers, widest at the bottom for plant and shortest at the top for human. The pyramid for plant/human should show two layers, the bottom one the same width as in the other pyramid, and the top one for humans may be wider than in the other. Explanation should indicate that eating the plants ourselves means more food available, as energy is not lost to the environment from an intermediary animal level.

Nutrient cycles

Page 378

1. a) Respiration releases carbon dioxide into the atmosphere from the breakdown of complex carbon compounds inside organisms.

b) Photosynthesis fixes/converts carbon dioxide from the atmosphere into complex carbon compounds in plant tissue.

c) Decomposition decays/breaks down dead plant and animal tissue by decomposers, releasing carbon dioxide into the atmosphere during respiration.

2. a) carbon dioxide, **b)** complex carbon compounds, **c)** complex carbon compounds

3. EXTENDED Combustion increases the carbon dioxide concentration in the atmosphere more rapidly than natural processes such as respiration. Deforestation removes trees, so this reduces the amount of oxygen taken from the atmosphere for photosynthesis and increases the amount of carbon dioxide released if the forest is burnt. So this can rapidly change the oxygen/carbon dioxide balance in the atmosphere near the forest.

Page 379

1. a) The conversion of liquid water on the Earth's surface to water vapour in the atmosphere.

b) The evaporation of water from the surface of leaves.

c) The conversion of water vapour in the atmosphere into liquid water droplets in clouds.

d) The falling of liquid (or solid) water to the Earth's surface from clouds.

2. Biotic route: drunk by an animal, or absorbed through a plant > water transpired by plant or evaporates from animal's skin > water vapour in atmosphere > condenses in cloud > falls as rain or snow to ground/pond.

Non-biotic route: water evaporates from pond > water vapour in atmosphere > condenses in cloud > falls as rain or snow to ground/pond.

3. All organisms need water in their bodies, to transport soluble materials around their bodies, and to allow cell reactions to take place. Plants also need water for photosynthesis.

Page 382

1. a) EXTENDED Bacteria that increase the amount of nitrate ions in the soil by converting ammonium ions to nitrite ions and then to nitrate ions.

b) Bacteria that convert atmospheric nitrogen gas directly into nitrates.

c) Bacteria that reduce the amount of nitrate ions in soil by converting them to nitrogen gas.

2. EXTENDED Nitrifying bacteria increase the fertility of soils because plants can only take in nitrogen in the form of nitrates dissolved in soil water. Without nitrogen the plants will not grow well, and become stunted.

3. EXTENDED Decomposers break down complex nitrogen compounds in dead plant and animal tissues and animal waste. This releases ammonium ions that nitrifying bacteria convert to nitrate ions that plants need. Without decomposers, the bacteria would have nothing to work on, and the concentration of nitrate ions in the soil would decrease.

Population size

Page 384

1. A group of organisms of the same species living in the same place at the same time.

2. EXTENDED All the organisms and the environmental factors that interact within in an area; examples include a lake, desert, tropical rainforest, coral reef, or anything similarly large-scale that has reasonably definable boundaries.

3. EXTENDED All the populations of organisms living within an ecosystem that form a food web.

4. EXTENDED Populations of different species that live in different habitats form the community of organisms that live in an ecosystem.

Page 387

1. Births and immigration increase population size; deaths and emigration decrease population size.

2. Food supply can increase population growth because it can increase birth rate and survival, reducing death rate. It can also cause an increase in immigration and decrease in emigration.

3. Predation and disease can decrease population growth because they increase the death rate.

Page 388

1. **EXTENDED** Log phase, exponential (lag) phase, stationary phase, death phase.

2. **EXTENDED** Microorganisms in a fermenter (or other suitable example), because conditions for growth are ideal and there is no other organism to predate on the populations.

3. **EXTENDED** The log phase is when the individuals in the population are preparing for growth and reproduction but population size is increasing very slowly.

   The exponential (lag) phase is where growth in population size is rapid because the birth rate is fast due to ideal conditions.

   The stationary phase is where growth levels off, and birth rate and death rate are equal, due to a limiting factor such as limited nutrients.

   The death phase is where population size falls because death rate is greater than birth rate, due to lack of a nutrient or increase in toxic conditions.

Page 391

1. The rate of growth shows exponential growth / the same shape as the log and exponential phases of a sigmoid growth curve.

2. because different estimates include predictions of different birth rates and death rates over this period

3. Any two of: different birth rates, immigration, death rates or emigration.

4. Any positive from: improved food availability, improved chances for work, improved health care (or similar).

   Any negative from: slum developments because city growing too rapidly, unrest leading to violence, increased risk of transmission of infectious disease.

SECTION 20 BIOTECHNOLOGY AND GENETIC ENGINEERING

Biotechnology and genetic engineering

Page 402

1. The use of organisms to make products, such as making bread or cheese or in genetic engineering.

2. They produce many complex chemicals and they grow and reproduce rapidly.

EXTENDED There are no ethical concerns about using bacteria, they have the same genetic code as other organisms, and they are easy to manipulate.

3. **EXTENDED** Animals need particular conditions in which to grow in order to remain healthy, and people get concerned when they see animals suffering. Bacteria are not thought to suffer as animals can do, so they are easier to work with.

Biotechnology

Page 407

1. a) carbon dioxide
   b) ethanol

2. It causes more juice to be released from a mass of fruit pulp because it breaks down the cell walls of uncrushed cells.

3. They contain enzymes that break down organic chemicals in stains more quickly and at lower temperatures than soap and hot water.

4. **EXTENDED** Lactase breaks down the lactose in milk, making it more suitable for drinking by people who are lactose-intolerant.

Page 408

1. **EXTENDED** A large vessel in which microorganisms are grown in large numbers under controlled conditions.

2. a) **EXTENDED** temperature, pH, oxygenation, nutrient concentration
   b) Temperature will increase due to the reactions of respiration and other reactions of the microorganisms. If temperature rises too high, it may reduce rate of growth or kill the microorganisms.

      pH may change because of substances released by the microorganisms into the solution. This may reduce rate of growth.

      Oxygen concentration might fall as oxygen is used for respiration. Microorganisms are aerobic, so rate of growth will reduce if oxygen concentration falls.

      Nutrient concentration will fall as microorganisms use nutrients to make new cells. Rate of growth will fall if nutrients are not added to replace what is used.

3. a) **EXTENDED** keeping things sterile
   b) It prevents other microorganisms growing rapidly in the fermenter and competing with the added microorganisms.

Genetic engineering

Page 413

1. Taking a gene out of one organism and putting it into the DNA of an organism of a different species, so that the gene produces its protein or characteristic in the new organism.

2. Any two suitable examples, such as: bacteria that produce human insulin, crop plants that are resistant to a herbicide, crop plants that are resistant to pest damage, crop plants that produce additional vitamins.

3. EXTENDED Any suitable advantage, such as: less use of chemicals so reduce effort and cost, less damage to environment, increased yield of crop.

   Any suitable disadvantage, such as: reduced biodiversity, increased seed cost, increased dependency on particular chemicals, risk of gene transfer to wild plants by pollination, possible health effects to people eating the GM products (although not proven).

4. EXTENDED The human insulin gene is cut out of a human chromosome > the gene is inserted into a bacterial plasmid > the plasmid is inserted back into a bacterium > the insulin gene causes the bacterium to make human insulin > when the bacterium divides, all the cells it produces contain the insulin gene.

SECTION 21 HUMAN INFLUENCES ON ECOSYSTEMS

Food supply

Page 424

1. Any four from: agricultural machinery increases speed at which farming tasks can be completed with fewer people; fertilisers improve yield of crop plants; pesticides reduce damage to crops by pests and so increase crop yield; herbicides kill competing weed plants, and so increase crop yields; artificial selection improves the plant and animals that we grow for food, so producing more food more easily.

2. a) Any one from: increased need for pesticides and other chemicals; reduced biodiversity.

   b) Any one from: soil erosion, habitat destruction, reduced biodiversity.

3. EXTENDED Farmers in poor countries do not have access to modern technologies that increase food production. Drought and flooding can destroy food production. Conflict (wars) can displace people and destroy food production.

Habitat destruction

Page 427

1. a) Any two such as: using land for building, extracting natural resources, pollution by chemicals, using land for growing crops, livestock production.

   b) Any two such as: pollution by chemicals including oil or discarded plastic waste, warming of oceans.

2. a) EXTENDED The destruction/cutting down of large areas of forest and woodland.

   b) The washing away of soil by heavy rainfall.

   c) When soluble nutrients dissolve in soil water and soak away deep into the ground.

3. a) EXTENDED Changes the amount of water transferred from soil to air through transpiration, so more water remains in soil and enters rivers.

   b) Soil washed away and nutrients leached from soil by increased water flow through ground, so decreasing soil fertility.

   c) Increases carbon dioxide concentration as less carbon dioxide taken from air through photosynthesis and stored as wood.

Pollution

Page 430

1. A chemical used to kill organisms that we don't want, including insects that eat our crops or weed plants that compete with our crops.

2. Using pesticides increases the yield of the crop by reducing the damage done by pests or making more water and nutrients available to a crop so that the crop plants grow better.

3. a) Any suitable answer, such as: kills other non-pest organisms so damages food webs; may kill of predators of the pest so that numbers of pests can increase even more rapidly; increasing resistance of pests to pesticides, so farmers use even more of the chemicals.

   b) Any suitable answer, such as: removes food and shelter plants for other insect species, which may include predators of the pests, so pest numbers will increase further; some herbicides can be toxic to other insects and soil organisms.

Page 431

1. The radioactive dust that falls out of the air after release from a power station, processing plant or bomb.

2. Accidental leakage or an explosion.

3. The radioactive dust was sent high into the atmosphere. Winds spread the dust across the continent. The areas with highest fall-out are those that are mountainous and nearest to the explosion.

4. Any suitable answer such as: burning by contact, causing cancers.

Page 433

1. They take a very long time to break down and they may leak poisonous chemicals into ground water, which can leak away into water systems.

2. EXTENDED The land cannot be used for many purposes for many years after the plastic has been dumped.

3. EXTENDED The plastics cause problems for wildlife in the oceans that eat them by accident, or become entangled in them.

Page 437

1. Any three such as: industrial chemical release, untreated sewage, fertilisers.

2. Poisoning of the water by toxic chemicals.

3. The addition of nutrients to water.

4. Run-off of fertiliser into water as a result of heavy rainfall; leaching of soluble nutrients in fertiliser through soil into water systems.

5. Eutrophication leads to the rapid growth of algae and other microorganisms, which remove large amounts of oxygen from the water for respiration. This does not leave enough oxygen in the water for the fish, so they die.

6. EXTENDED Sewage added to water > adds nutrients to water = eutrophication > plant and microorganism growth rate increases > respiration rate of microorganisms increases, removing dissolved oxygen from water > less dissolved oxygen for other organisms, which die = water pollution.

Air pollution

Page 440

1. It is produced by human activities in large enough amounts to harm organisms and the environment.

2. a) EXTENDED Smoke/emissions from factories contains acidic gases, such as sulfur dioxide, which dissolve in water droplets in clouds, which then fall as acid rain.

   b) The clouds containing the acidic water droplets can be blown over great distances away from the industrial areas by wind.

3. EXTENDED Direct damage to delicate tissues in lungs, of soft-skinned organisms such as fish and amphibians, and of single-celled organisms; indirect damage by changing the acidity of the soil, affecting its fertility due to leaching of minerals, or making poisonous minerals more soluble; effects as a result to changes in food web may affect other organisms due to interdependency.

Page 443

1. a) Natural: respiration; human: combustion of fossil fuels

   b) Natural: soil bacteria in the nitrogen cycle; human: addition of nitrogen-containing fertilisers to soil

   c) Natural: digestion of food in animal guts and decay of waterlogged vegetation; human: increase in livestock and artificial waterlogged vegetation in rice paddy fields

2. Any from: increase in number and intensity of storms, more drought, more flooding, change to summer/winter temperatures and precipitation.

3. EXTENDED The greenhouse effect is a natural process that warms the Earth's surface when greenhouse gases in the atmosphere prevent longer wavelength radiation escaping into space. The enhanced greenhouse effect is the additional warming caused by the addition of greenhouse gases to the atmosphere as a result of human activity.

Conservation

Page 448

1. a) Protection so that something isn't damaged.

   b) A resource that can be used without running out and without long-term damage to the environment.

2. EXTENDED technology and use of the environment to meet growing human needs without damaging the environment

3. They are non renewable, so they will eventually run out. Conserving them will mean that they last longer.

4. a) EXTENDED replacing trees that have been cut down, and only buying wood products from forests that are managed, to prevent long-term damage

   b) making sure that enough breeding fish remain after fishing to produce the next generation, preventing overfishing by fishing quotas, re-stocking rivers and lakes where fish numbers have decreased

Page 451

1. Humans use a large proportion of the freshwater resources that are available, and our population size is still increasing. We also need to avoid pollution of water by our activities.

2. They are non-renewable, and we use them for much of our energy needs and as a raw material for products such as plastics.

3. **EXTENDED** It is cleaned of large material; the organic material is then broken down by microorganisms in treatment beds; it is then treated with chemicals to kill any microorganisms and to remove toxic dissolved minerals.

4. **EXTENDED** It uses less energy than making paper from wood, and fewer chemicals, so also reduces pollution.

Page 453

1. a) At risk of extinction/dying out.
   b) Breeding animals in captivity, such as in zoos or wildlife parks.
   c) A collection of seeds of many plant species stored for use in the future.

2. Any three from: climate change, hunting, habitat destruction, pollution, introduction of foreign species.

3. Prevent species from becoming extinct, prevent damaging human activities in vulnerable areas, preparing for environmental change by collecting and storing genetic material.

Index

monocotyledons 32
monocultures 423, 424
monohybrid crosses 324–9
monohybrid inheritance 323–9
morphology 17
motor neurones 240–11, 243
mouth 129
movement 13
    in and out of cells 60–75
mRNA 321–22
MRSA 268
Mucor 22, 282
mucus 49, 201
multiple births 309
muscle cells 47, 219–20, 249
mushrooms 22
mutation 190, 344–6
mycelium 22
myriapods 28–9

N

natural selection 349–52
negative feedback 253
nerve cells 50
nerves 239, 240
nervous system 239, 240–11, 249
neurones 240–42, 243
neurotransmitters 241, 242
nicotine 272
nitrate ions 380, 381
nitrifying bacteria 380
nitrogen cycle 379–82
nitrogen fertilisers 381
nitrogen-fixing bacteria 380, 382
non-biodegradable 431
non-renewable resources 444, 445
nuclear fall-out 430–11
nucleus 43, 44, 81
nutrients
    in a balanced diet 125–6
    cycles 375–82
    essential 123–4
nutrition 14
    human 121–43
    malnutrition 124, 126
    plants 102–19
    saprotrophic 22
    see also food

O

obesity 126
oesophagus 129
oestrogen 249, 303–4, 306
offshoots 282–3
oils 79

omnivores 366
oral rehydration salts 131
order 15, 25
organ systems 42, 48
organ transplants 168, 169,
    232–3, 271
organs 48
    sense organs 240, 244–8
    target organs 248
osmosis 65–8, 104, 149, 154
    in animal cells 71
    and plant water uptake 69–10
ovary (flower) 286
ovary (human) 296, 297
oviduct 296, 298
ovulation 297, 304
oxygen
    in the blood 162, 174
    diffusion 62, 63
    and germination 217–18, 294
    from photosynthesis 103, 108,
    110
    in respiration 216
    see also gas exchange
oxygen debt 220

P

palisade cells 50, 113
pancreas 129, 136
paper recycling 448–9
parasites 346
partially permeable 62, 64
passive immunity 193
passive process 62
pathogens 20, 80, 175, 185–7,
    300
    defence against 189
    immunity to 191
    mutating 190
pectinase 404
penicillin 266, 352, 407–8
penis 296
pepsin 95, 137
peripheral nervous system 240
peristalsis 129, 130
pesticides 423
    pollution from 427–10
pH
    acid rain 437, 439
    and enzymes 94–5, 96–7, 137
    indicator 110, 111
phagocytes 175–6, 189
phenotype 324–6, 330–11
phloem 113, 147

photosynthesis 44, 103–11
    investigating 104–5
    rate of 106–10
phototropism 255
phylum 15–16, 25
physical digestion 132, 133–5
placenta 298, 300, 302
plant cells 20, 43, 44
    osmosis in 65–8
    water potential 69
plants 20–21
    adaptive features 348
    anatomy 103
    artificial selection 353–4
    energy transfer losses 370
    features and adaptations 31–32
    in the food chain 364
    gas exchange 110–11
    mineral requirements 114–15
    natural selection 350–11
    nutrition 102–19
    sexual reproduction in 285–95
    species 10
    transport in 146–57
    tropic responses 254–8
    tuber formation 282
    water uptake 69–10, 149–10
    see also flowering plants; leaf
plasma 174–5
plasmids 23, 402, 411
plastics 431–32, 448
platelets 176, 180
pollen tube 292
pollination 285, 286, 287–11
    fertilisation from 292
pollution 425, 427–43
    air 437–43
    from nuclear fall-out 430–11
    from pesticides 427–10
    from plastics 431–32
    water 433–7
population 383, 384
population size 383–11
    birds on farmland 458–9
    see also human population size
potometer 153
precipitation 378
predators 365, 386–7, 429
predictions 326–7
pregnancy 300–11
    smoking and 272
premolars 133
prey 386–7
primary consumers 364, 372

Notes

Notes

Notes

Notes

Notes

Notes

Notes

Notes

Notes